Translator : Jay Chung

Editors : Shawn Sanders / Kevin P. Croall /
          Duncan Cameron / Angel Cheng

Production Artist : Hung-Ya Lin

US Cover Design : Hung-Ya Lin

Production Manager : Janice Chang

Art Director : Yuki Chung

Marketing : Nicole Curry

President : Robin Kuo

Publisher
ComicsOne Corporation
48531 Warm Springs Blvd.,
Suite 408
Fremont, CA 94539
www.ComicsOne.com

First Edition: March 2004
ISDN 1-58899-329-9

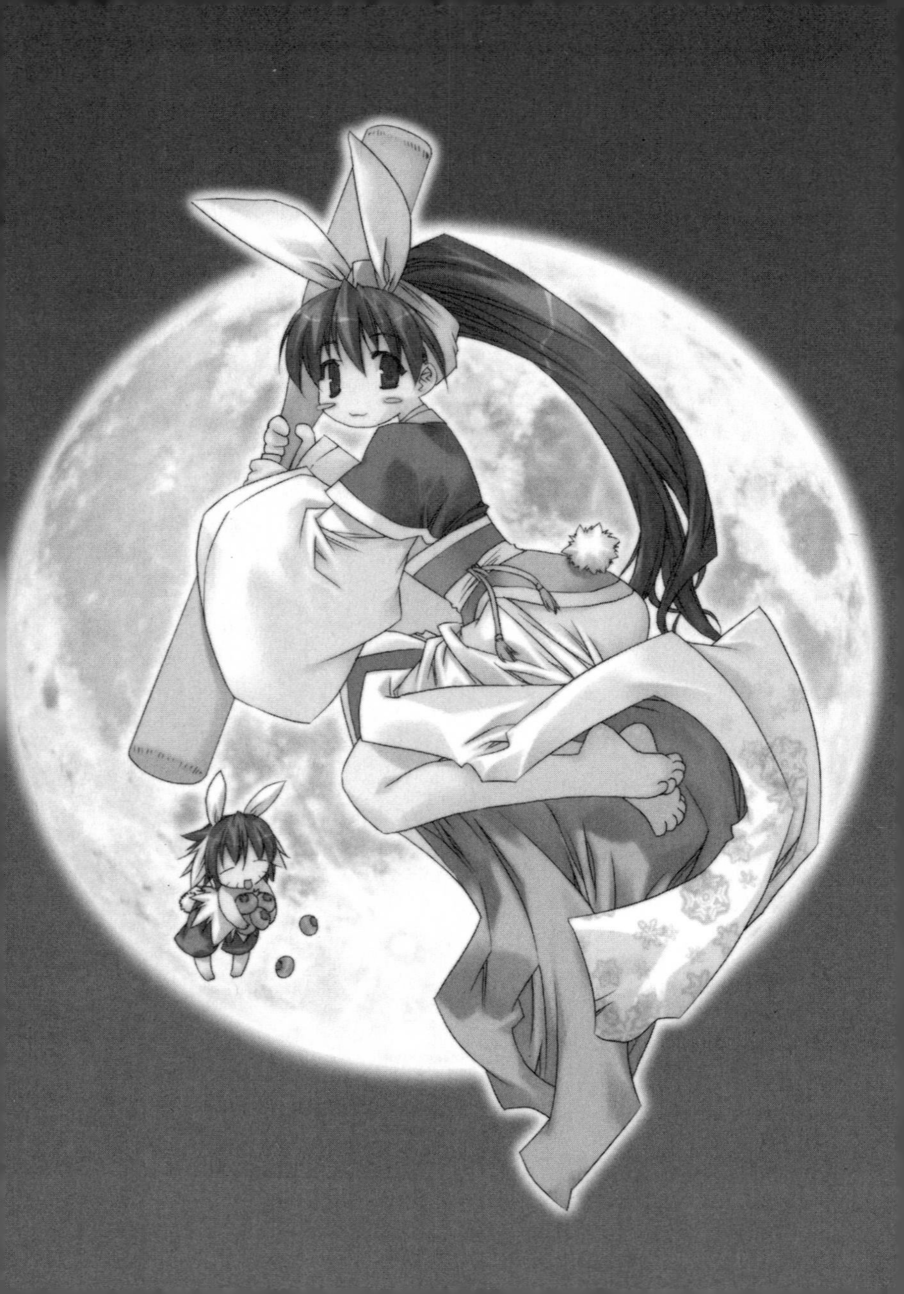

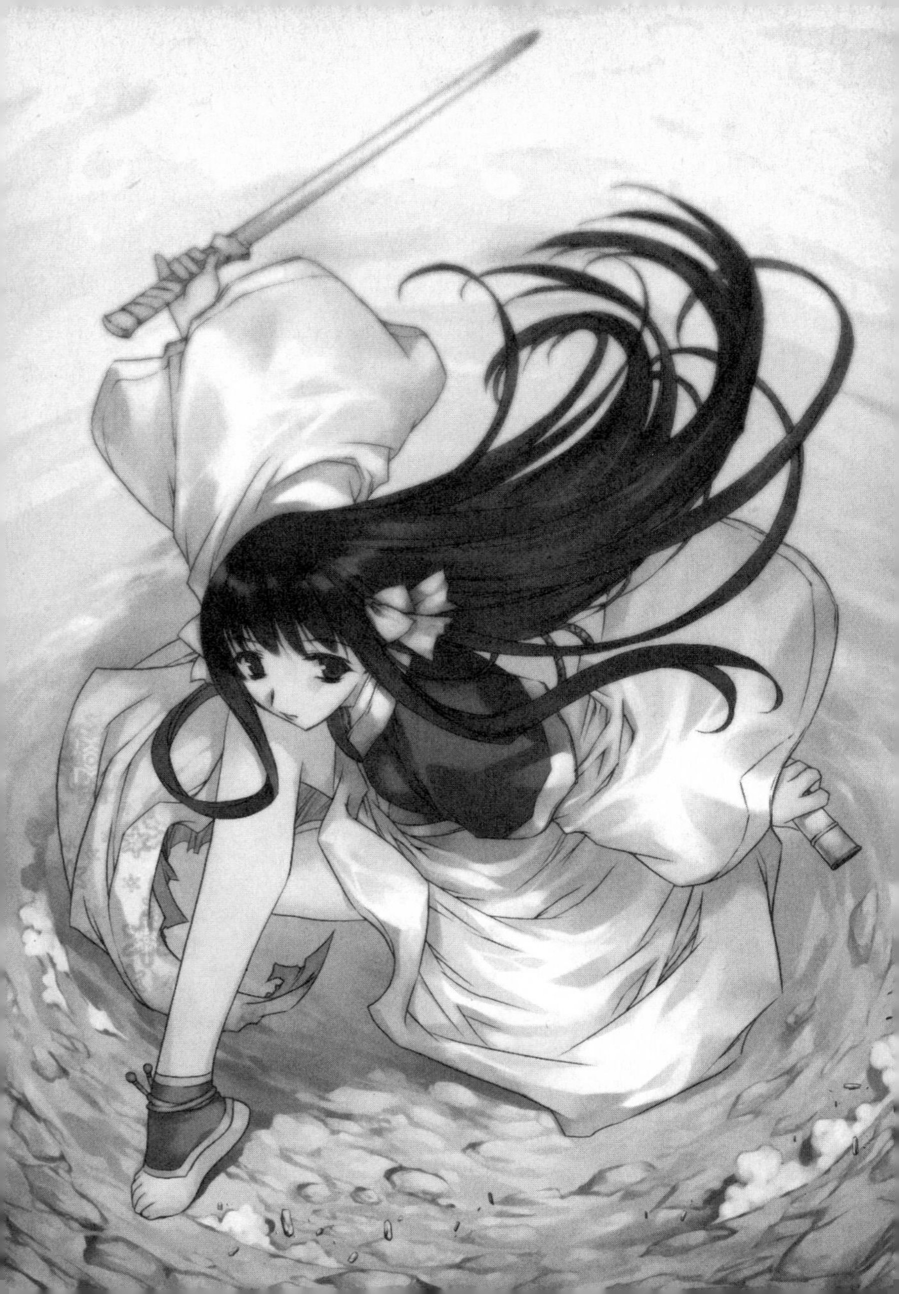

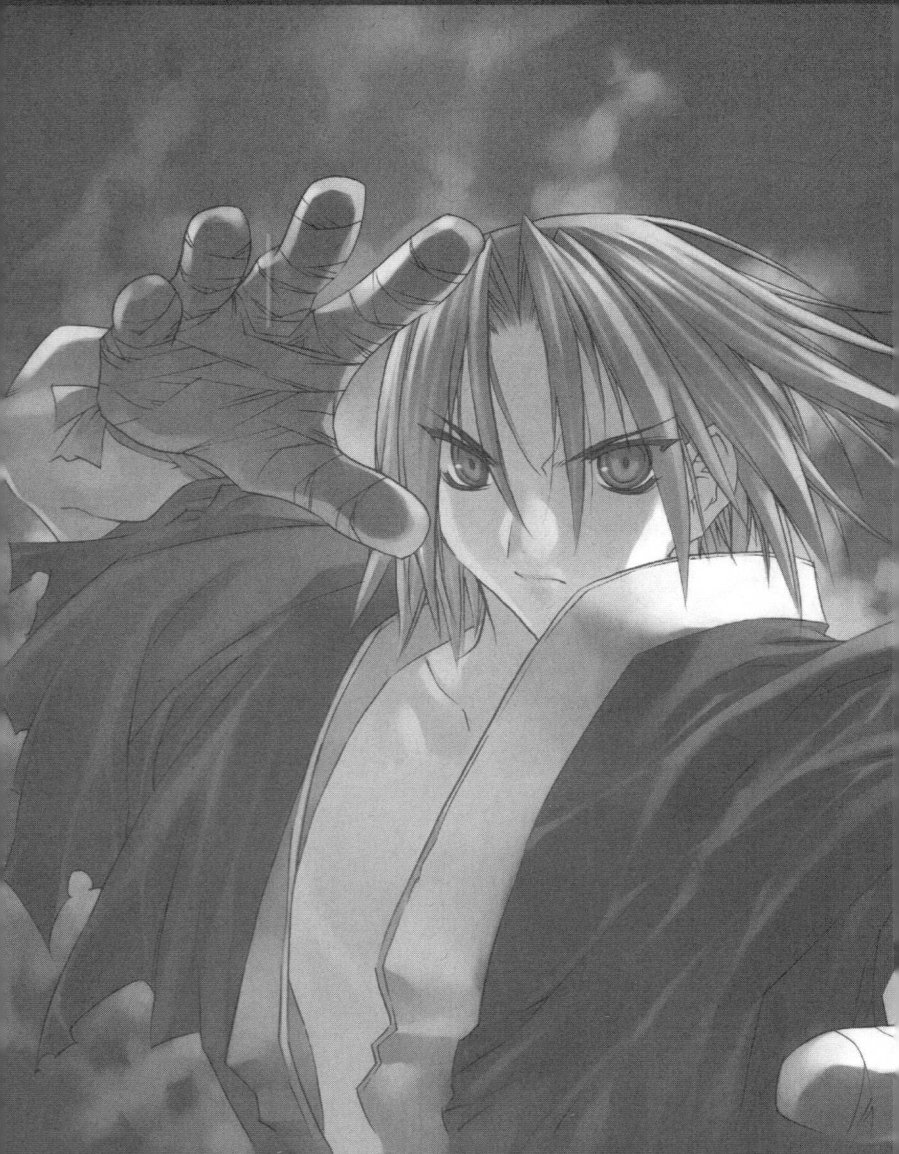

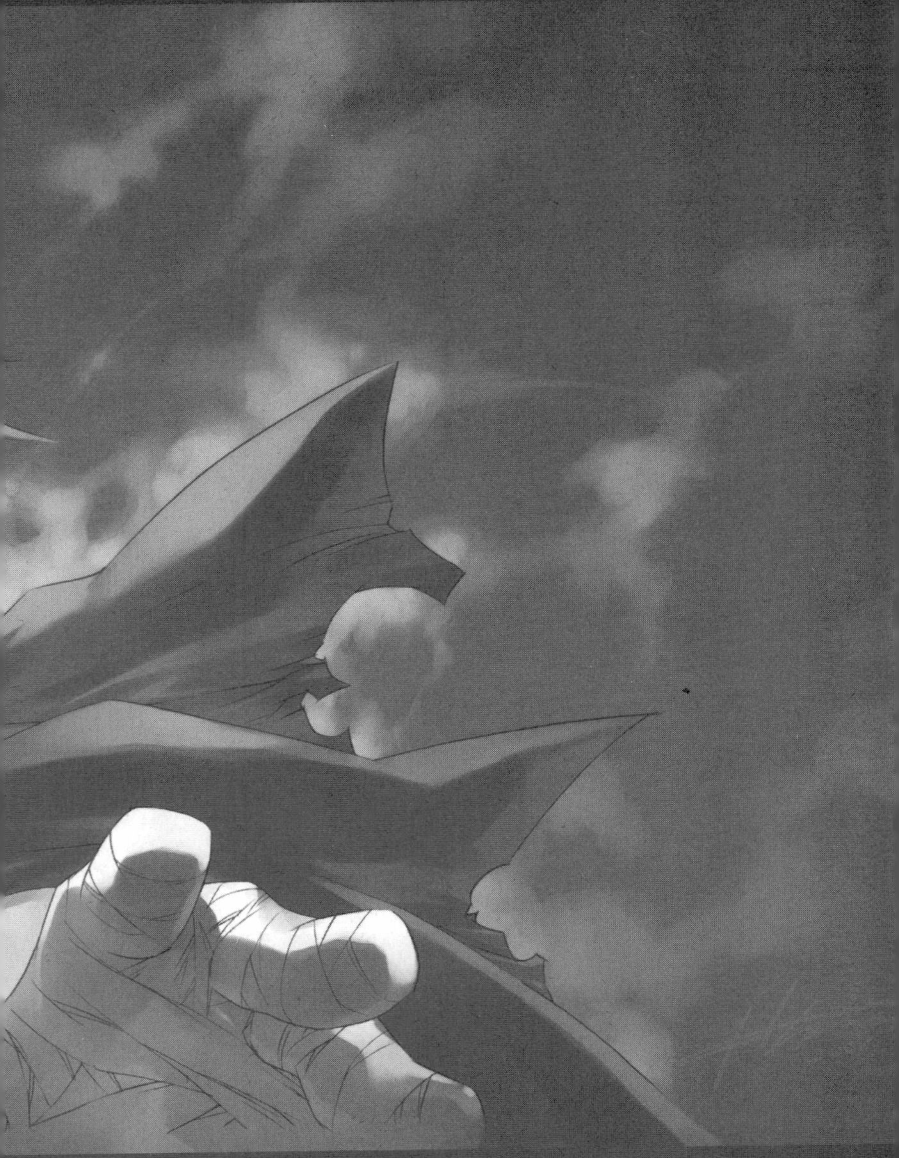

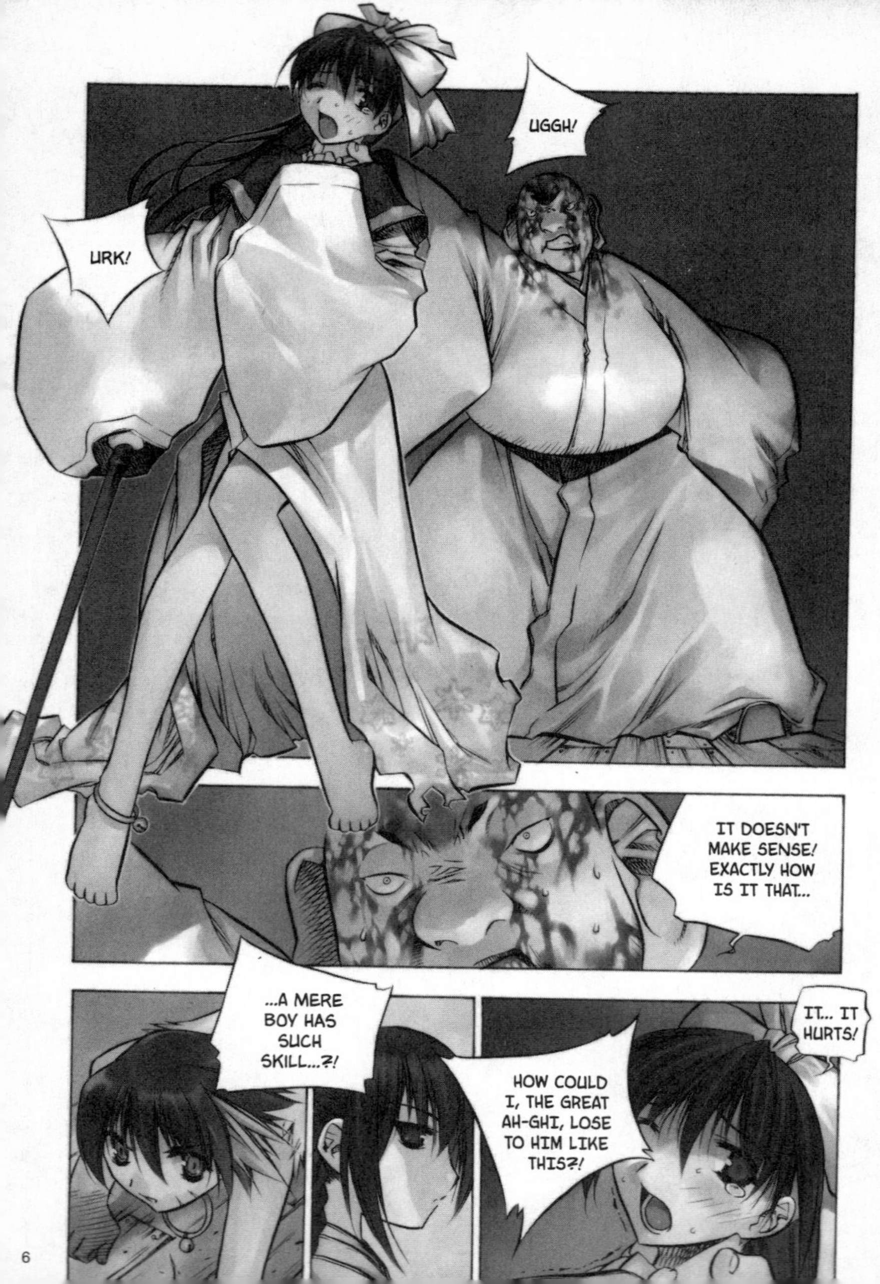
UGGH!
URK!
IT DOESN'T MAKE SENSE! EXACTLY HOW IS IT THAT...
...A MERE BOY HAS SUCH SKILL...?!
IT... IT HURTS!
HOW COULD I, THE GREAT AH-GHI, LOSE TO HIM LIKE THIS?!

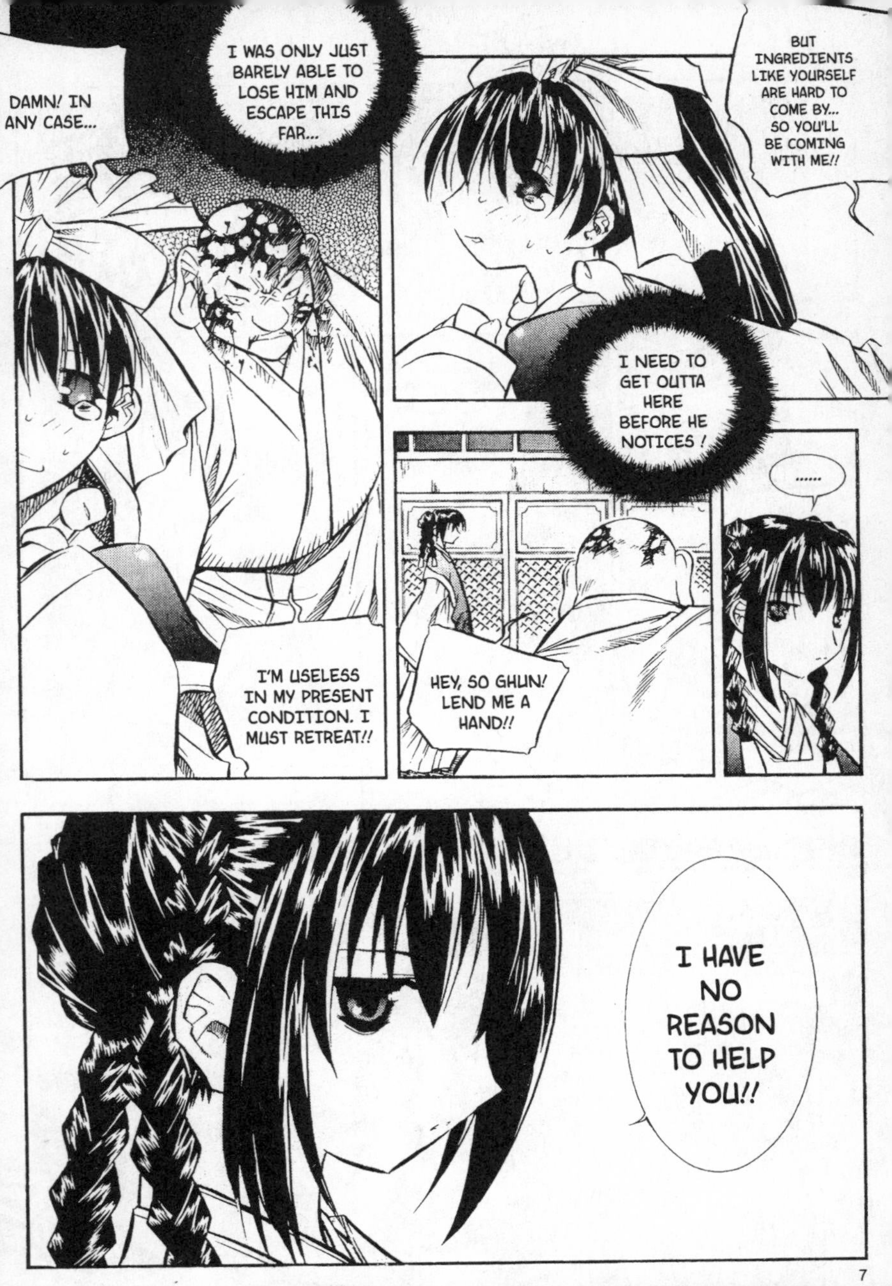
DAMN! IN ANY CASE...
I WAS ONLY JUST BARELY ABLE TO LOSE HIM AND ESCAPE THIS FAR...
BUT INGREDIENTS LIKE YOURSELF ARE HARD TO COME BY... SO YOU'LL BE COMING WITH ME!!
I NEED TO GET OUTTA HERE BEFORE HE NOTICES !
I'M USELESS IN MY PRESENT CONDITION. I MUST RETREAT!!
HEY, SO GHUN! LEND ME A HAND!!
......
I HAVE NO REASON TO HELP YOU!!

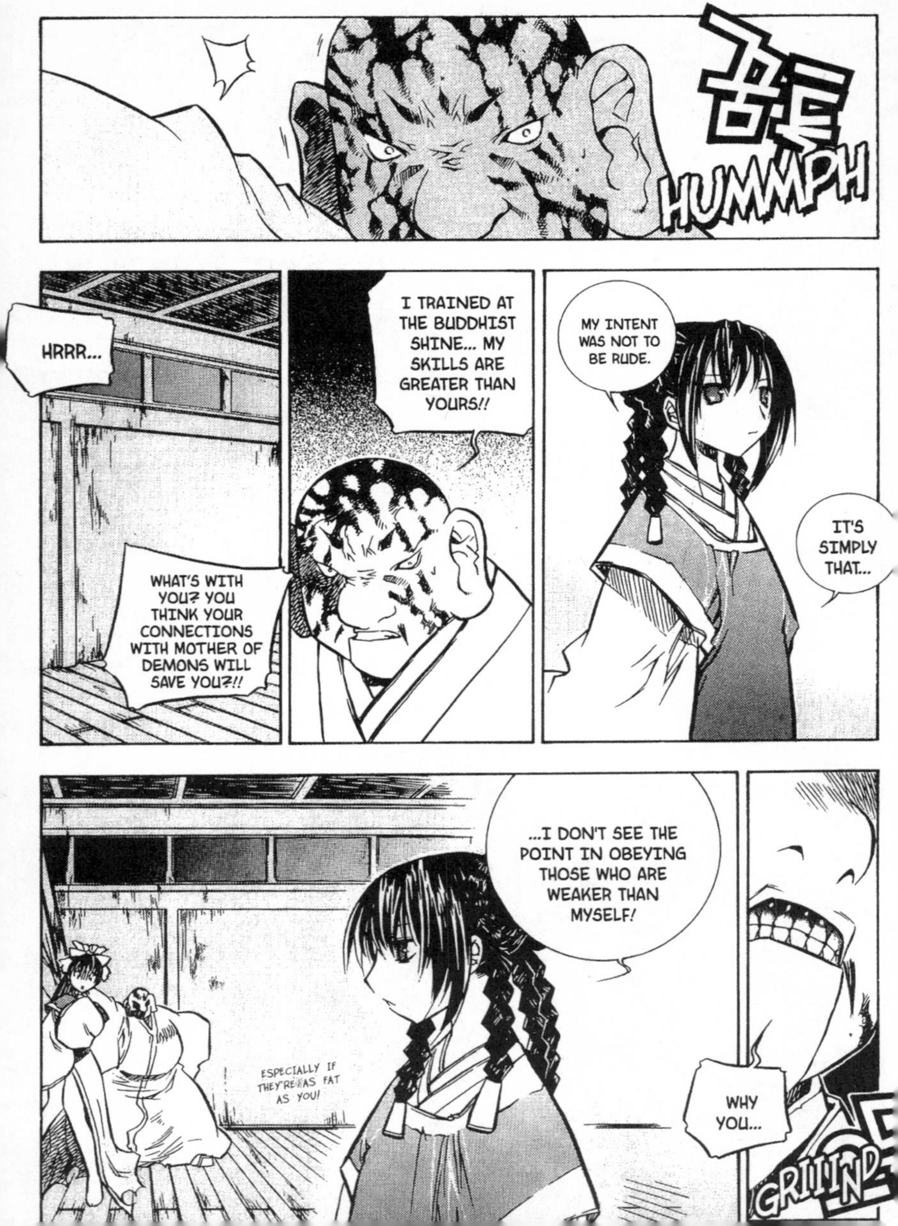
HUMMPH
HRRR...
WHAT'S WITH YOU? YOU THINK YOUR CONNECTIONS WITH MOTHER OF DEMONS WILL SAVE YOU?!!
I TRAINED AT THE BUDDHIST SHINE... MY SKILLS ARE GREATER THAN YOURS!!
MY INTENT WAS NOT TO BE RUDE.
IT'S SIMPLY THAT...
...I DON'T SEE THE POINT IN OBEYING THOSE WHO ARE WEAKER THAN MYSELF!
ESPECIALLY IF THEY'RE AS FAT AS YOU!
WHY YOU...
GRIIIND

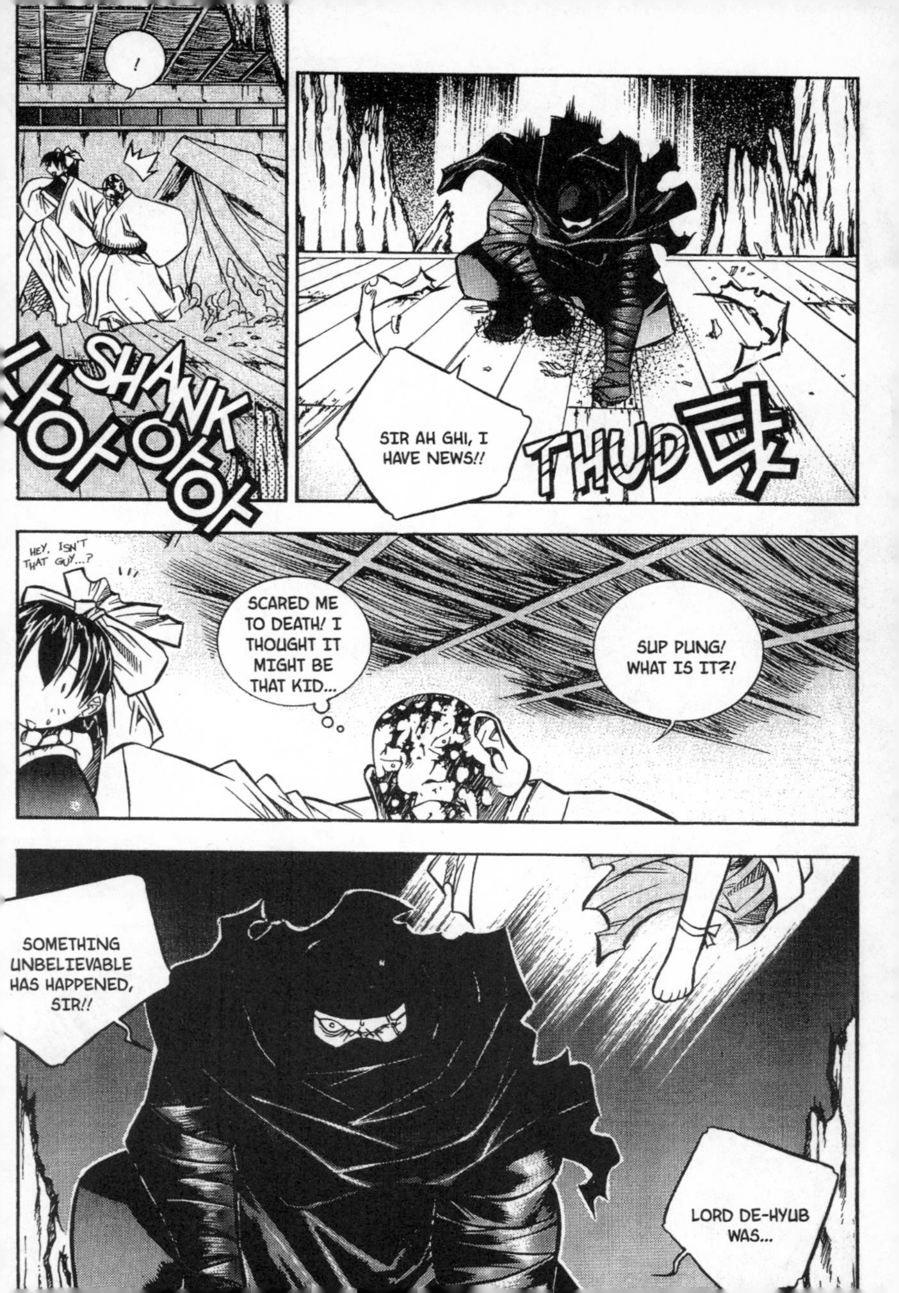
!
SHANK
THUD
SIR AH GHI, I HAVE NEWS!!
HEY, ISN'T THAT GUY...?
SCARED ME TO DEATH! I THOUGHT IT MIGHT BE THAT KID...
SUP PUNG! WHAT IS IT?!
SOMETHING UNBELIEVABLE HAS HAPPENED, SIR!!
LORD DE-HYUB WAS...

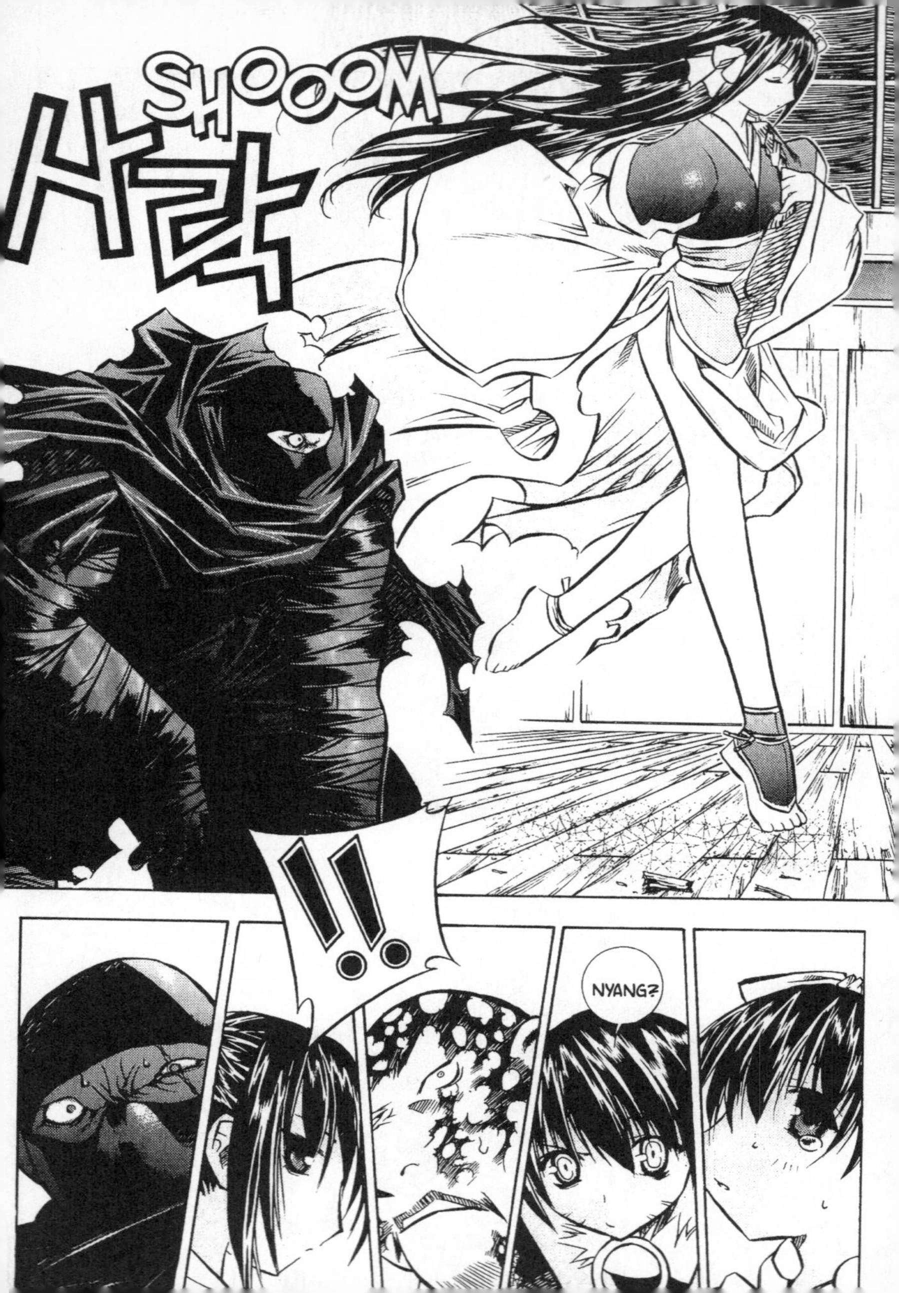

SHOOOM
!!
NYANG?

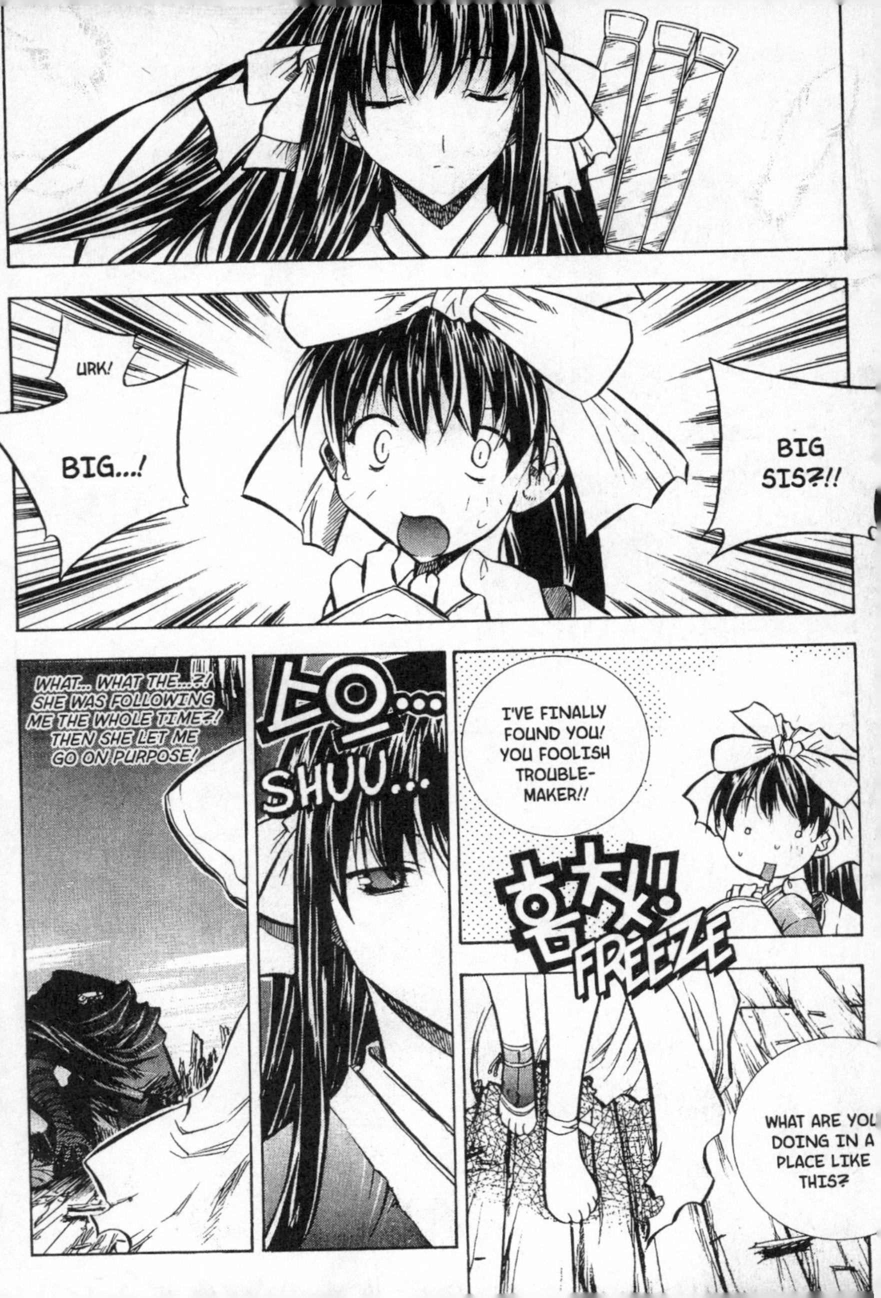
URK!
BIG...!
BIG SIS?!!
WHAT... WHAT THE...?! SHE WAS FOLLOWING ME THE WHOLE TIME?! THEN SHE LET ME GO ON PURPOSE!
스으...
SHUU...
I'VE FINALLY FOUND YOU! YOU FOOLISH TROUBLE-MAKER!!
FREEZE
WHAT ARE YOU DOING IN A PLACE LIKE THIS?

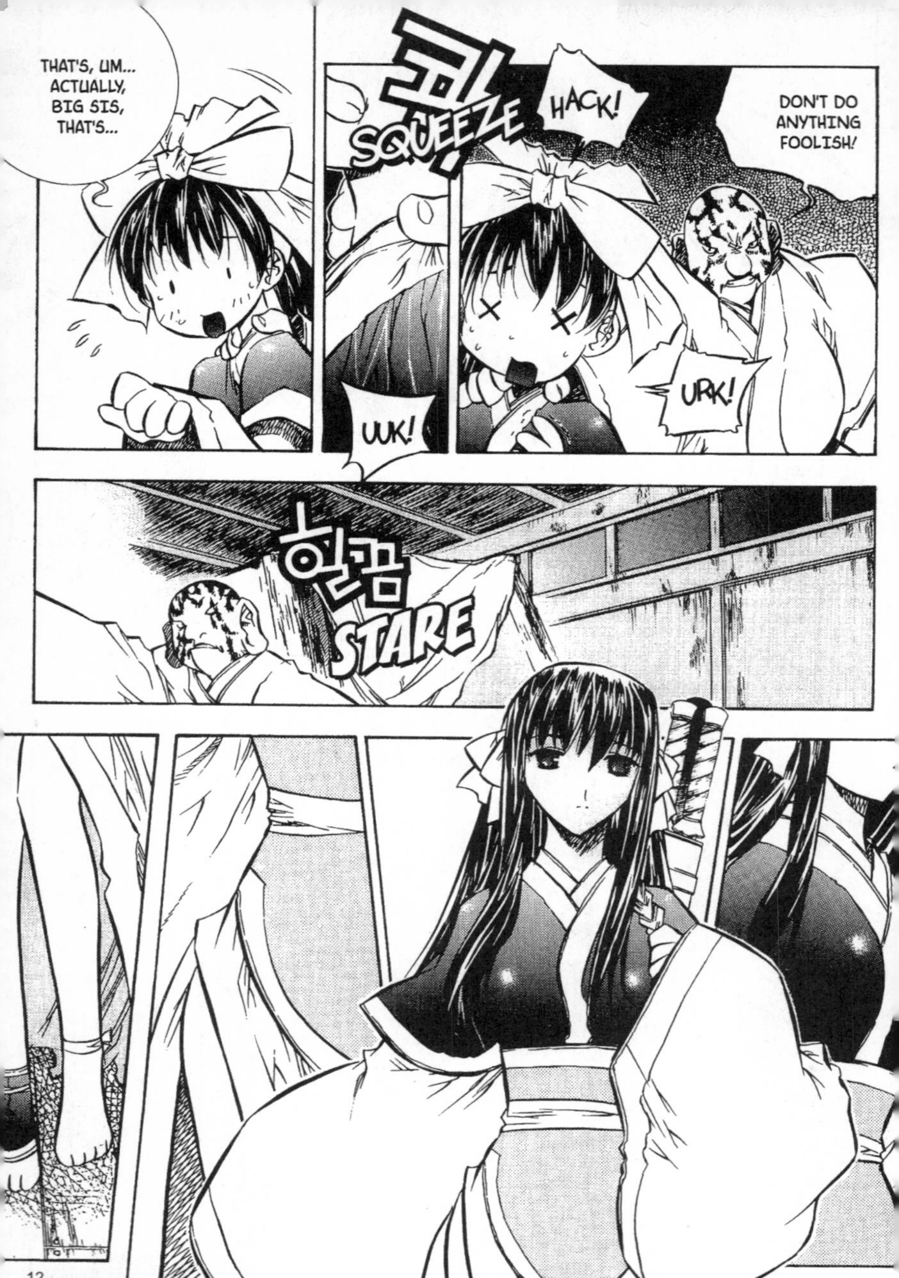
THAT'S, UM... ACTUALLY, BIG SIS, THAT'S...
SQUEEZE
HACK!
DON'T DO ANYTHING FOOLISH!
UUK!
URK!
힐끔
STARE

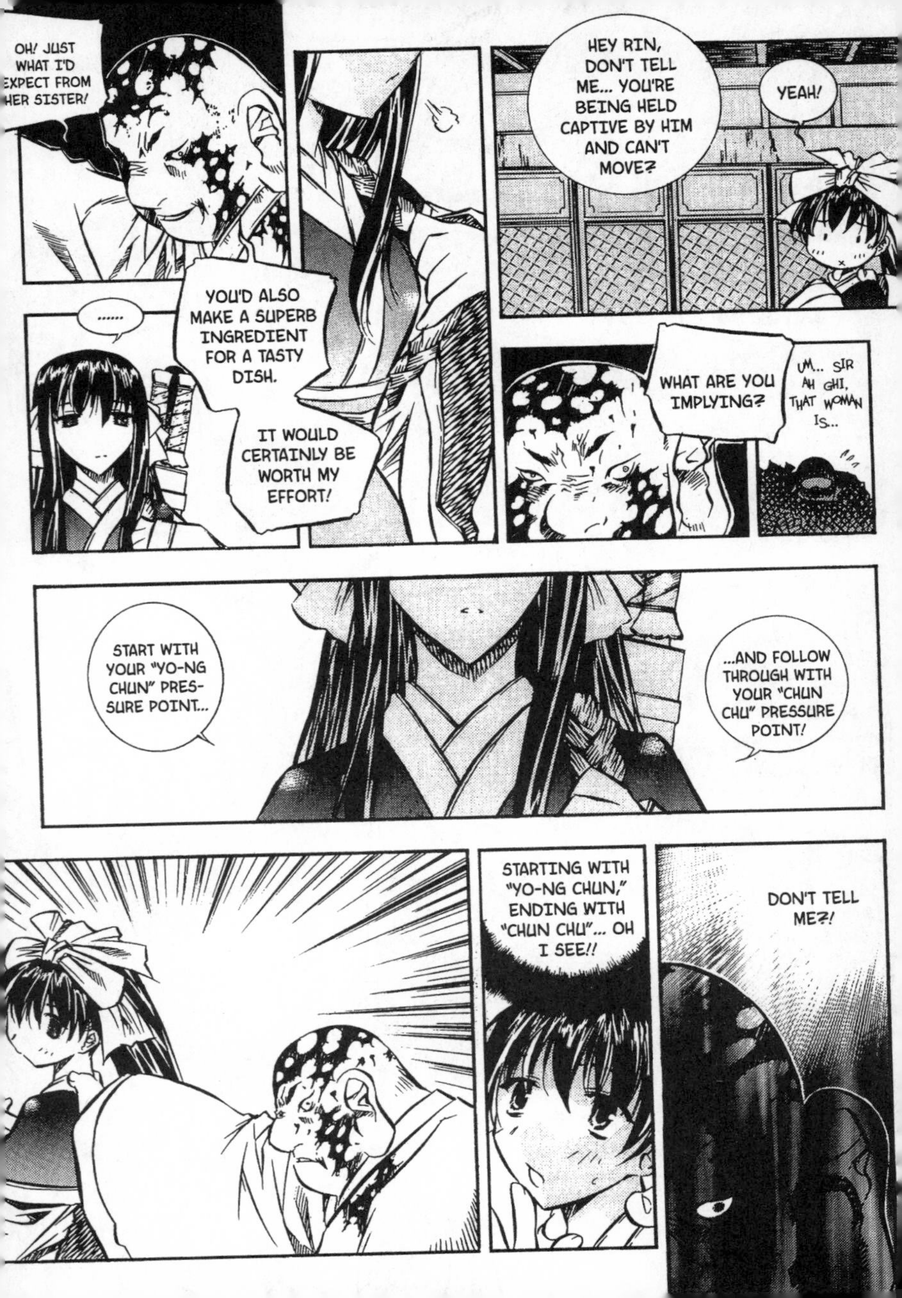
OH! JUST WHAT I'D EXPECT FROM HER SISTER!
......
YOU'D ALSO MAKE A SUPERB INGREDIENT FOR A TASTY DISH.
IT WOULD CERTAINLY BE WORTH MY EFFORT!
HEY RIN, DON'T TELL ME... YOU'RE BEING HELD CAPTIVE BY HIM AND CAN'T MOVE?
YEAH!
WHAT ARE YOU IMPLYING?
UM... SIR AH GHI, THAT WOMAN IS...
START WITH YOUR "YO-NG CHUN" PRES-SURE POINT...
...AND FOLLOW THROUGH WITH YOUR "CHUN CHU" PRESSURE POINT!
STARTING WITH "YO-NG CHUN," ENDING WITH "CHUN CHU"... OH I SEE!!
DON'T TELL ME?!

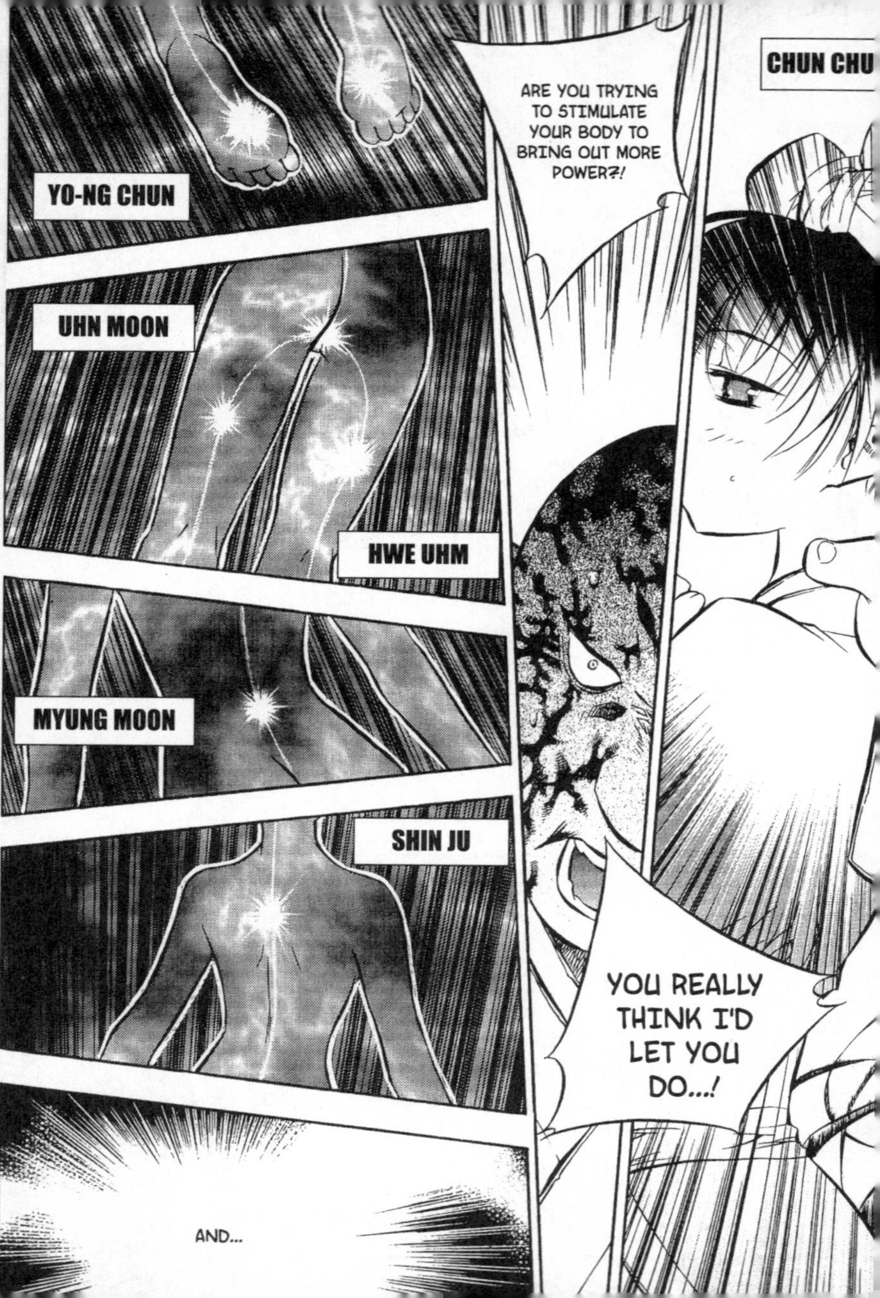
CHUN CHU
ARE YOU TRYING TO STIMULATE YOUR BODY TO BRING OUT MORE POWER?!
YO-NG CHUN
UHN MOON
HWE UHM
MYUNG MOON
SHIN JU
YOU REALLY THINK I'D LET YOU DO...!
AND...

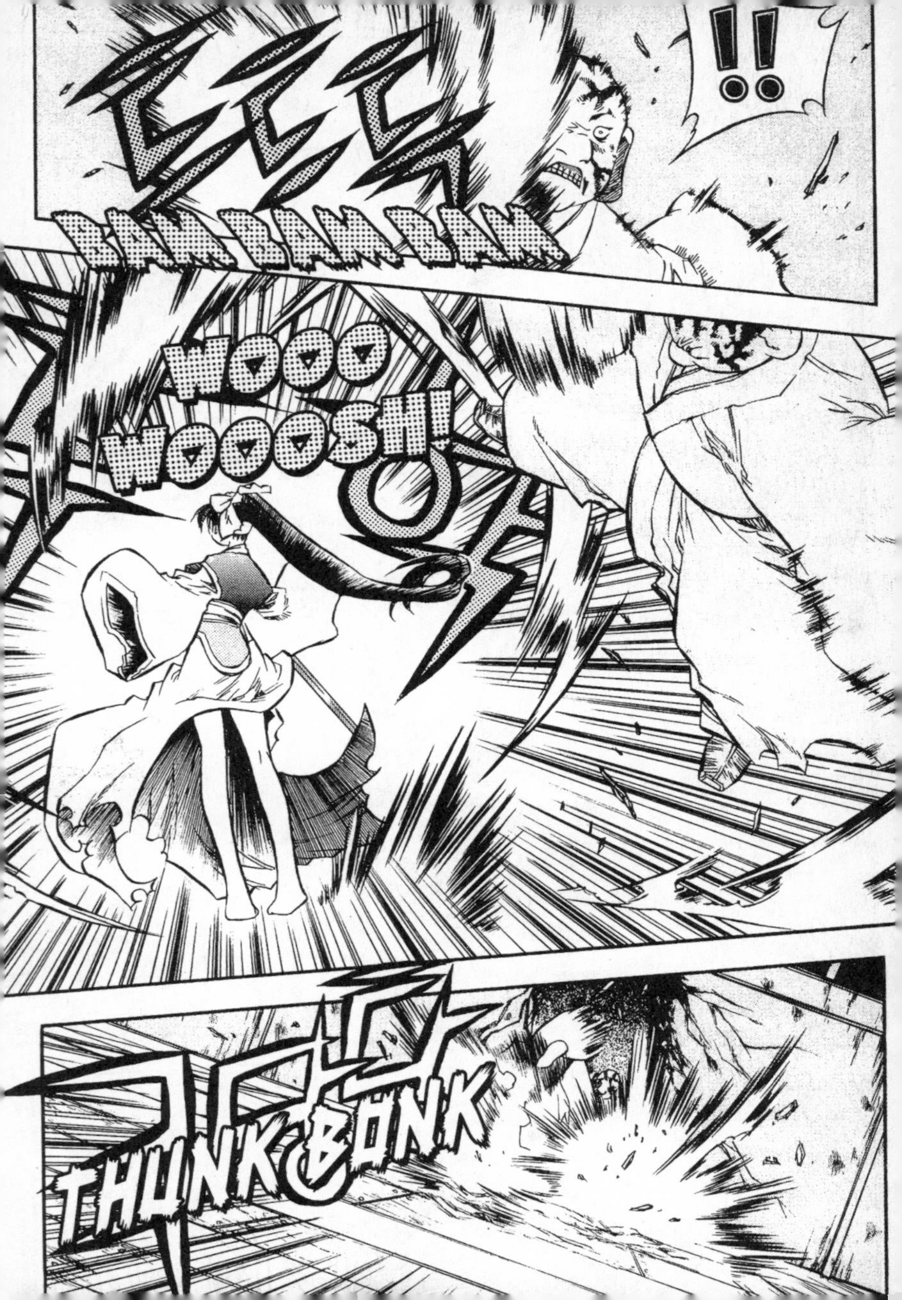
!!
BAMBAMBAM
WOOO WOOOSH!
THUNK BONK

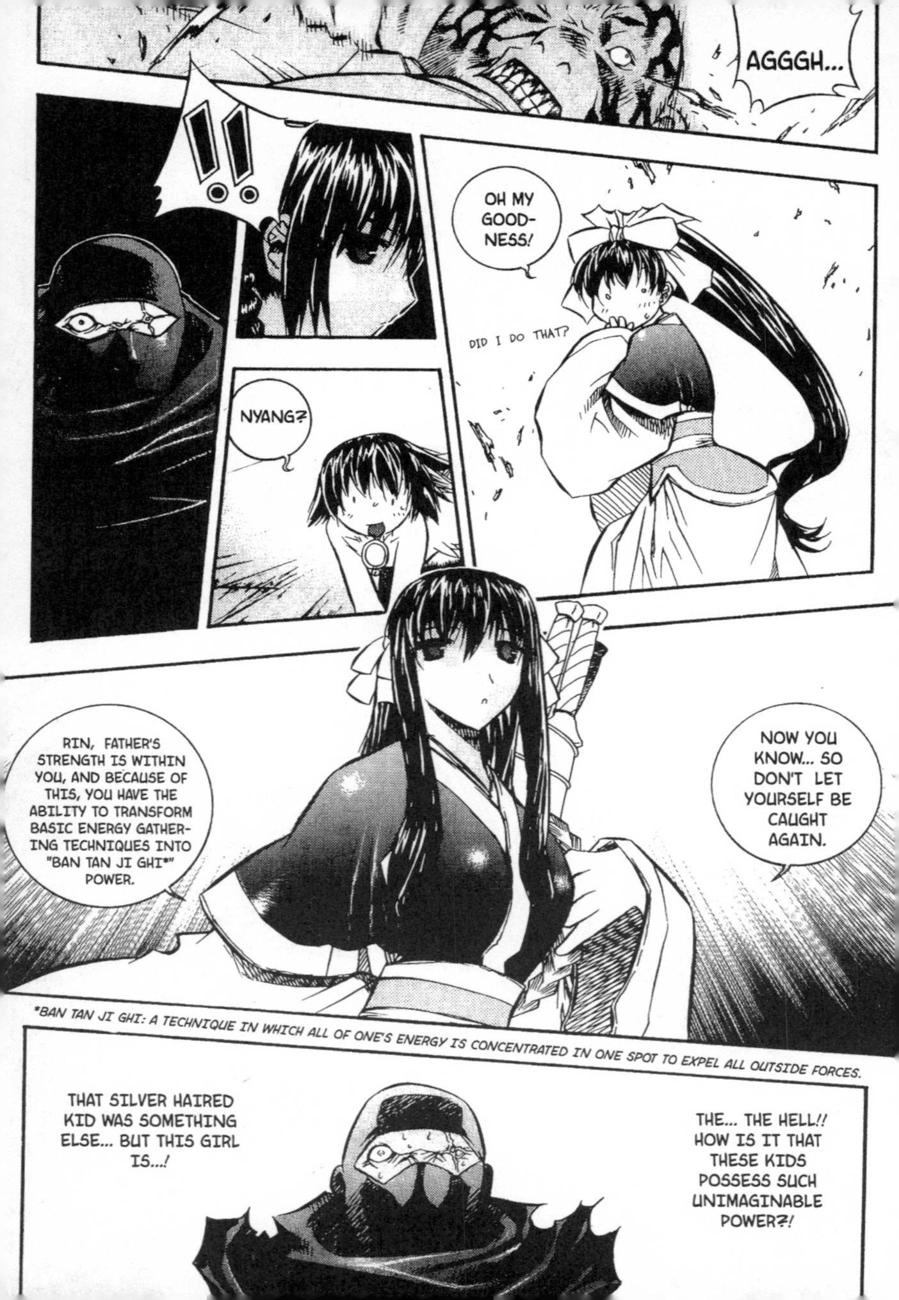
AGGGH...
!!
OH MY GOODNESS!
DID I DO THAT?
NYANG?
RIN, FATHER'S STRENGTH IS WITHIN YOU, AND BECAUSE OF THIS, YOU HAVE THE ABILITY TO TRANSFORM BASIC ENERGY GATHERING TECHNIQUES INTO "BAN TAN JI GHI*" POWER.
NOW YOU KNOW... SO DON'T LET YOURSELF BE CAUGHT AGAIN.
THE... THE HELL!! HOW IS IT THAT THESE KIDS POSSESS SUCH UNIMAGINABLE POWER?!
THAT SILVER HAIRED KID WAS SOMETHING ELSE... BUT THIS GIRL IS...!

*BAN TAN JI GHI: A TECHNIQUE IN WHICH ALL OF ONE'S ENERGY IS CONCENTRATED IN ONE SPOT TO EXPEL ALL OUTSIDE FORCES.

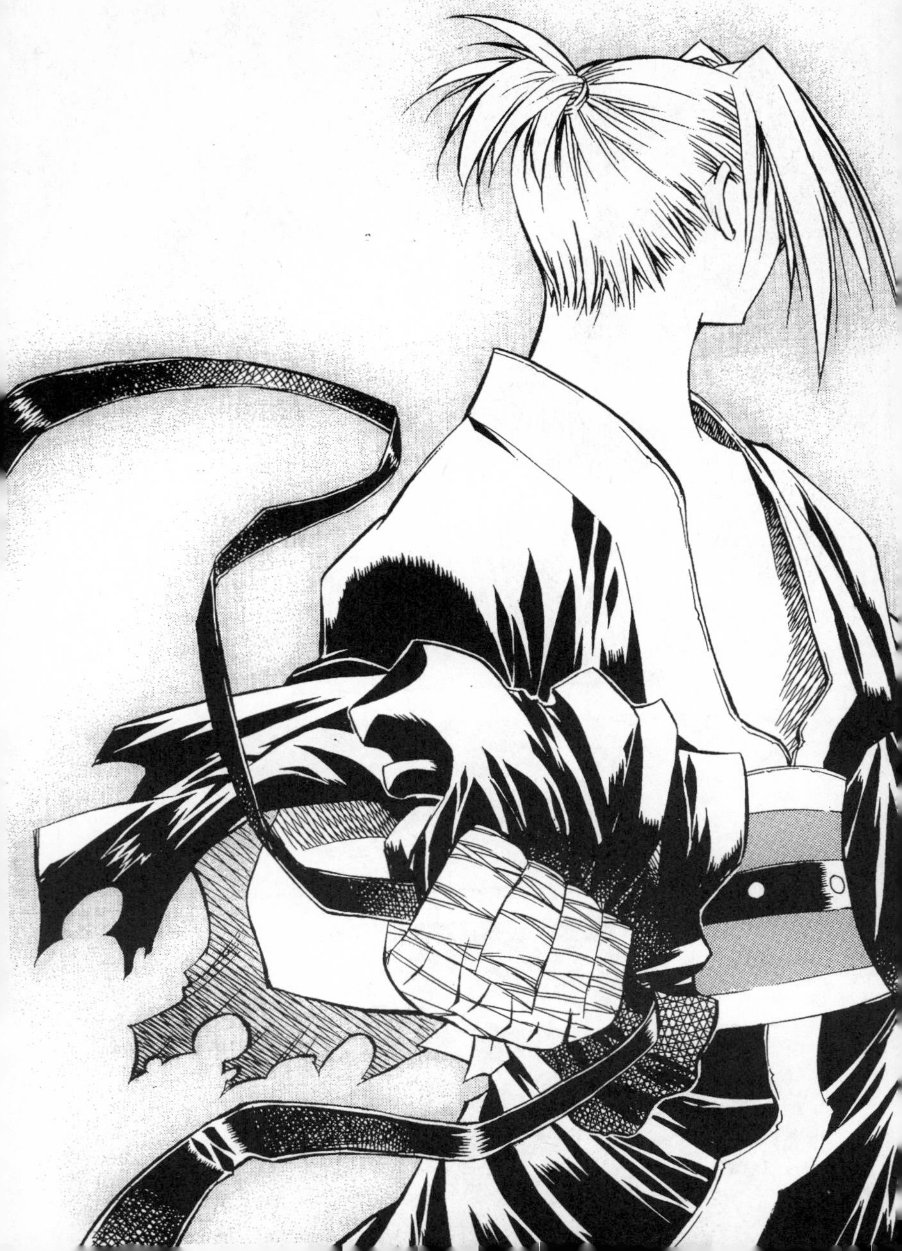

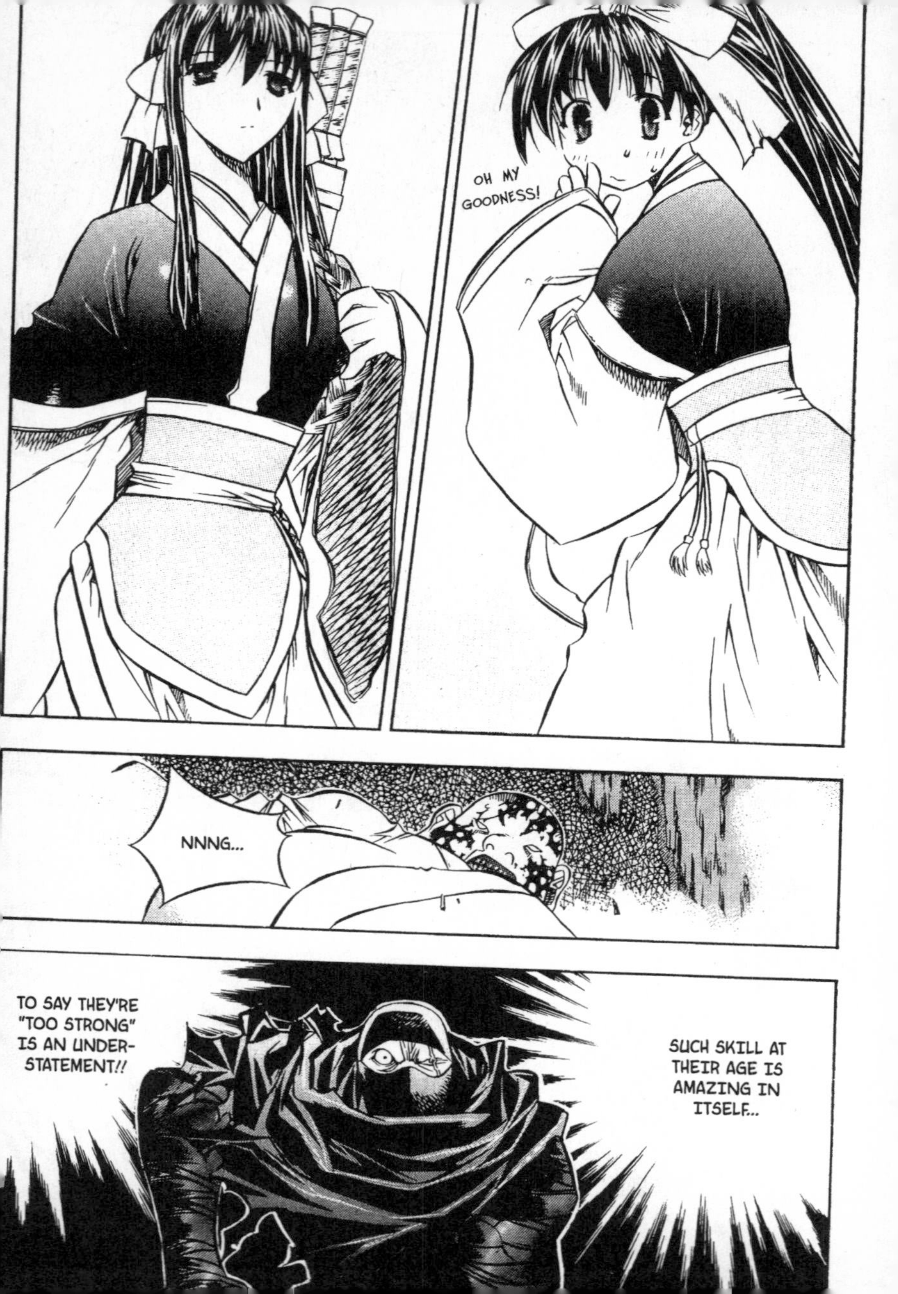
OH MY GOODNESS!
NNNG...
SUCH SKILL AT THEIR AGE IS AMAZING IN ITSELF...
TO SAY THEY'RE "TOO STRONG" IS AN UNDER-STATEMENT!!

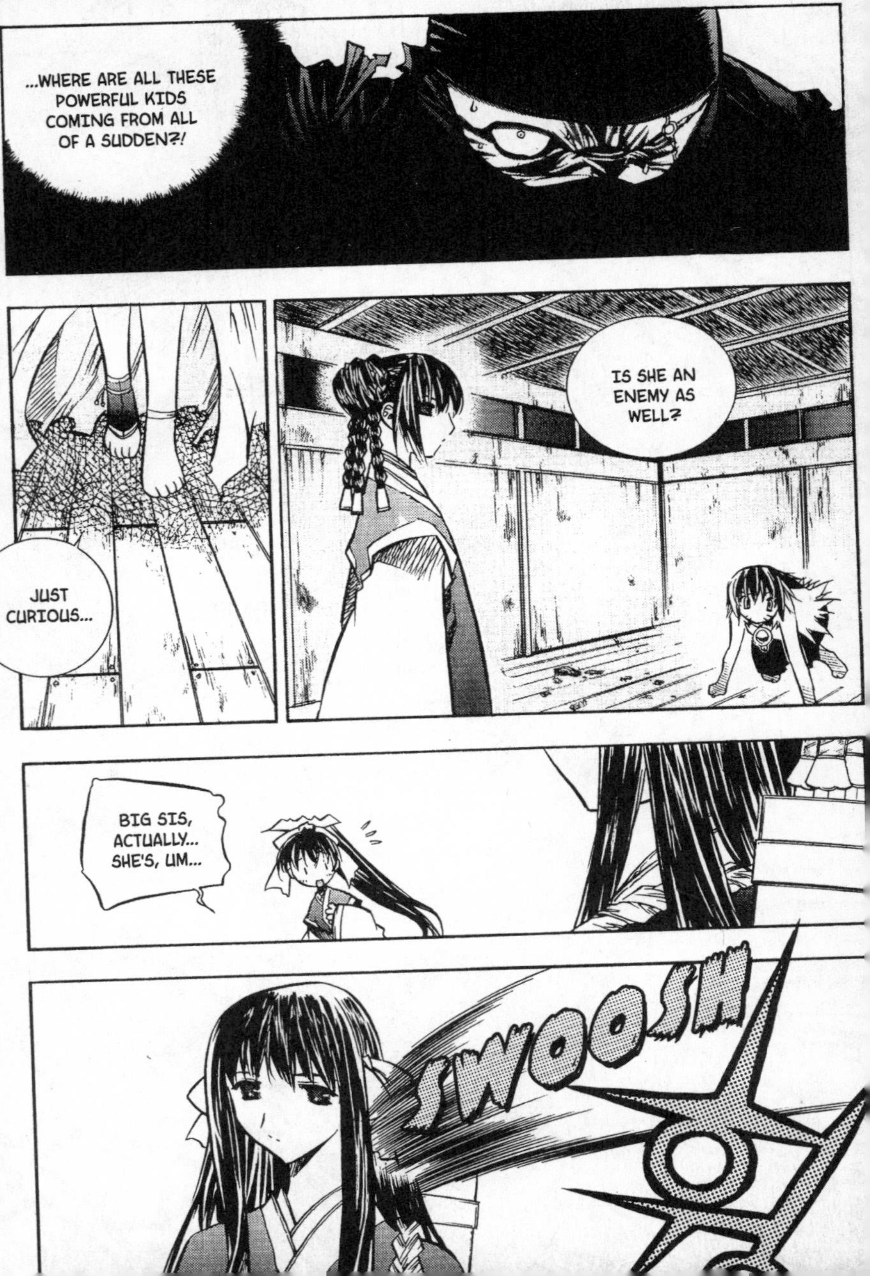
...WHERE ARE ALL THESE POWERFUL KIDS COMING FROM ALL OF A SUDDEN?!
IS SHE AN ENEMY AS WELL?
JUST CURIOUS...
BIG SIS, ACTUALLY... SHE'S, UM...
SWOOSH

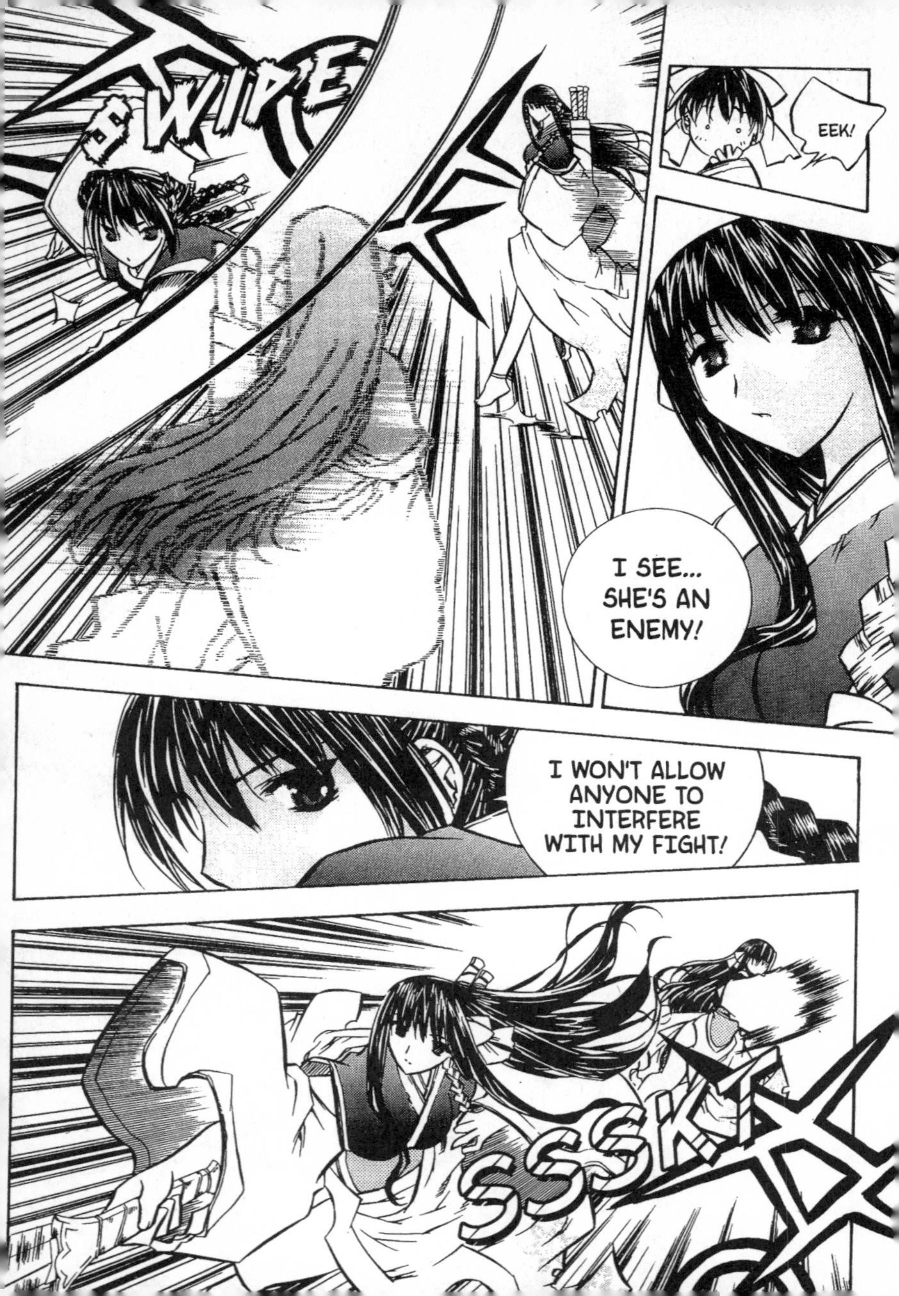
EEK!
TWIPE
I SEE... SHE'S AN ENEMY!
I WON'T ALLOW ANYONE TO INTERFERE WITH MY FIGHT!
SSSKT

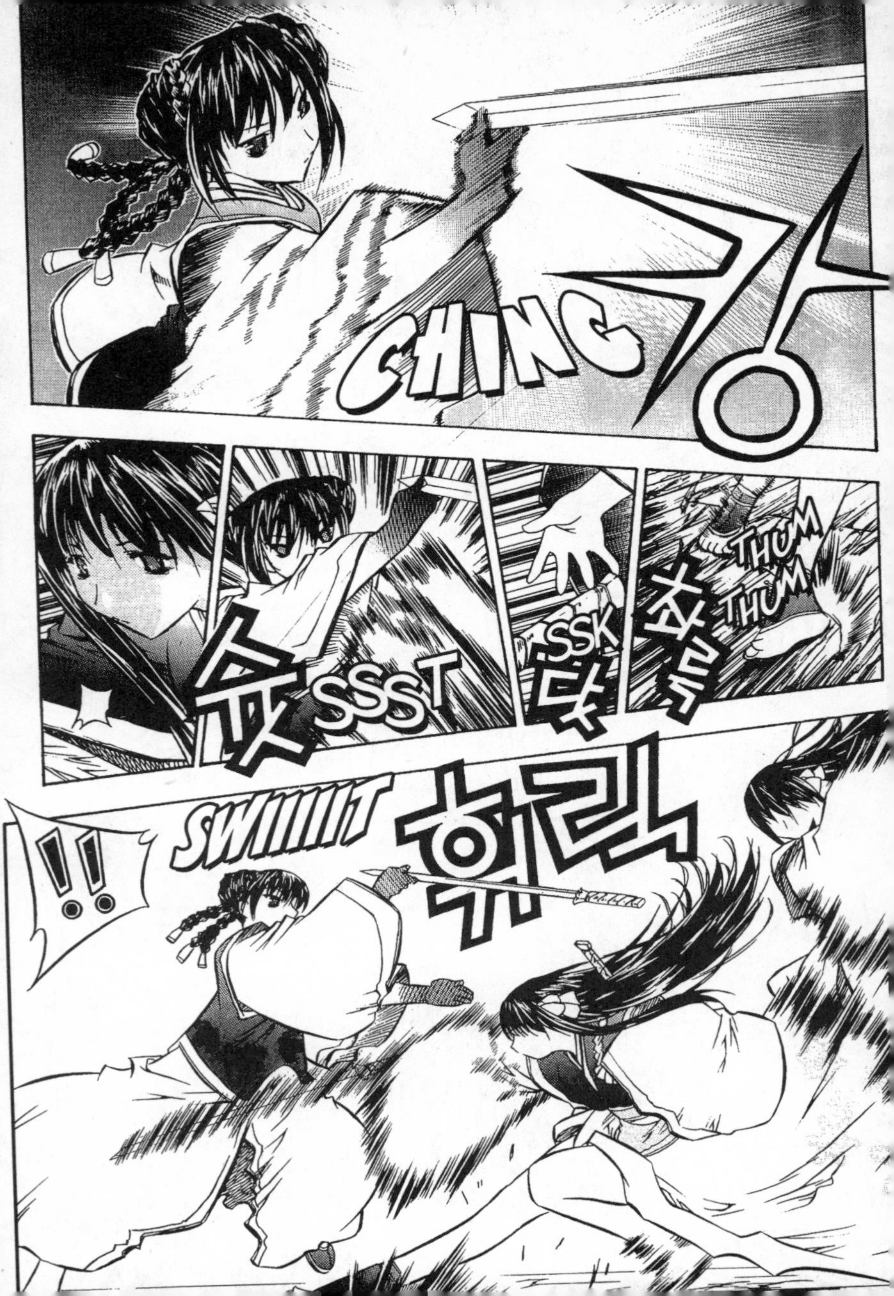
CHING
SSSST
SSK
THUM THUM
SWIIIIT
!!

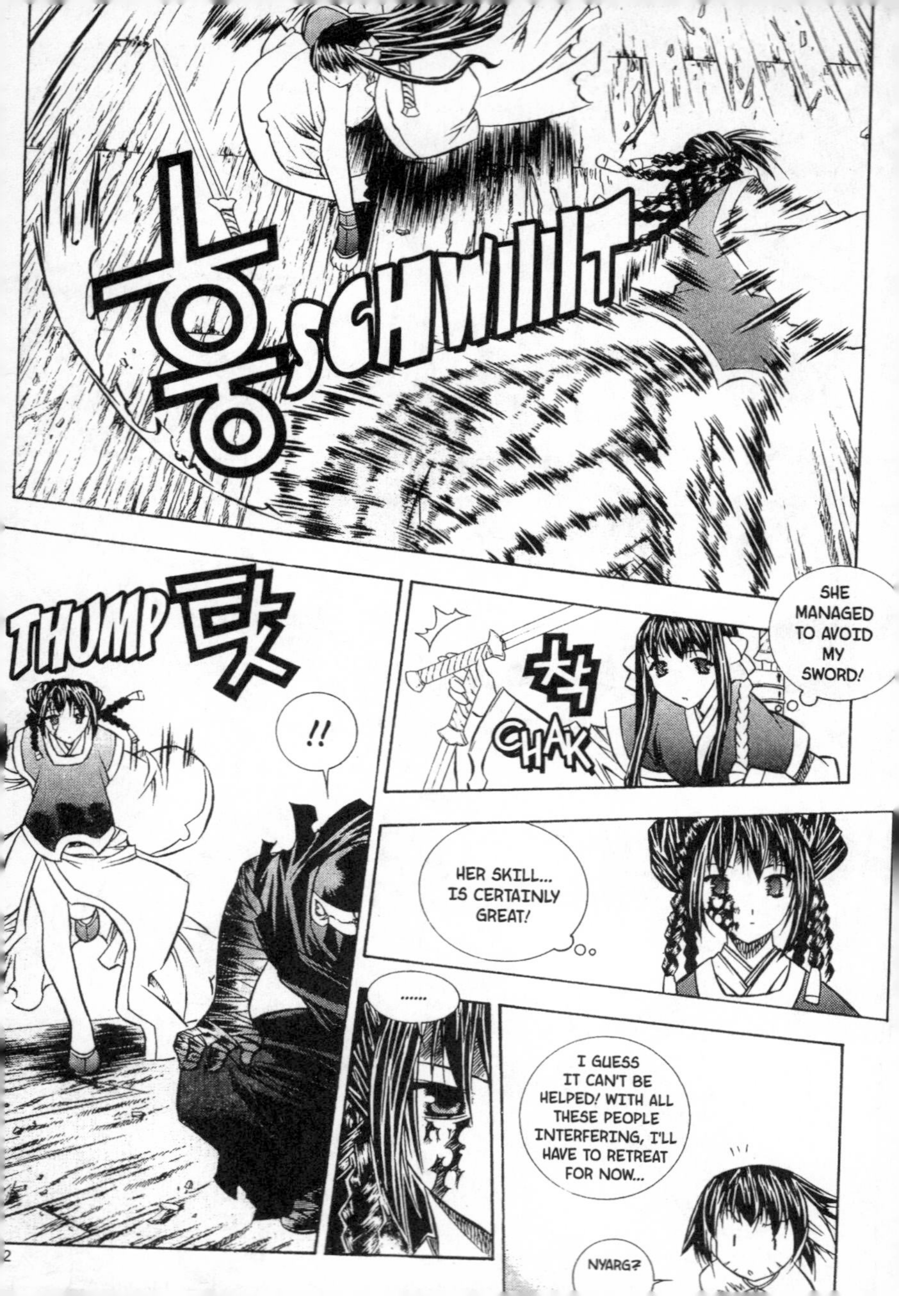

SCHWIIIT
THUMP
!!
착
CHAK
SHE MANAGED TO AVOID MY SWORD!
HER SKILL... IS CERTAINLY GREAT!
......
I GUESS IT CAN'T BE HELPED! WITH ALL THESE PEOPLE INTERFERING, I'LL HAVE TO RETREAT FOR NOW...
NYARG?

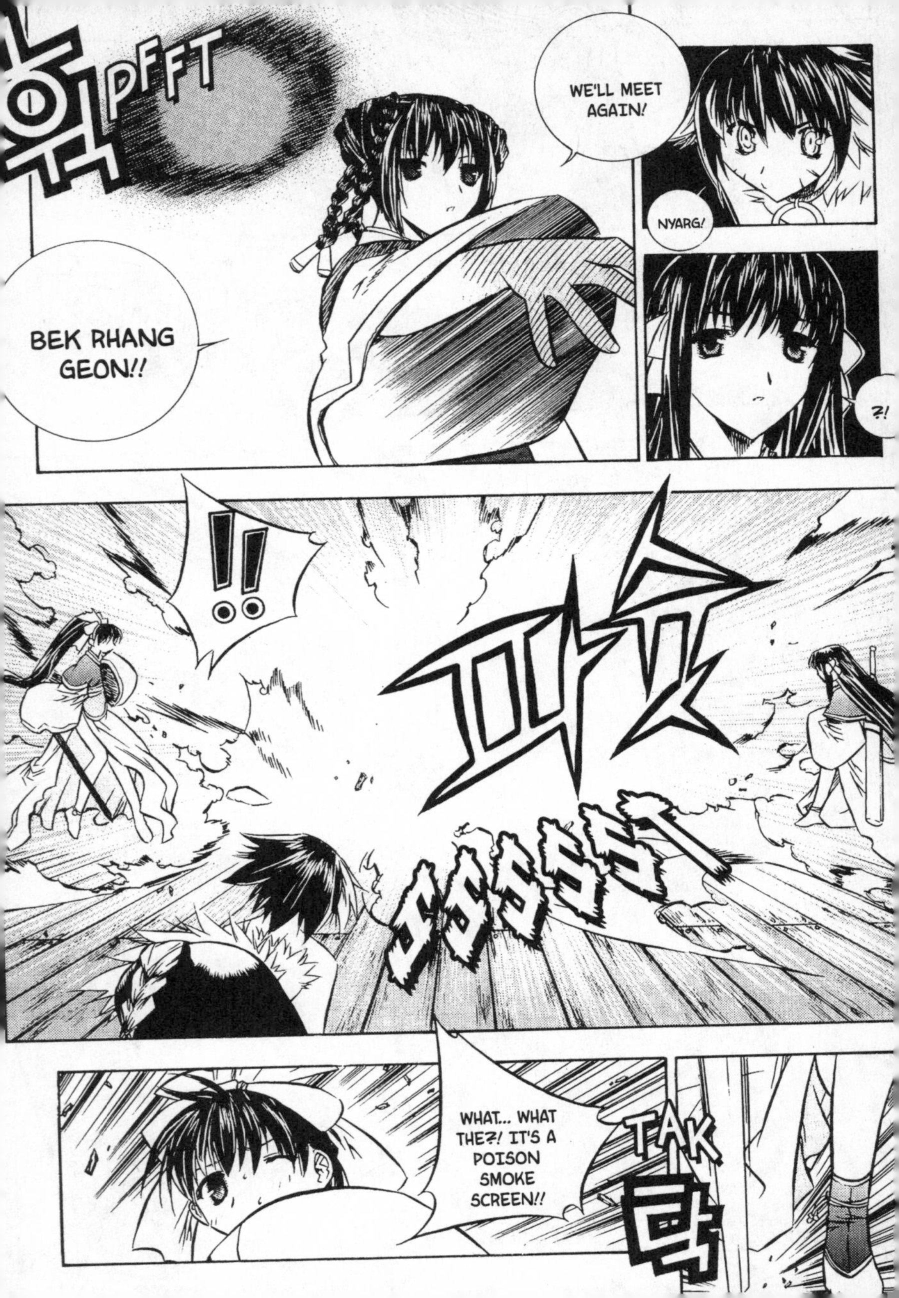

WE'LL MEET AGAIN!
NYARG!
PFFT
BEK RHANG GEON!!
?!
!!
SSSSST
WHAT... WHAT THE?! IT'S A POISON SMOKE SCREEN!!
TAK

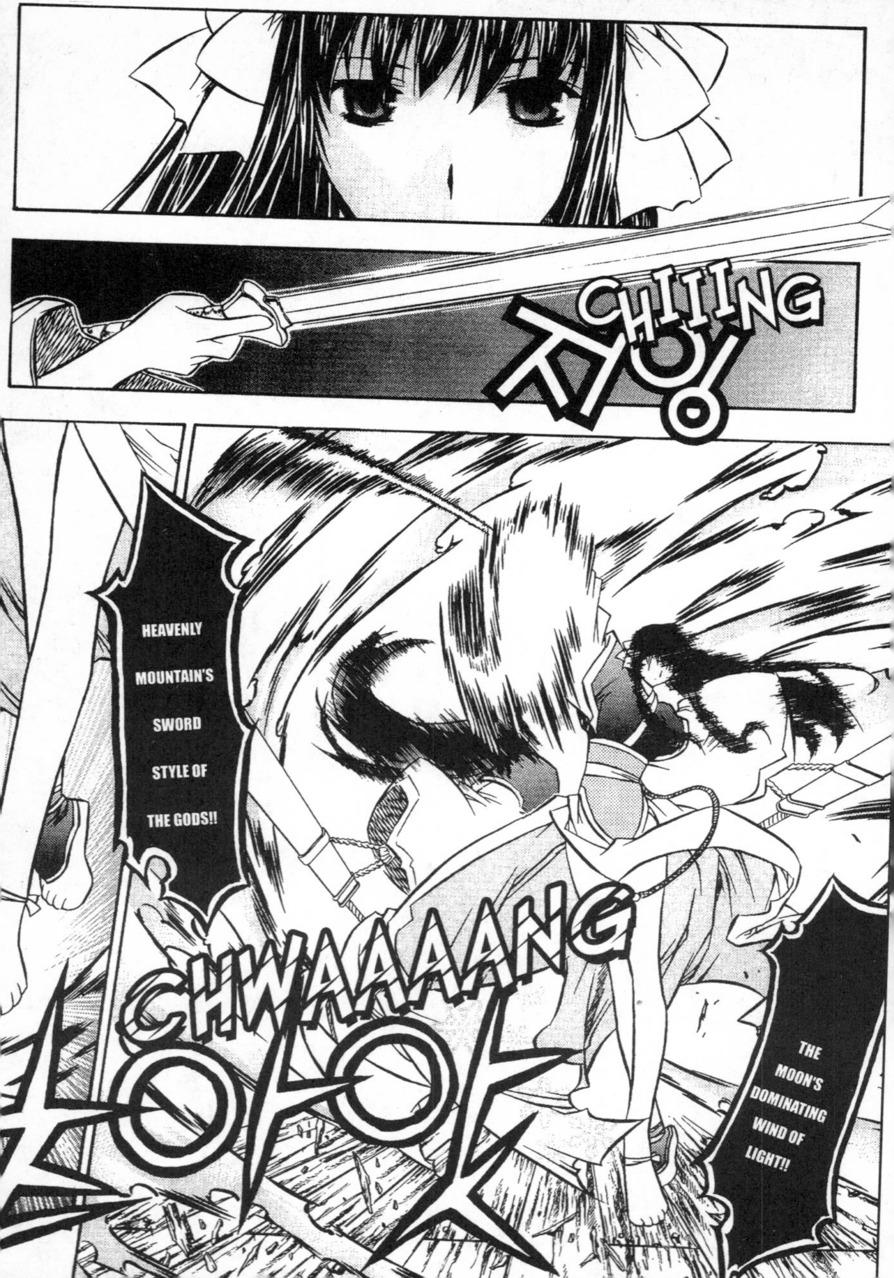
CHIIING
징
HEAVENLY MOUNTAIN'S SWORD STYLE OF THE GODS!!
THE MOON'S DOMINATING WIND OF LIGHT!!
CHWAAAAANG
촤아악

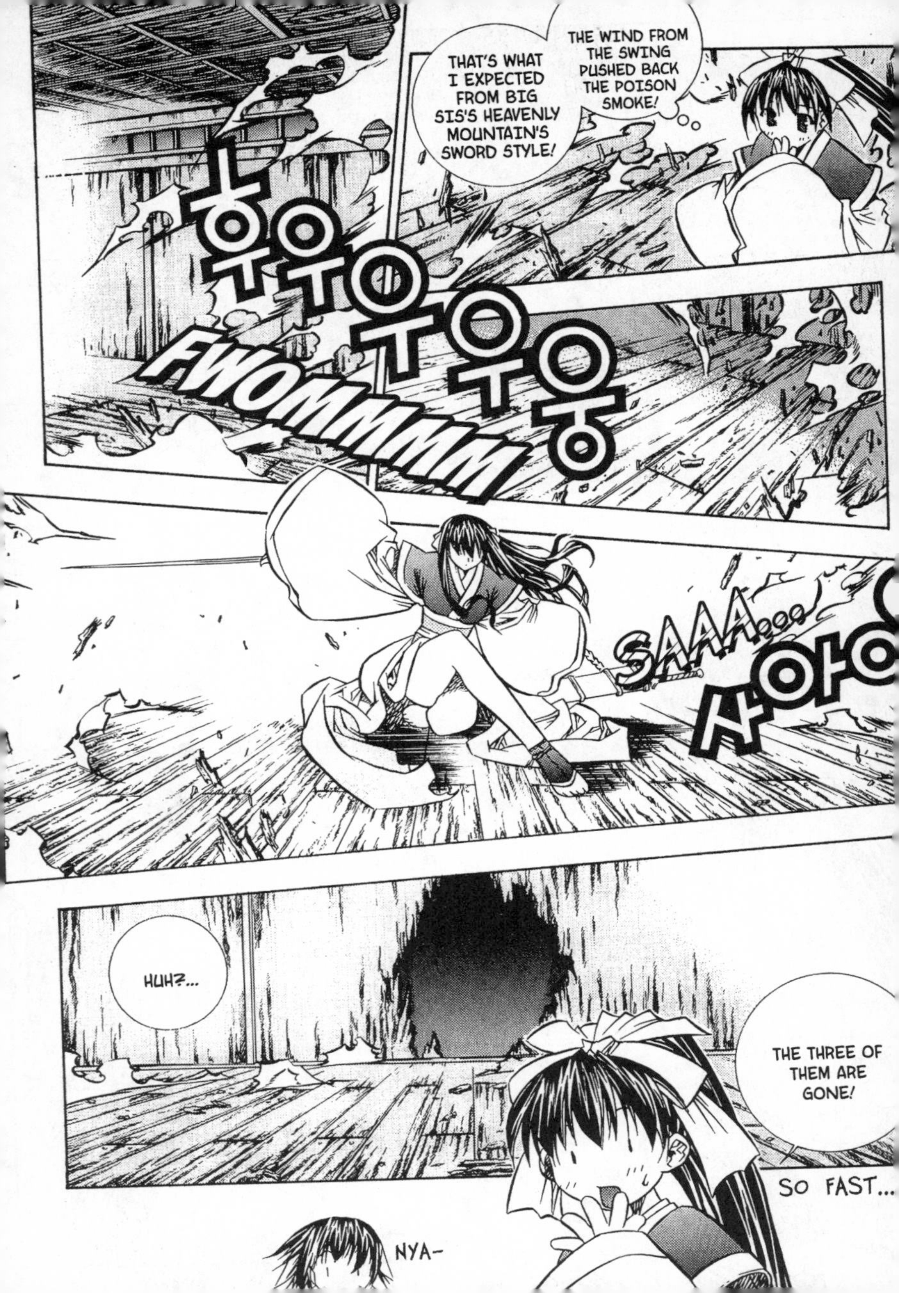
THE WIND FROM THE SWING PUSHED BACK THE POISON SMOKE!
THAT'S WHAT I EXPECTED FROM BIG SIS'S HEAVENLY MOUNTAIN'S SWORD STYLE!
FWOMMMMM
SAAA...
THE THREE OF THEM ARE GONE!
SO FAST...
HUH?...
NYA-

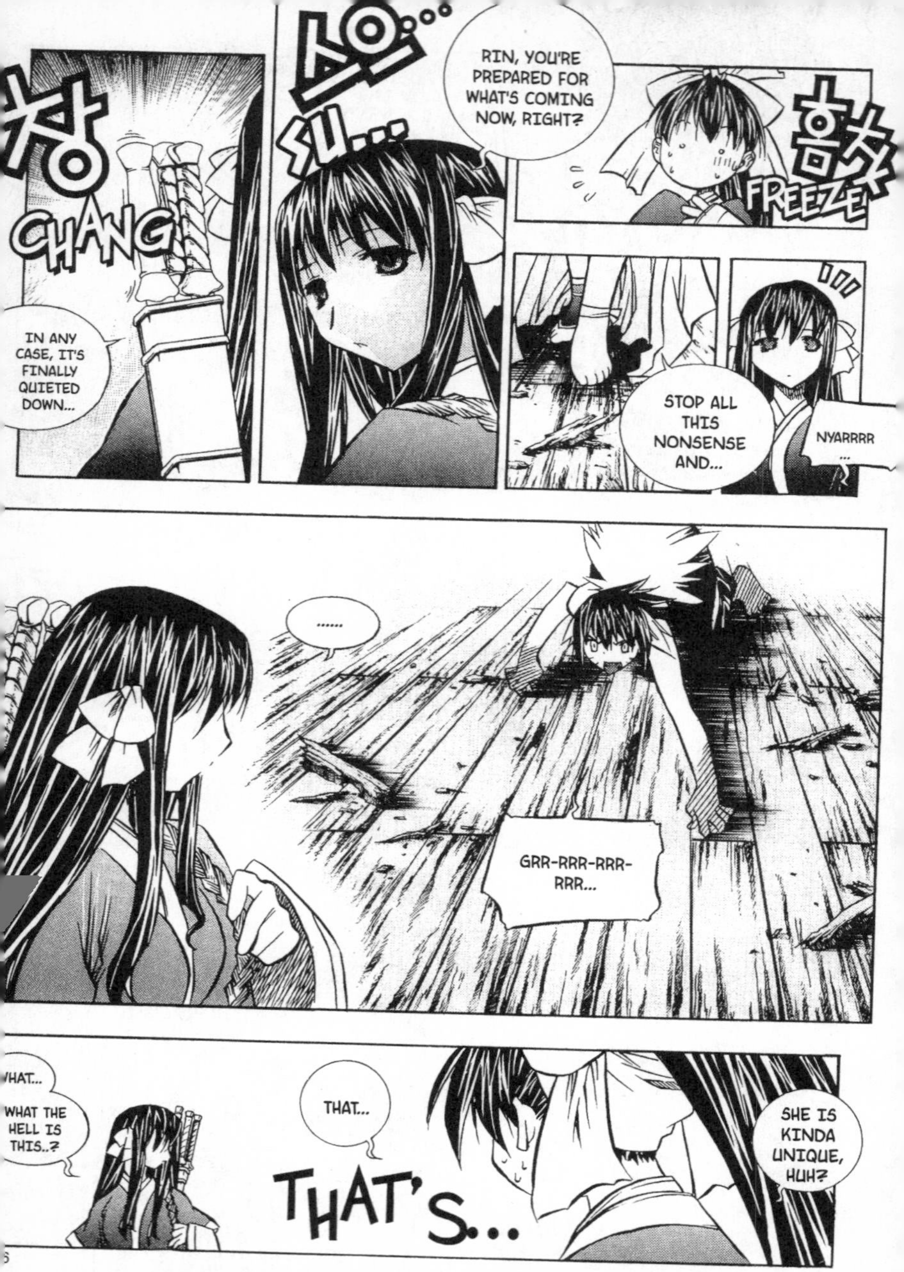
창
CHANG!
IN ANY CASE, IT'S FINALLY QUIETED DOWN...
스으...
SU...
RIN, YOU'RE PREPARED FOR WHAT'S COMING NOW, RIGHT?
흠칫
FREEZE
STOP ALL THIS NONSENSE AND...
NYARRRR ...
......
GRR-RRR-RRR-RRR...
HAT...
WHAT THE HELL IS THIS..?
THAT...
THAT'S...
SHE IS KINDA UNIQUE, HUH?

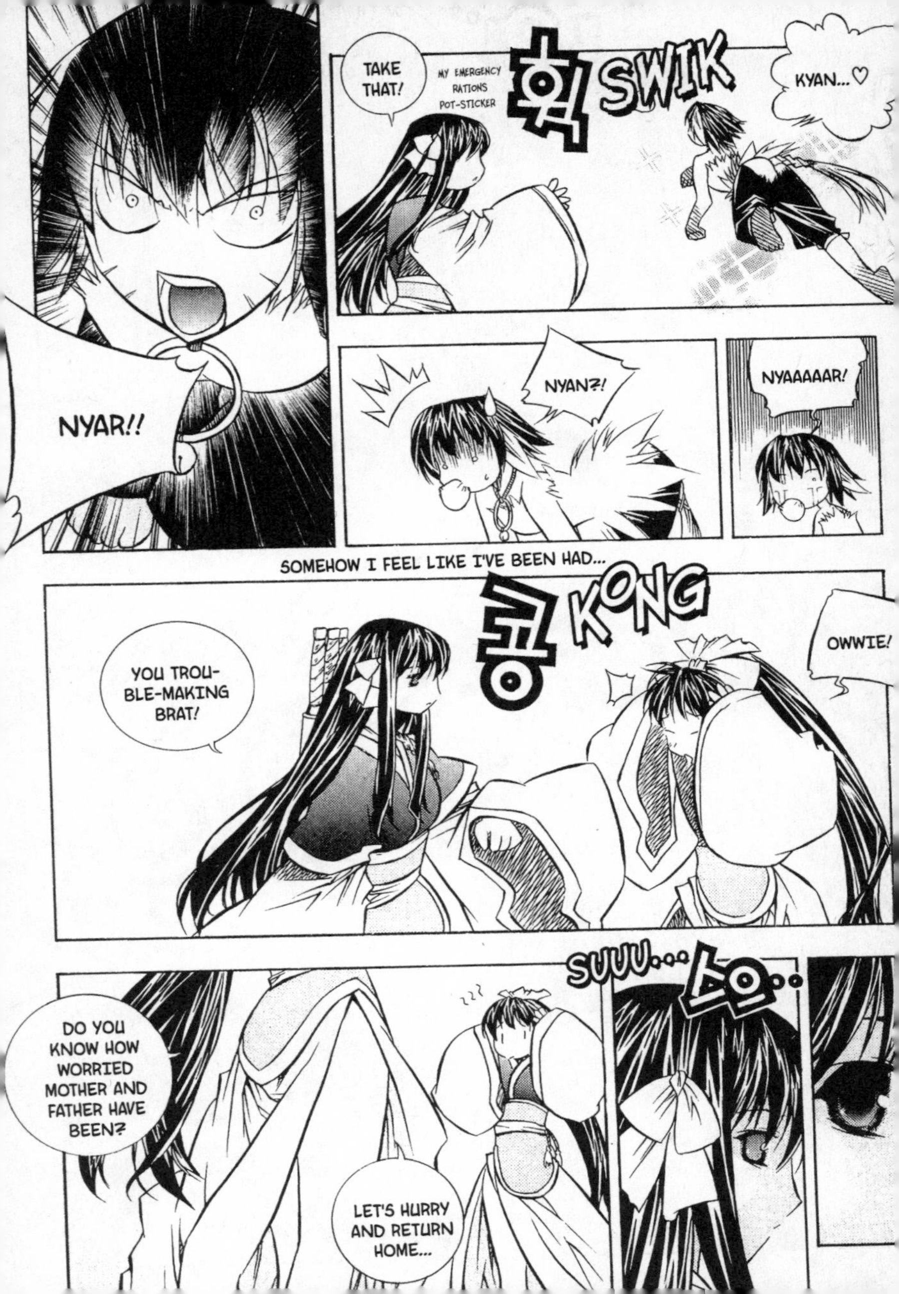
NYAR!!
TAKE THAT!
MY EMERGENCY RATIONS POT-STICKER
휙 SWIK
KYAN...♡
NYAN?!
NYAAAAAR!
SOMEHOW I FEEL LIKE I'VE BEEN HAD...
콩 KONG
YOU TROUBLE-MAKING BRAT!
OWWIE!
DO YOU KNOW HOW WORRIED MOTHER AND FATHER HAVE BEEN?
LET'S HURRY AND RETURN HOME...
SUUU...

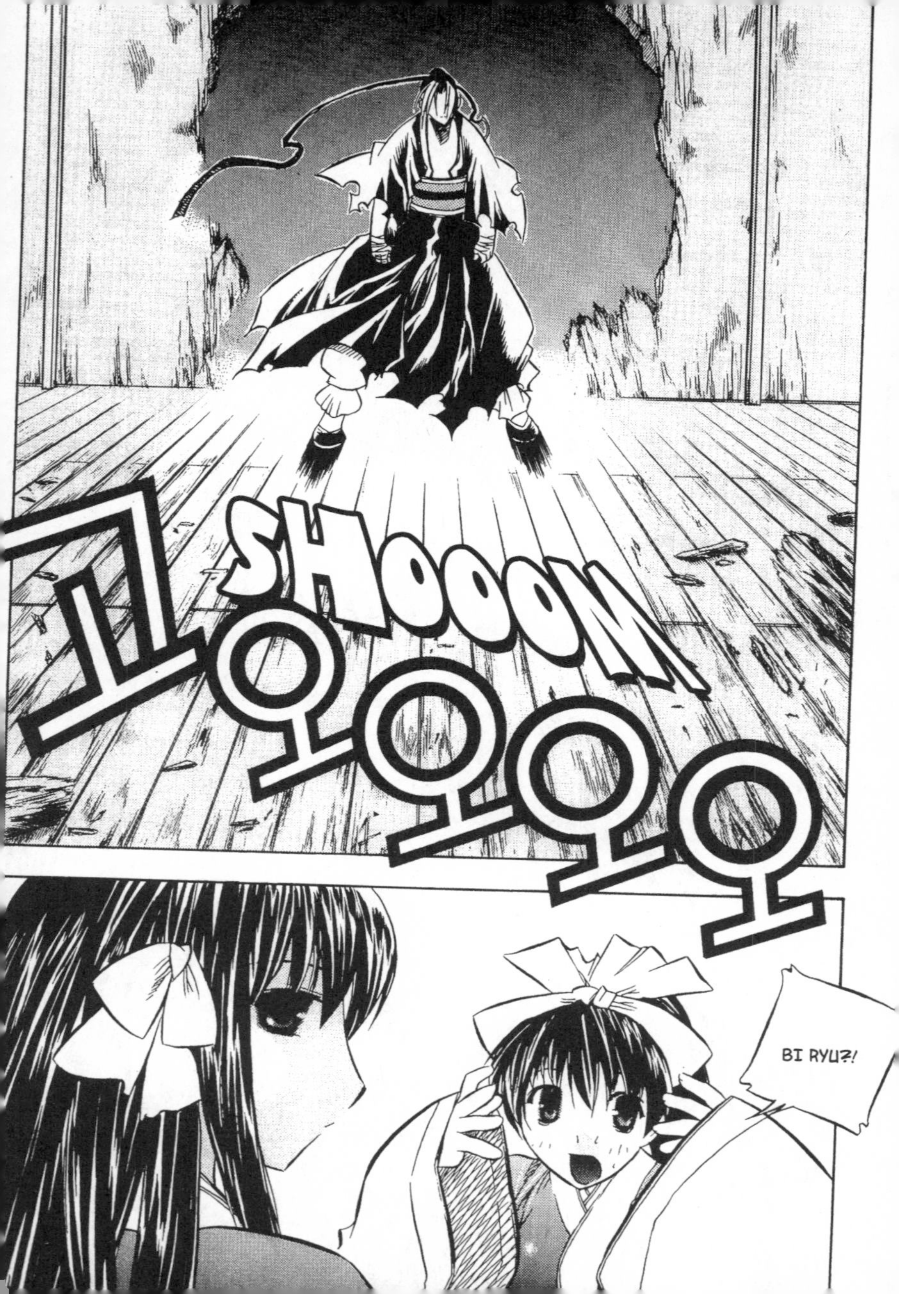
SHOOOM
BI RYU?!

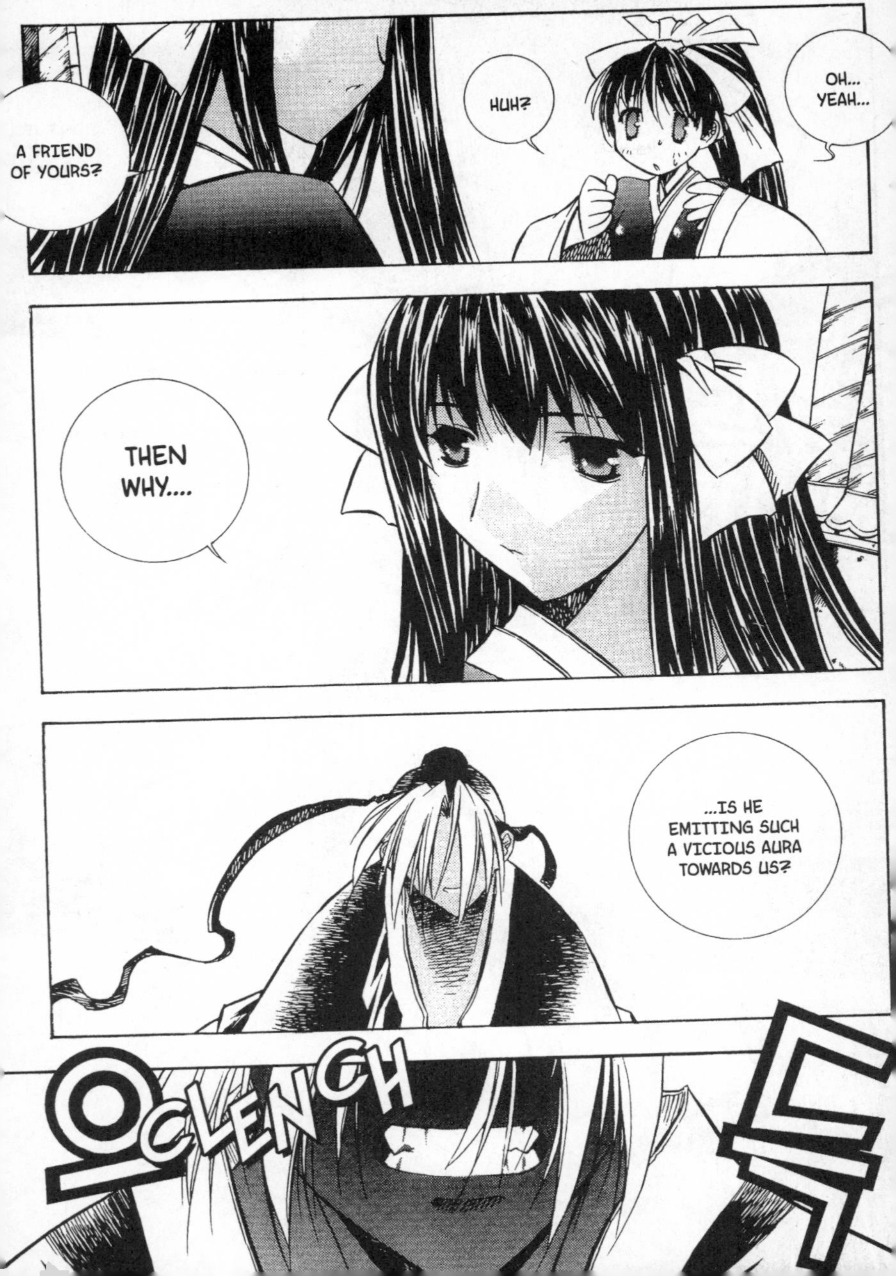
A FRIEND OF YOURS?
HUH?
OH... YEAH...
THEN WHY....
...IS HE EMITTING SUCH A VICIOUS AURA TOWARDS US?
CLENCH

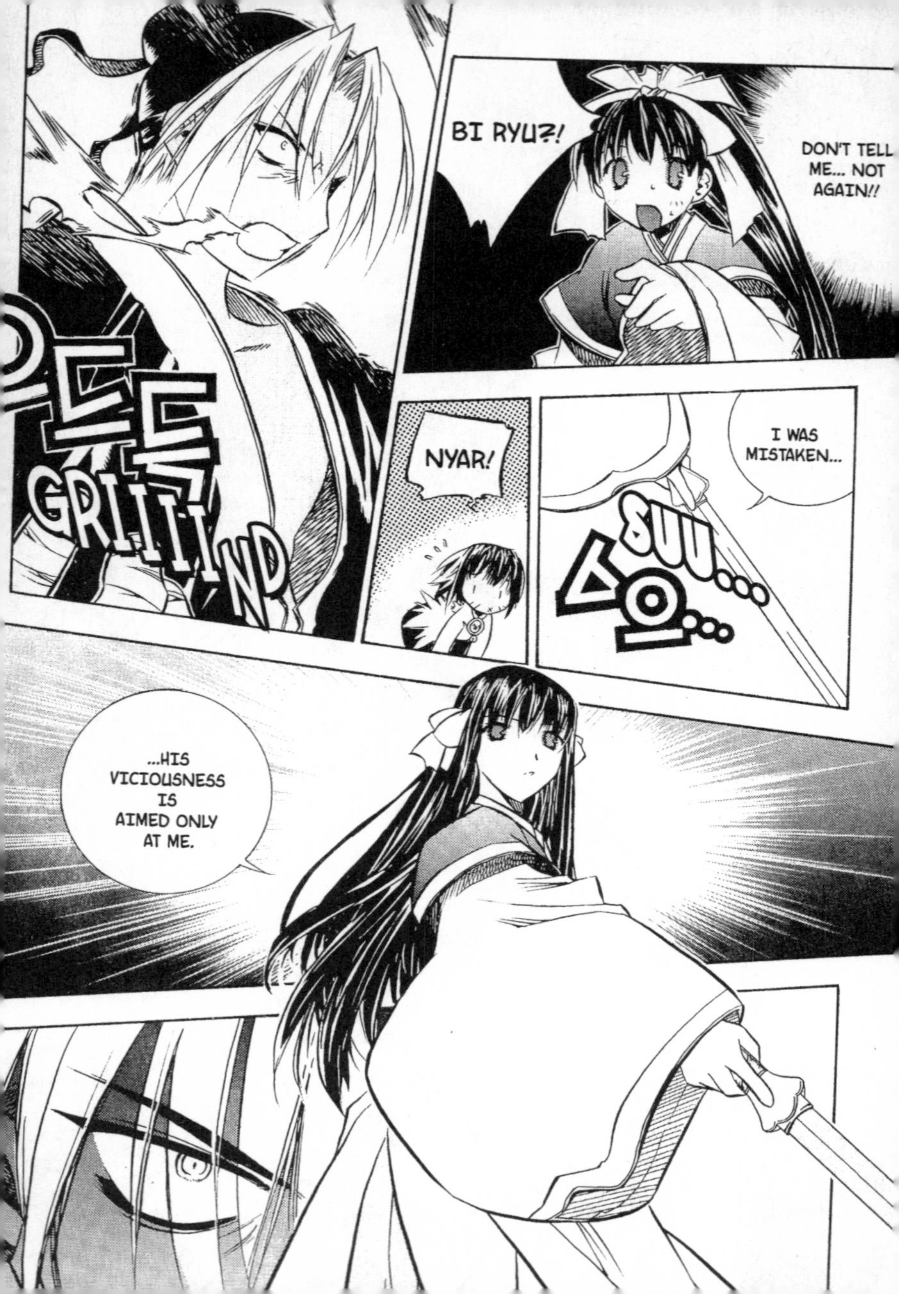
DON'T TELL ME... NOT AGAIN!!
BI RYU?!
GRIIIIND
I WAS MISTAKEN...
SUU...
NYAR!
...HIS VICIOUSNESS IS AIMED ONLY AT ME.

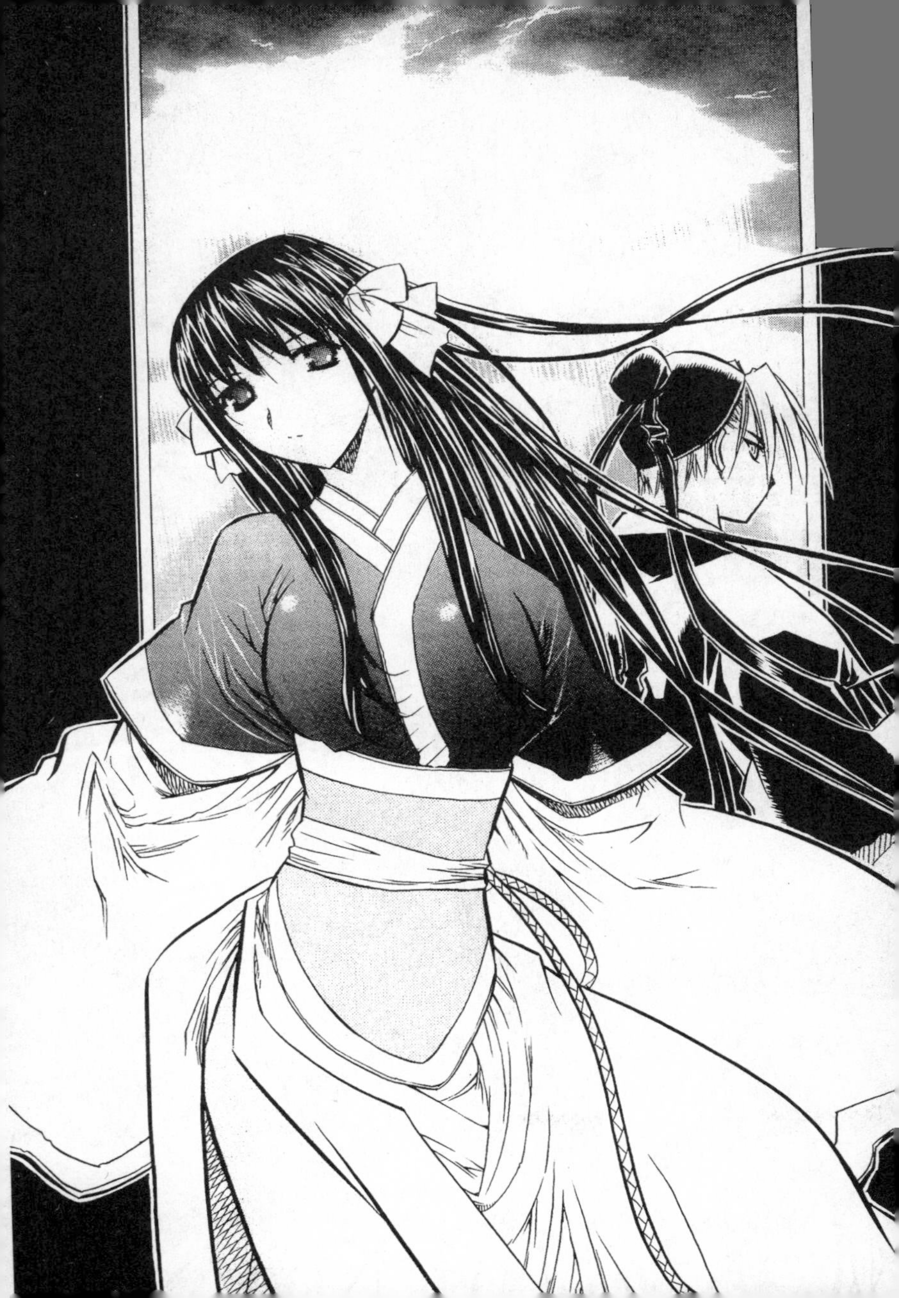

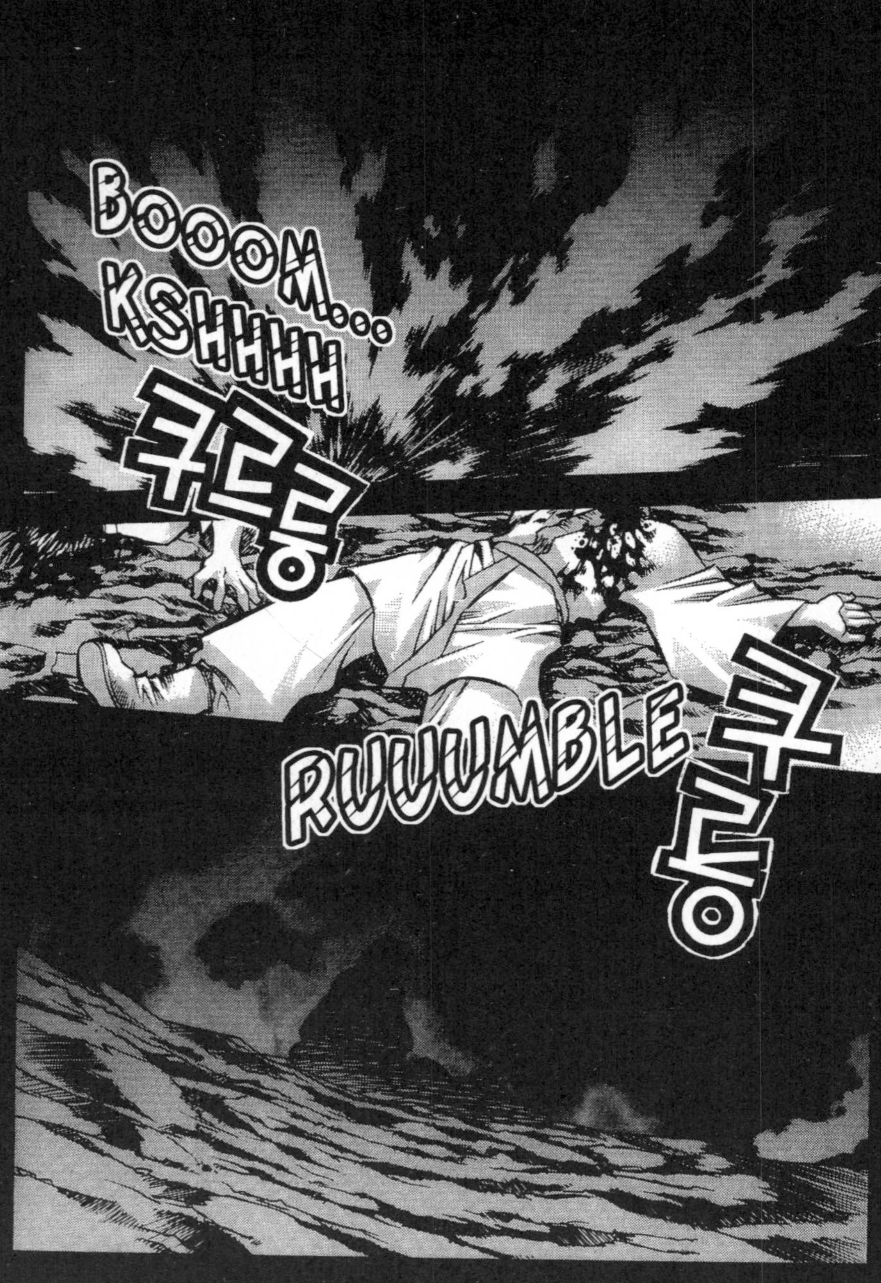
BOOOM...
KSHHHHH
RUUUMBLE

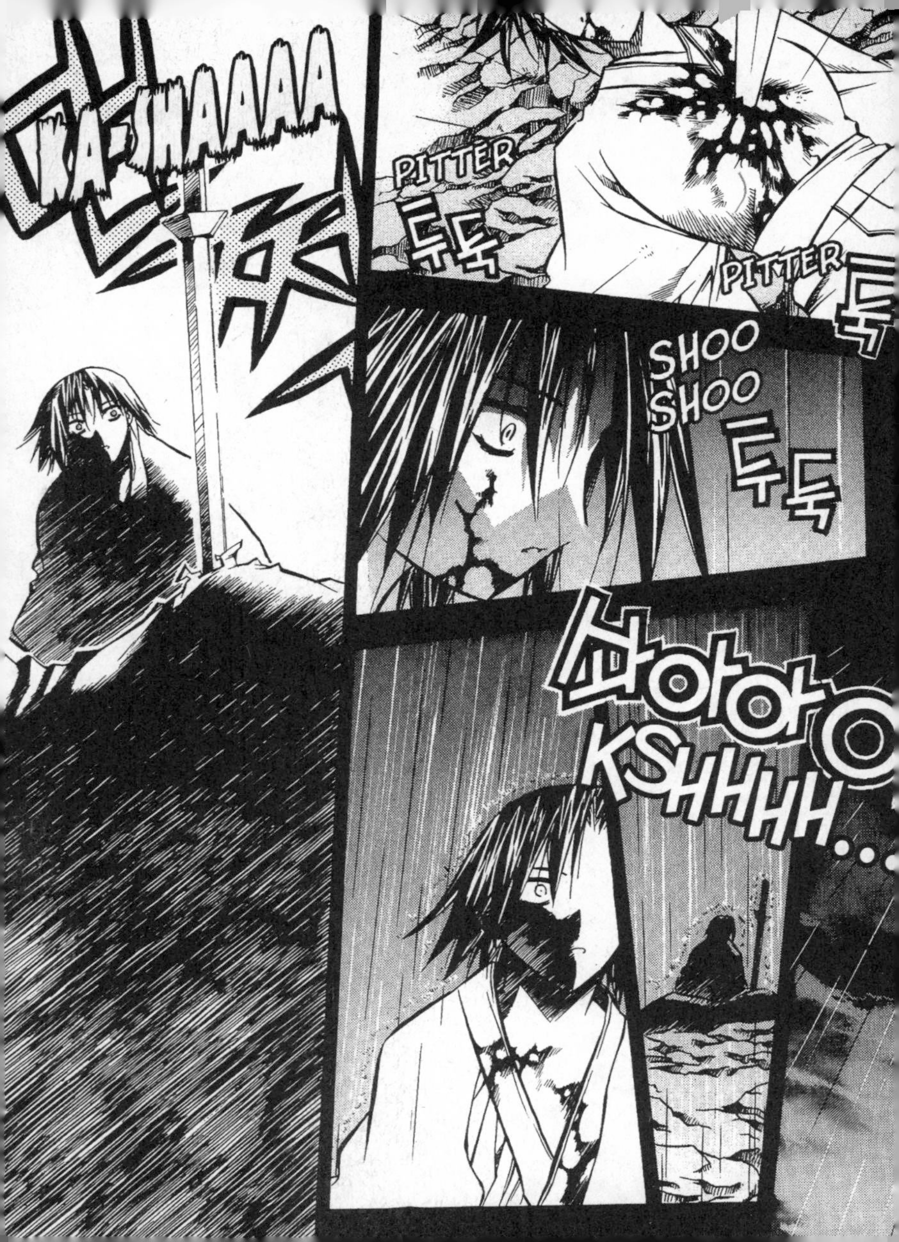
KA-SHAAAA
PITTER
PITTER
SHOO
SHOO
KSHHHH...

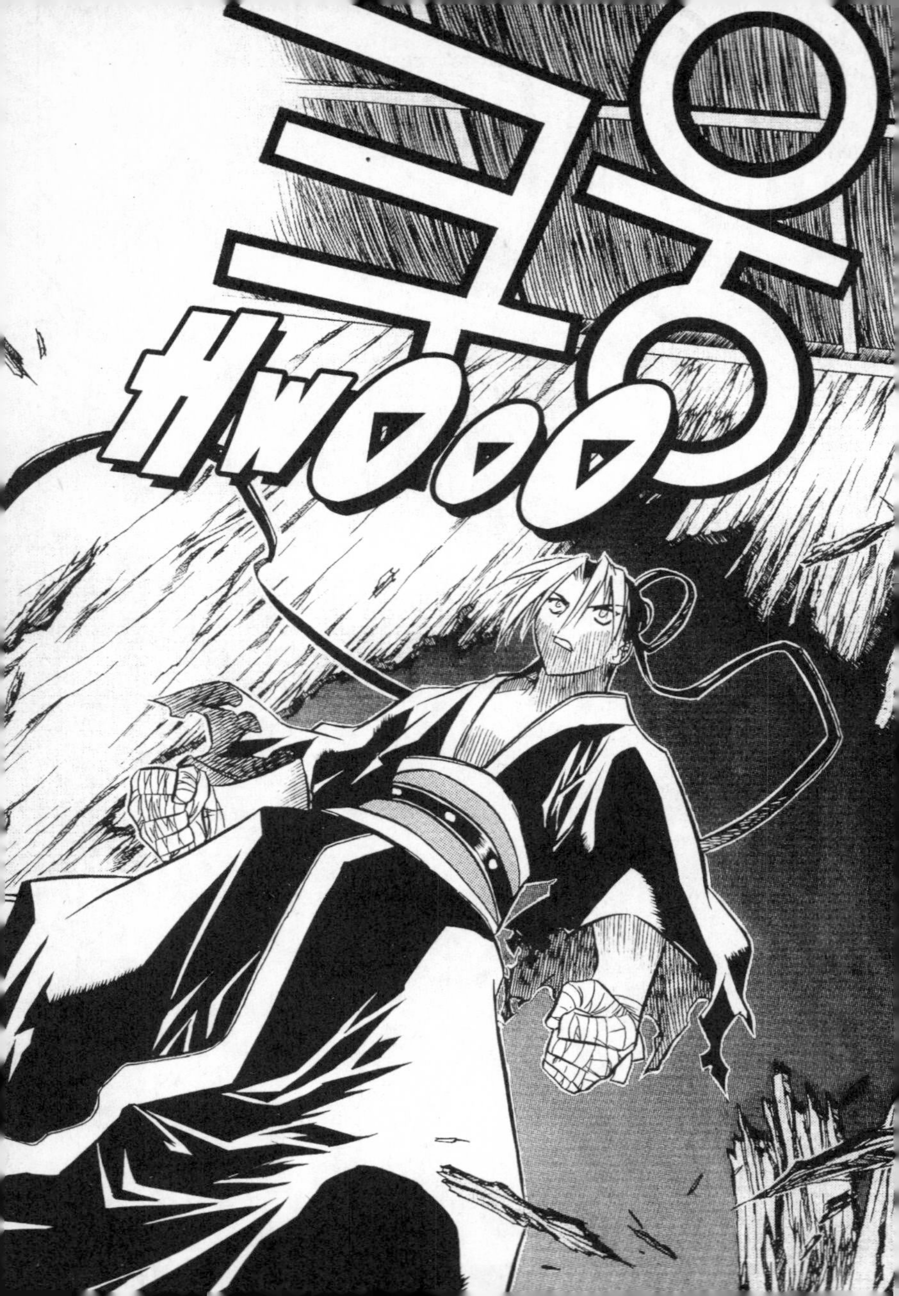
HWOOO

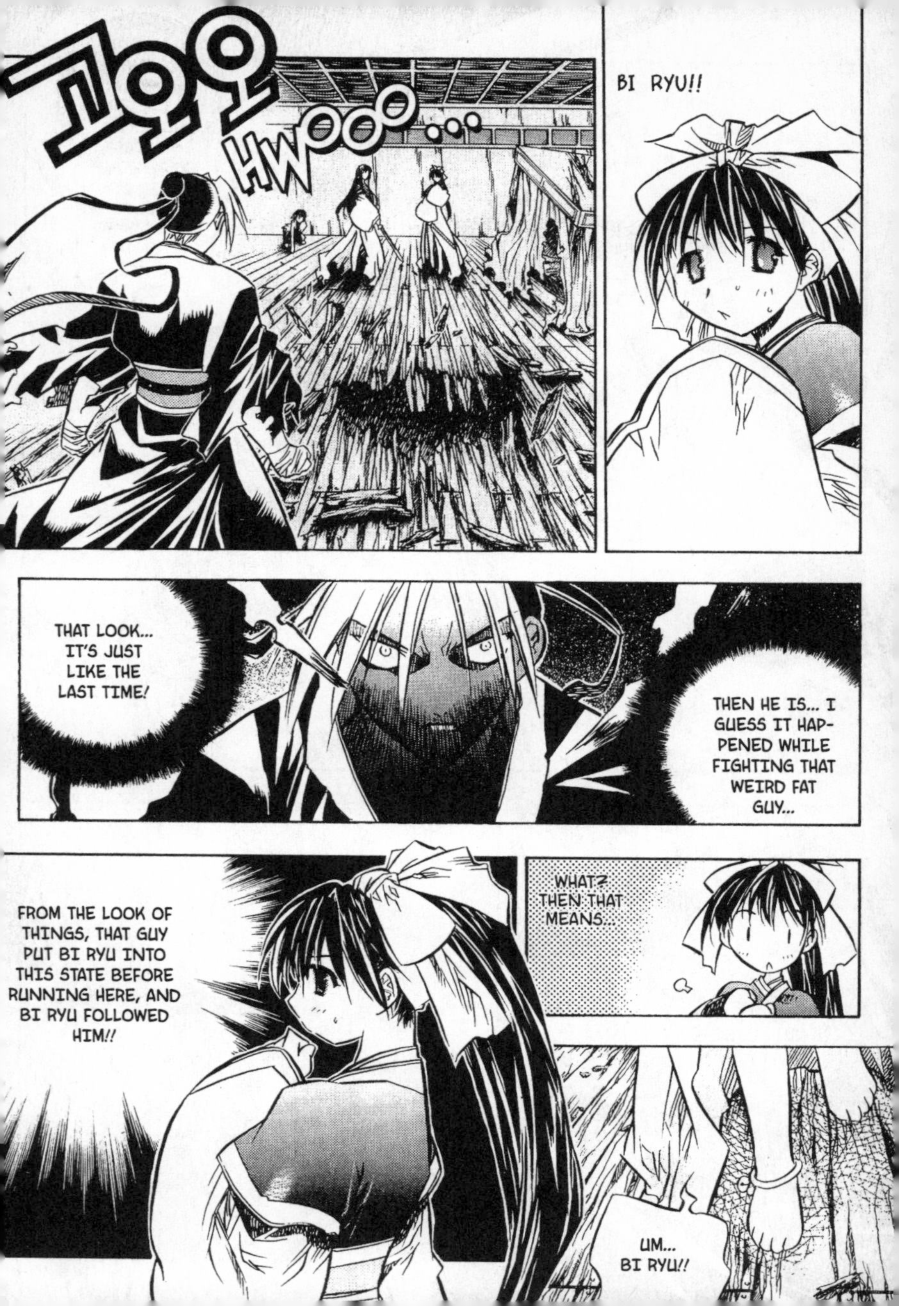
BI RYU!!
HWOOO...
THAT LOOK... IT'S JUST LIKE THE LAST TIME!
THEN HE IS... I GUESS IT HAPPENED WHILE FIGHTING THAT WEIRD FAT GUY...
WHAT? THEN THAT MEANS...
FROM THE LOOK OF THINGS, THAT GUY PUT BI RYU INTO THIS STATE BEFORE RUNNING HERE, AND BI RYU FOLLOWED HIM!!
UM... BI RYU!!

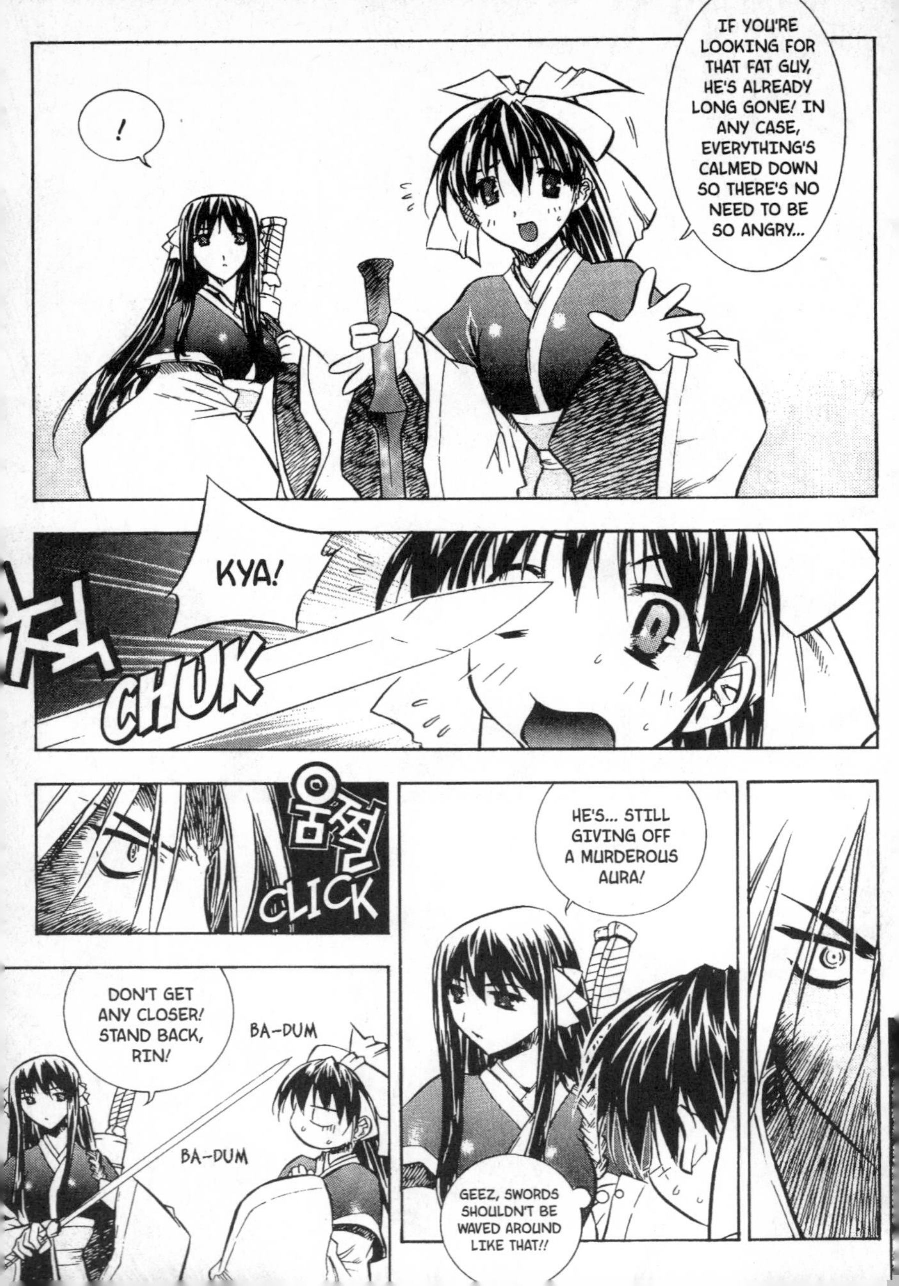
IF YOU'RE LOOKING FOR THAT FAT GUY, HE'S ALREADY LONG GONE! IN ANY CASE, EVERYTHING'S CALMED DOWN SO THERE'S NO NEED TO BE SO ANGRY...
!
KYA!
척
CHUK
HE'S... STILL GIVING OFF A MURDEROUS AURA!
움찔
CLICK
GEEZ, SWORDS SHOULDN'T BE WAVED AROUND LIKE THAT!!
DON'T GET ANY CLOSER! STAND BACK, RIN!
BA-DUM
BA-DUM

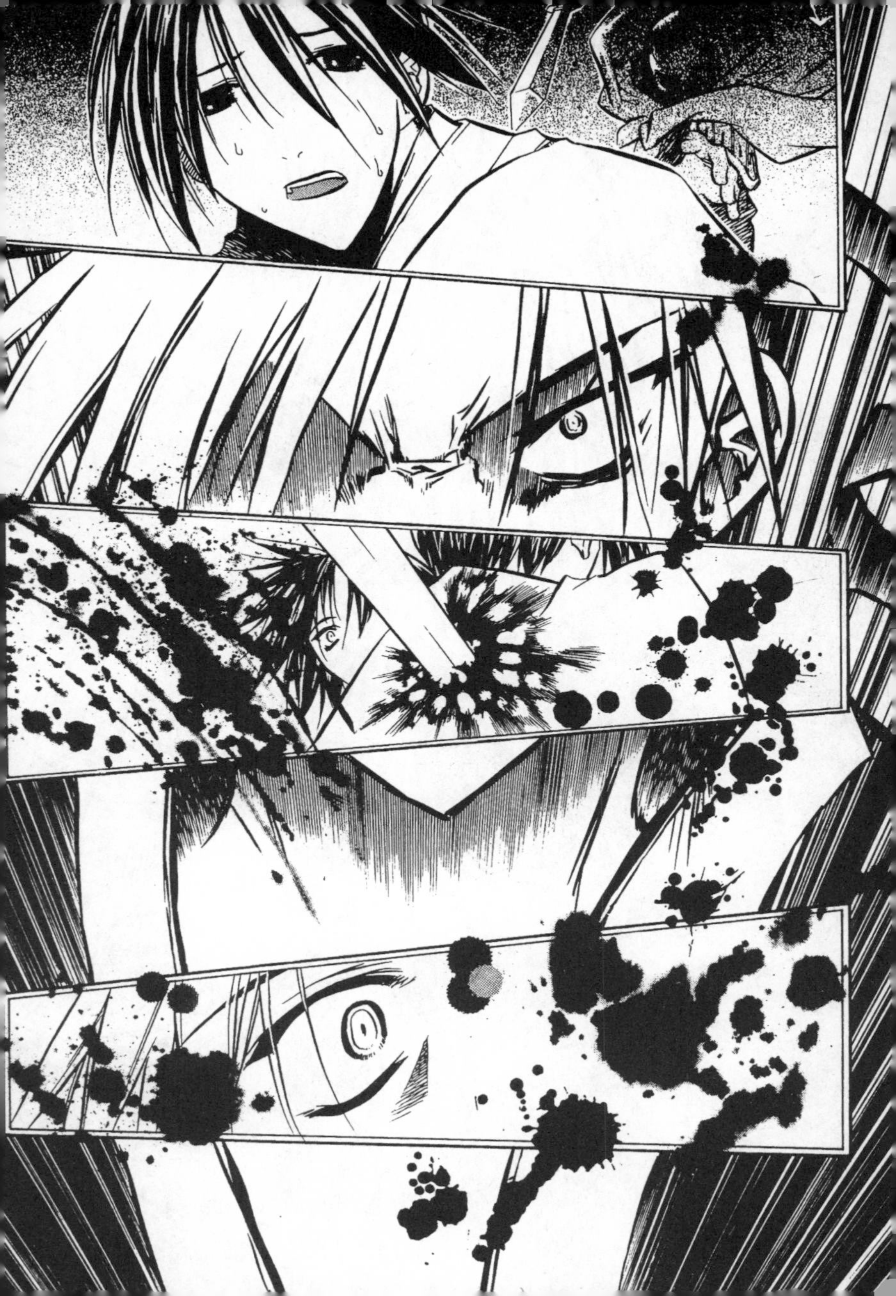

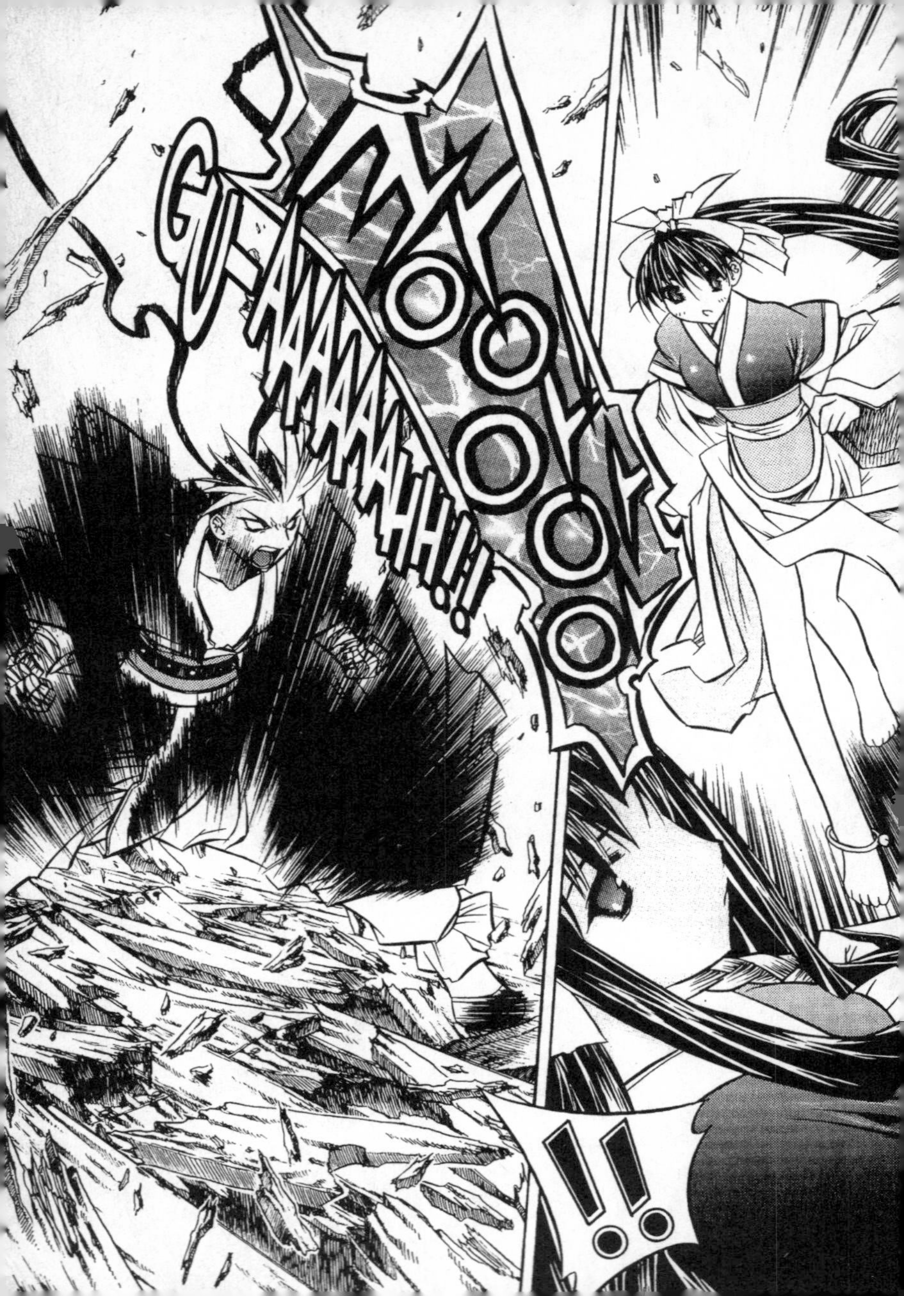
GUHAAAAAAAAAAAHH!!
!!

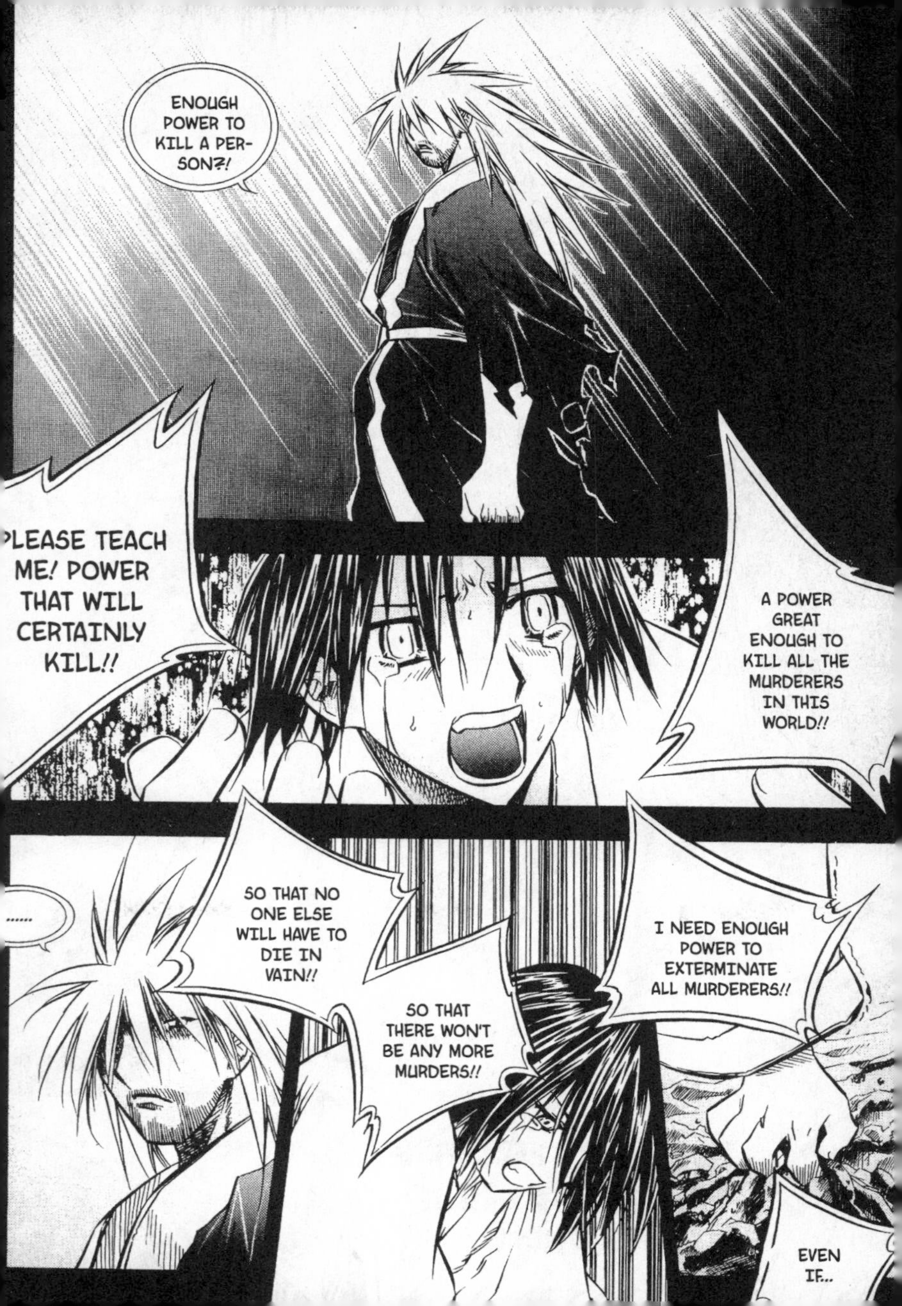

ENOUGH POWER TO KILL A PERSON?!
A POWER GREAT ENOUGH TO KILL ALL THE MURDERERS IN THIS WORLD!!
PLEASE TEACH ME! POWER THAT WILL CERTAINLY KILL!!
I NEED ENOUGH POWER TO EXTERMINATE ALL MURDERERS!!
SO THAT NO ONE ELSE WILL HAVE TO DIE IN VAIN!!
SO THAT THERE WON'T BE ANY MORE MURDERS!!
......
EVEN IF...

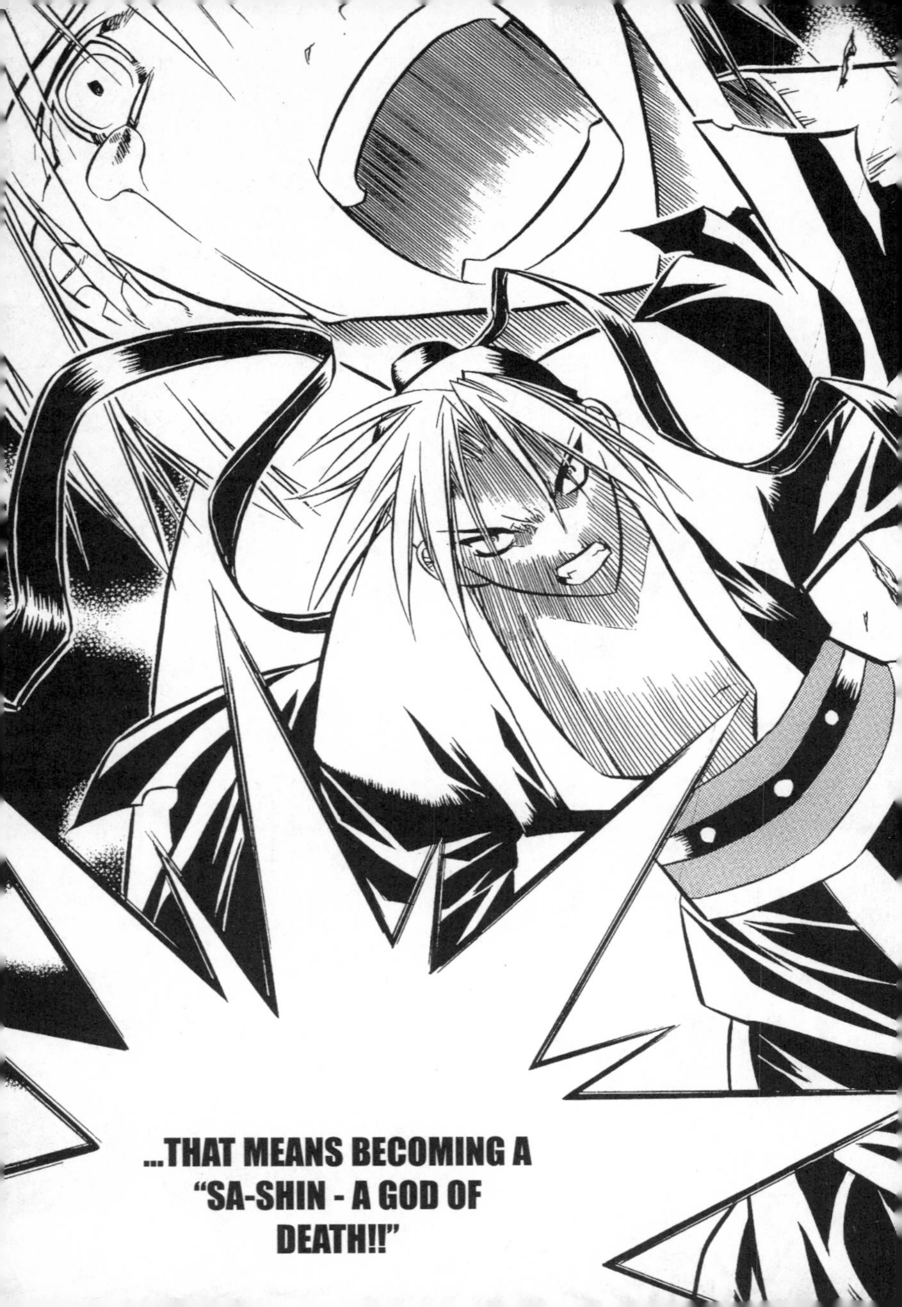
...THAT MEANS BECOMING A "SA-SHIN - A GOD OF DEATH!!"

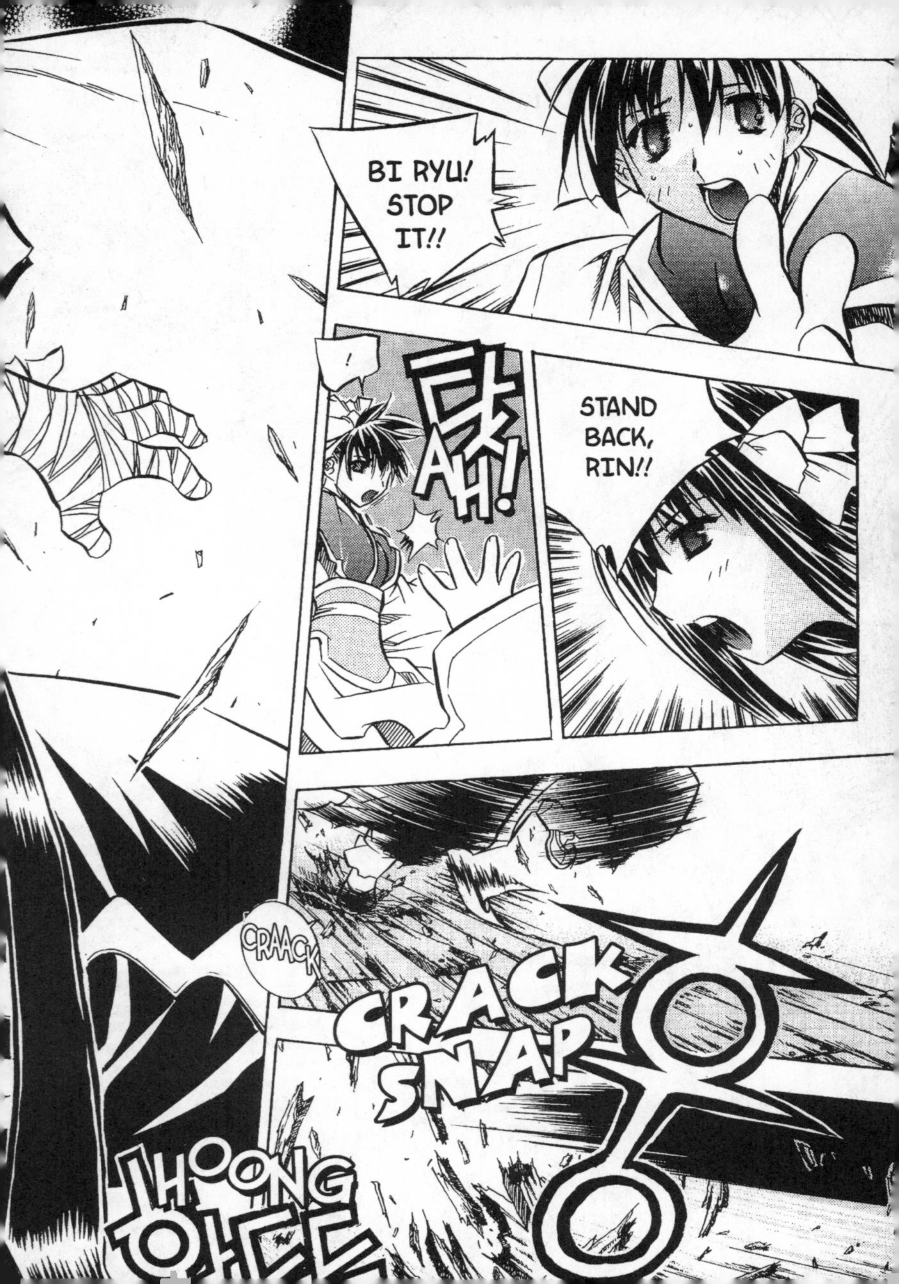
BI RYU! STOP IT!!
!
STAND BACK, RIN!!
AH!
CRAACK
CRACK SNAP
HOONG

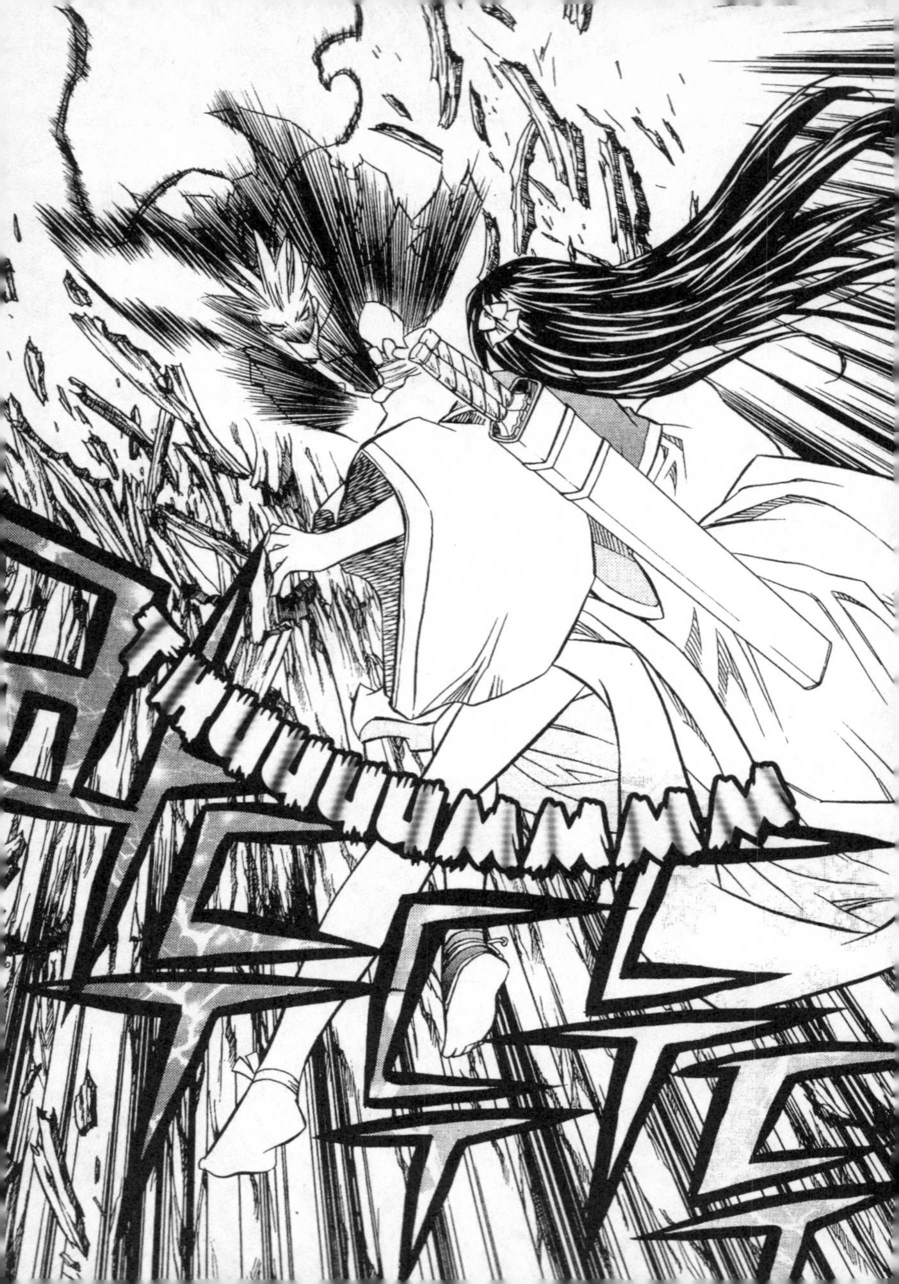
FUUUUUMMMN

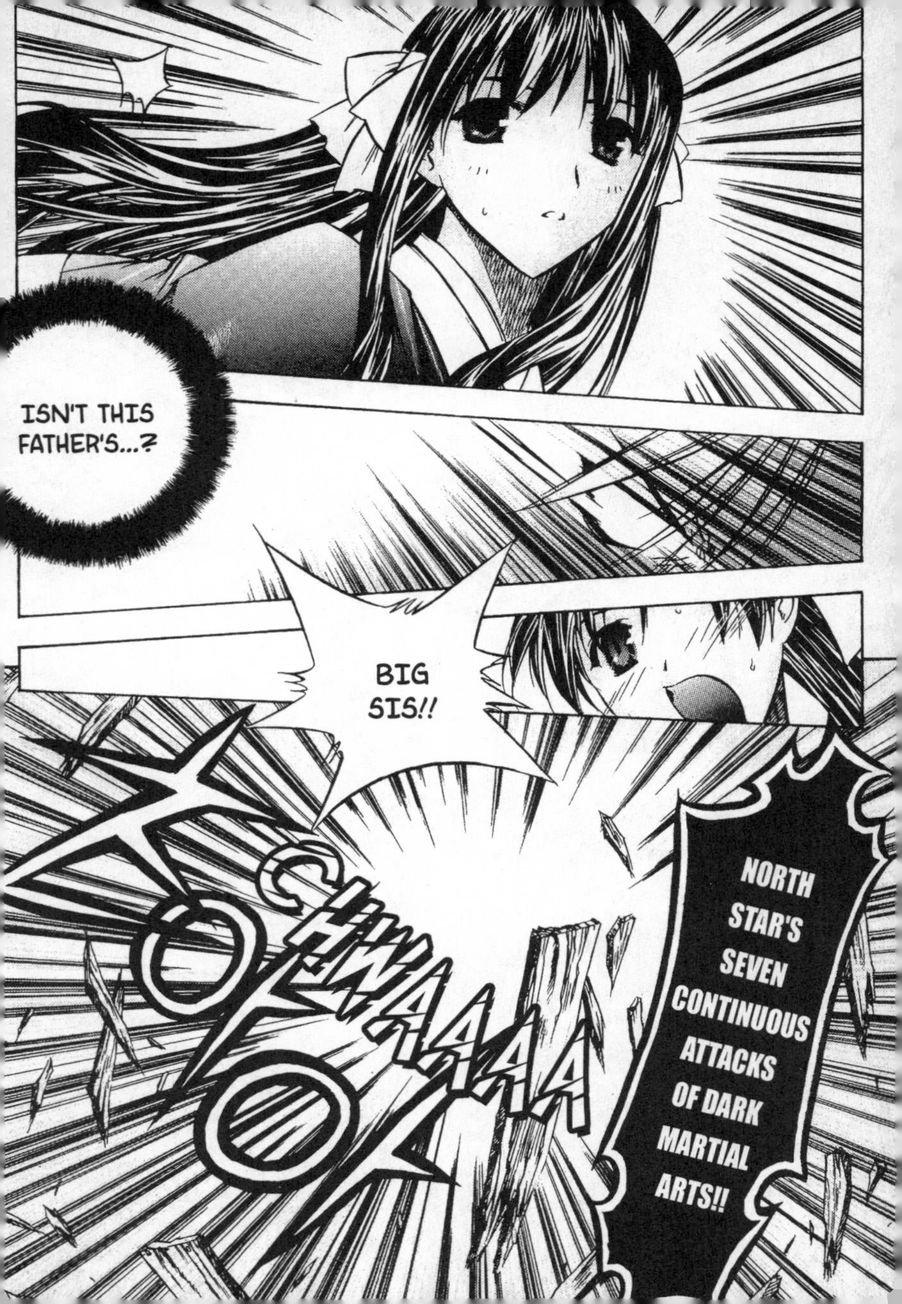
ISN'T THIS FATHER'S...?
BIG SIS!!
NORTH STAR'S SEVEN CONTINUOUS ATTACKS OF DARK MARTIAL ARTS!!
CHWAAAA

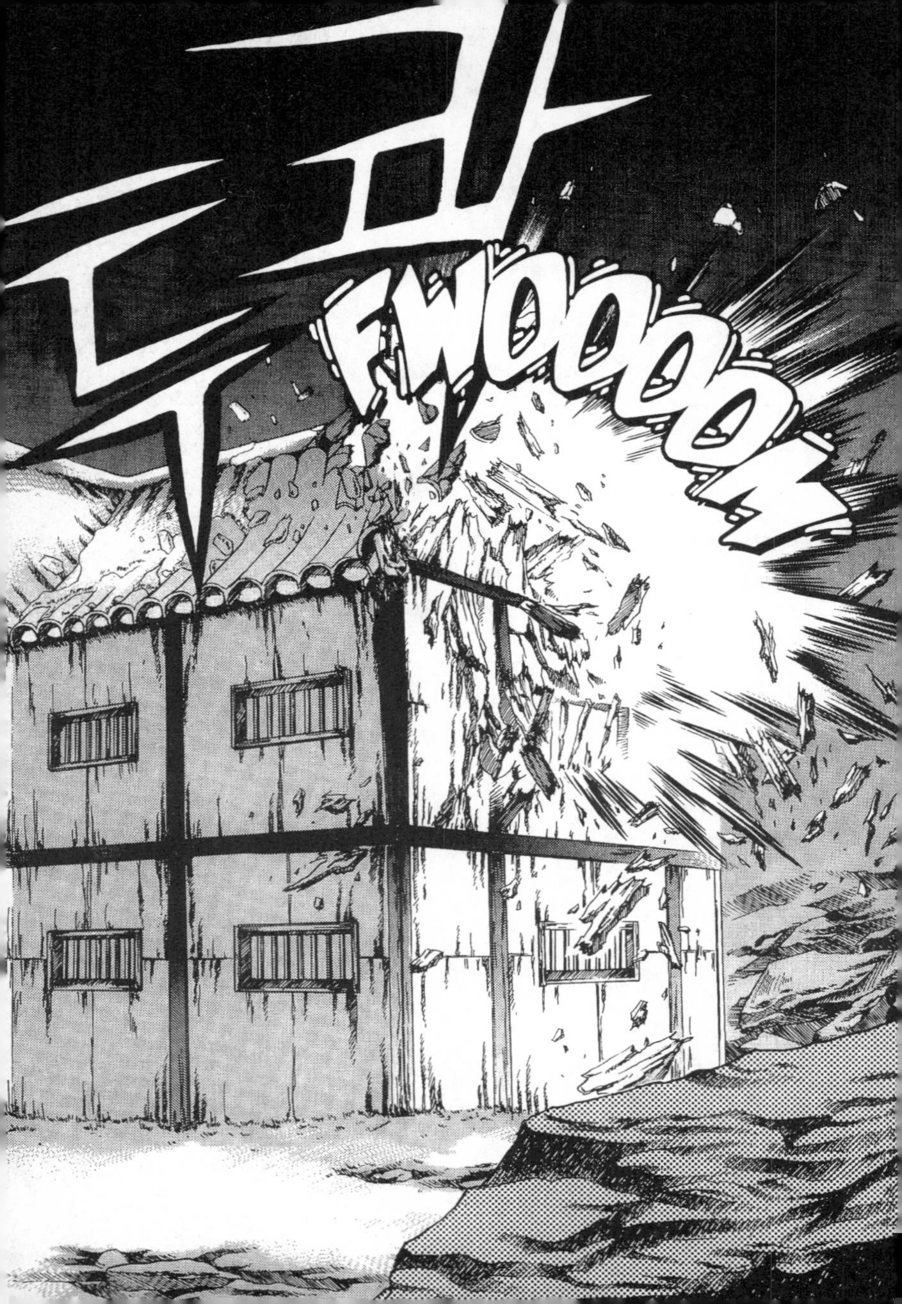
FWOOOOM

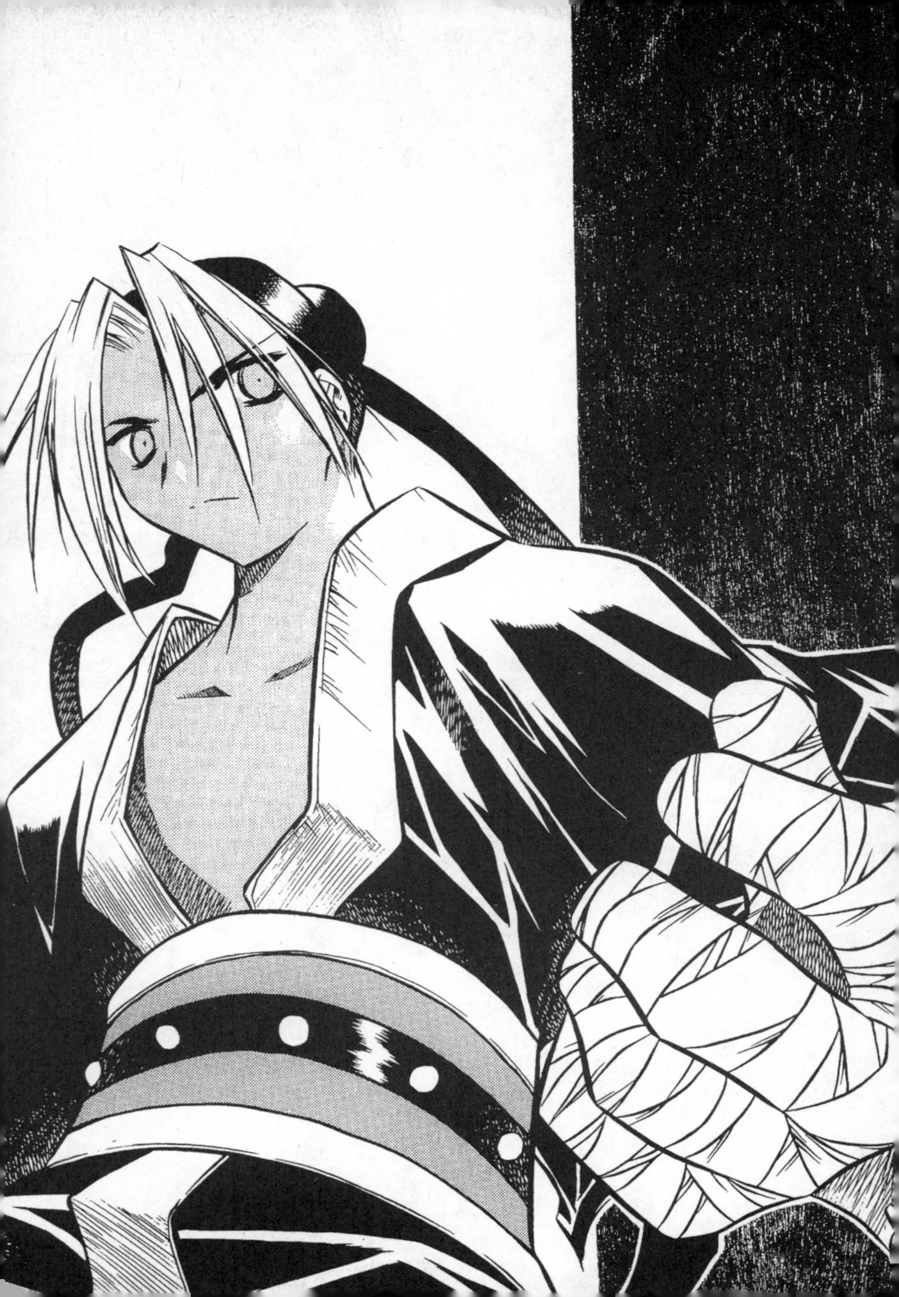

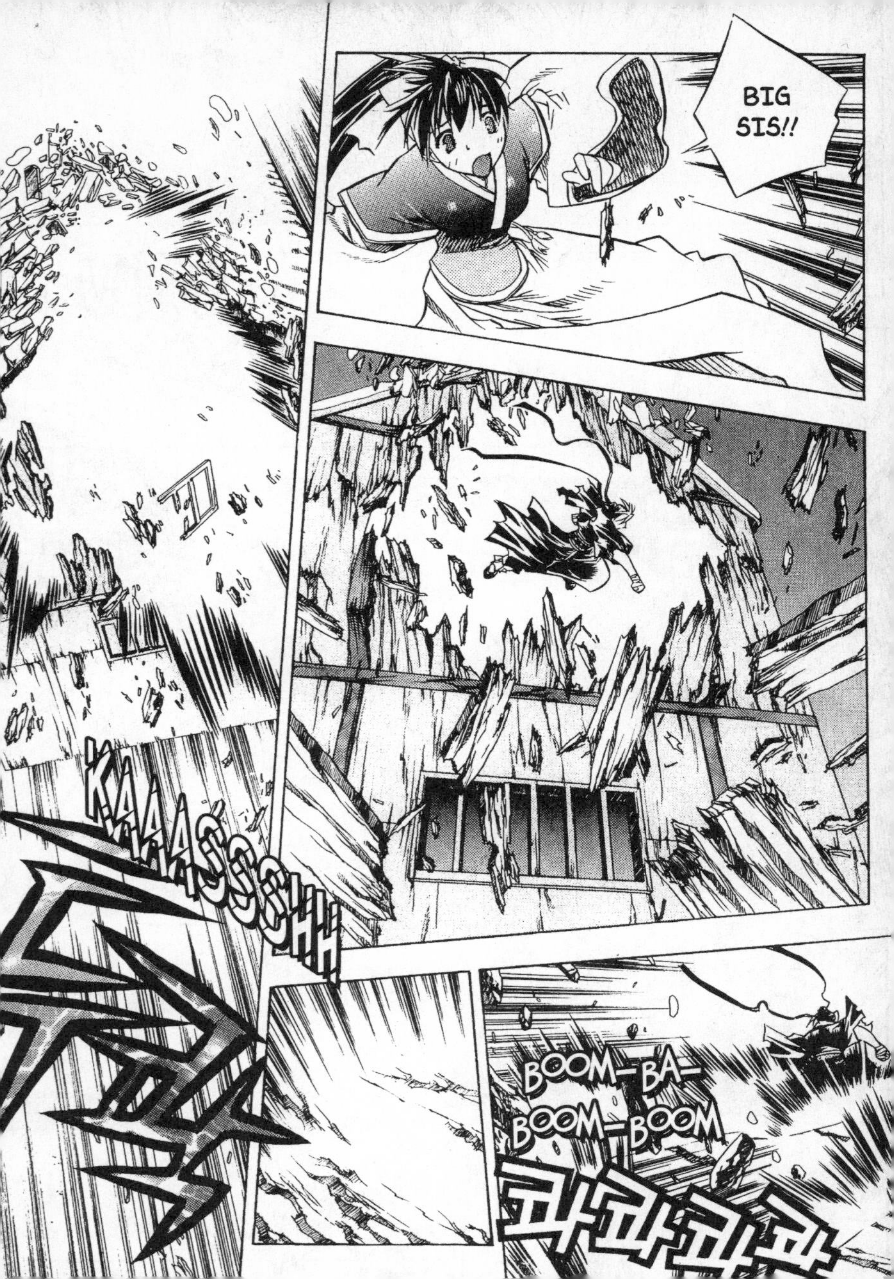
BIG SIS!!
KAAASSSHH
BOOM-BA-BOOM-BOOM
파파파파

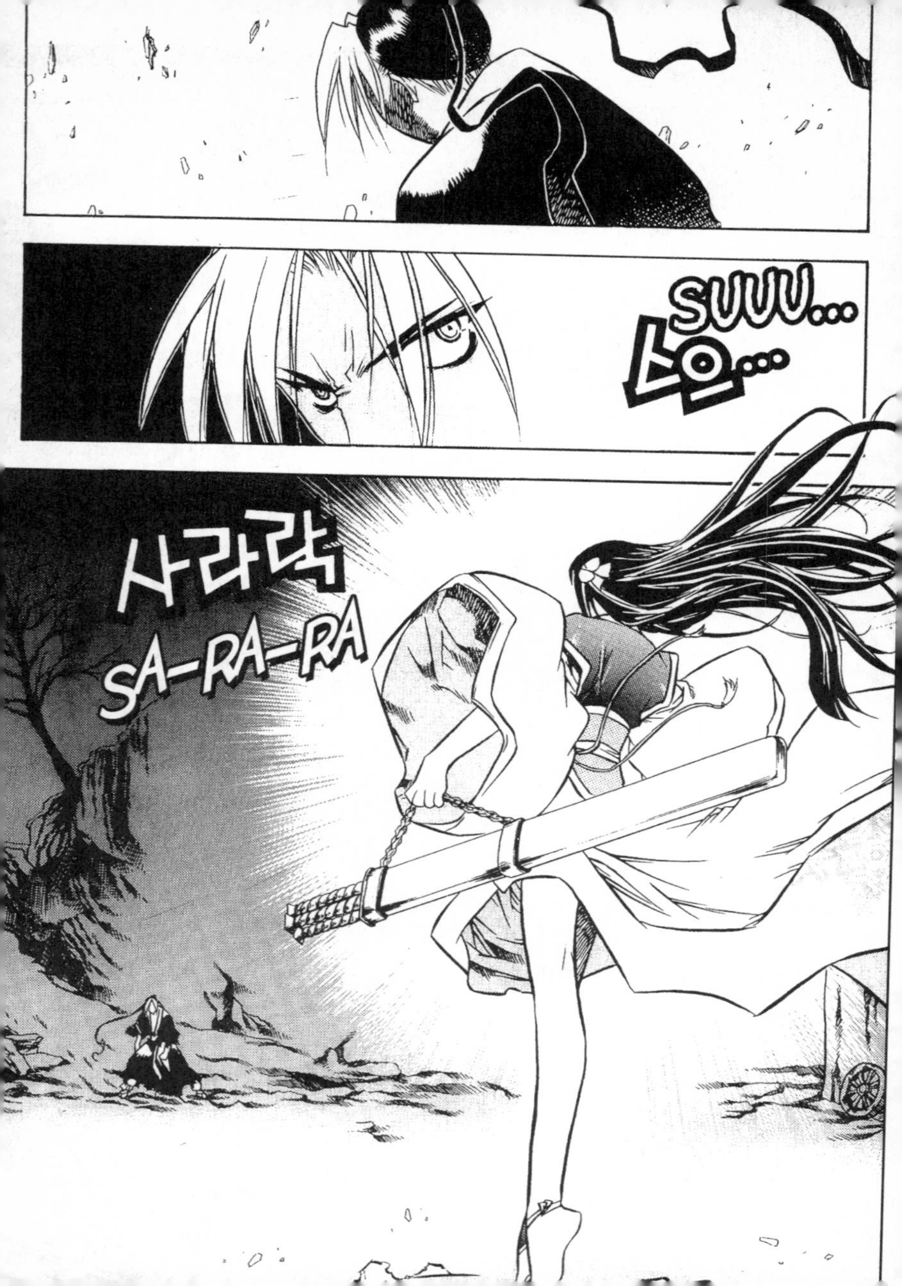
SUUU...
스으...
사라락
SA-RA-RA

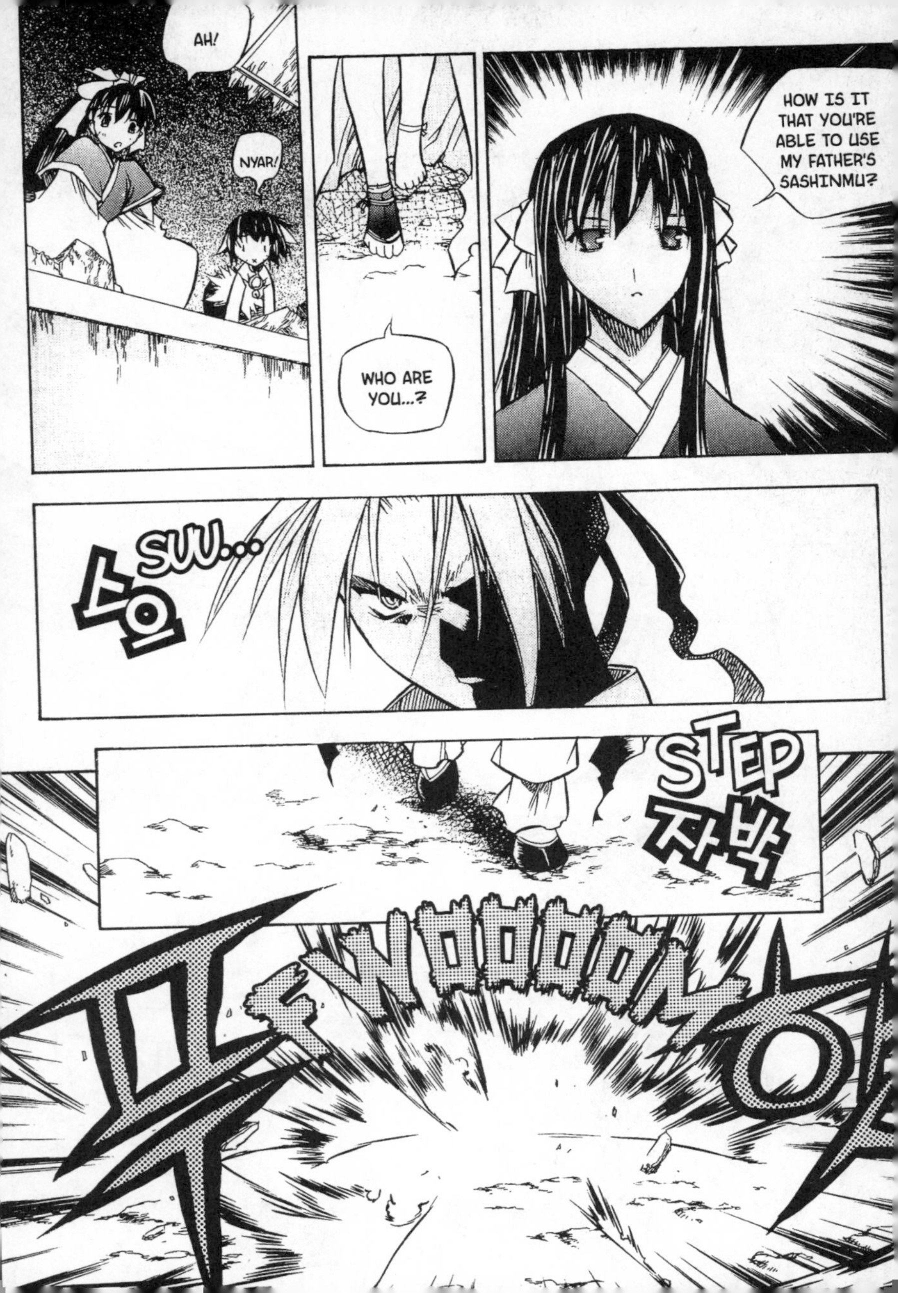
AH!
NYAR!
WHO ARE YOU...?
HOW IS IT THAT YOU'RE ABLE TO USE MY FATHER'S SASHINMU?
SUU...
STEP
자박
SWOOOOOM

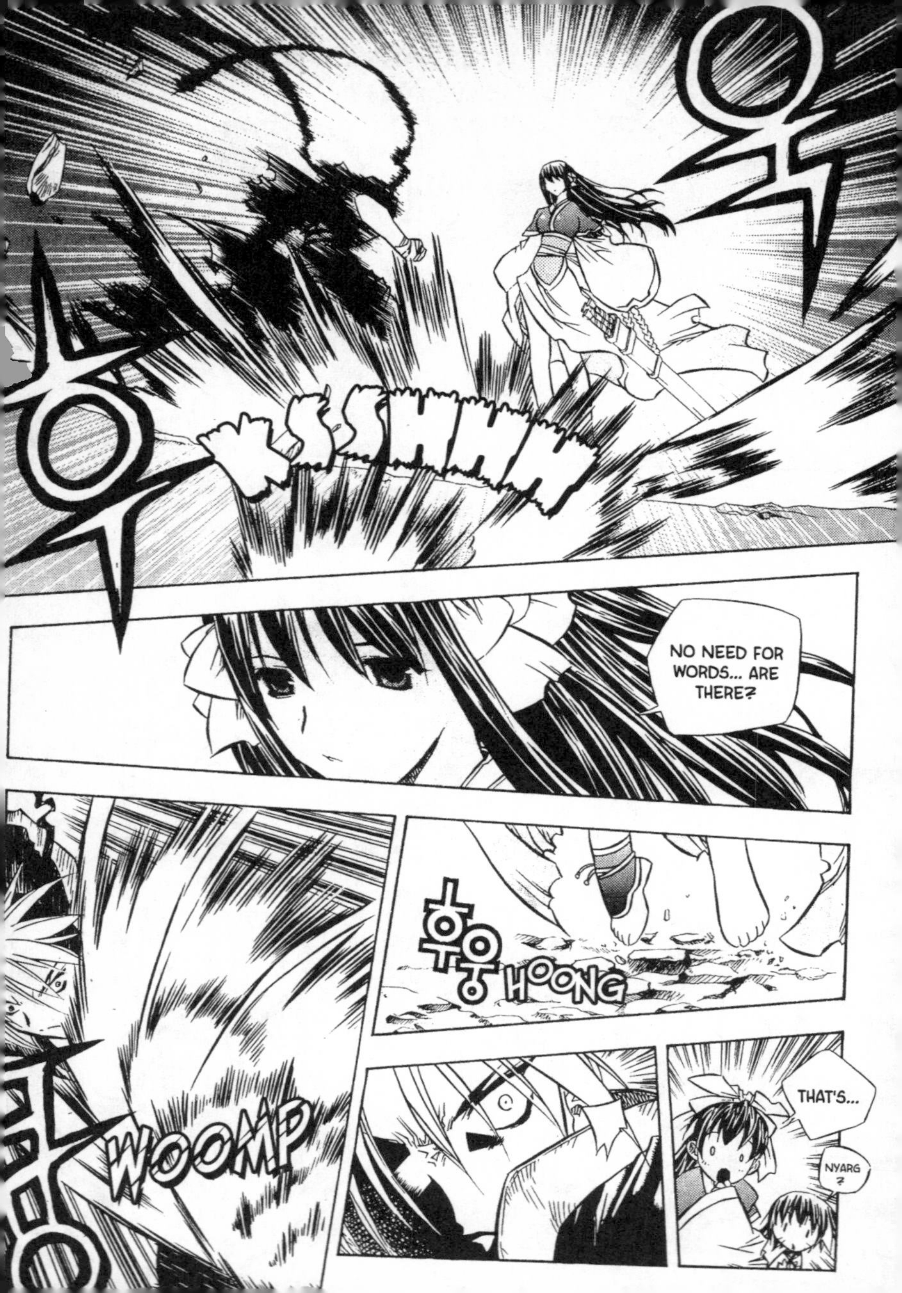
우
WSSHHH
NO NEED FOR WORDS... ARE THERE?
후웅 HOONG
WOOMP
THAT'S...
NYARG?

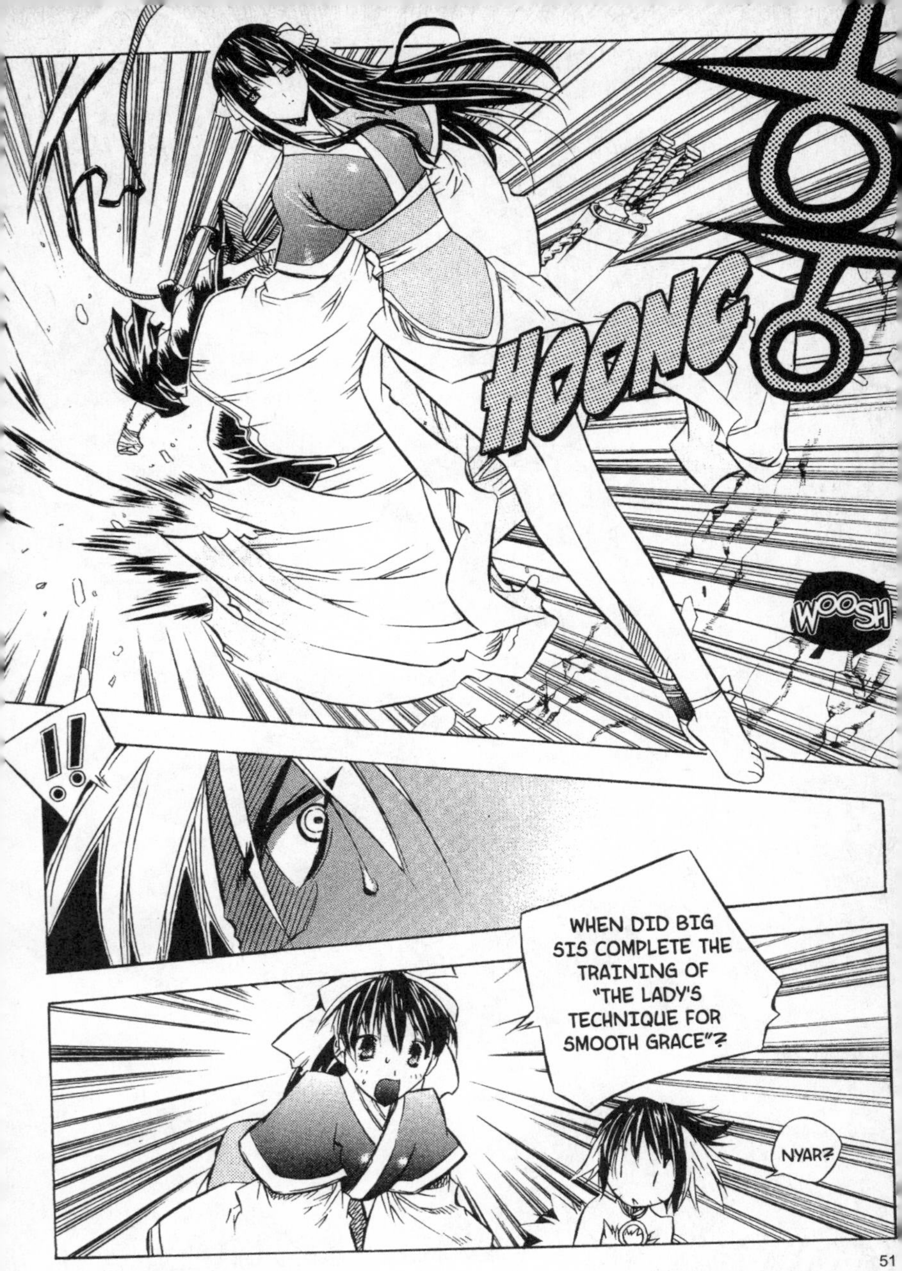
HOONG
WOOSH
!!
WHEN DID BIG SIS COMPLETE THE TRAINING OF "THE LADY'S TECHNIQUE FOR SMOOTH GRACE"?
NYAR?

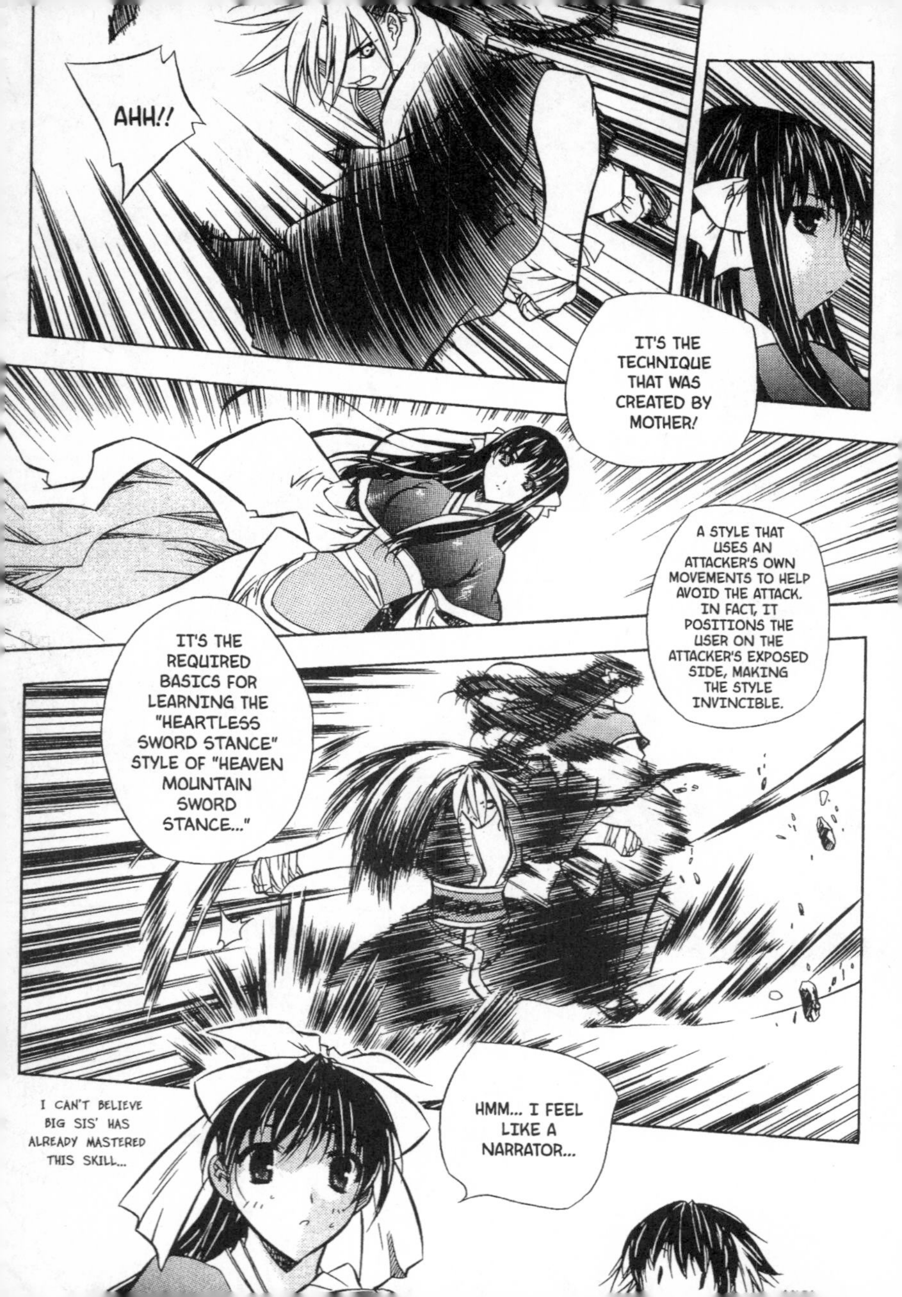
AHH!!
IT'S THE TECHNIQUE THAT WAS CREATED BY MOTHER!
A STYLE THAT USES AN ATTACKER'S OWN MOVEMENTS TO HELP AVOID THE ATTACK. IN FACT, IT POSITIONS THE USER ON THE ATTACKER'S EXPOSED SIDE, MAKING THE STYLE INVINCIBLE.
IT'S THE REQUIRED BASICS FOR LEARNING THE "HEARTLESS SWORD STANCE" STYLE OF "HEAVEN MOUNTAIN SWORD STANCE..."
HMM... I FEEL LIKE A NARRATOR...
I CAN'T BELIEVE BIG SIS' HAS ALREADY MASTERED THIS SKILL...

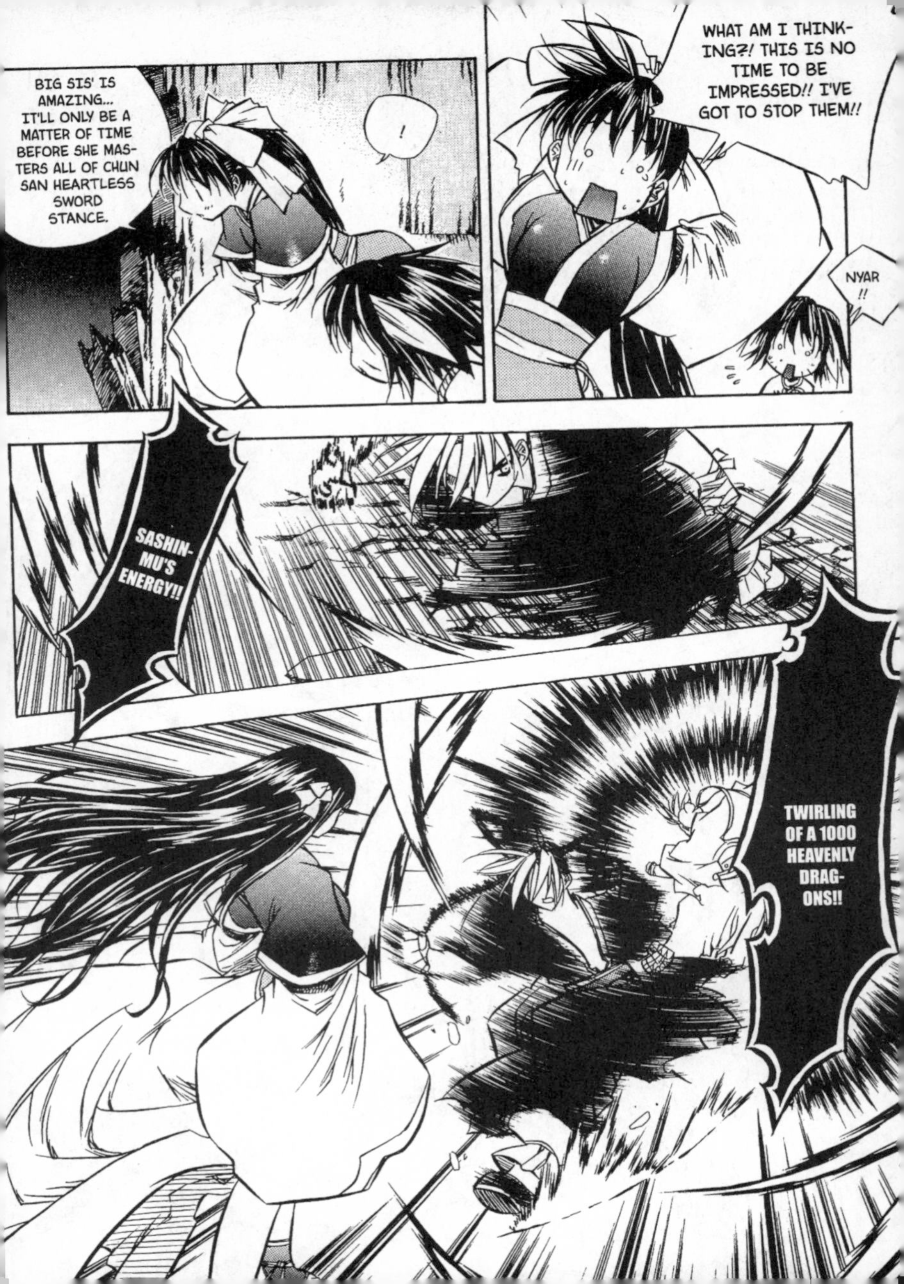
WHAT AM I THINK-ING?! THIS IS NO TIME TO BE IMPRESSED!! I'VE GOT TO STOP THEM!!
NYAR !!
!
BIG SIS' IS AMAZING... IT'LL ONLY BE A MATTER OF TIME BEFORE SHE MAS-TERS ALL OF CHUN SAN HEARTLESS SWORD STANCE.
SASHIN-MU'S ENERGY!!
TWIRLING OF A 1000 HEAVENLY DRAG-ONS!!

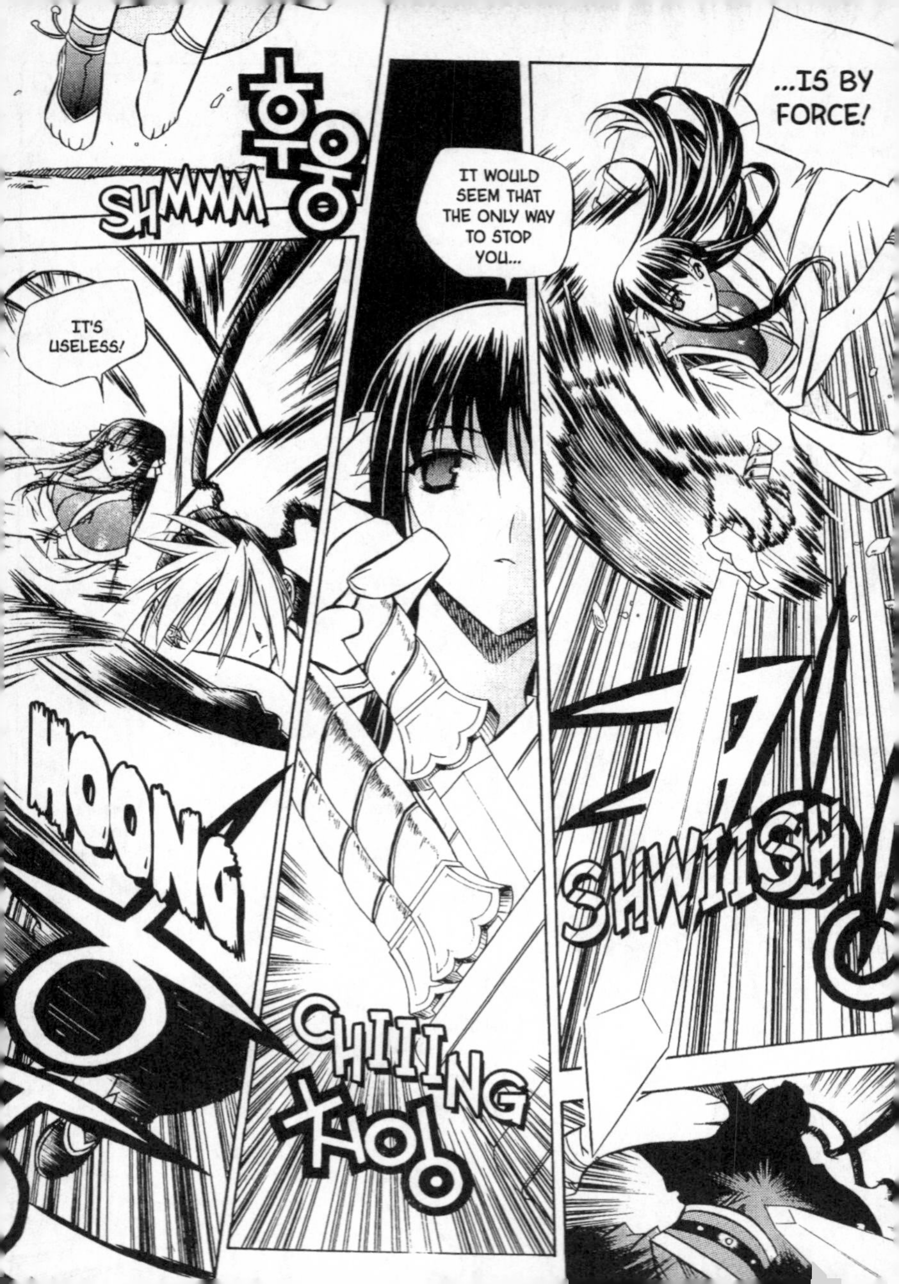
후웅
SHMMM
IT'S USELESS!
HOONG
IT WOULD SEEM THAT THE ONLY WAY TO STOP YOU...
CHIIING
...IS BY FORCE!
SHWIISH

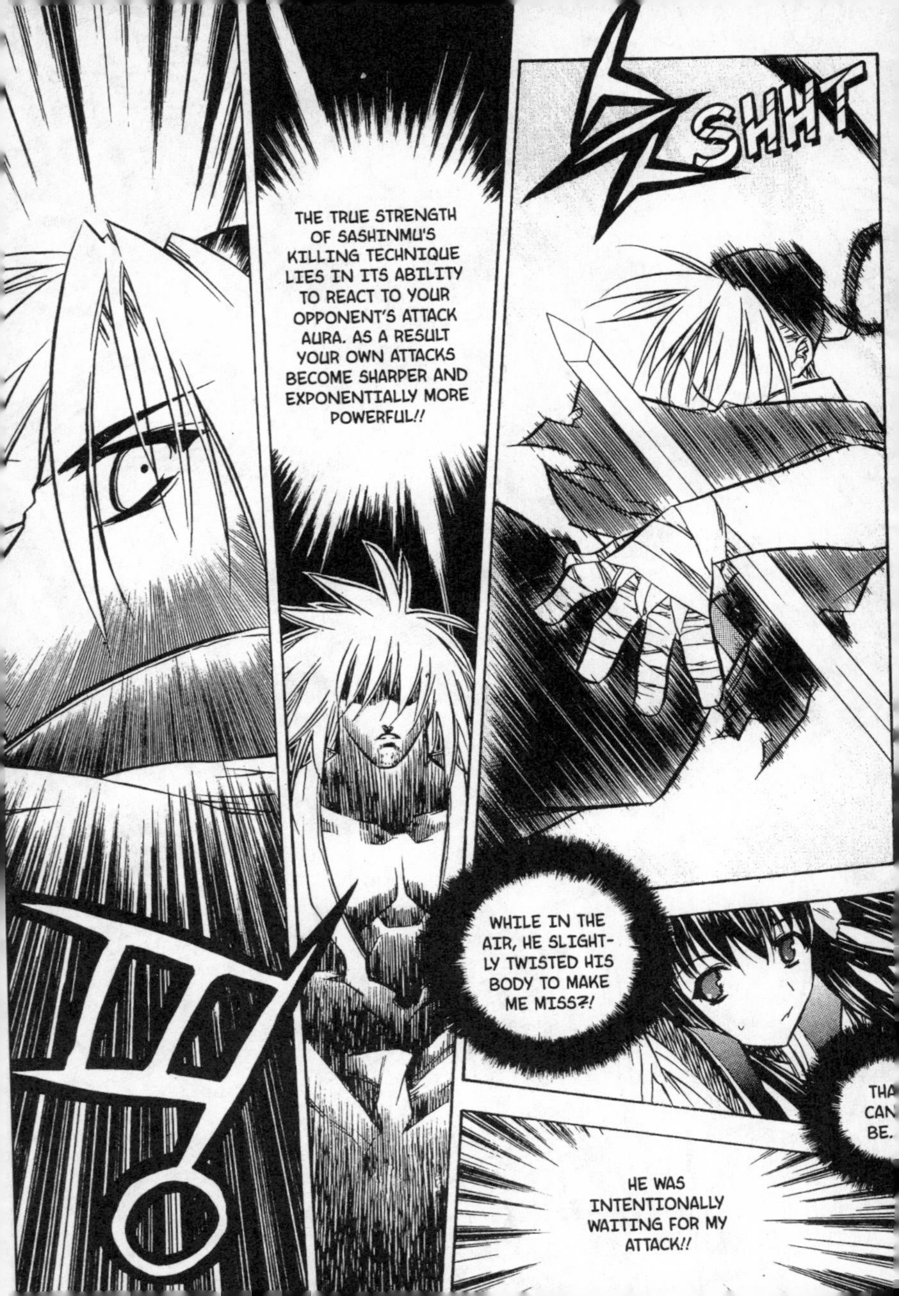
SHHT
THE TRUE STRENGTH OF SASHINMU'S KILLING TECHNIQUE LIES IN ITS ABILITY TO REACT TO YOUR OPPONENT'S ATTACK AURA. AS A RESULT YOUR OWN ATTACKS BECOME SHARPER AND EXPONENTIALLY MORE POWERFUL!!
WHILE IN THE AIR, HE SLIGHT-LY TWISTED HIS BODY TO MAKE ME MISS?!
HE WAS INTENTIONALLY WAITING FOR MY ATTACK!!

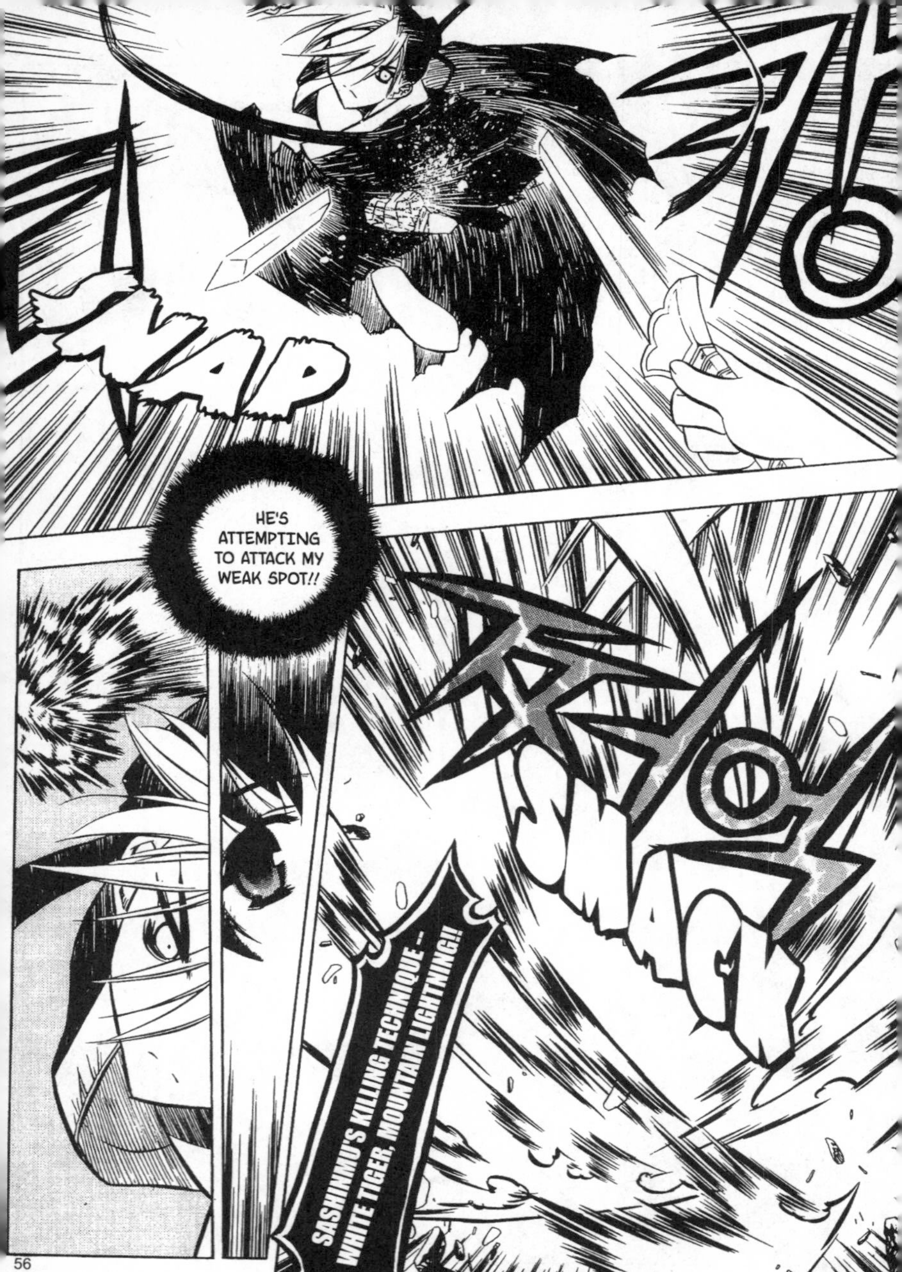
HE'S ATTEMPTING TO ATTACK MY WEAK SPOT!!
SASHINMU'S KILLING TECHNIQUE – WHITE TIGER, MOUNTAIN LIGHTNING!!

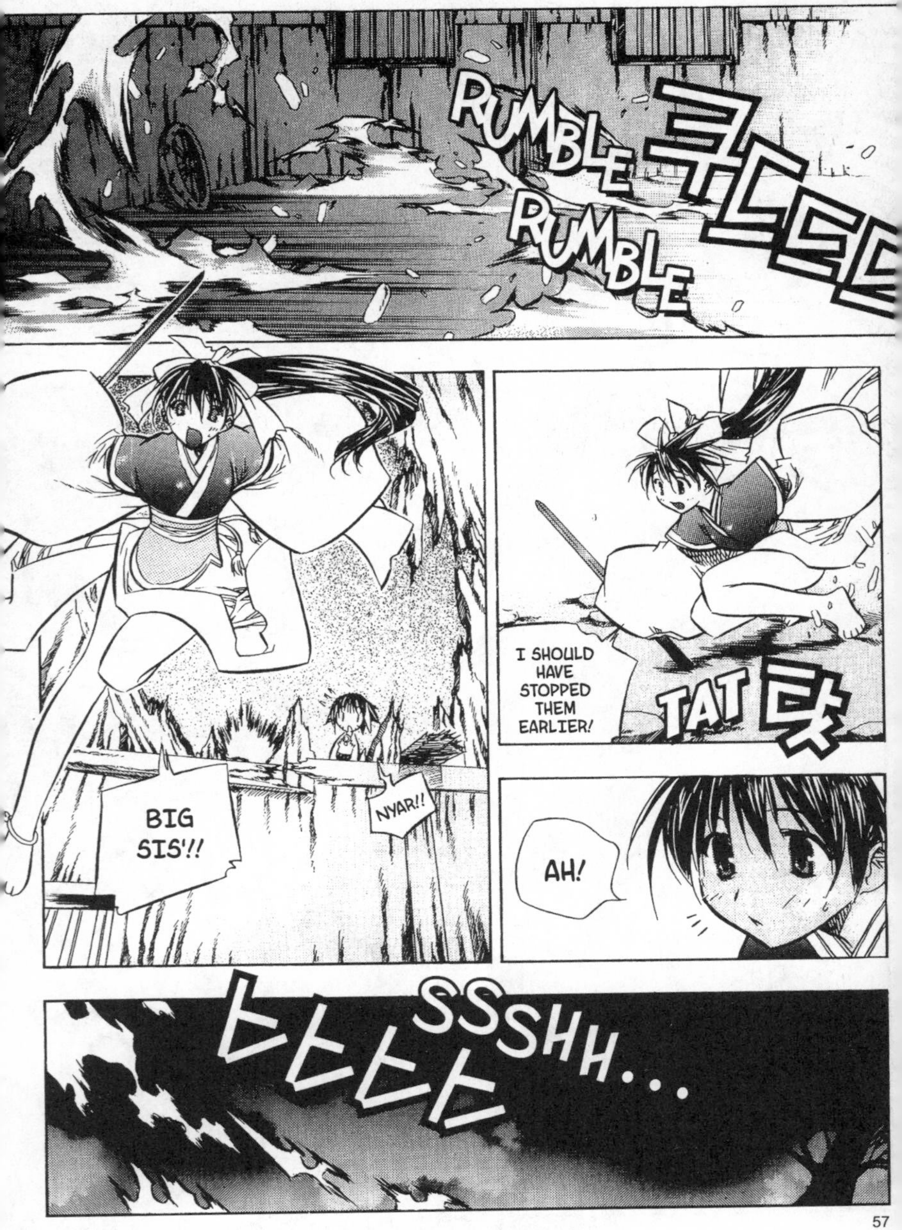

RUMBLE 쿠ㄷㄷㄷ
RUMBLE
I SHOULD HAVE STOPPED THEM EARLIER!
TAT 탓
BIG SIS'!!
NYAR!!
AH!
SSSHH... ㅏㅏㅏㅏ

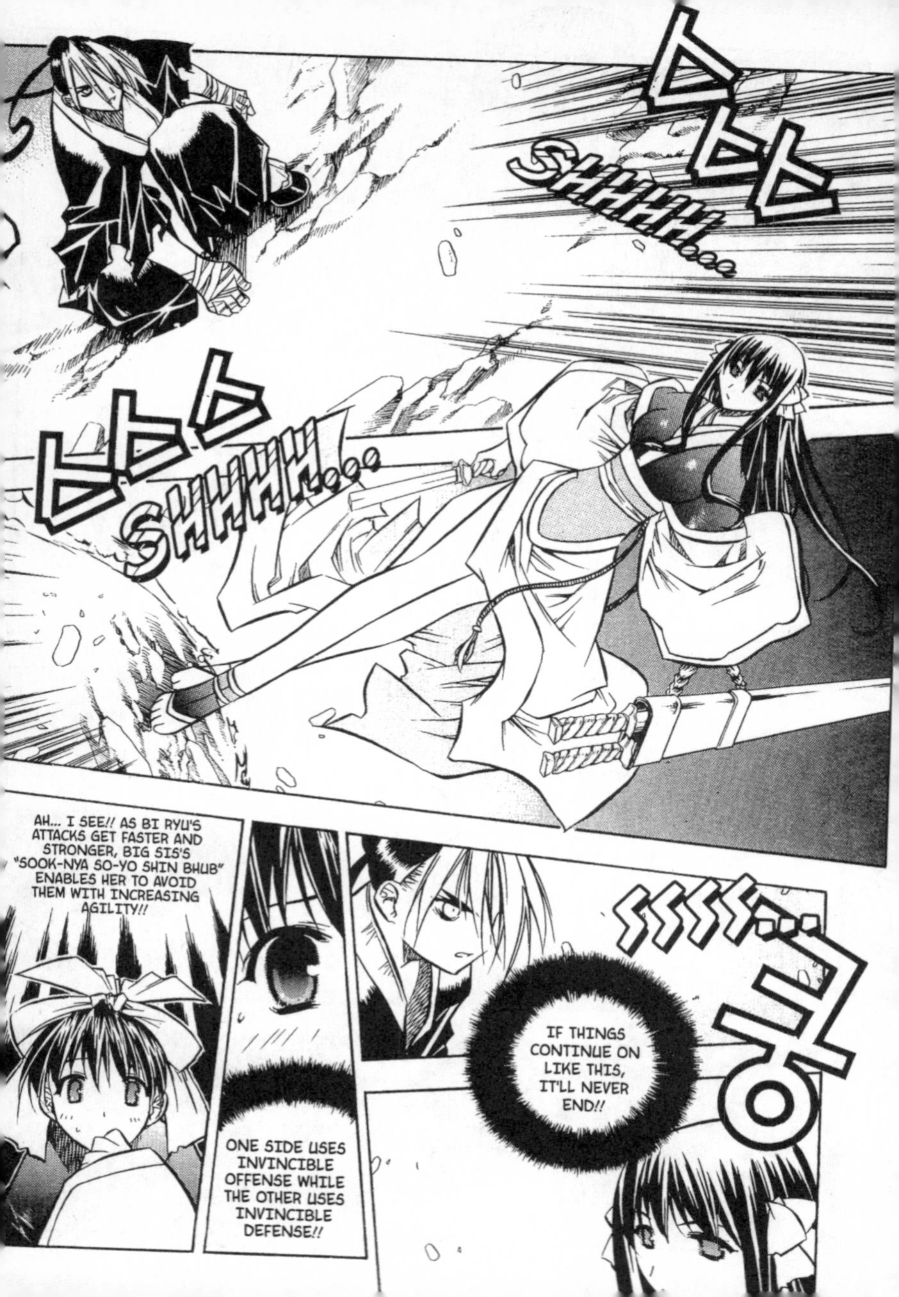
SHHHHH...
SHHHHH...
AH... I SEE!! AS BI RYU'S ATTACKS GET FASTER AND STRONGER, BIG SIS'S "SOOK-NYA SO-YO SHIN BHUB" ENABLES HER TO AVOID THEM WITH INCREASING AGILITY!!
ONE SIDE USES INVINCIBLE OFFENSE WHILE THE OTHER USES INVINCIBLE DEFENSE!!
IF THINGS CONTINUE ON LIKE THIS, IT'LL NEVER END!!
SSSSS...

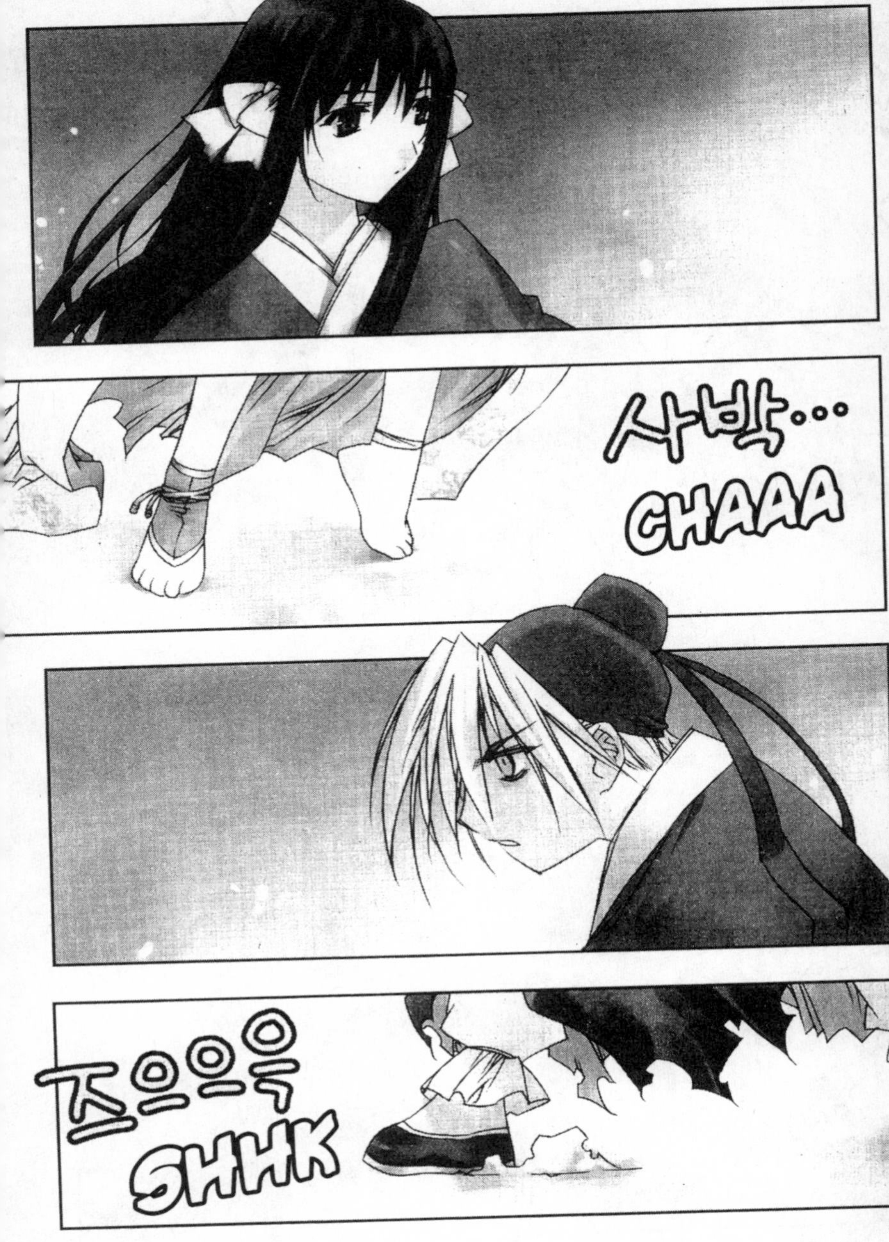
사박...
CHAAA
즈으으윽
SHHK

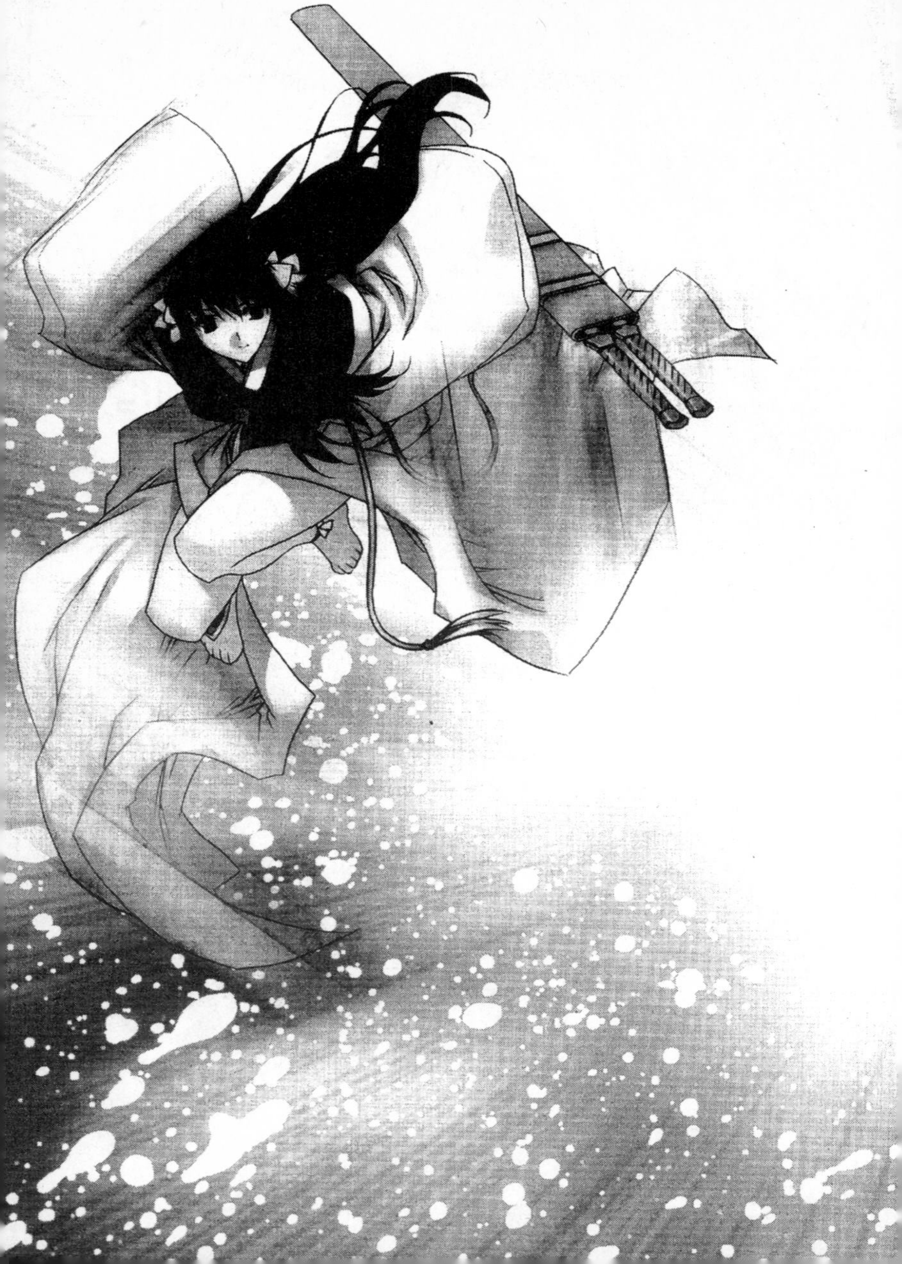

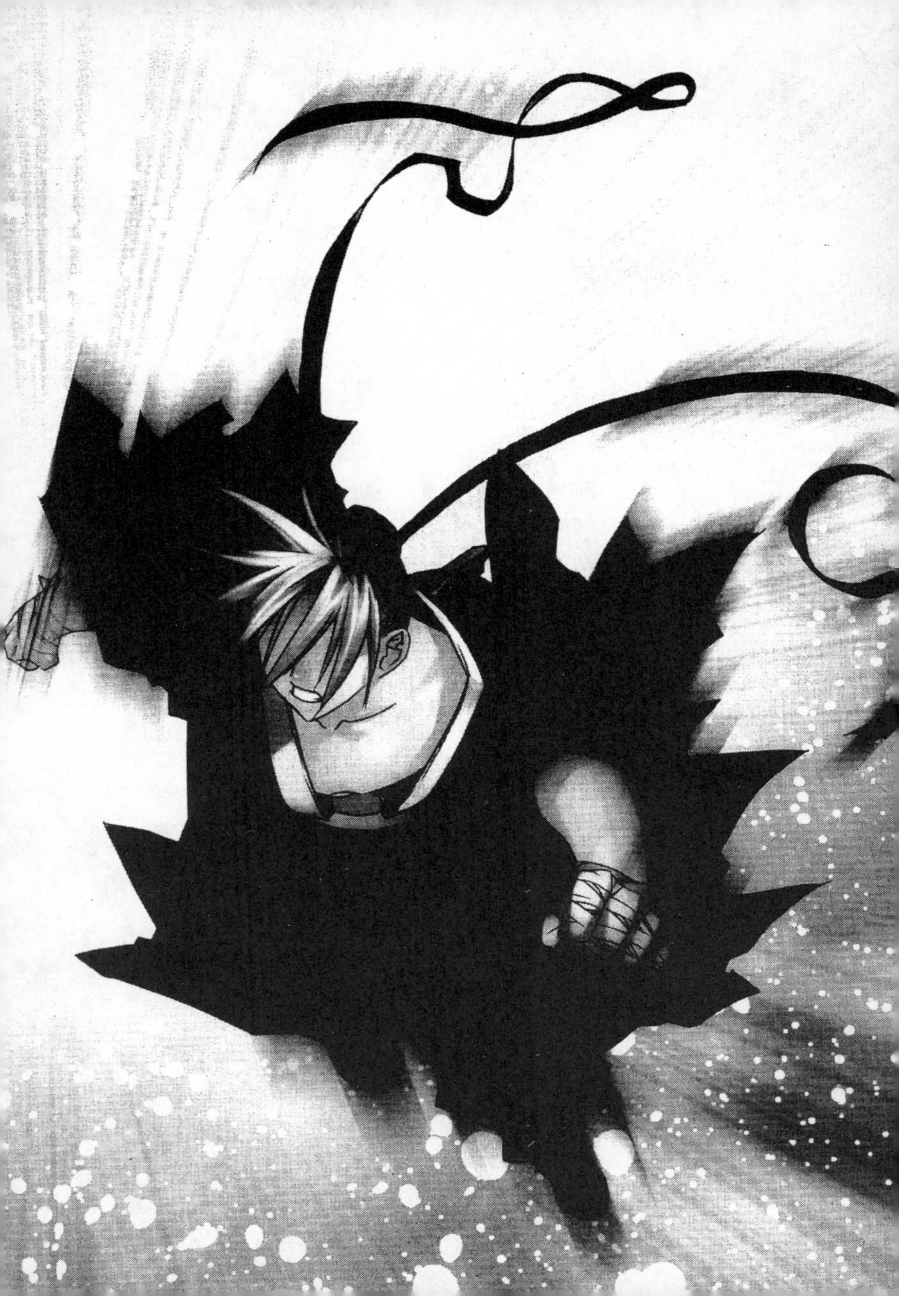

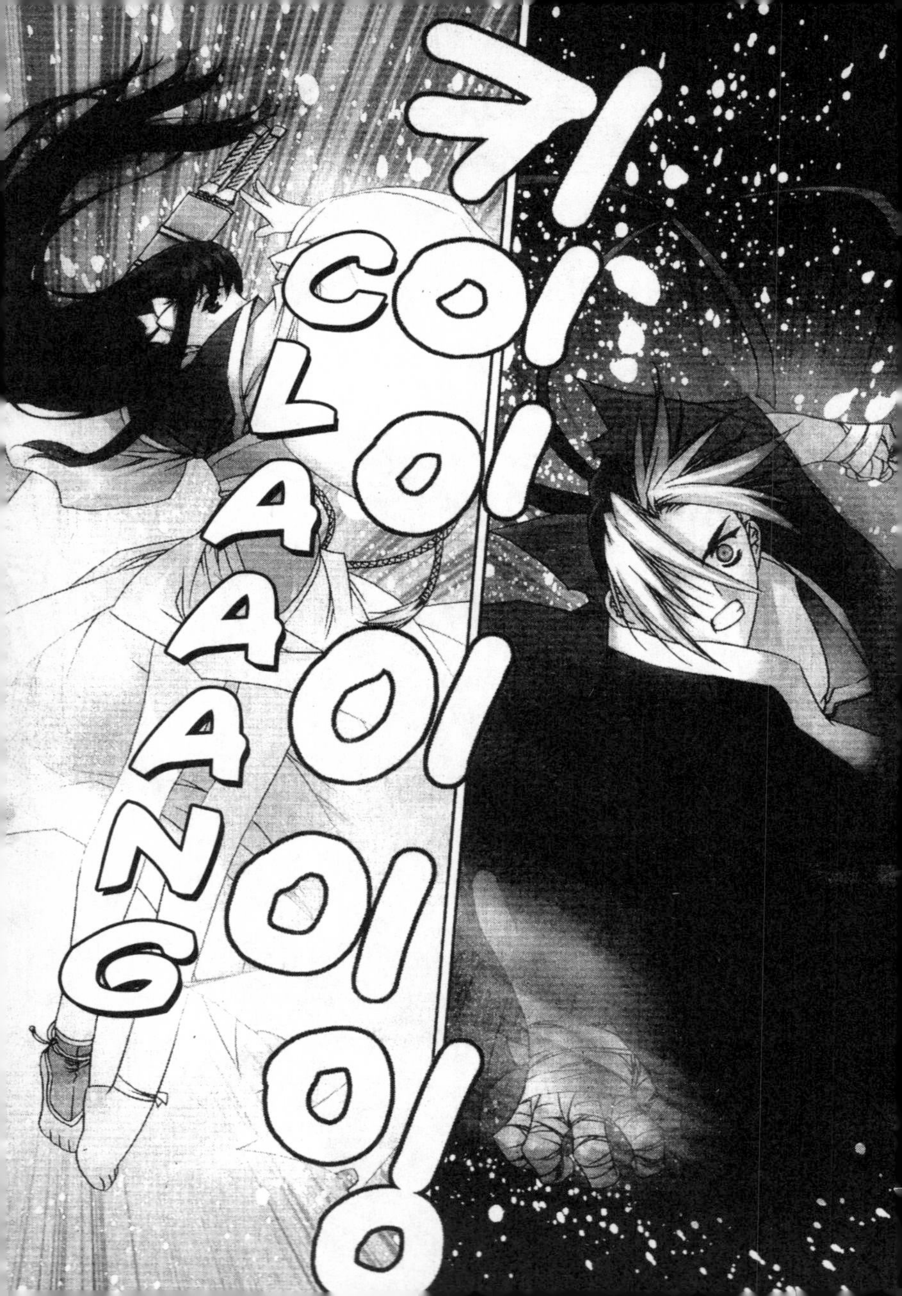
CLAAANG

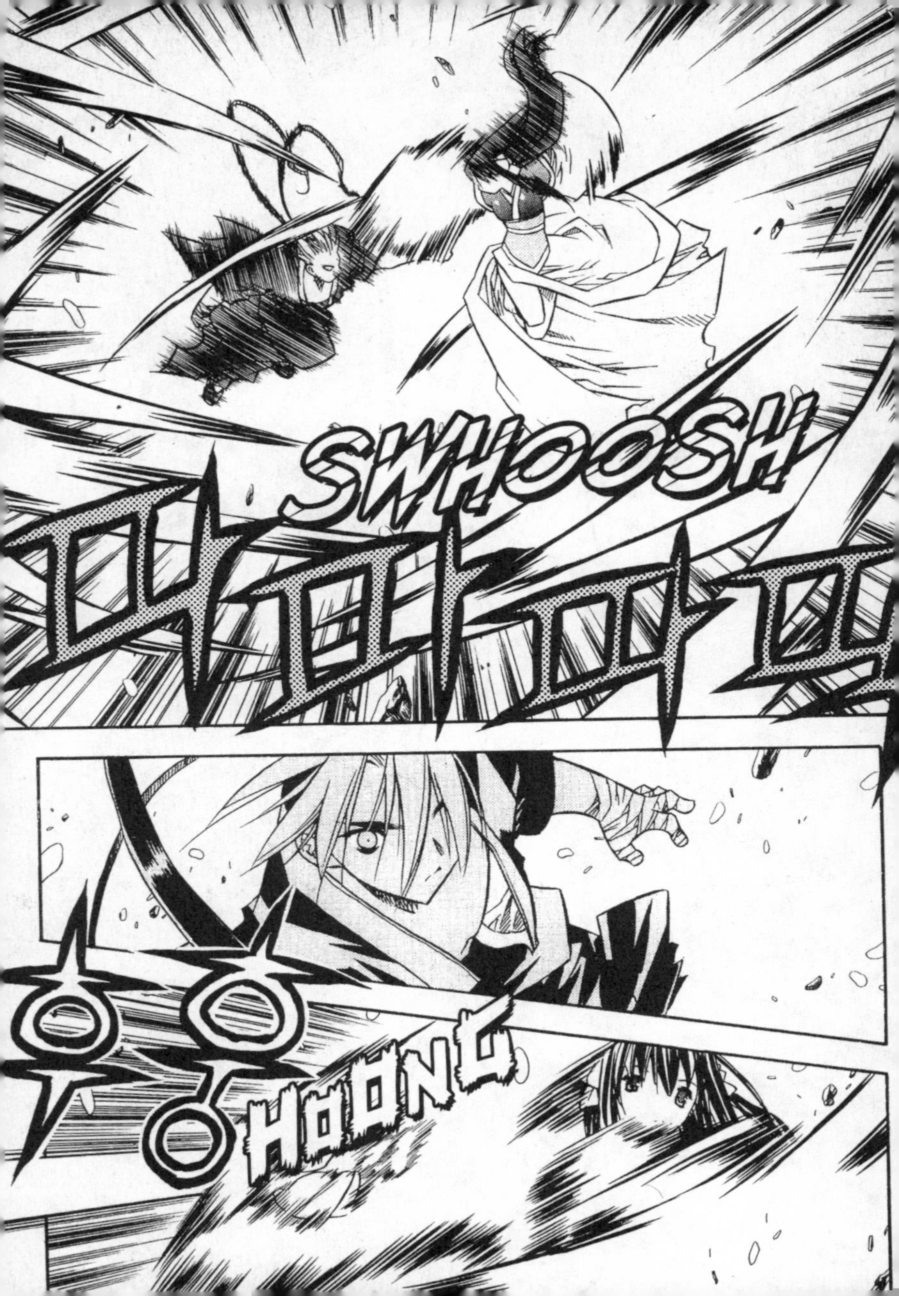
SWHOOSH
HOONG

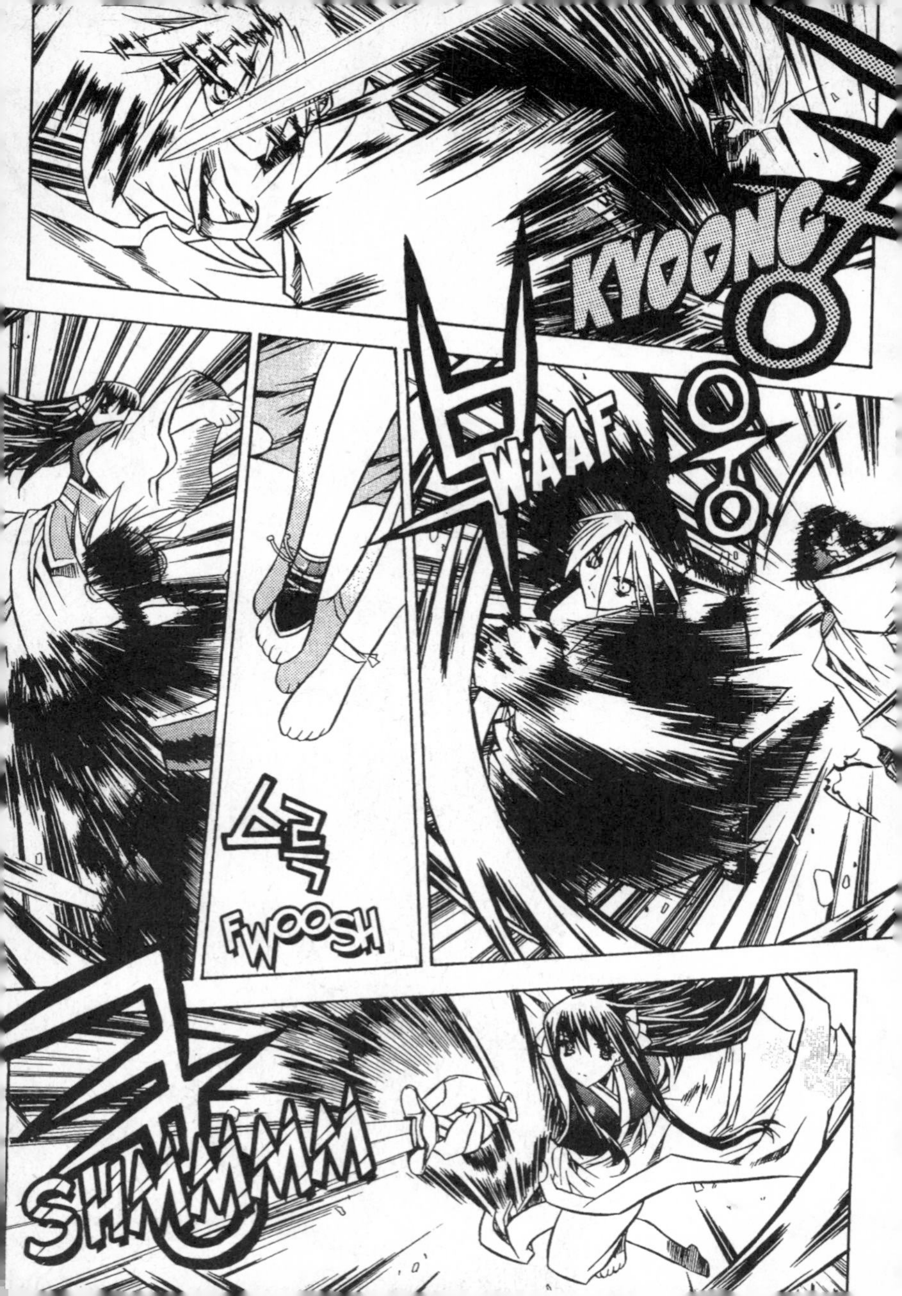
KYOONG
WAAF
FWOOSH
SHMMMM

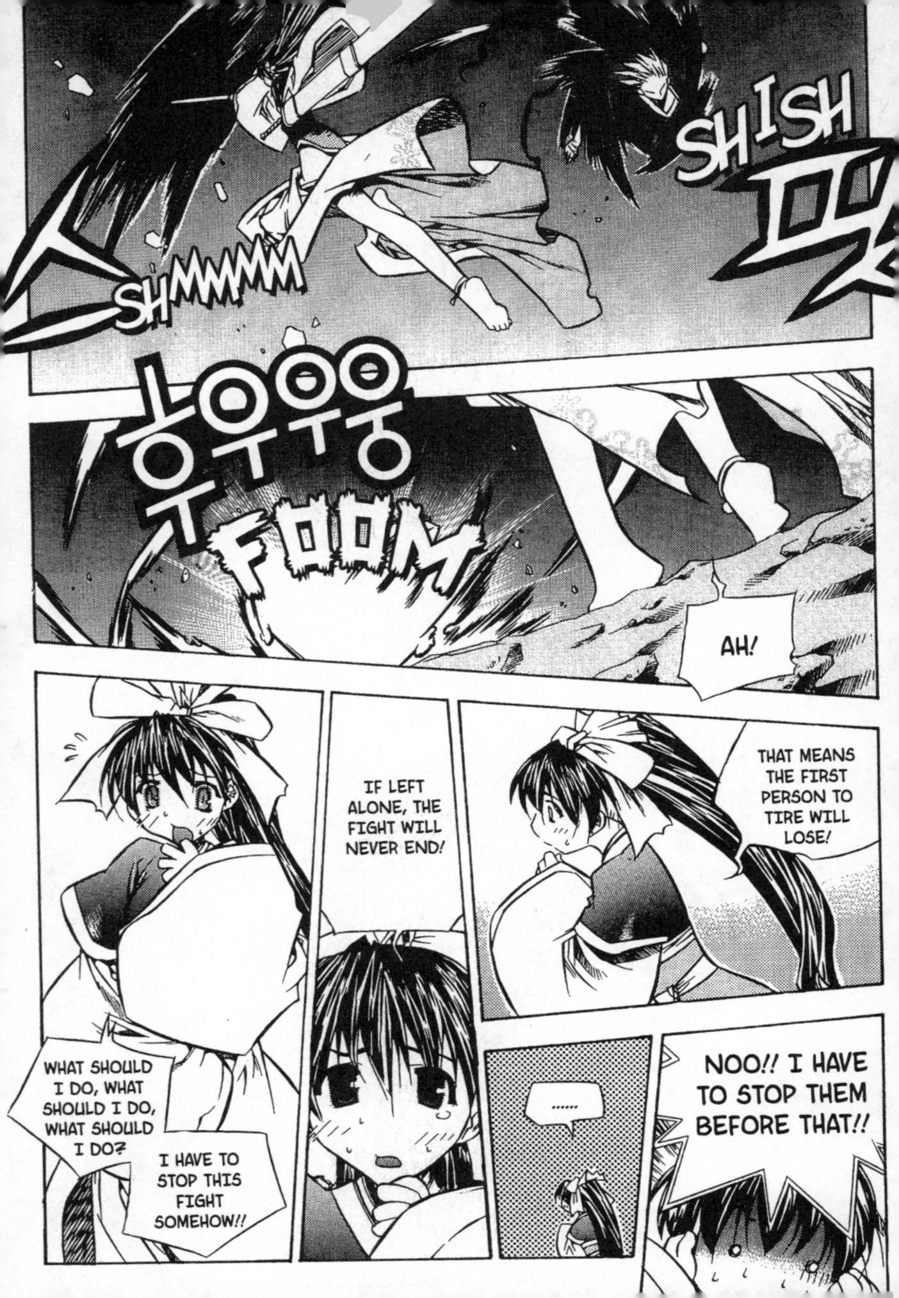
SHISH
SHMMMM
FOOM
AH!
THAT MEANS THE FIRST PERSON TO TIRE WILL LOSE!
IF LEFT ALONE, THE FIGHT WILL NEVER END!
WHAT SHOULD I DO, WHAT SHOULD I DO, WHAT SHOULD I DO?
I HAVE TO STOP THIS FIGHT SOMEHOW!!
......
NOO!! I HAVE TO STOP THEM BEFORE THAT!!

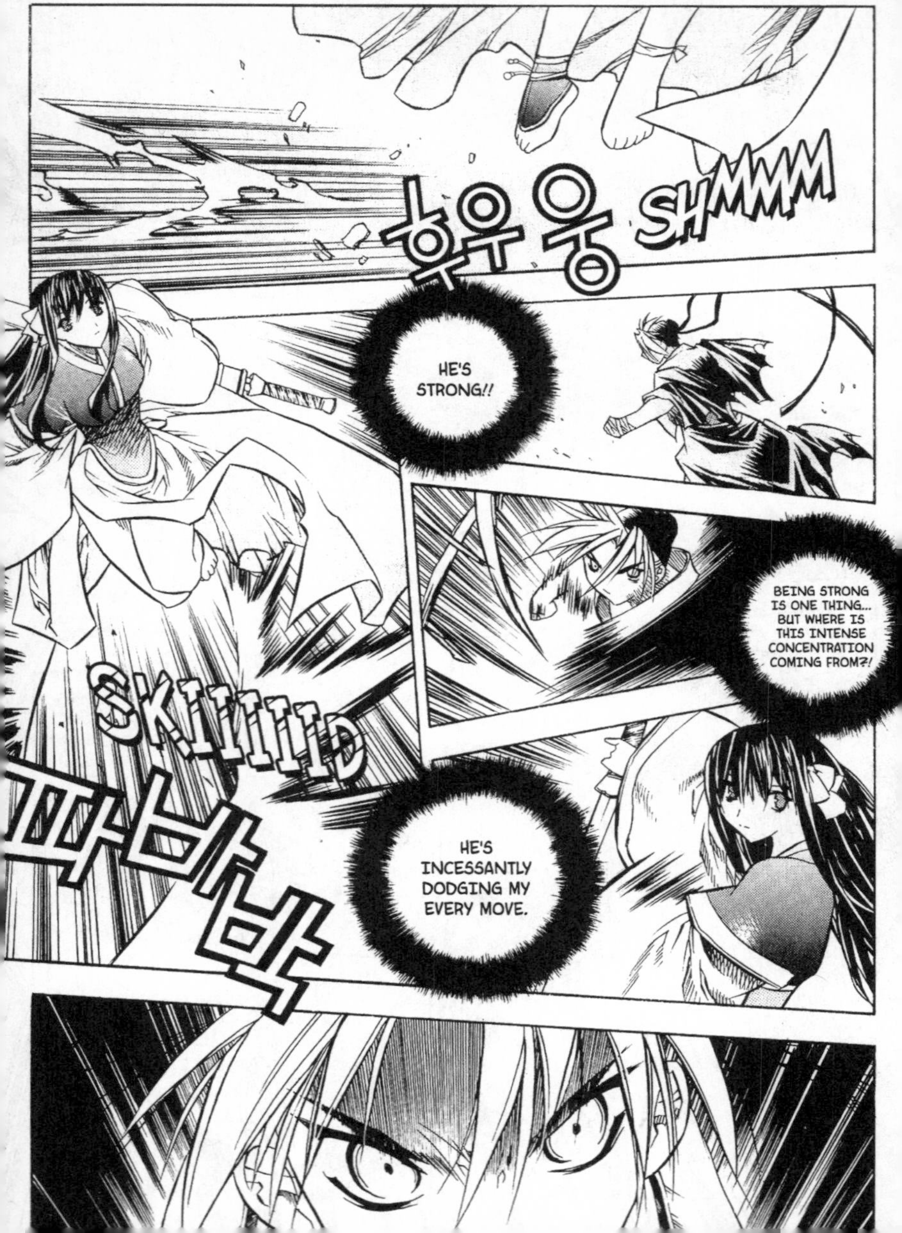

훙웅
SHMMM
HE'S STRONG!!
BEING STRONG IS ONE THING... BUT WHERE IS THIS INTENSE CONCENTRATION COMING FROM?!
SKIIIID
파박
HE'S INCESSANTLY DODGING MY EVERY MOVE.

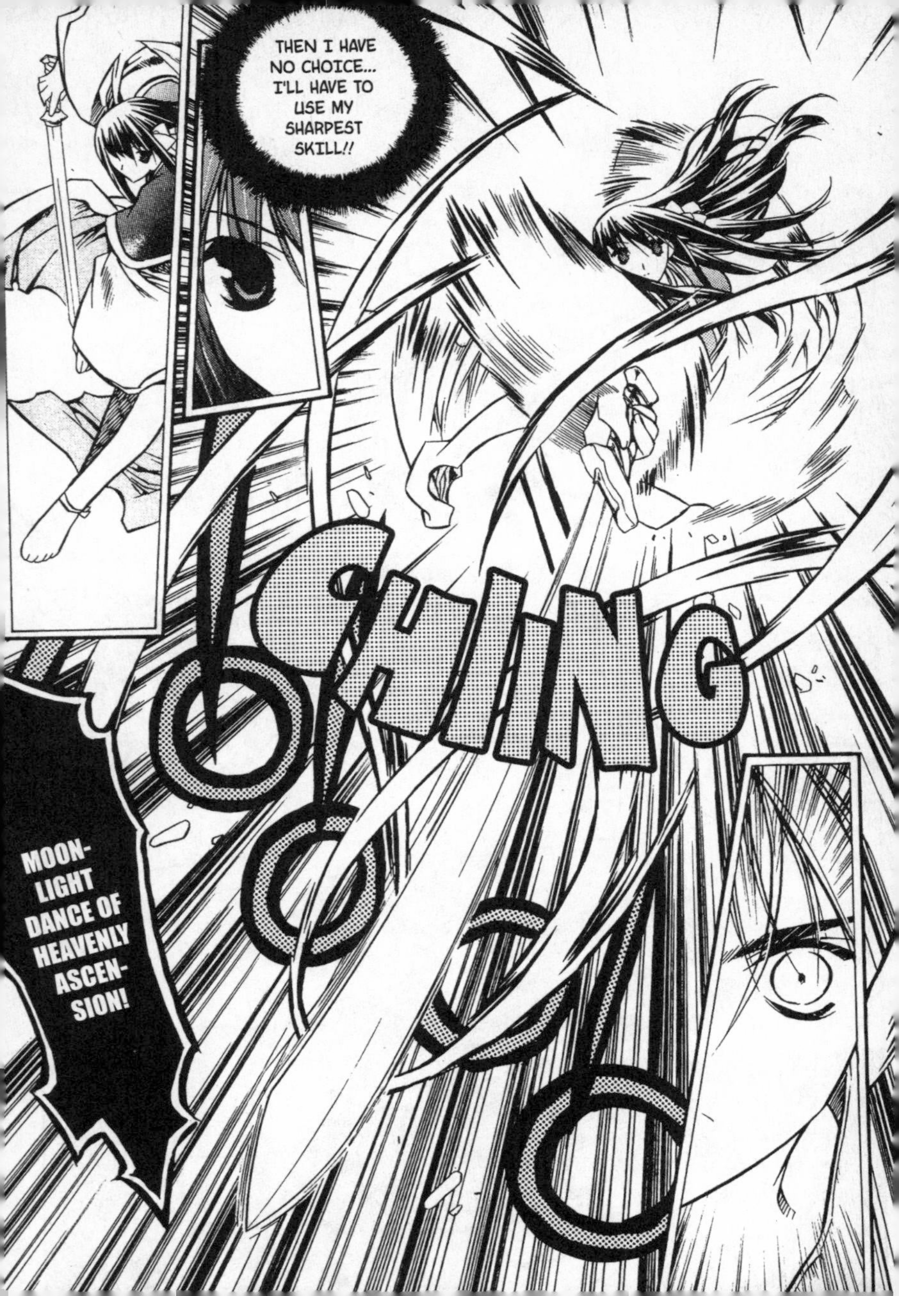
THEN I HAVE NO CHOICE... I'LL HAVE TO USE MY SHARPEST SKILL!!
CHIING
MOON-LIGHT DANCE OF HEAVENLY ASCEN-SION!

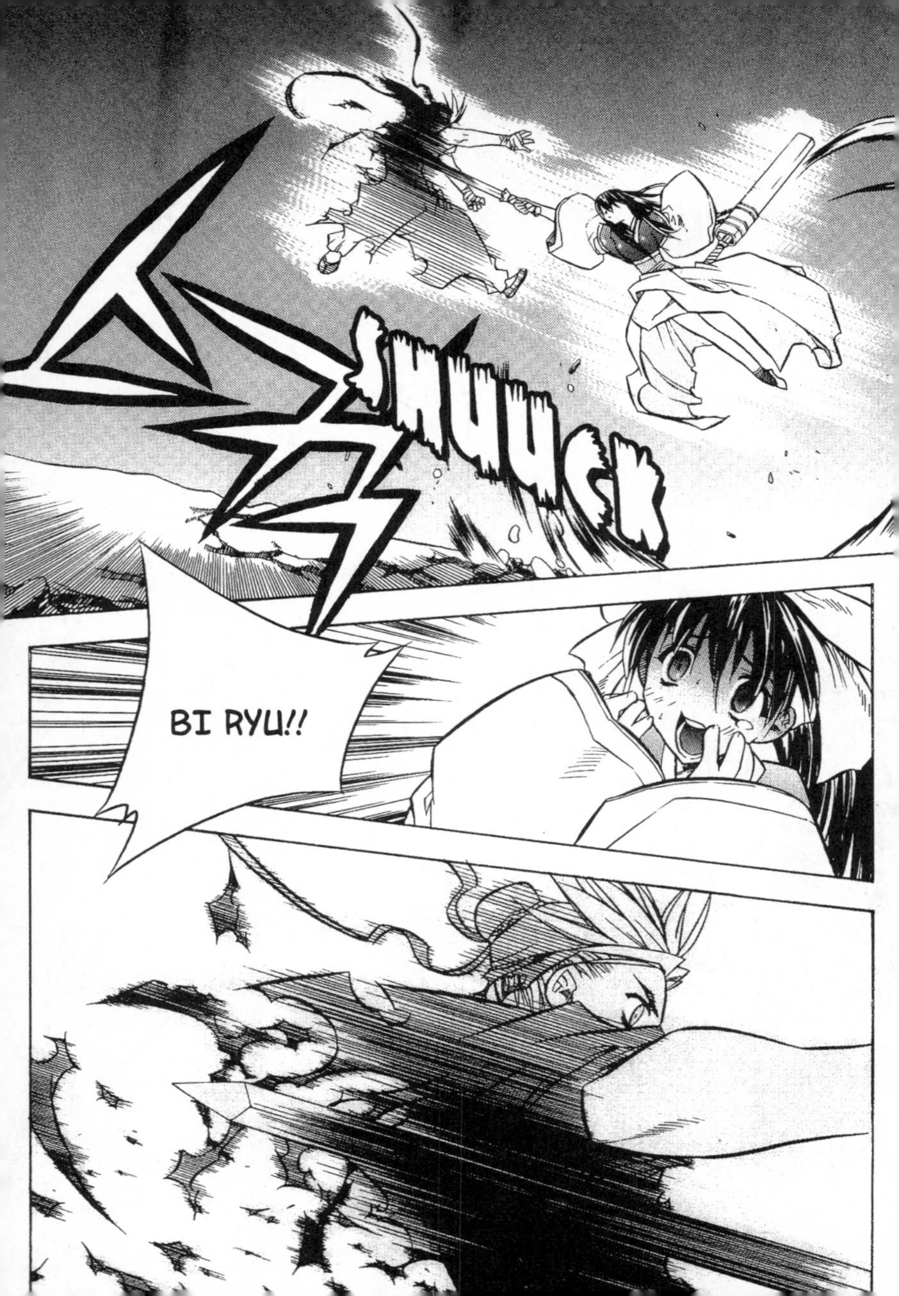
SHUUCK
BI RYU!!

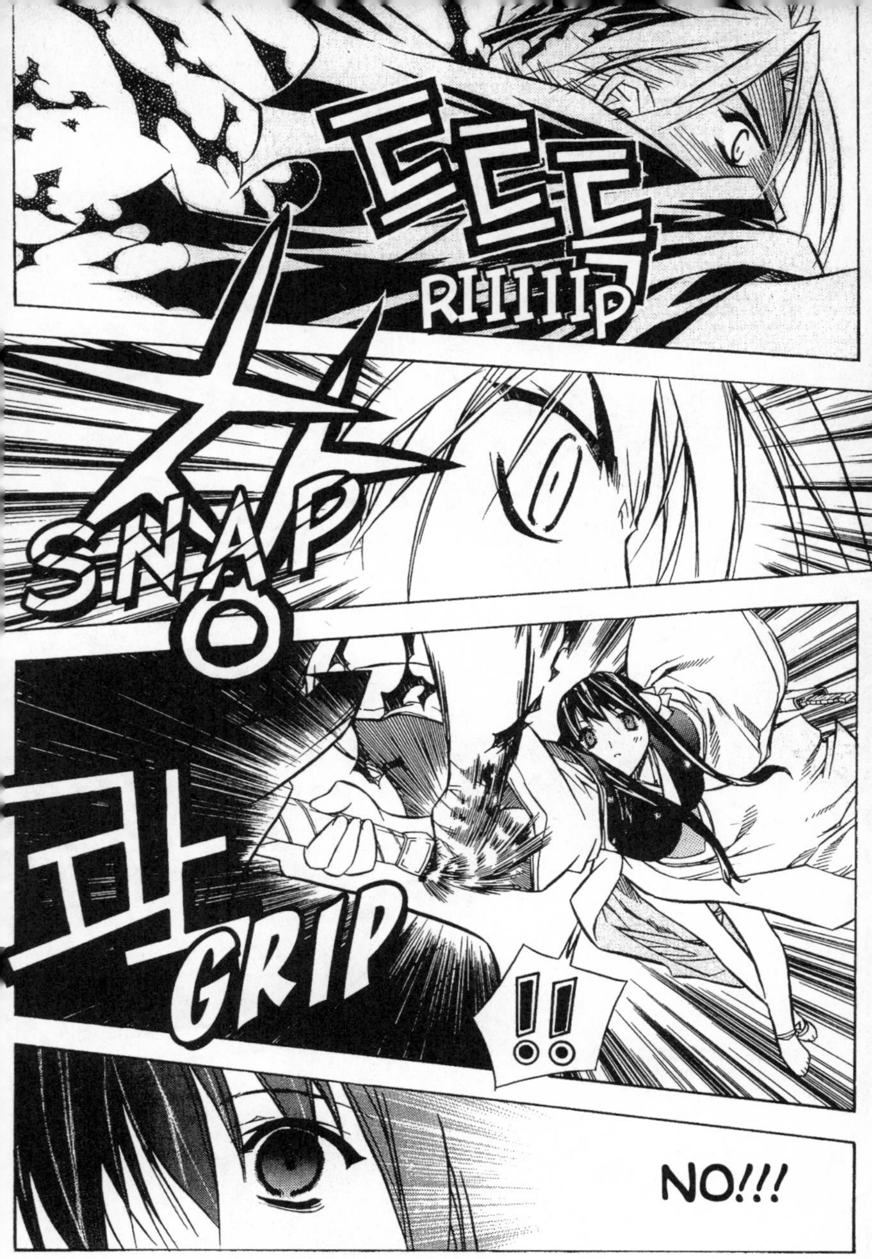
RIIIIp
SNAP
GRIP
!!
NO!!!

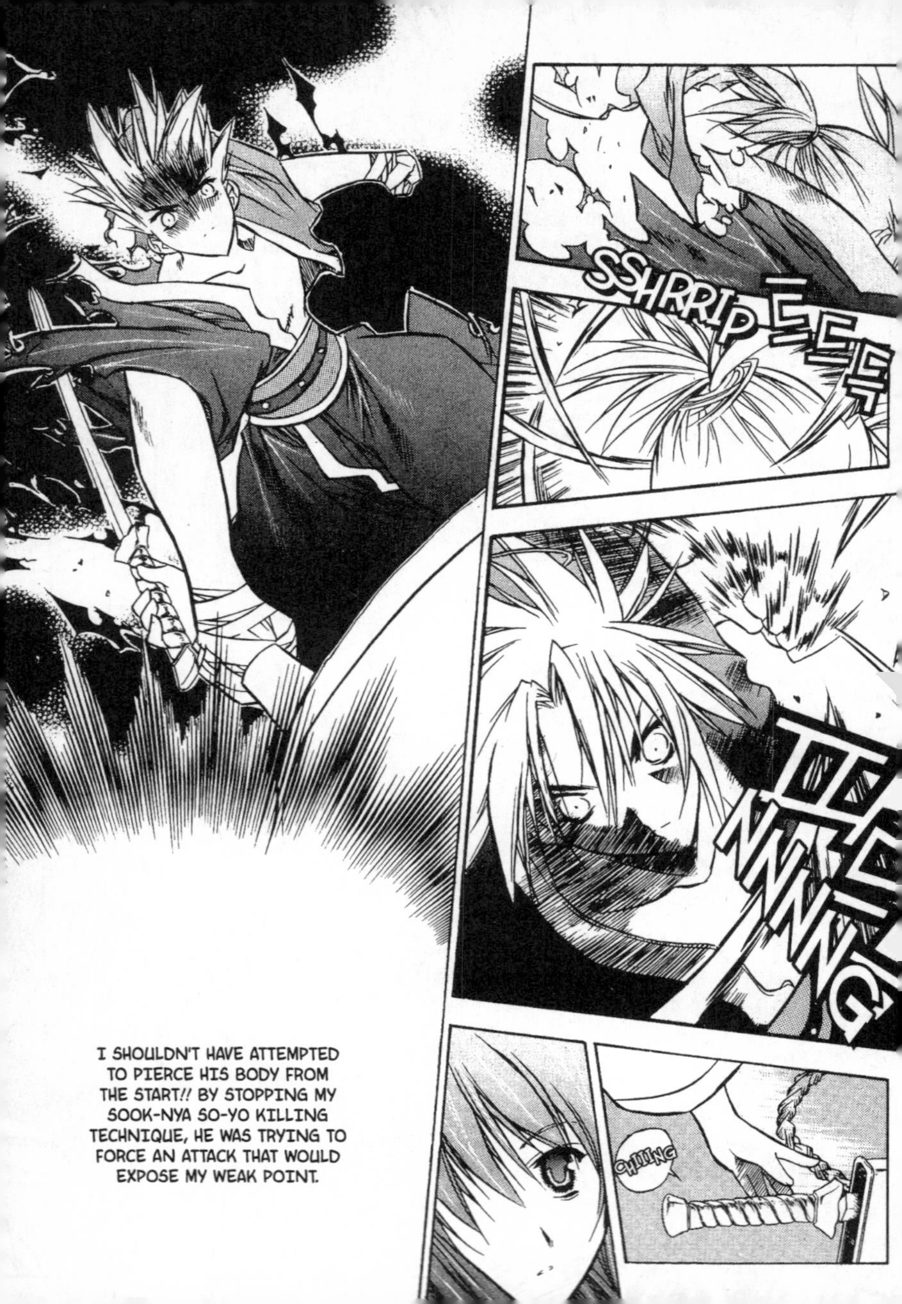
SSHRRIPEEEE
NNNNG
I SHOULDN'T HAVE ATTEMPTED TO PIERCE HIS BODY FROM THE START!! BY STOPPING MY SOOK-NYA SO-YO KILLING TECHNIQUE, HE WAS TRYING TO FORCE AN ATTACK THAT WOULD EXPOSE MY WEAK POINT.
CHIIING

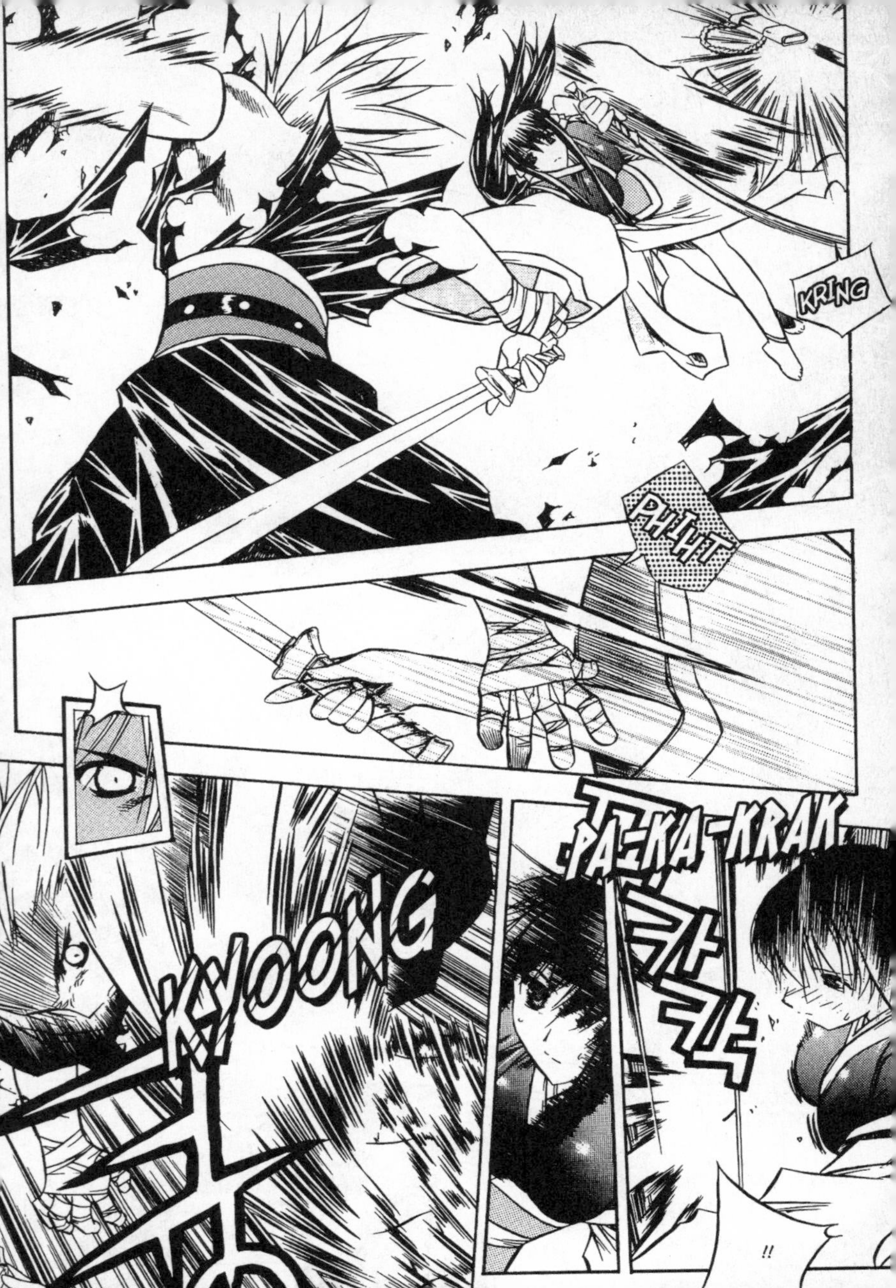
KRING
PHIHT
PA-KA-KRAK
KYOONG
!!

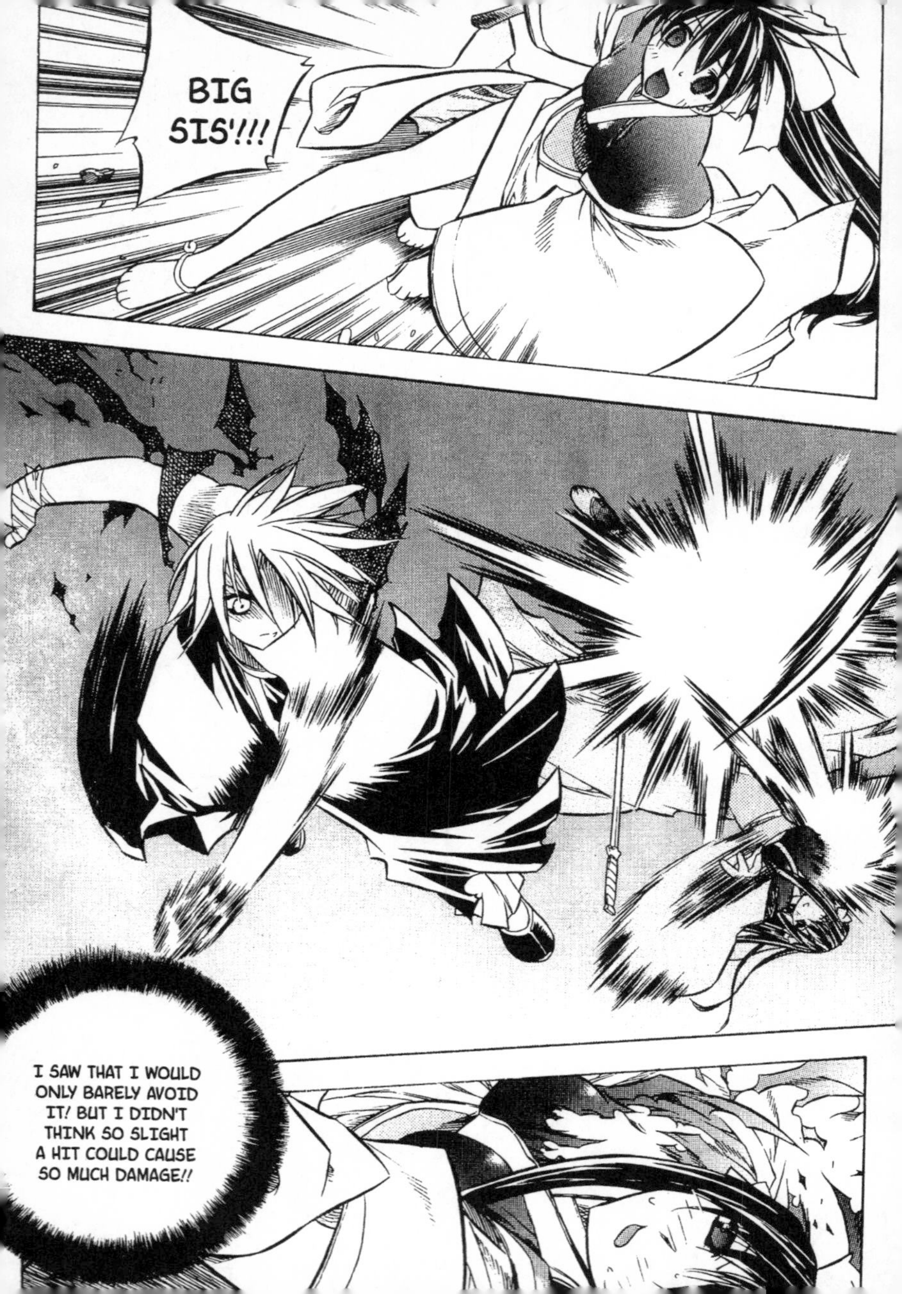
BIG SIS'!!!
I SAW THAT I WOULD ONLY BARELY AVOID IT! BUT I DIDN'T THINK SO SLIGHT A HIT COULD CAUSE SO MUCH DAMAGE!!

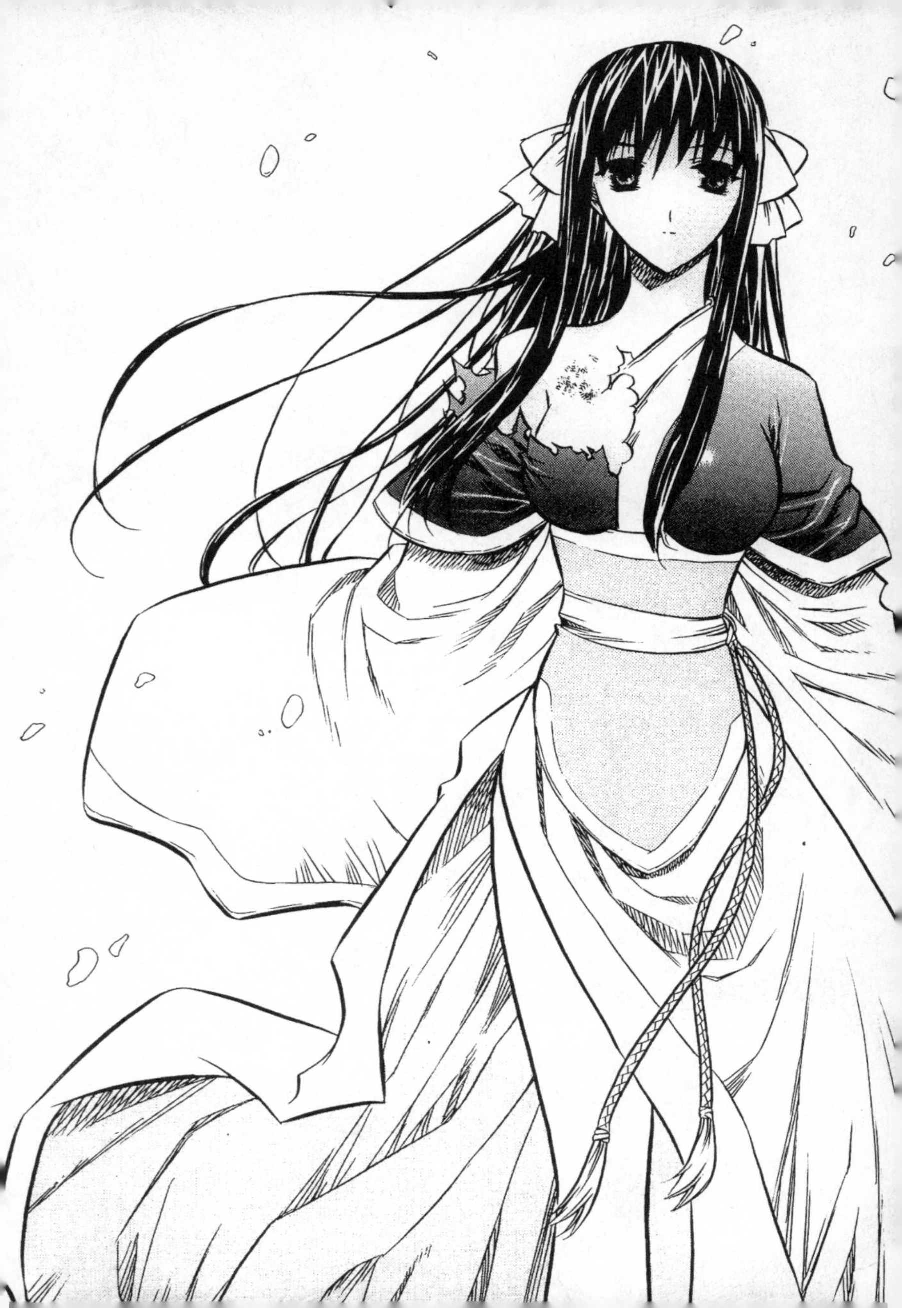

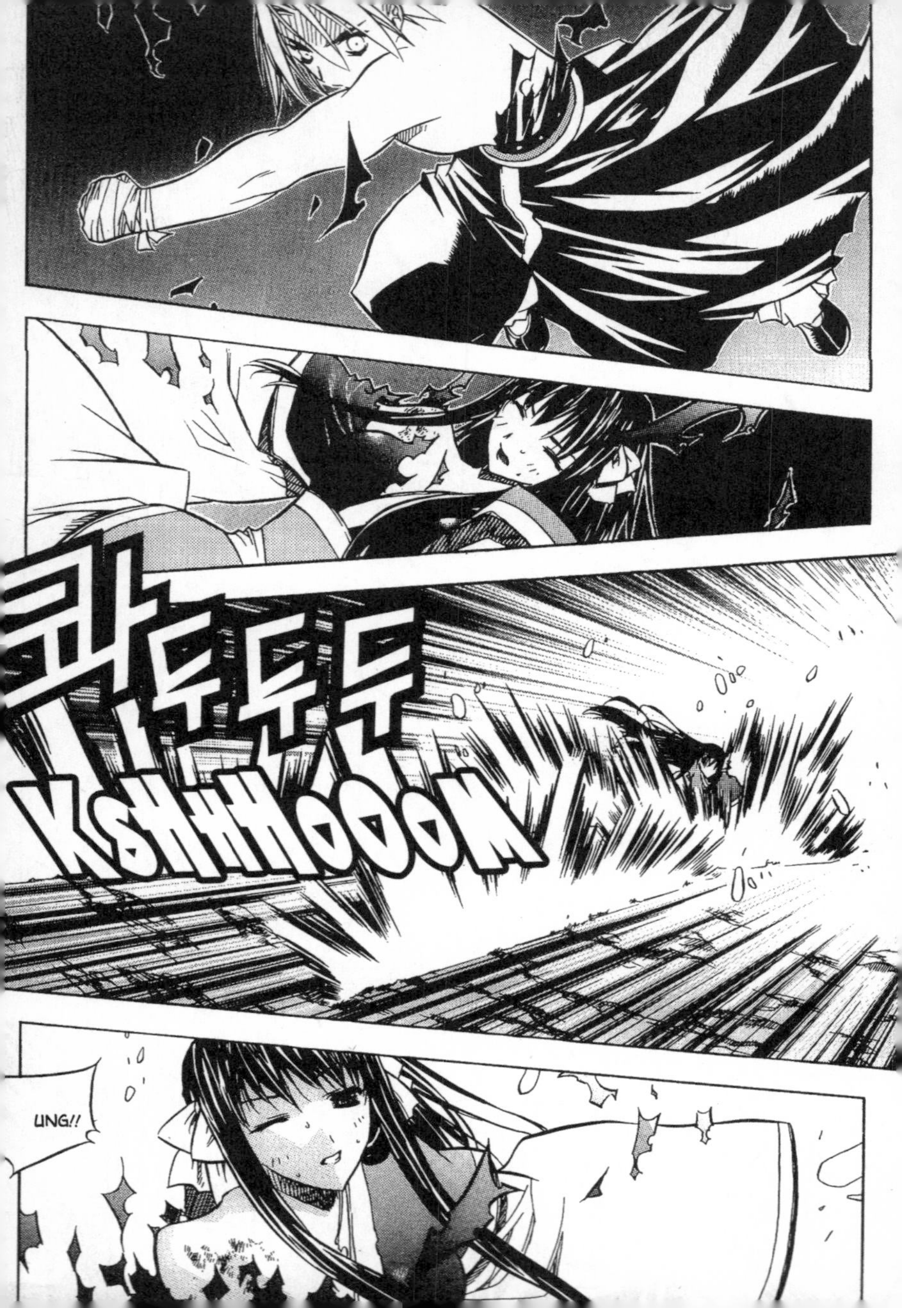

콰두두
KSHHHOOOOM
UNG!!

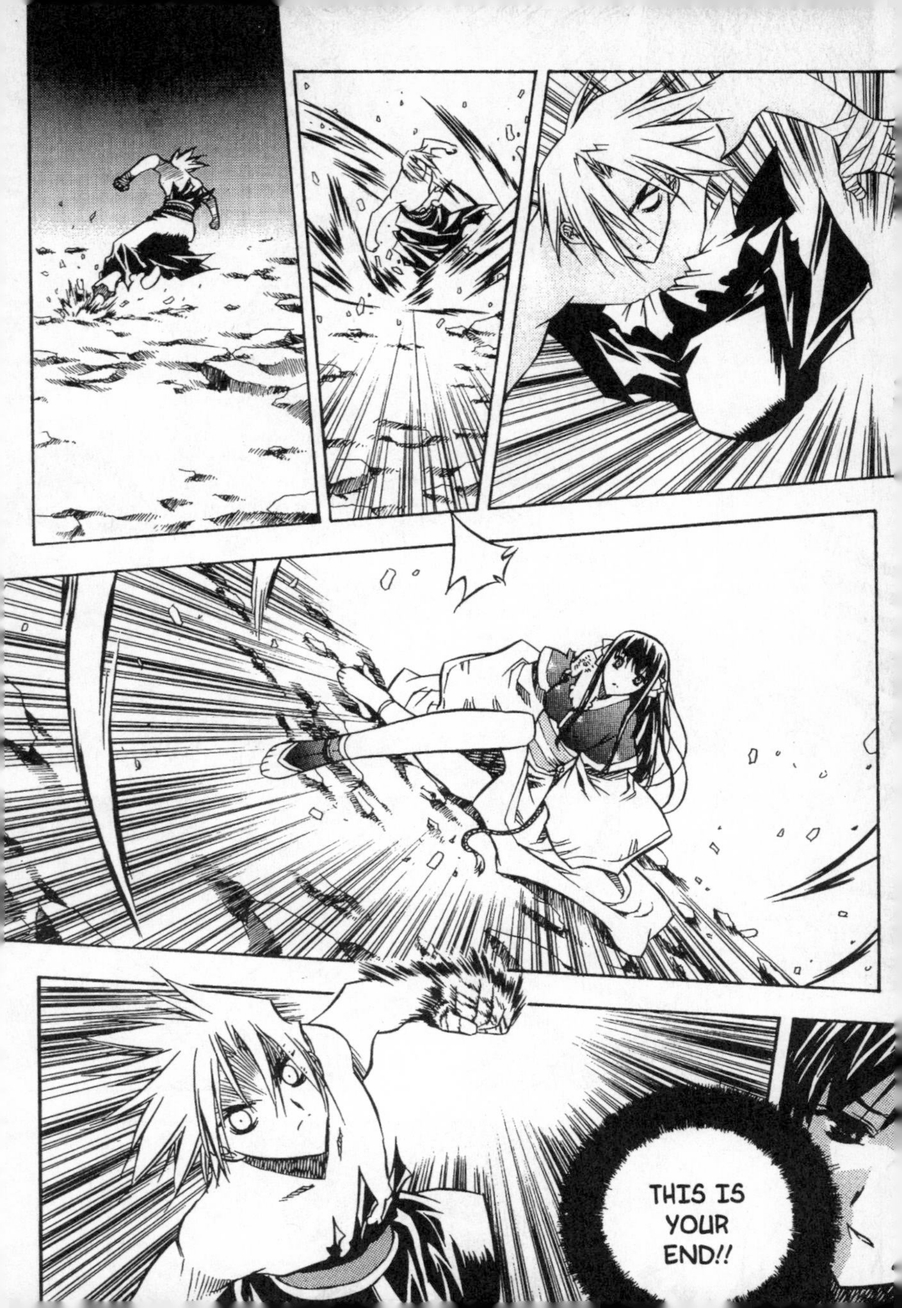
THIS IS YOUR END!!

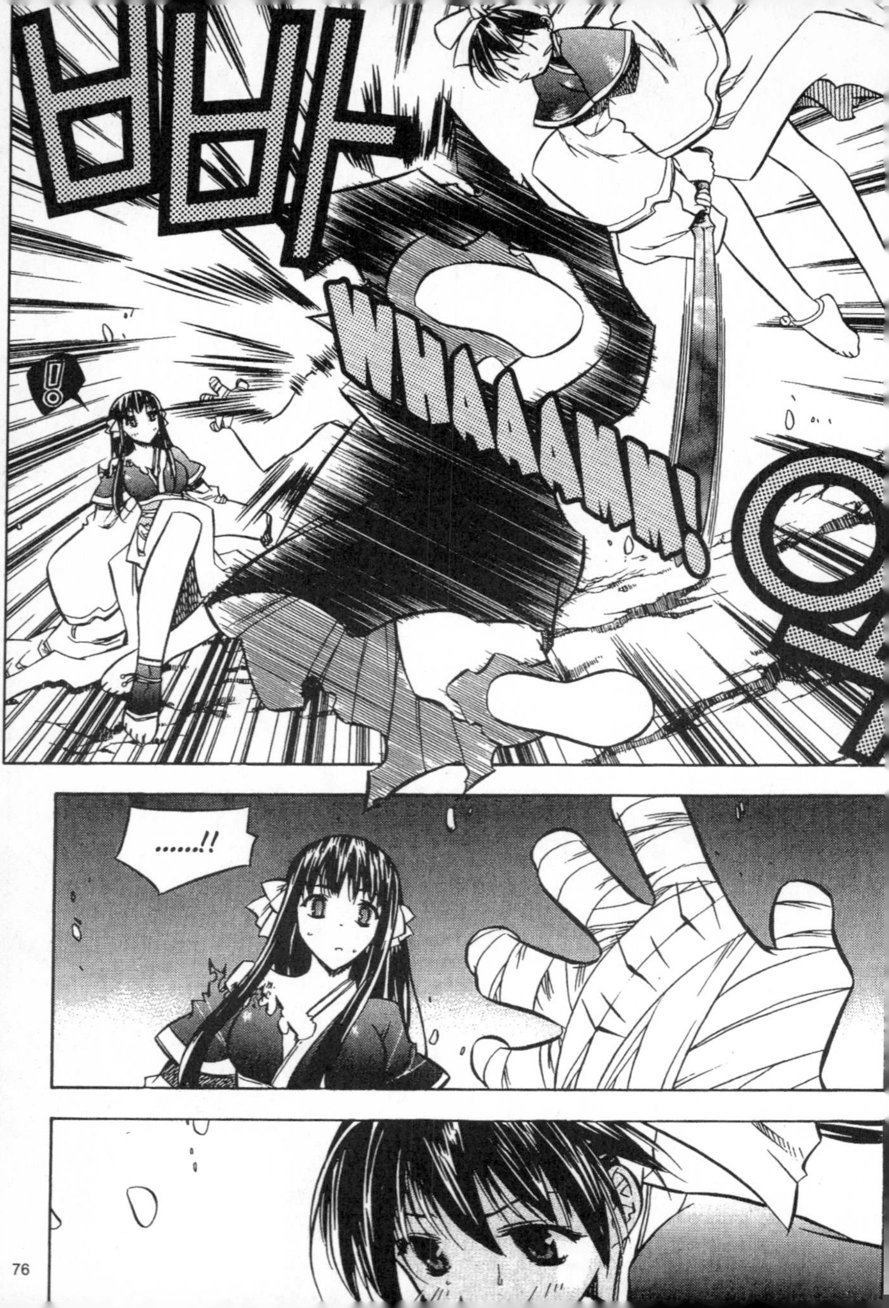
WHAAAAM!!
!
.......!!

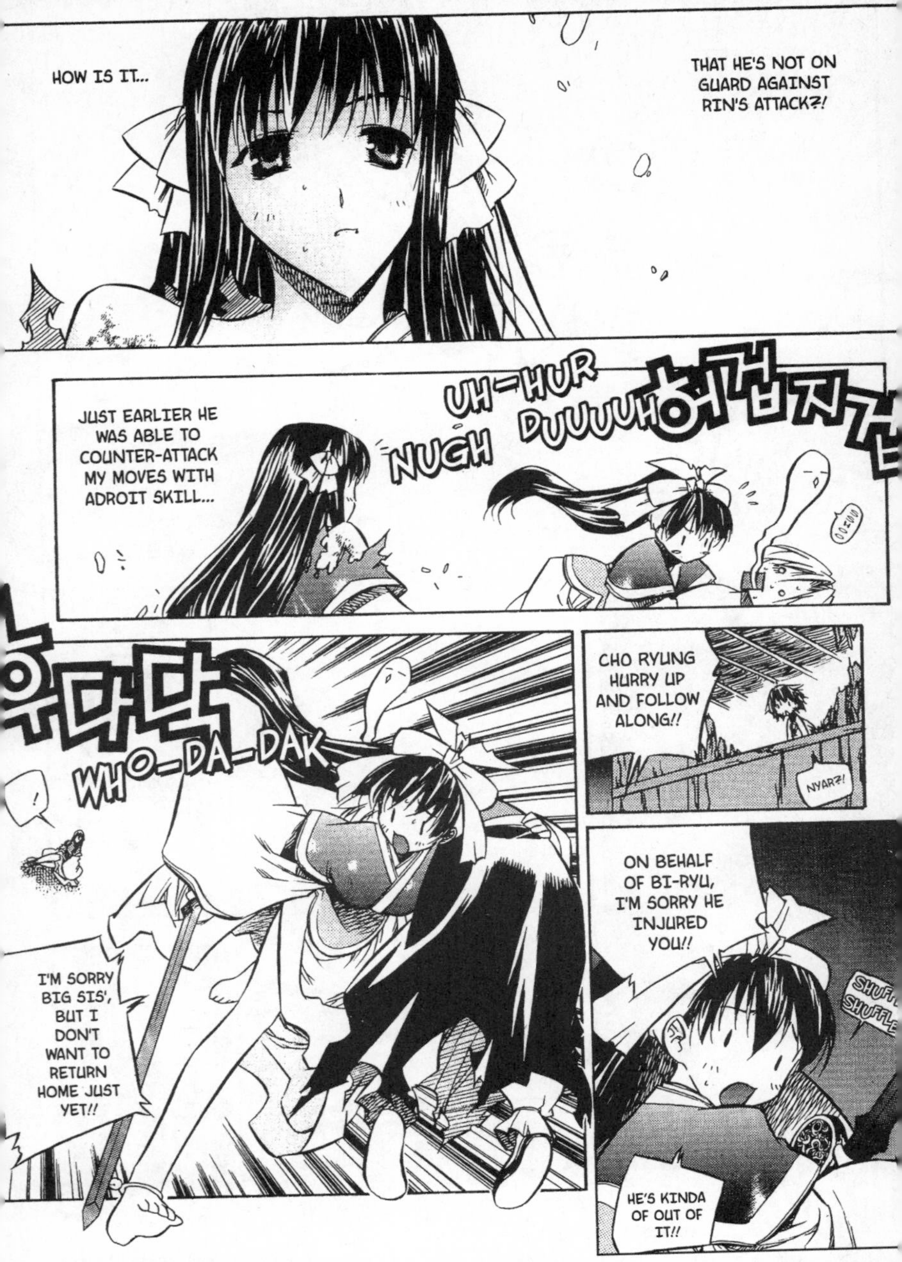
HOW IS IT...
THAT HE'S NOT ON GUARD AGAINST RIN'S ATTACK?!
JUST EARLIER HE WAS ABLE TO COUNTER-ATTACK MY MOVES WITH ADROIT SKILL...
UH-HUR NUGH DUUUUH
허겁지
후다닥
WHO-DA-DAK
!
CHO RYUNG HURRY UP AND FOLLOW ALONG!!
NYAR?!
I'M SORRY BIG SIS', BUT I DON'T WANT TO RETURN HOME JUST YET!!
ON BEHALF OF BI-RYU, I'M SORRY HE INJURED YOU!!
SHUFFLE
HE'S KINDA OF OUT OF IT!!

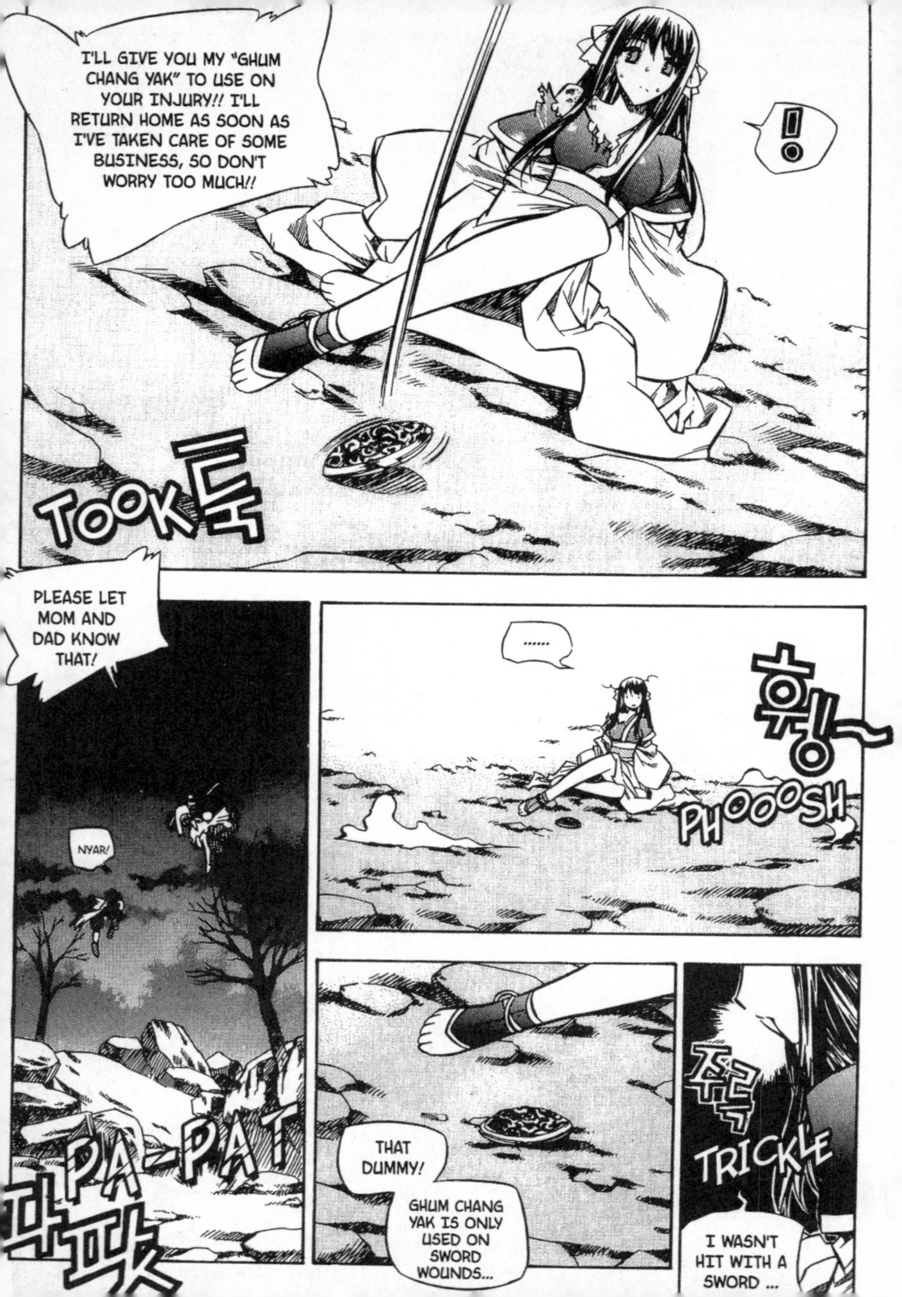
I'LL GIVE YOU MY "GHUM CHANG YAK" TO USE ON YOUR INJURY!! I'LL RETURN HOME AS SOON AS I'VE TAKEN CARE OF SOME BUSINESS, SO DON'T WORRY TOO MUCH!!
!
TOOK 톡
PLEASE LET MOM AND DAD KNOW THAT!
NYAR!
PA-PAT 파팟
......
휭~
PHOOOSH
THAT DUMMY!
GHUM CHANG YAK IS ONLY USED ON SWORD WOUNDS...
주르륵
TRICKLE
I WASN'T HIT WITH A SWORD ...

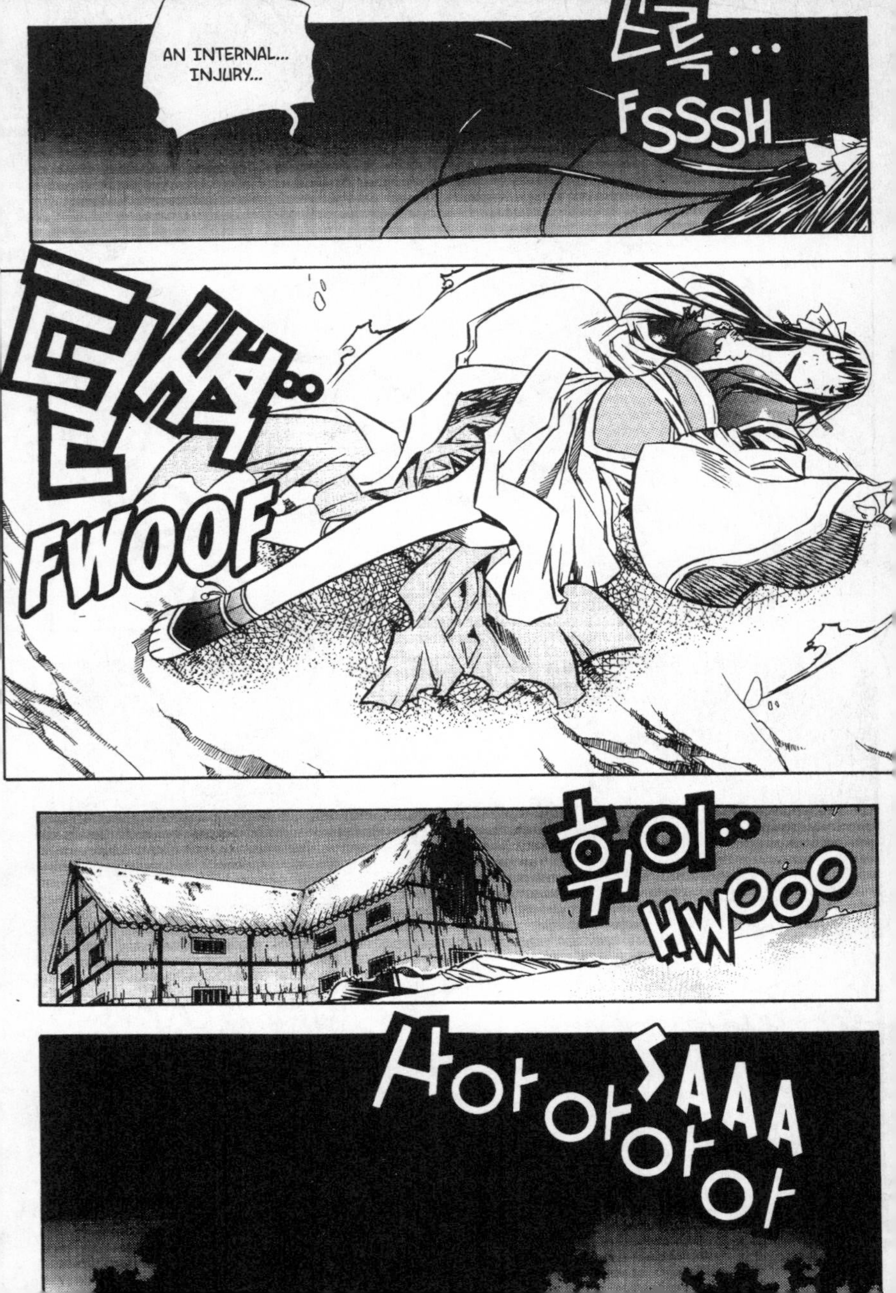
AN INTERNAL... INJURY...
FSSSH
털썩..
FWOOF
휘이..
HWOOO
사아아아아
SAAA

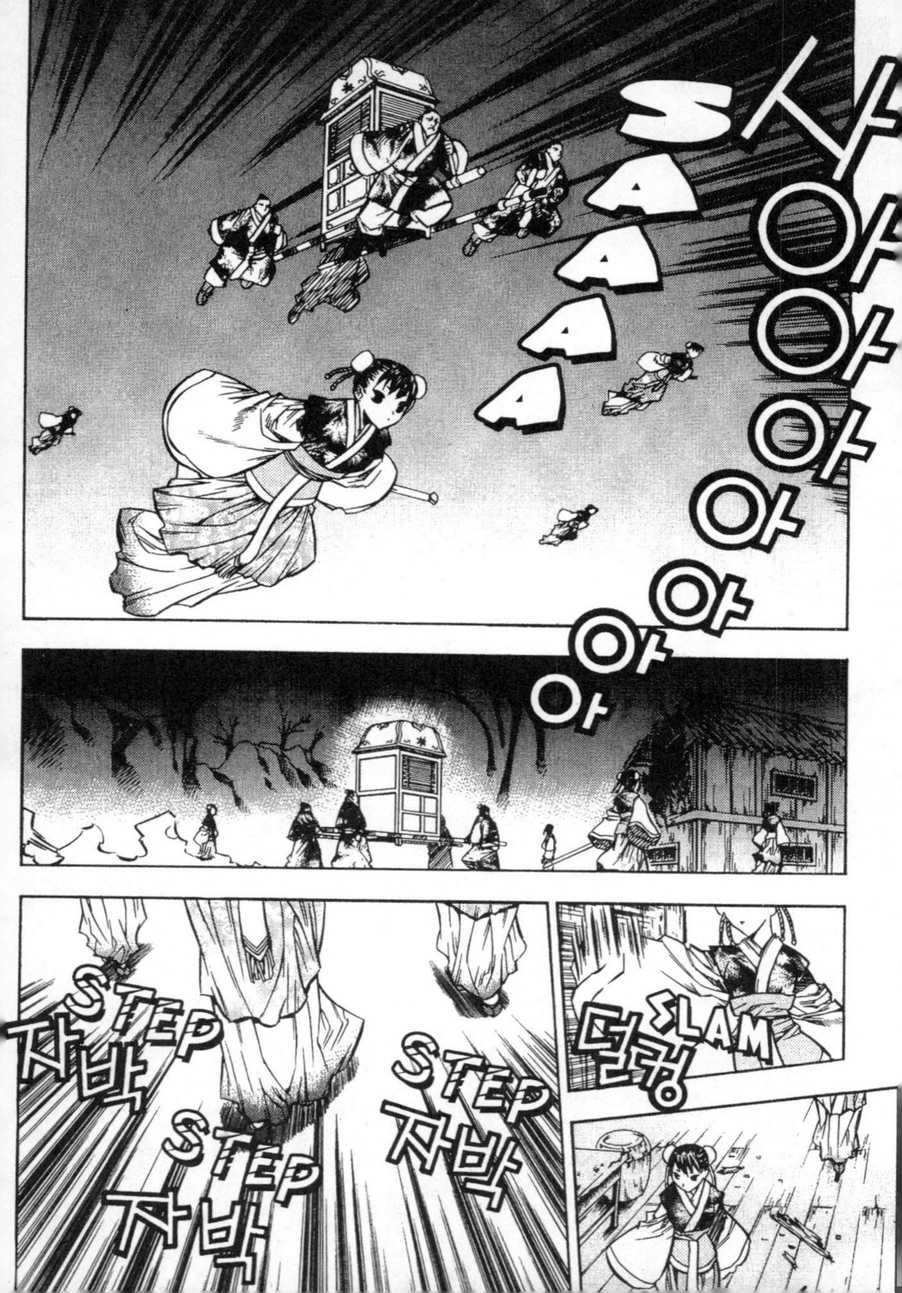
사아아아아아아아
SAAAA
자박 STEP
자박 STEP
자박 STEP
덜컹 SLAM

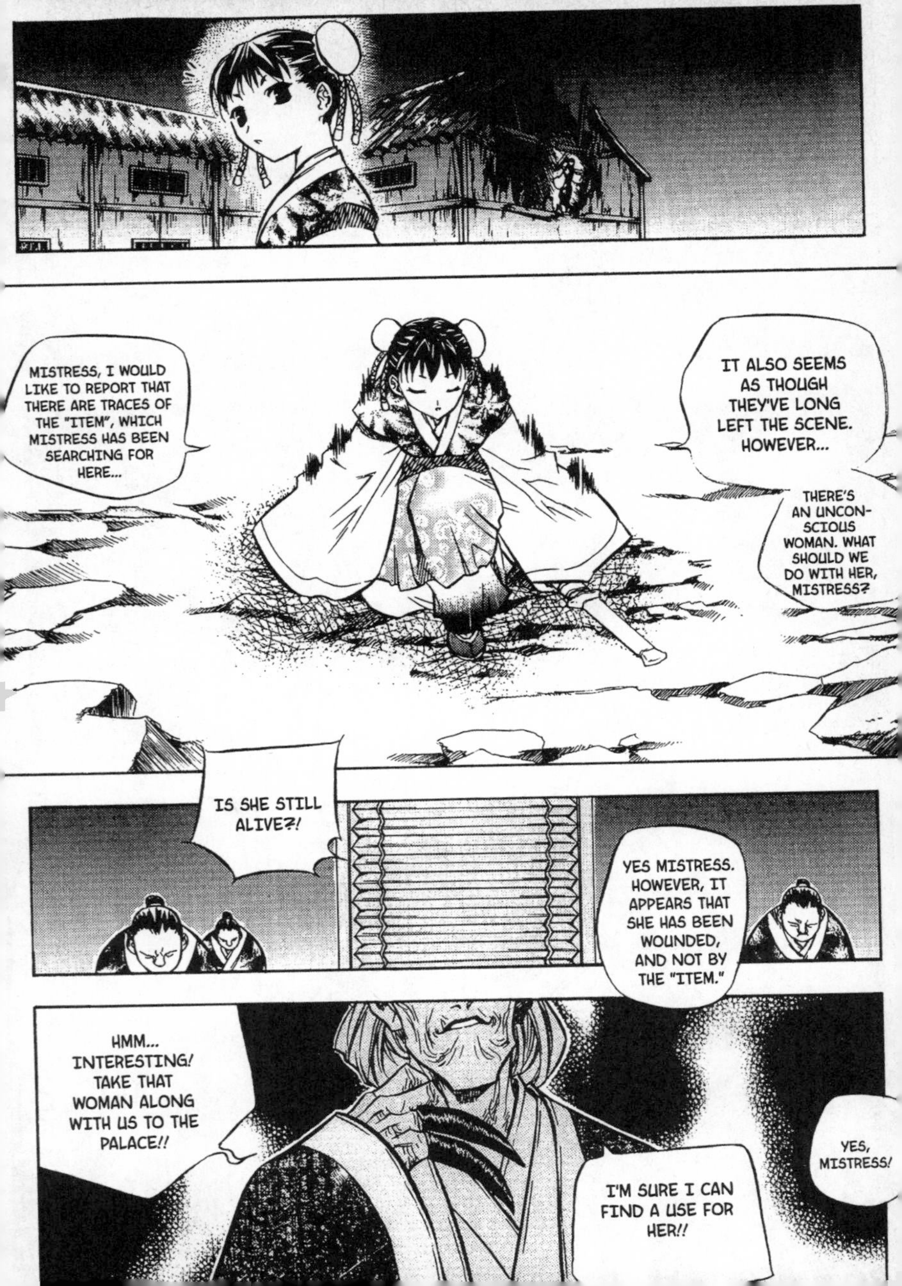
MISTRESS, I WOULD LIKE TO REPORT THAT THERE ARE TRACES OF THE "ITEM", WHICH MISTRESS HAS BEEN SEARCHING FOR HERE...
IT ALSO SEEMS AS THOUGH THEY'VE LONG LEFT THE SCENE. HOWEVER...
THERE'S AN UNCON-SCIOUS WOMAN. WHAT SHOULD WE DO WITH HER, MISTRESS?
IS SHE STILL ALIVE?!
YES MISTRESS. HOWEVER, IT APPEARS THAT SHE HAS BEEN WOUNDED, AND NOT BY THE "ITEM."
HMM... INTERESTING! TAKE THAT WOMAN ALONG WITH US TO THE PALACE!!
I'M SURE I CAN FIND A USE FOR HER!!
YES, MISTRESS!

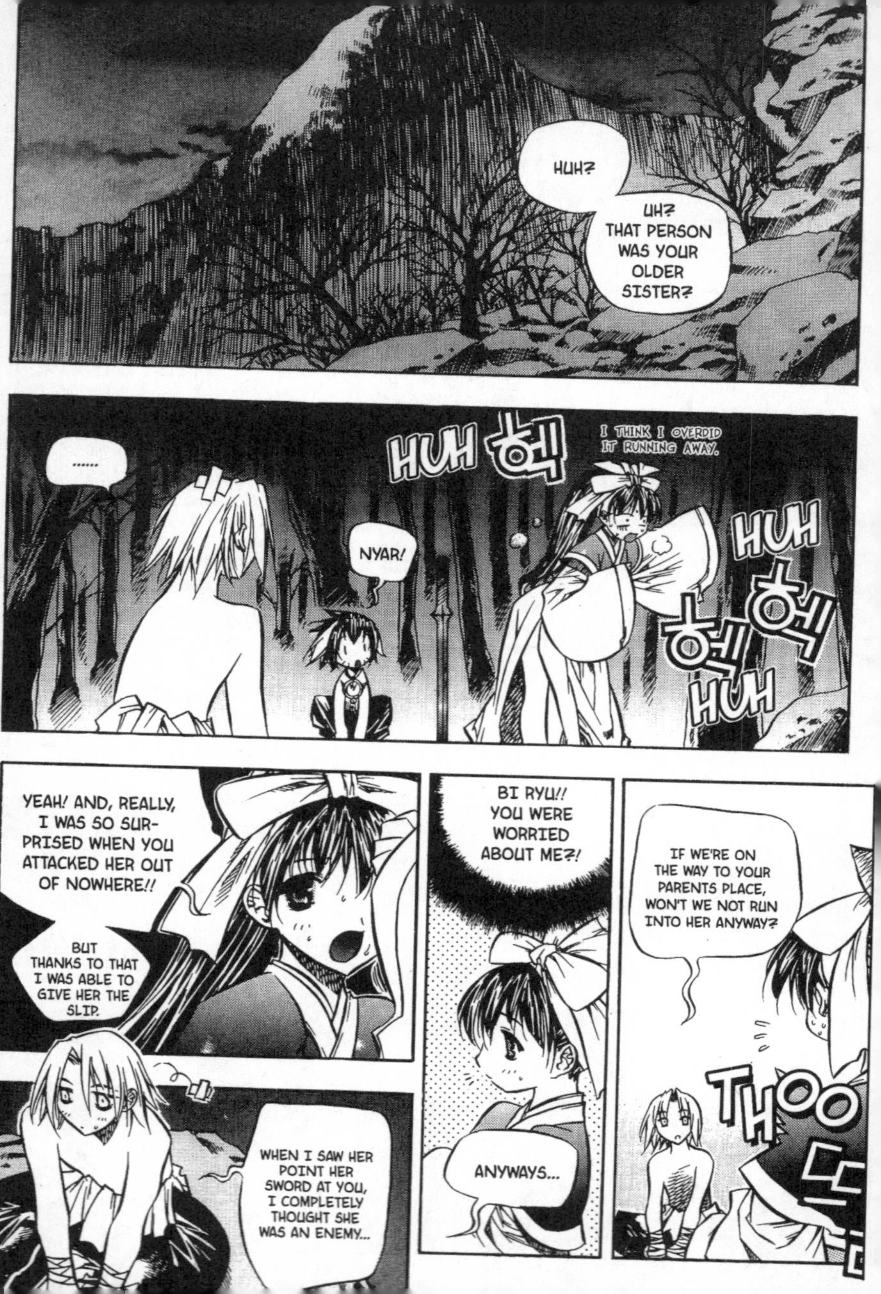
HUH?
UH?
THAT PERSON WAS YOUR OLDER SISTER?
......
HUH 헥
I THINK I OVERDID IT RUNNING AWAY.
NYAR!
HUH 헥
헥 HUH
YEAH! AND, REALLY, I WAS SO SUR-PRISED WHEN YOU ATTACKED HER OUT OF NOWHERE!!
BUT THANKS TO THAT I WAS ABLE TO GIVE HER THE SLIP.
WHEN I SAW HER POINT HER SWORD AT YOU, I COMPLETELY THOUGHT SHE WAS AN ENEMY...
BI RYU!! YOU WERE WORRIED ABOUT ME?!
ANYWAYS...
IF WE'RE ON THE WAY TO YOUR PARENTS PLACE, WON'T WE NOT RUN INTO HER ANYWAY?
THOO

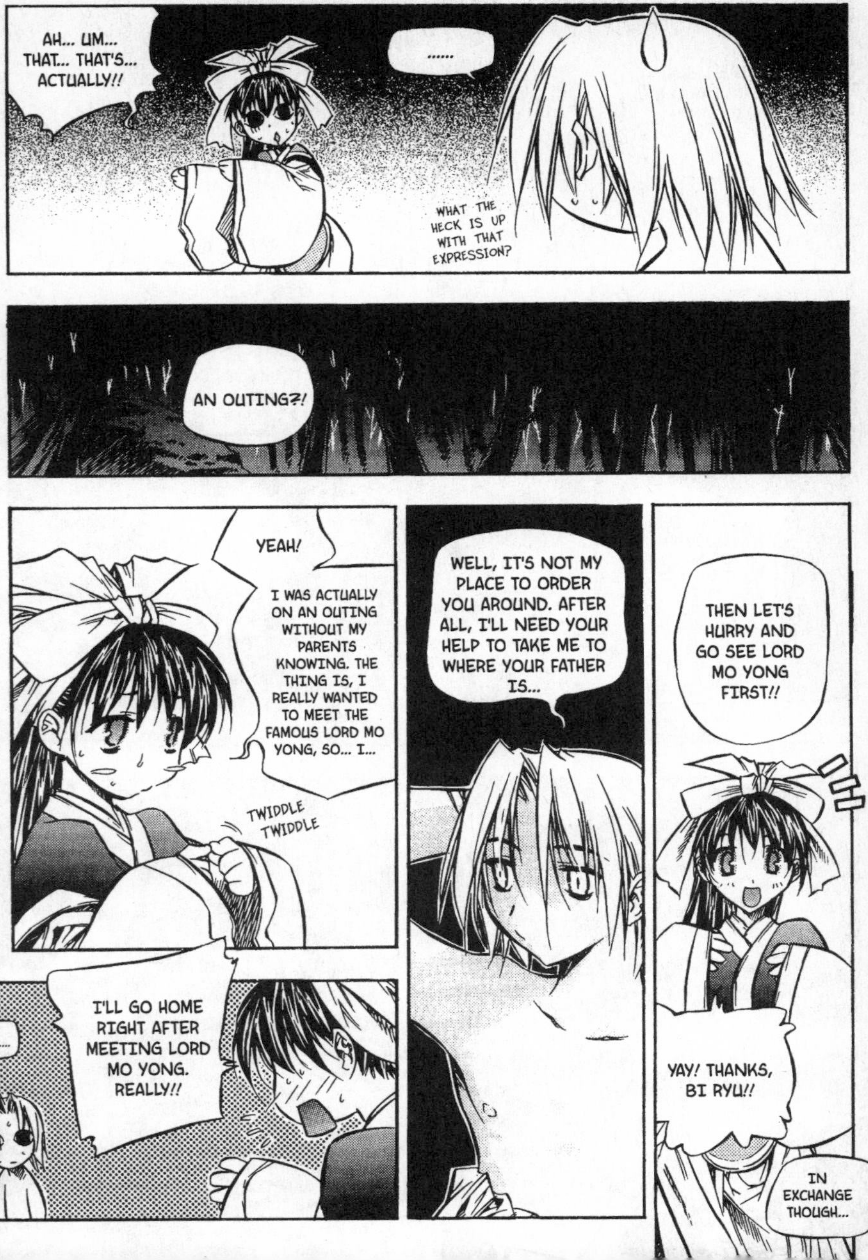
AH... UM... THAT... THAT'S... ACTUALLY!!
......
WHAT THE HECK IS UP WITH THAT EXPRESSION?
AN OUTING?!
YEAH!
I WAS ACTUALLY ON AN OUTING WITHOUT MY PARENTS KNOWING. THE THING IS, I REALLY WANTED TO MEET THE FAMOUS LORD MO YONG, SO... I...
TWIDDLE TWIDDLE
......
I'LL GO HOME RIGHT AFTER MEETING LORD MO YONG. REALLY!!
WELL, IT'S NOT MY PLACE TO ORDER YOU AROUND. AFTER ALL, I'LL NEED YOUR HELP TO TAKE ME TO WHERE YOUR FATHER IS...
THEN LET'S HURRY AND GO SEE LORD MO YONG FIRST!!
YAY! THANKS, BI RYU!!
IN EXCHANGE THOUGH...

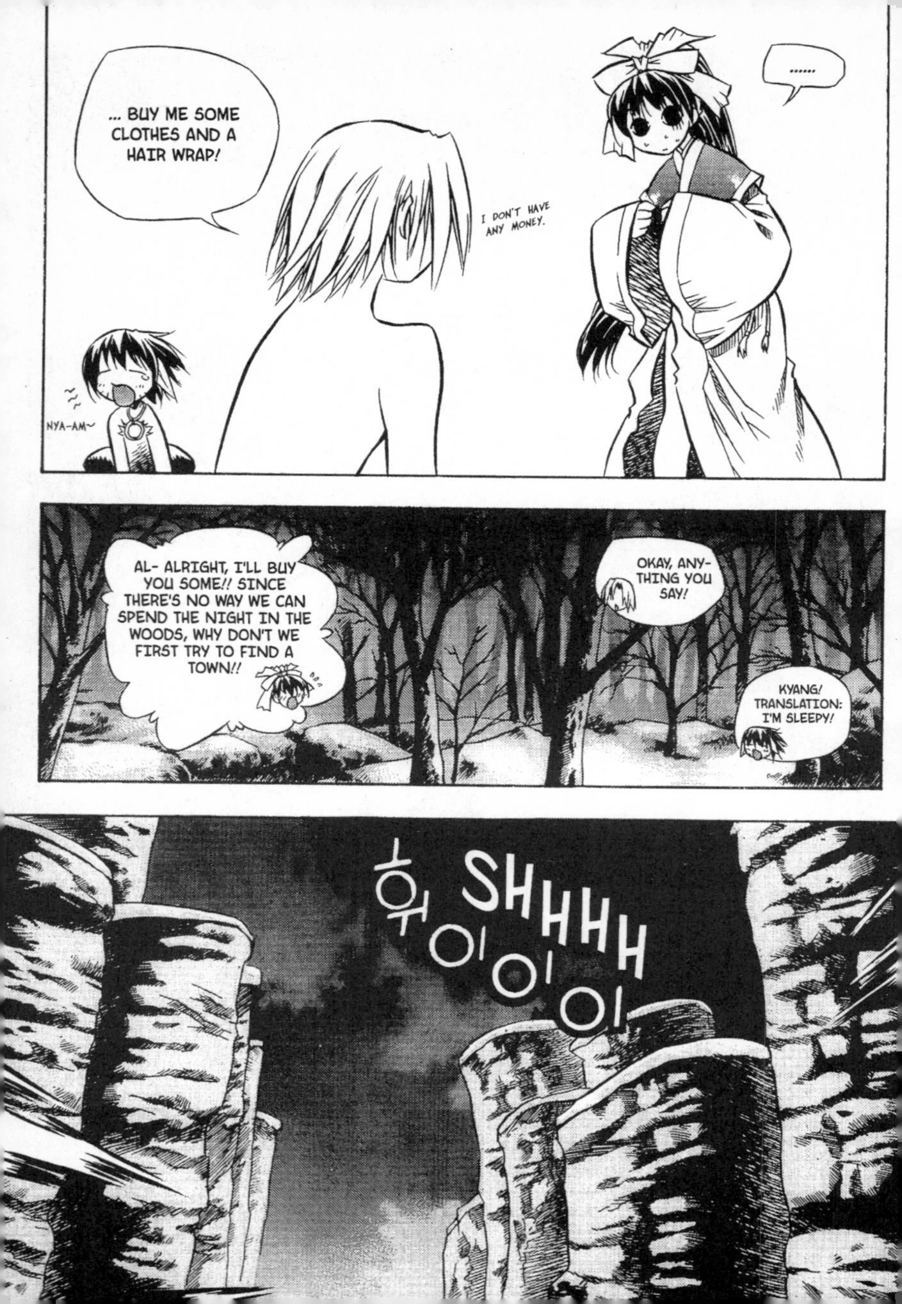
......
I DON'T HAVE ANY MONEY.
... BUY ME SOME CLOTHES AND A HAIR WRAP!
NYA-AM~
OKAY, ANY-THING YOU SAY!
KYANG! TRANSLATION: I'M SLEEPY!
AL- ALRIGHT, I'LL BUY YOU SOME!! SINCE THERE'S NO WAY WE CAN SPEND THE NIGHT IN THE WOODS, WHY DON'T WE FIRST TRY TO FIND A TOWN!!
SHHHH

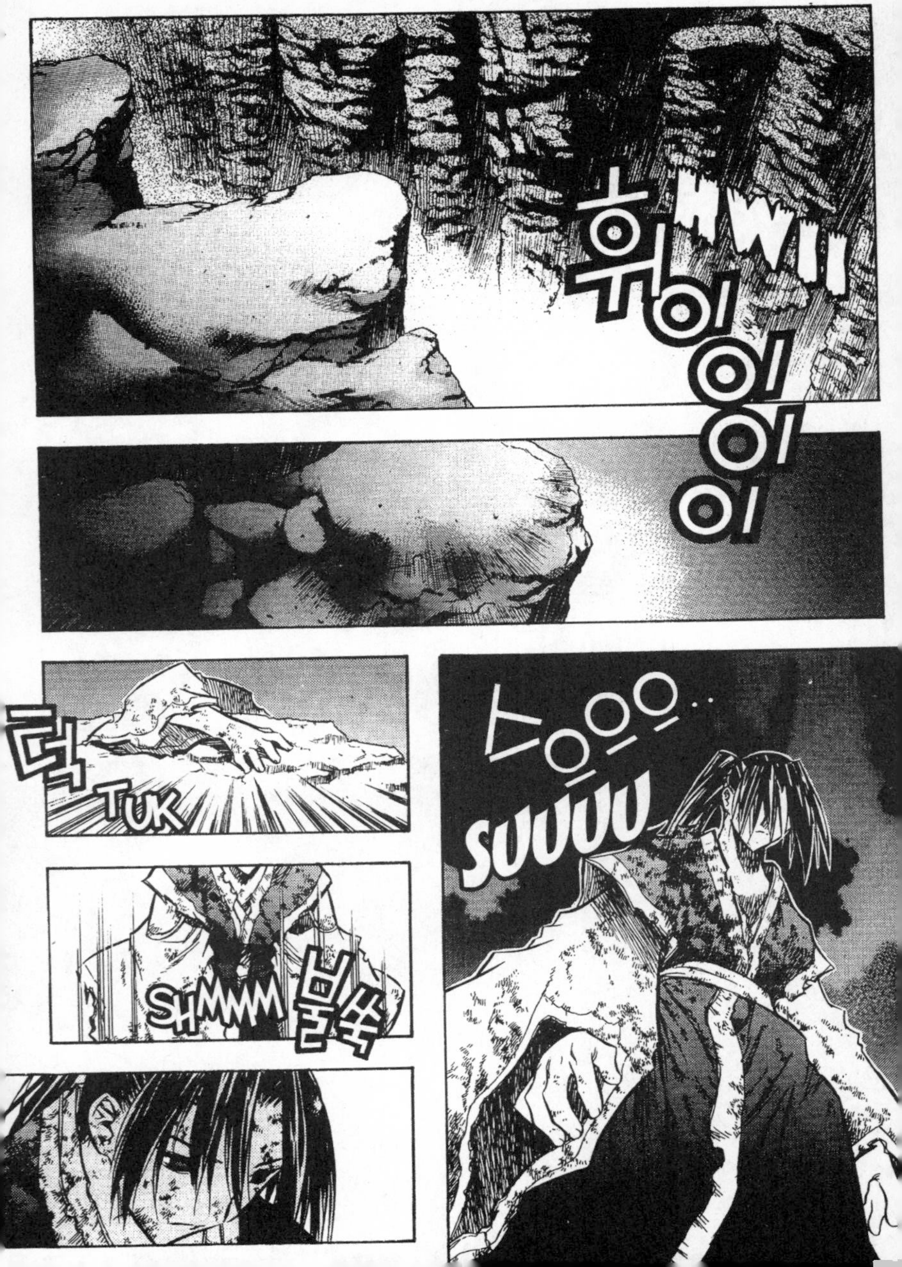
휘이이이이
HWII
스으으으..
SUUUU
턱
TUK
불쑥
SHMMM

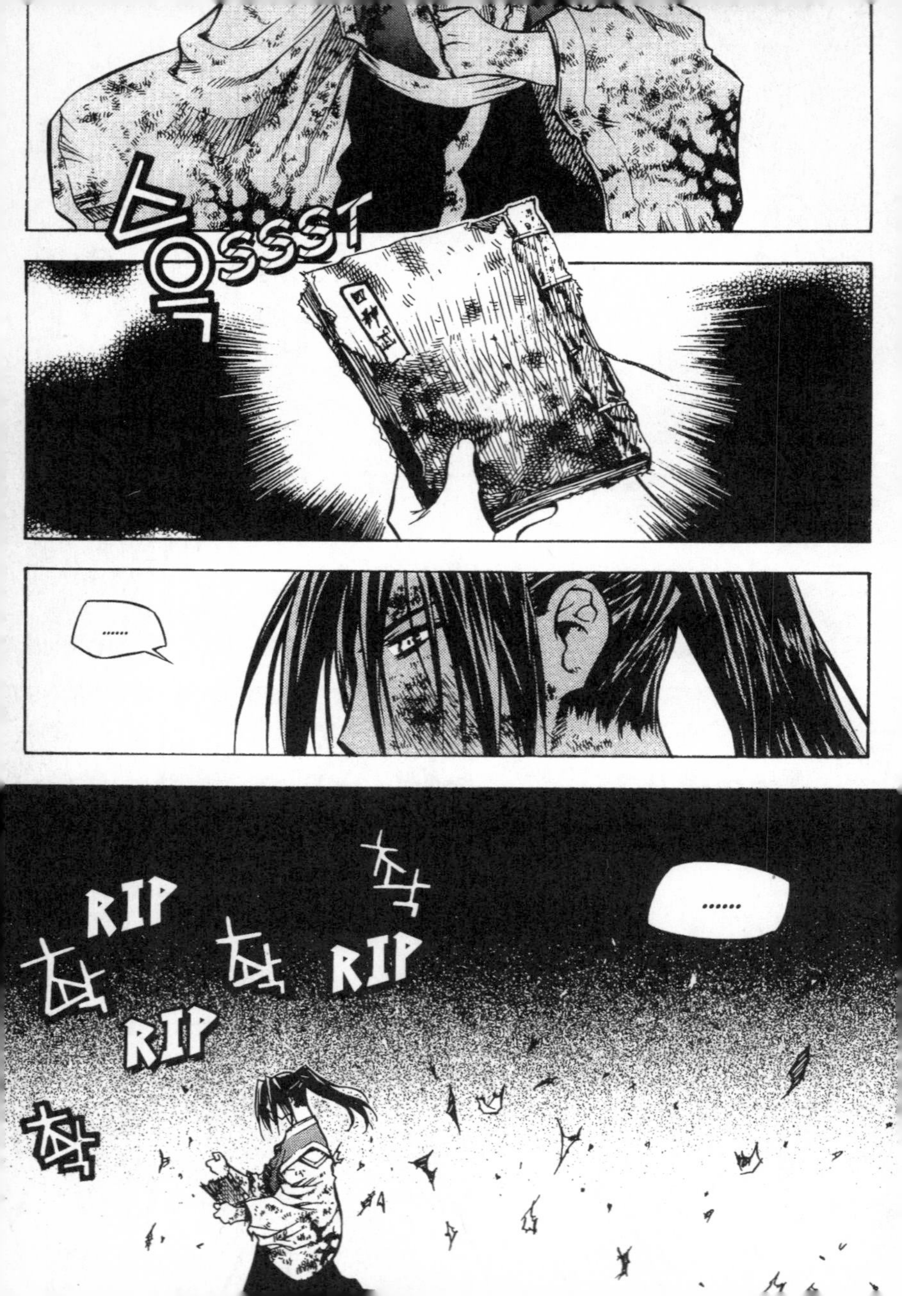
......
......
RIP
RIP
RIP

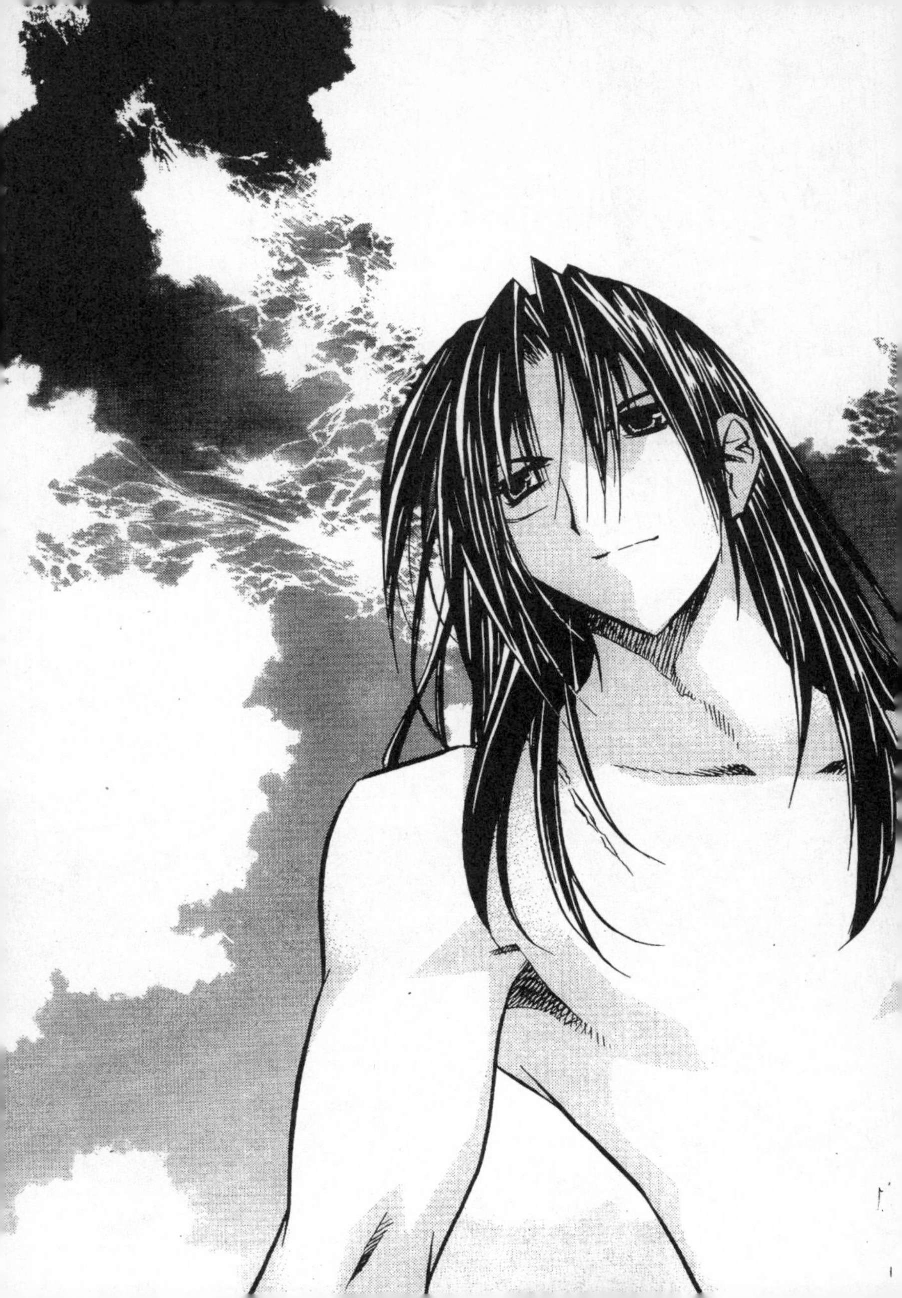

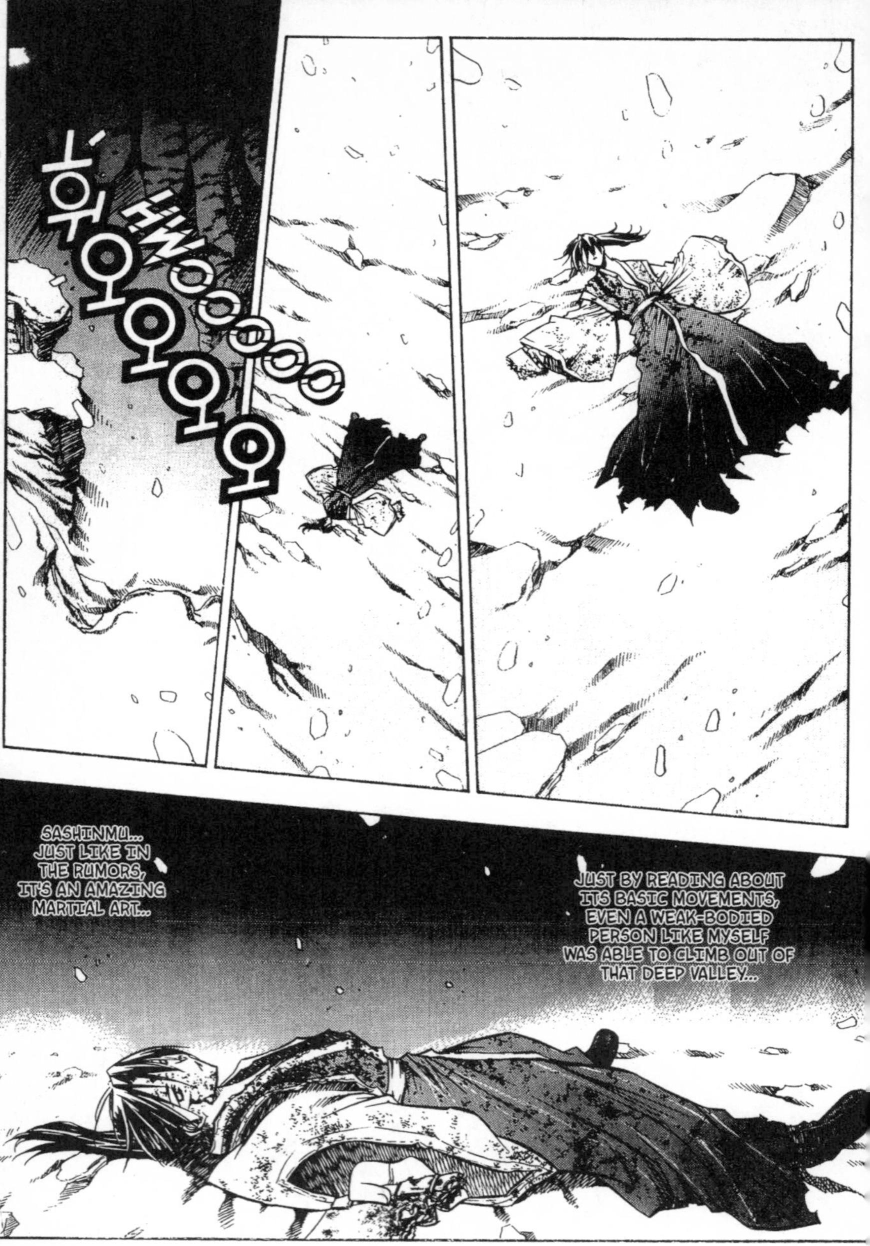
HWOOOOOO
SASHINMU... JUST LIKE IN THE RUMORS, IT'S AN AMAZING MARTIAL ART...
JUST BY READING ABOUT ITS BASIC MOVEMENTS, EVEN A WEAK-BODIED PERSON LIKE MYSELF WAS ABLE TO CLIMB OUT OF THAT DEEP VALLEY...

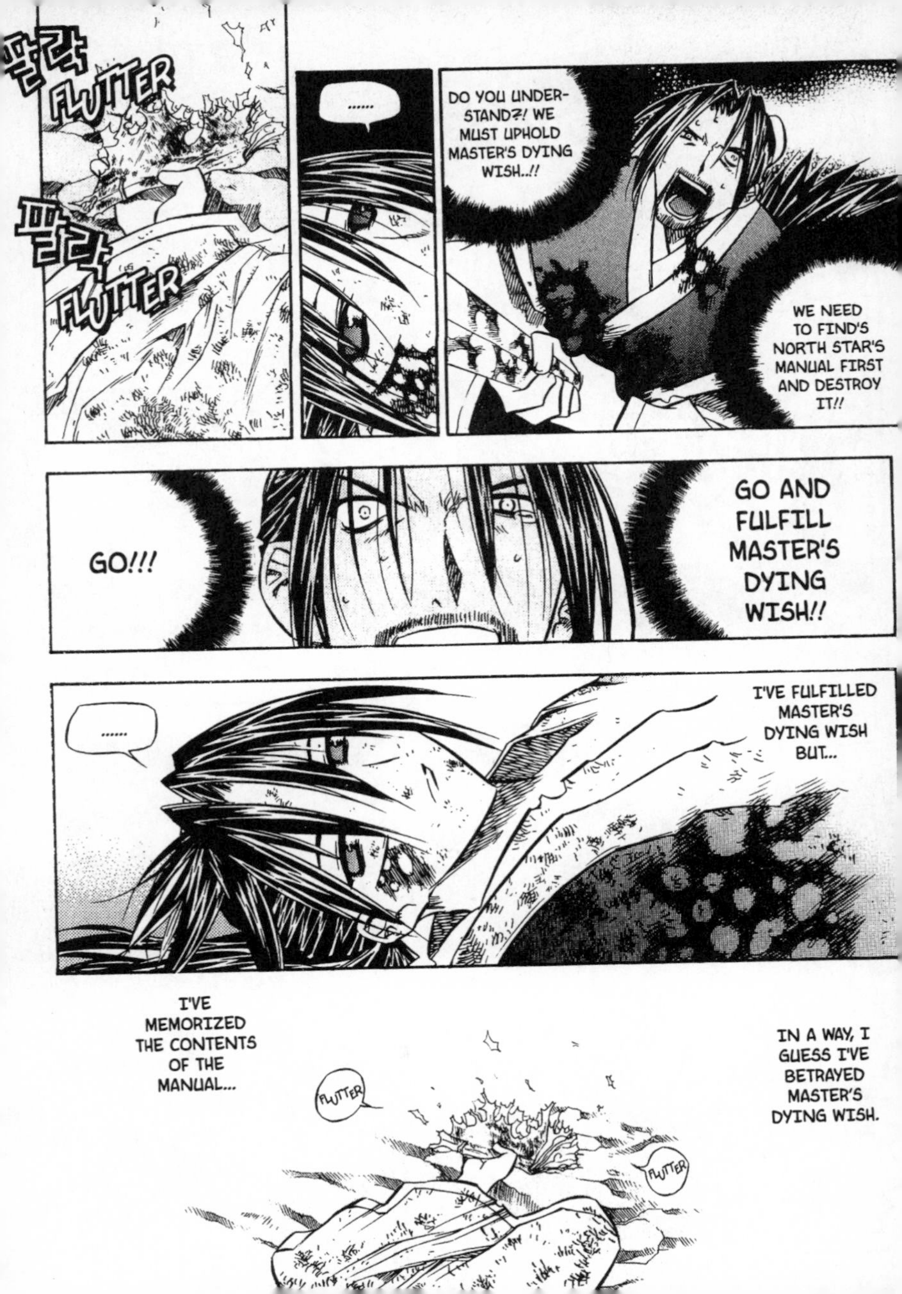

펄럭
FLUTTER
팔락
FLUTTER
......
DO YOU UNDERSTAND?! WE MUST UPHOLD MASTER'S DYING WISH..!!
WE NEED TO FIND'S NORTH STAR'S MANUAL FIRST AND DESTROY IT!!
GO!!!
GO AND FULFILL MASTER'S DYING WISH!!
......
I'VE FULFILLED MASTER'S DYING WISH BUT...
I'VE MEMORIZED THE CONTENTS OF THE MANUAL...
FLUTTER
FLUTTER
IN A WAY, I GUESS I'VE BETRAYED MASTER'S DYING WISH.

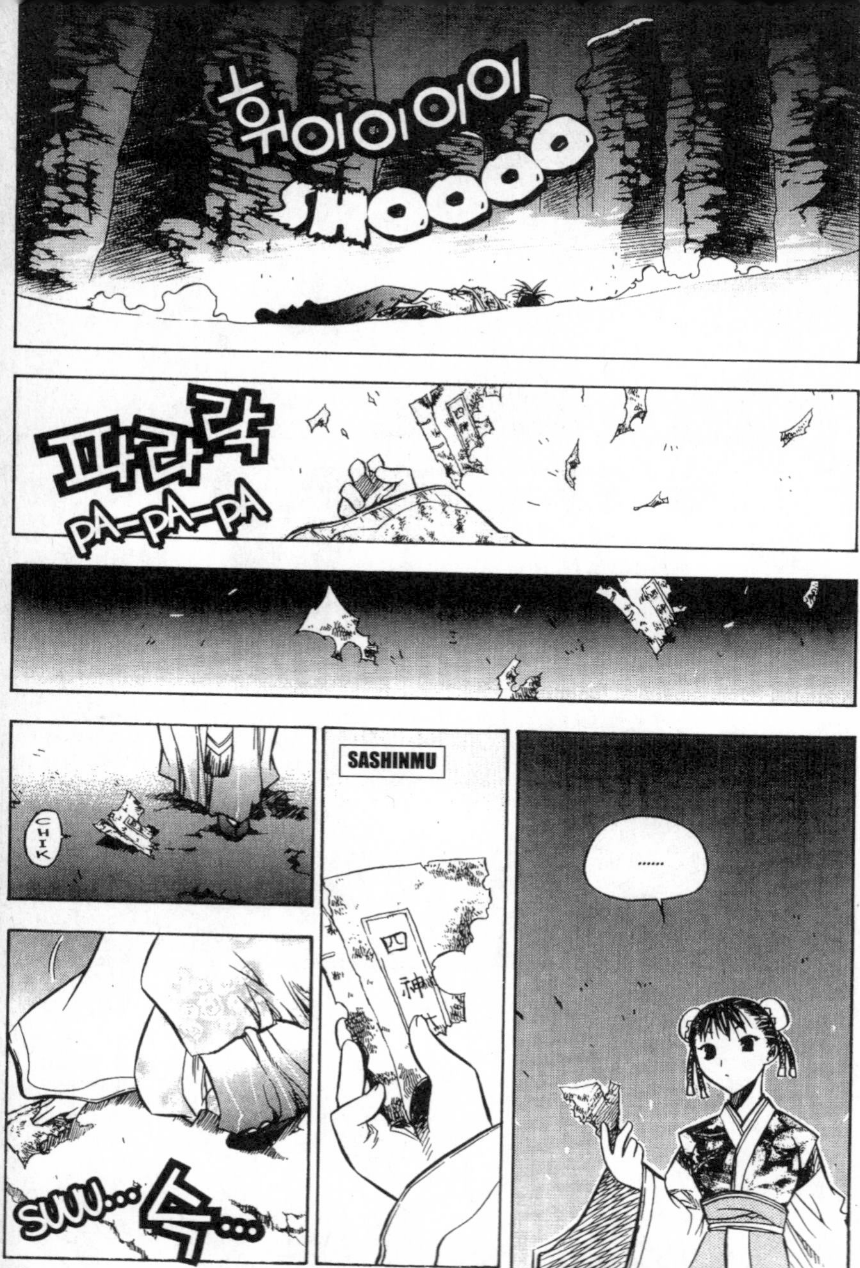

솨아이이이이
SHOOOO
파라락
PA-PA-PA
CHIK
SASHINMU
......
SUUU...
스...

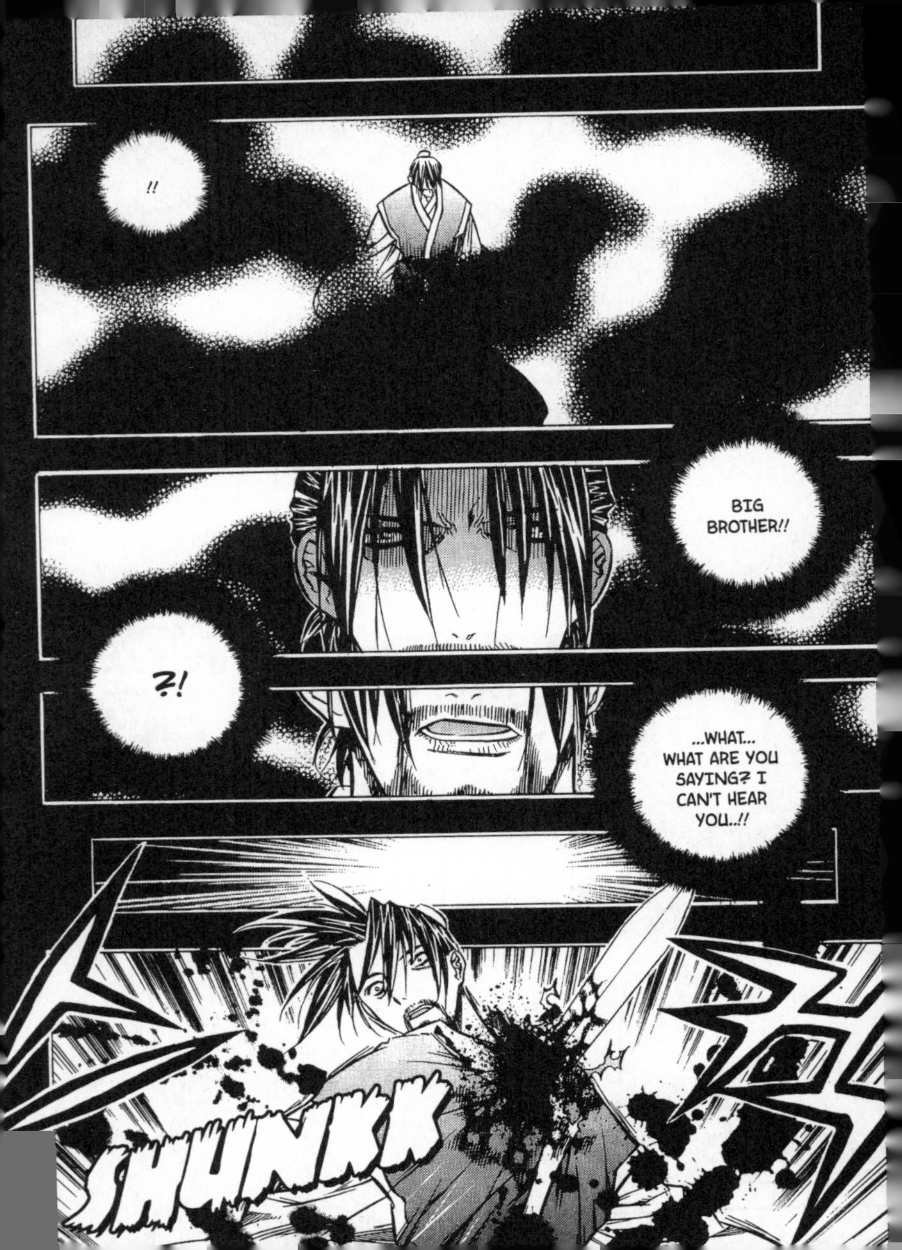
!!
BIG BROTHER!!
?!
...WHAT... WHAT ARE YOU SAYING? I CAN'T HEAR YOU..!!
SHUNKK

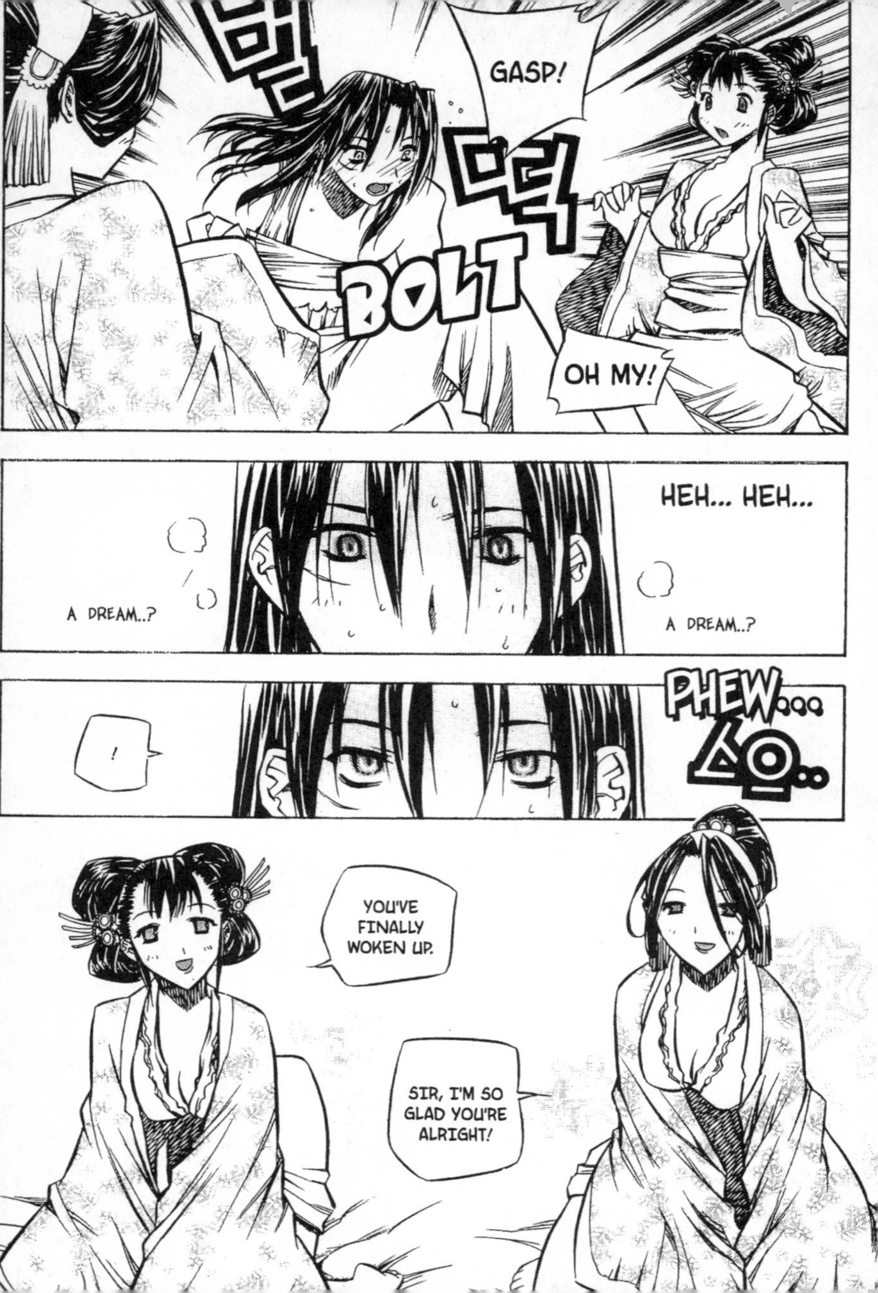
GASP!
BOLT
OH MY!
HEH... HEH...
A DREAM..?
A DREAM..?
PHEW...
!
YOU'VE FINALLY WOKEN UP.
SIR, I'M SO GLAD YOU'RE ALRIGHT!

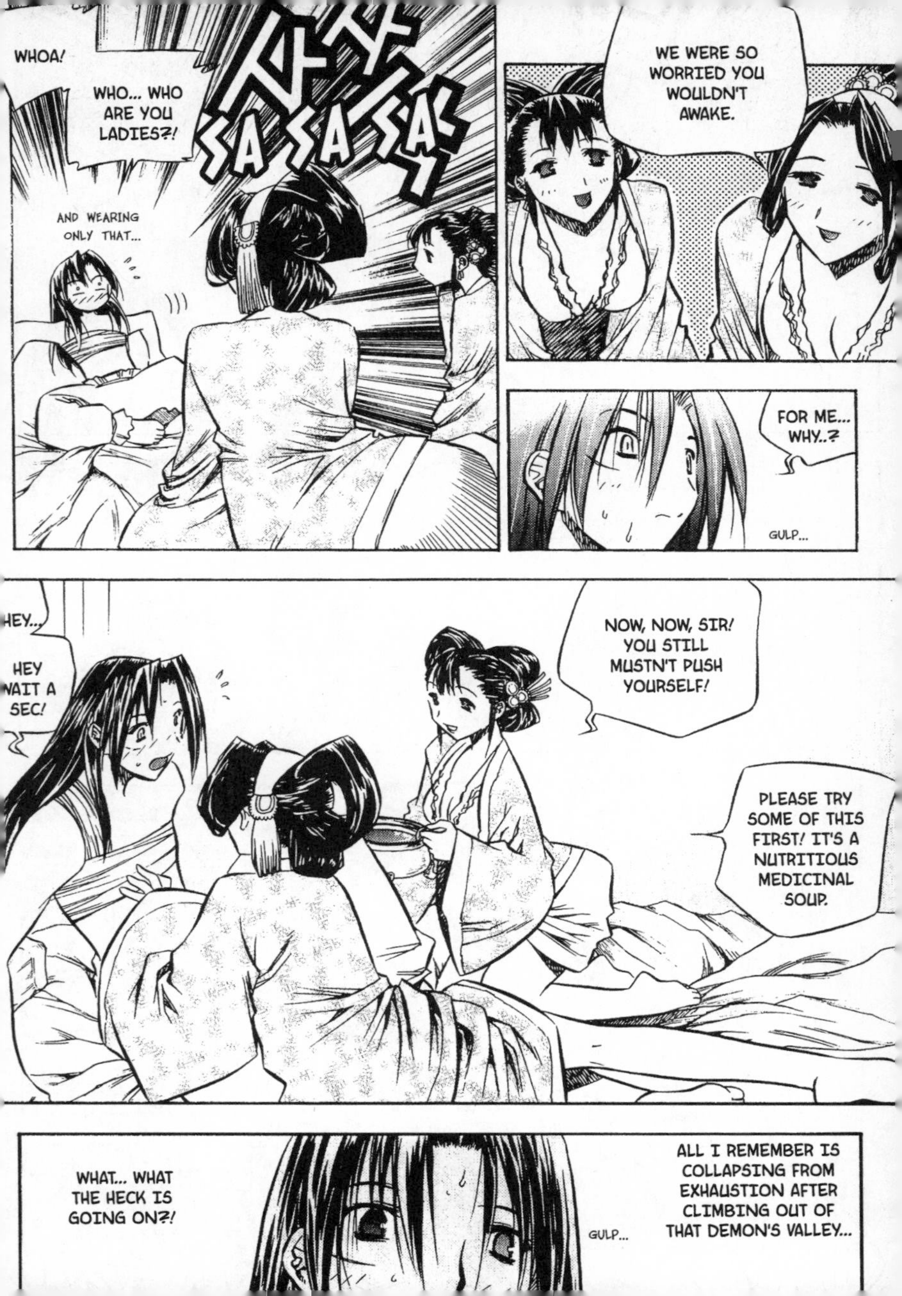

WHOA!
WHO... WHO ARE YOU LADIES?!
AND WEARING ONLY THAT...
SA SA SA SA
WE WERE SO WORRIED YOU WOULDN'T AWAKE.
FOR ME... WHY..?
GULP...
HEY...
HEY WAIT A SEC!
NOW, NOW, SIR! YOU STILL MUSTN'T PUSH YOURSELF!
PLEASE TRY SOME OF THIS FIRST! IT'S A NUTRITIOUS MEDICINAL SOUP.
WHAT... WHAT THE HECK IS GOING ON?!
GULP...
ALL I REMEMBER IS COLLAPSING FROM EXHAUSTION AFTER CLIMBING OUT OF THAT DEMON'S VALLEY...

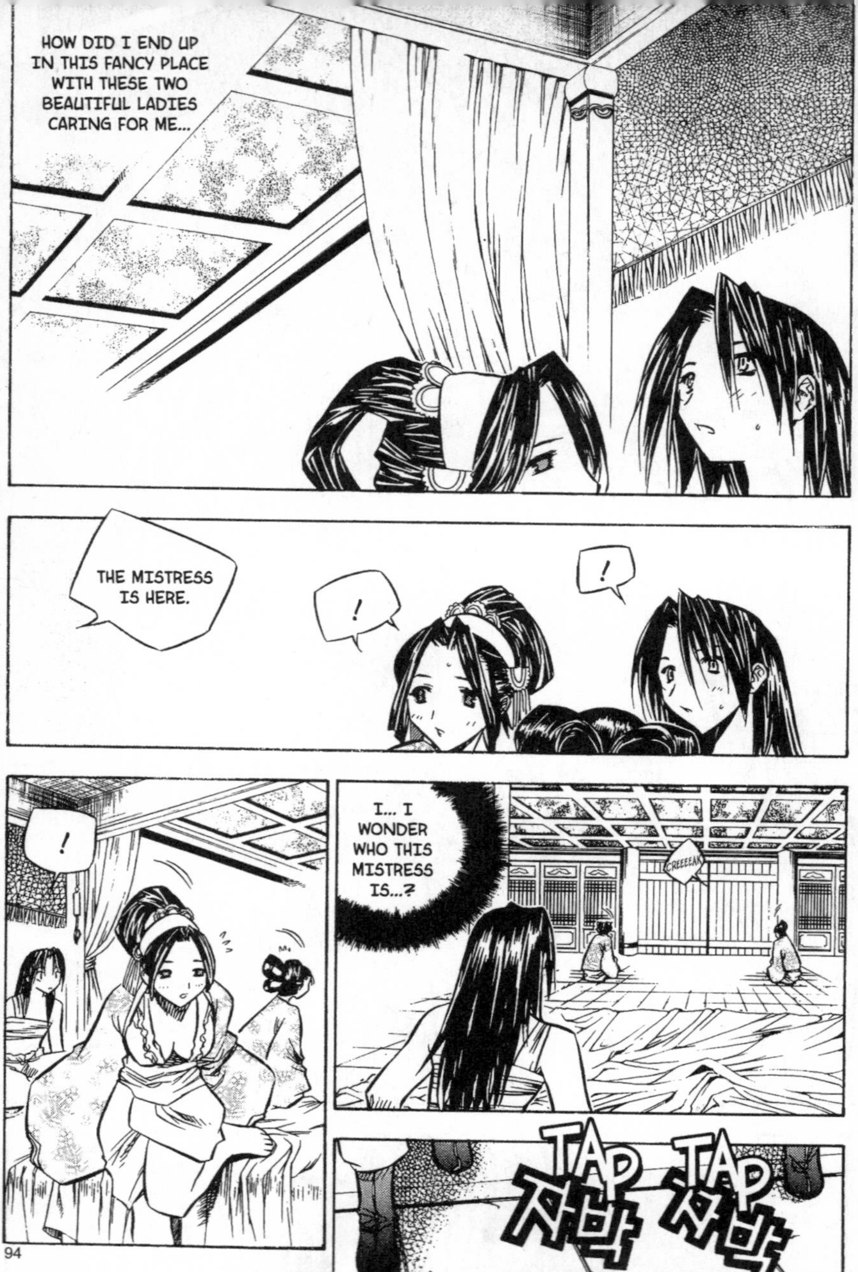
HOW DID I END UP IN THIS FANCY PLACE WITH THESE TWO BEAUTIFUL LADIES CARING FOR ME...
!
!
THE MISTRESS IS HERE.
I... I WONDER WHO THIS MISTRESS IS...?
CREEEEAK
!
TAP TAP
자박 자박

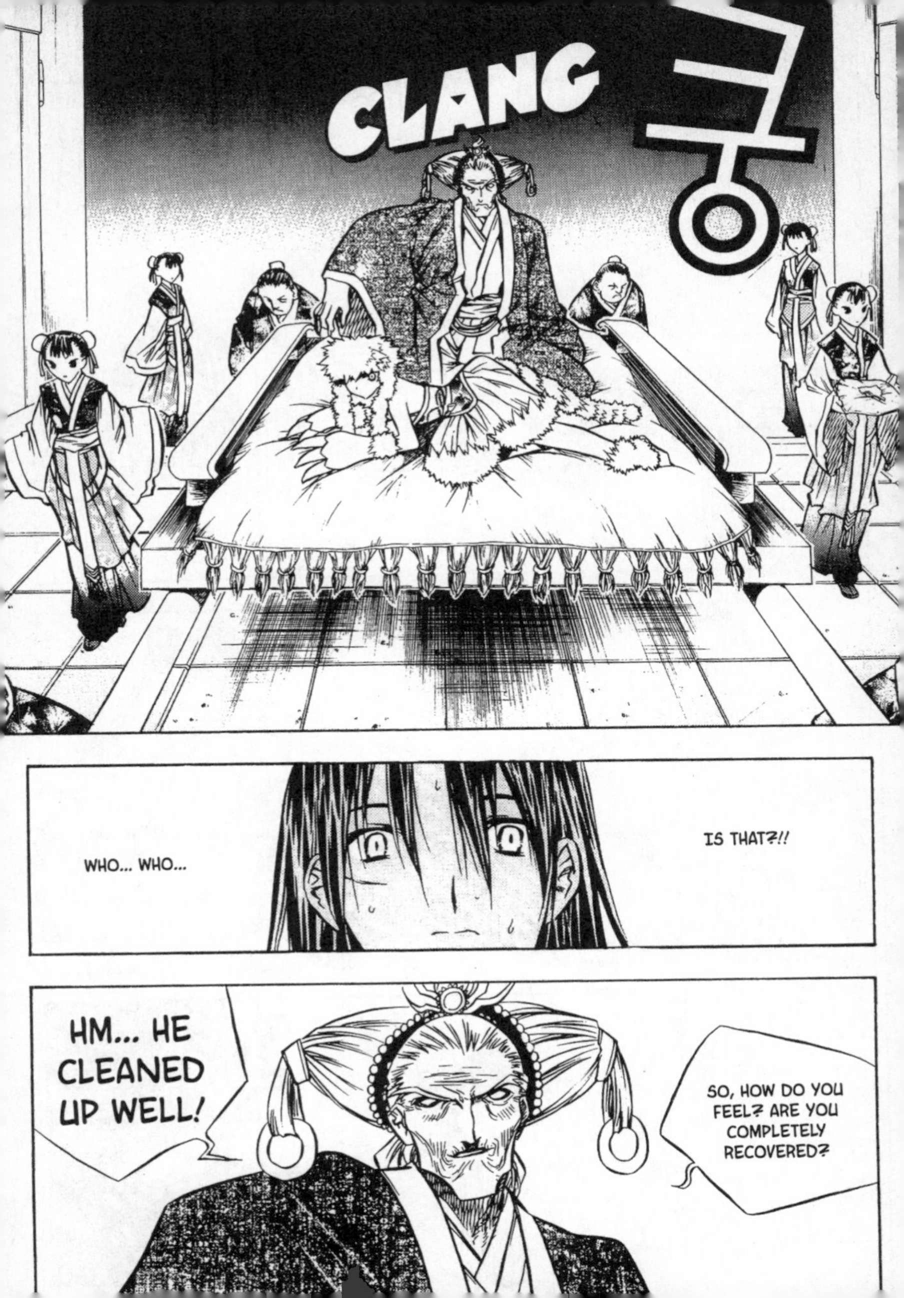
CLANG
WHO... WHO...
IS THAT?!!
HM... HE CLEANED UP WELL!
SO, HOW DO YOU FEEL? ARE YOU COMPLETELY RECOVERED?

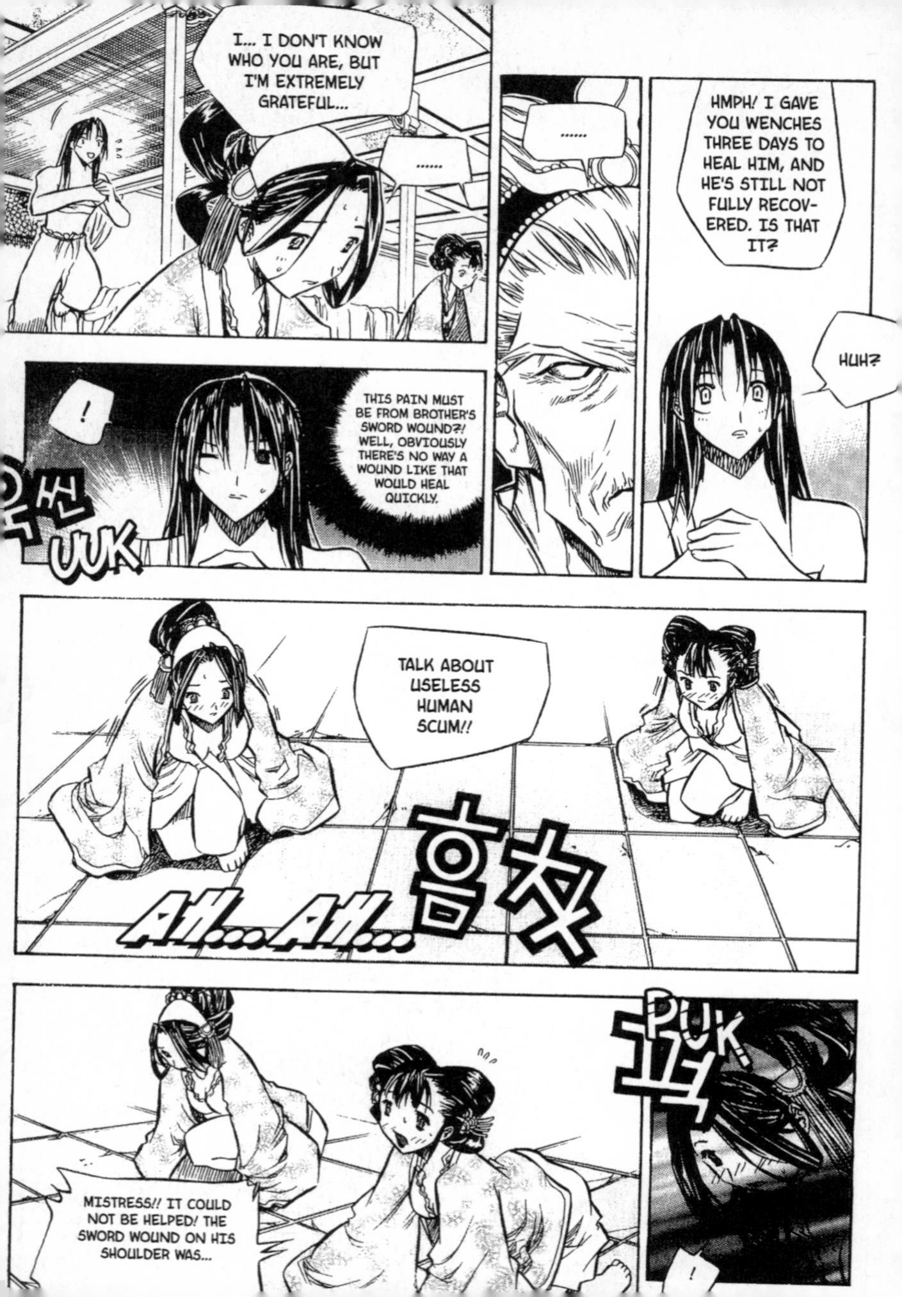
HMPH! I GAVE YOU WENCHES THREE DAYS TO HEAL HIM, AND HE'S STILL NOT FULLY RECOVERED. IS THAT IT?
......
......
I... I DON'T KNOW WHO YOU ARE, BUT I'M EXTREMELY GRATEFUL...
HUH?
THIS PAIN MUST BE FROM BROTHER'S SWORD WOUND?! WELL, OBVIOUSLY THERE'S NO WAY A WOUND LIKE THAT WOULD HEAL QUICKLY.
!
UUK
TALK ABOUT USELESS HUMAN SCUM!!
AH... AH...
PUK
MISTRESS!! IT COULD NOT BE HELPED! THE SWORD WOUND ON HIS SHOULDER WAS...
!

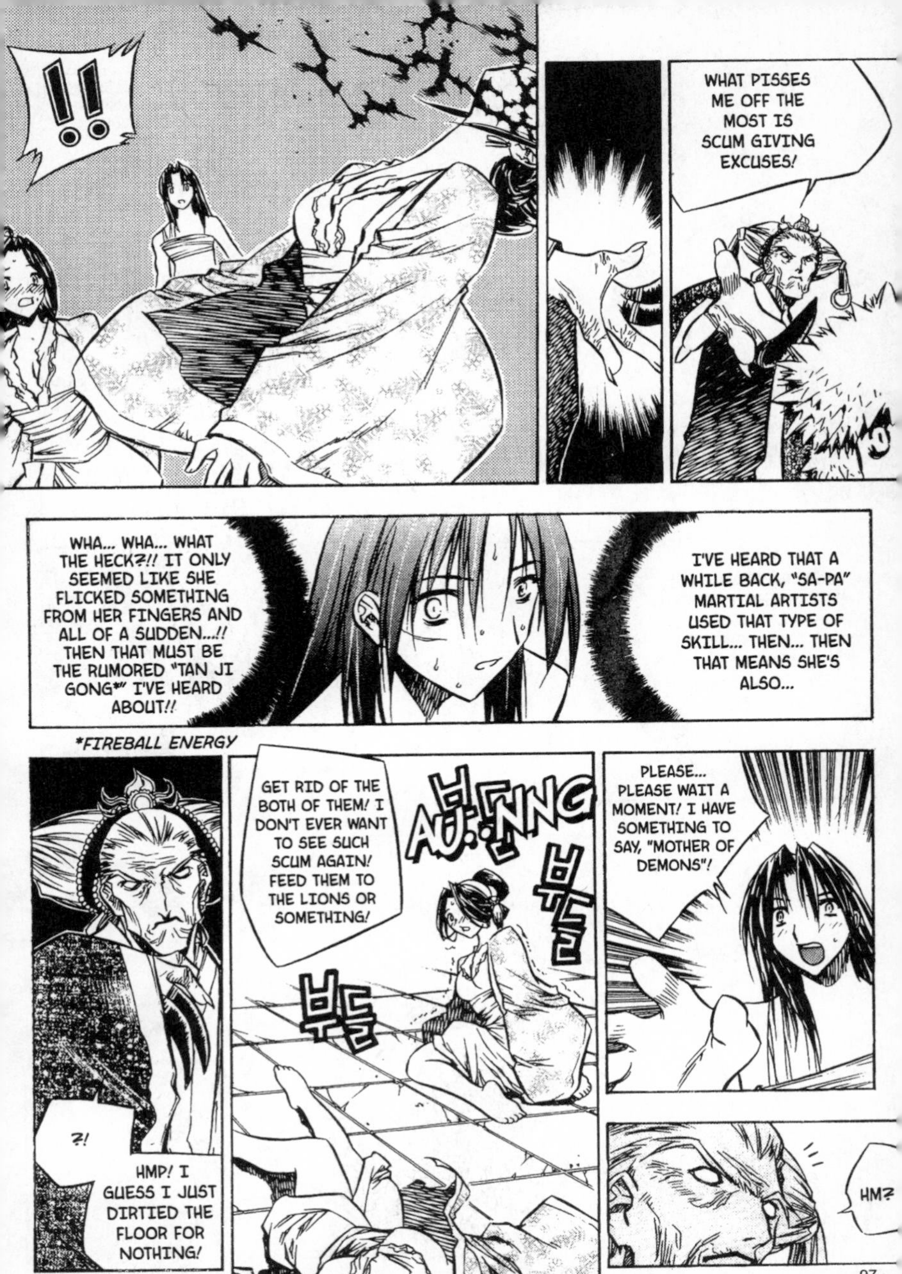
!!
WHAT PISSES ME OFF THE MOST IS SCUM GIVING EXCUSES!
WHA... WHA... WHAT THE HECK?!! IT ONLY SEEMED LIKE SHE FLICKED SOMETHING FROM HER FINGERS AND ALL OF A SUDDEN...!! THEN THAT MUST BE THE RUMORED "TAN JI GONG*" I'VE HEARD ABOUT!!
I'VE HEARD THAT A WHILE BACK, "SA-PA" MARTIAL ARTISTS USED THAT TYPE OF SKILL... THEN... THEN THAT MEANS SHE'S ALSO...
*FIREBALL ENERGY
?!
HMP! I GUESS I JUST DIRTIED THE FLOOR FOR NOTHING!
GET RID OF THE BOTH OF THEM! I DON'T EVER WANT TO SEE SUCH SCUM AGAIN! FEED THEM TO THE LIONS OR SOMETHING!
PLEASE... PLEASE WAIT A MOMENT! I HAVE SOMETHING TO SAY, "MOTHER OF DEMONS"!
HM?

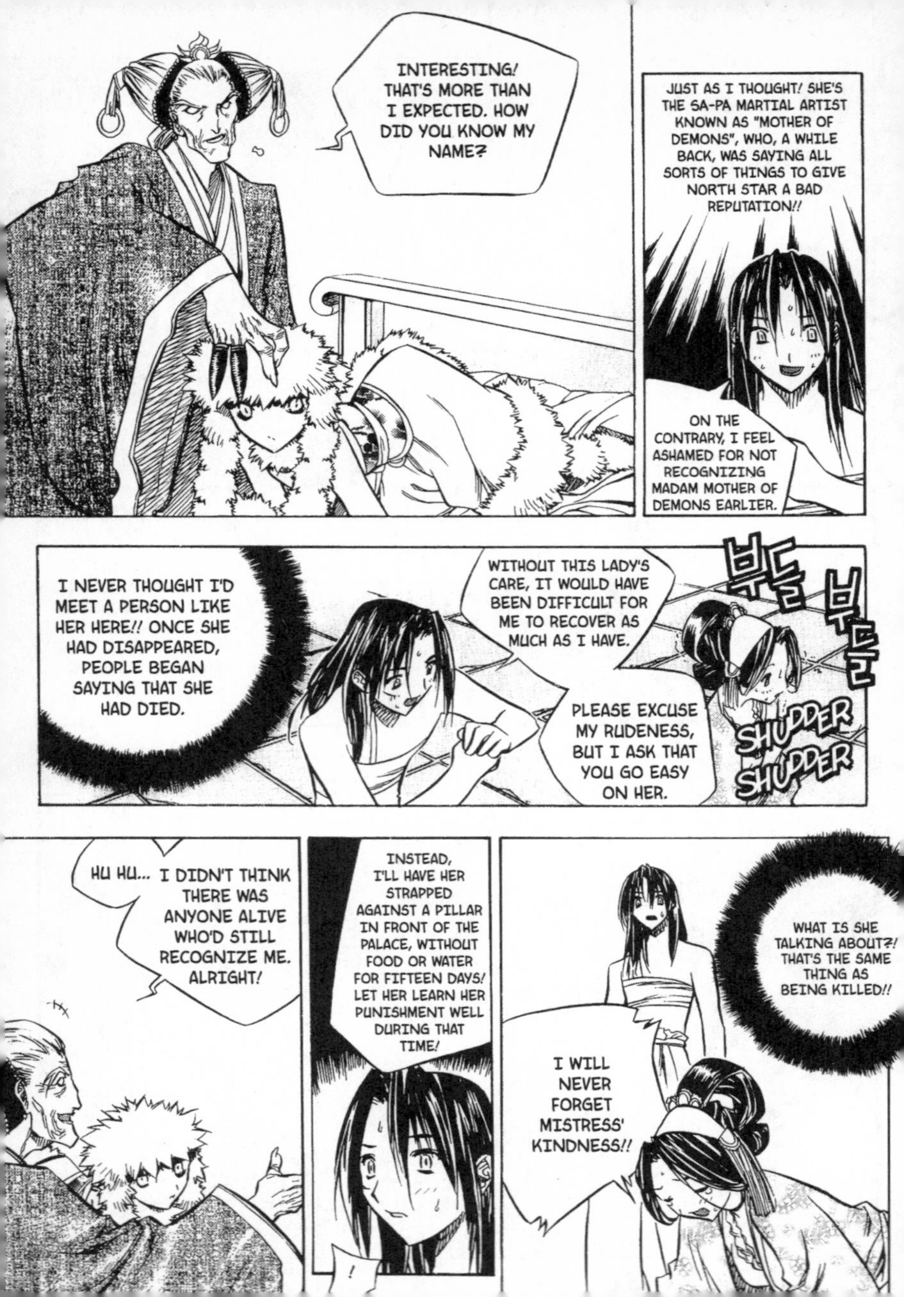

INTERESTING! THAT'S MORE THAN I EXPECTED. HOW DID YOU KNOW MY NAME?
JUST AS I THOUGHT! SHE'S THE SA-PA MARTIAL ARTIST KNOWN AS "MOTHER OF DEMONS", WHO, A WHILE BACK, WAS SAYING ALL SORTS OF THINGS TO GIVE NORTH STAR A BAD REPUTATION!!
ON THE CONTRARY, I FEEL ASHAMED FOR NOT RECOGNIZING MADAM MOTHER OF DEMONS EARLIER.
I NEVER THOUGHT I'D MEET A PERSON LIKE HER HERE!! ONCE SHE HAD DISAPPEARED, PEOPLE BEGAN SAYING THAT SHE HAD DIED.
WITHOUT THIS LADY'S CARE, IT WOULD HAVE BEEN DIFFICULT FOR ME TO RECOVER AS MUCH AS I HAVE.
PLEASE EXCUSE MY RUDENESS, BUT I ASK THAT YOU GO EASY ON HER.
부들 부들
SHUDDER SHUDDER
HU HU... I DIDN'T THINK THERE WAS ANYONE ALIVE WHO'D STILL RECOGNIZE ME. ALRIGHT!
INSTEAD, I'LL HAVE HER STRAPPED AGAINST A PILLAR IN FRONT OF THE PALACE, WITHOUT FOOD OR WATER FOR FIFTEEN DAYS! LET HER LEARN HER PUNISHMENT WELL DURING THAT TIME!
WHAT IS SHE TALKING ABOUT?! THAT'S THE SAME THING AS BEING KILLED!!
I WILL NEVER FORGET MISTRESS' KINDNESS!!

I DON'T WANT TO SEE HER ANY LONGER, TAKE HER AWAY!

AND...

FWISH

...SINCE YOU KNOW MY NAME, YOU PROBABLY KNOW WHAT KIND OF PERSON I AM.

IN SPITE OF THAT, AREN'T YOU CURIOUS TO KNOW WHY I LET YOU LIVE?!

THAT...

THAT'S..?!

SHAAA

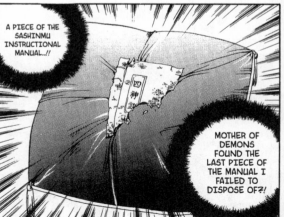

A PIECE OF THE SASHINMU INSTRUCTIONAL MANUAL..!!

MOTHER OF DEMONS FOUND THE LAST PIECE OF THE MANUAL I FAILED TO DISPOSE OF?!

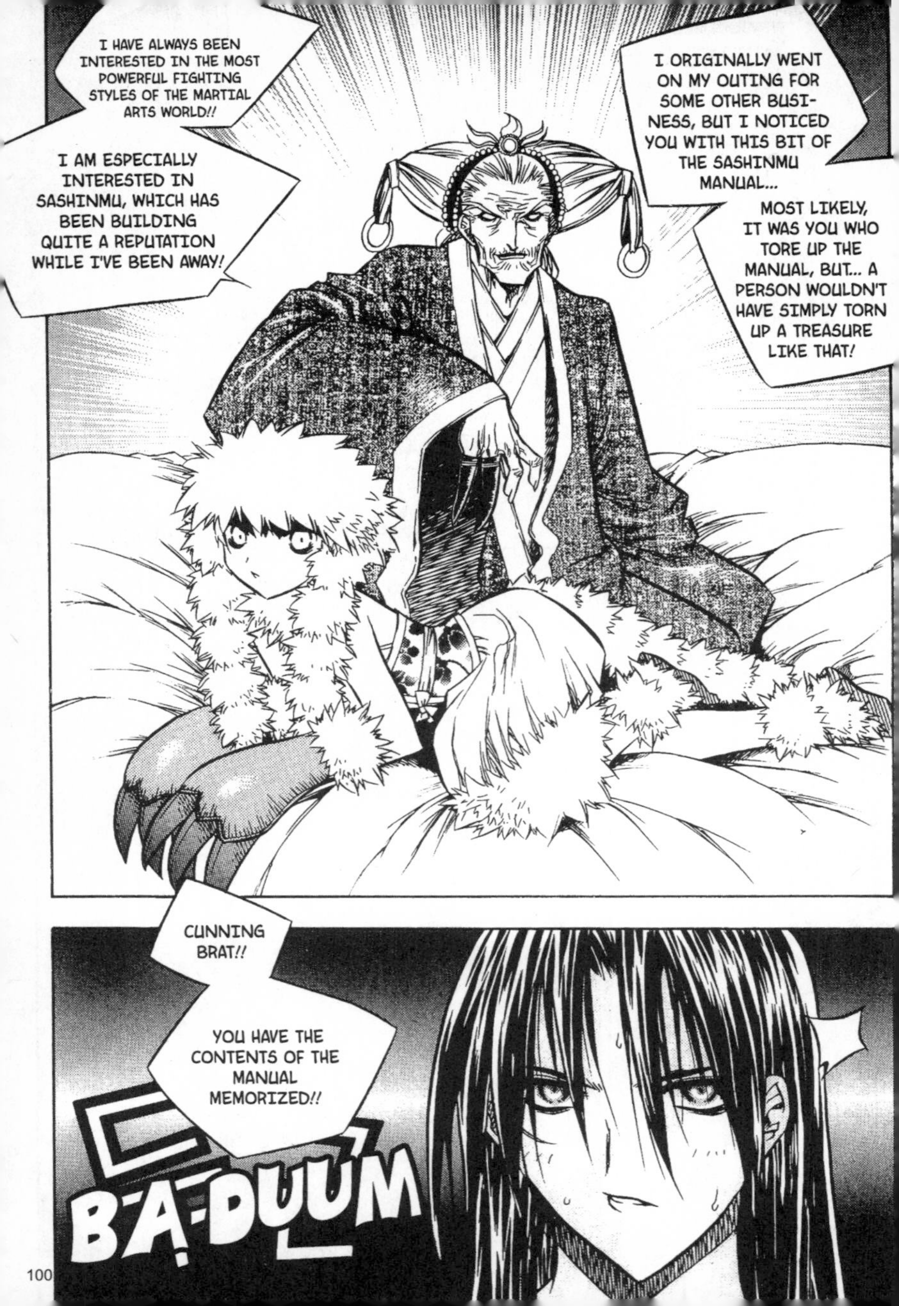
I ORIGINALLY WENT ON MY OUTING FOR SOME OTHER BUSINESS, BUT I NOTICED YOU WITH THIS BIT OF THE SASHINMU MANUAL...
MOST LIKELY, IT WAS YOU WHO TORE UP THE MANUAL, BUT... A PERSON WOULDN'T HAVE SIMPLY TORN UP A TREASURE LIKE THAT!
I HAVE ALWAYS BEEN INTERESTED IN THE MOST POWERFUL FIGHTING STYLES OF THE MARTIAL ARTS WORLD!!
I AM ESPECIALLY INTERESTED IN SASHINMU, WHICH HAS BEEN BUILDING QUITE A REPUTATION WHILE I'VE BEEN AWAY!
CUNNING BRAT!!
YOU HAVE THE CONTENTS OF THE MANUAL MEMORIZED!!
B-A-DUUM

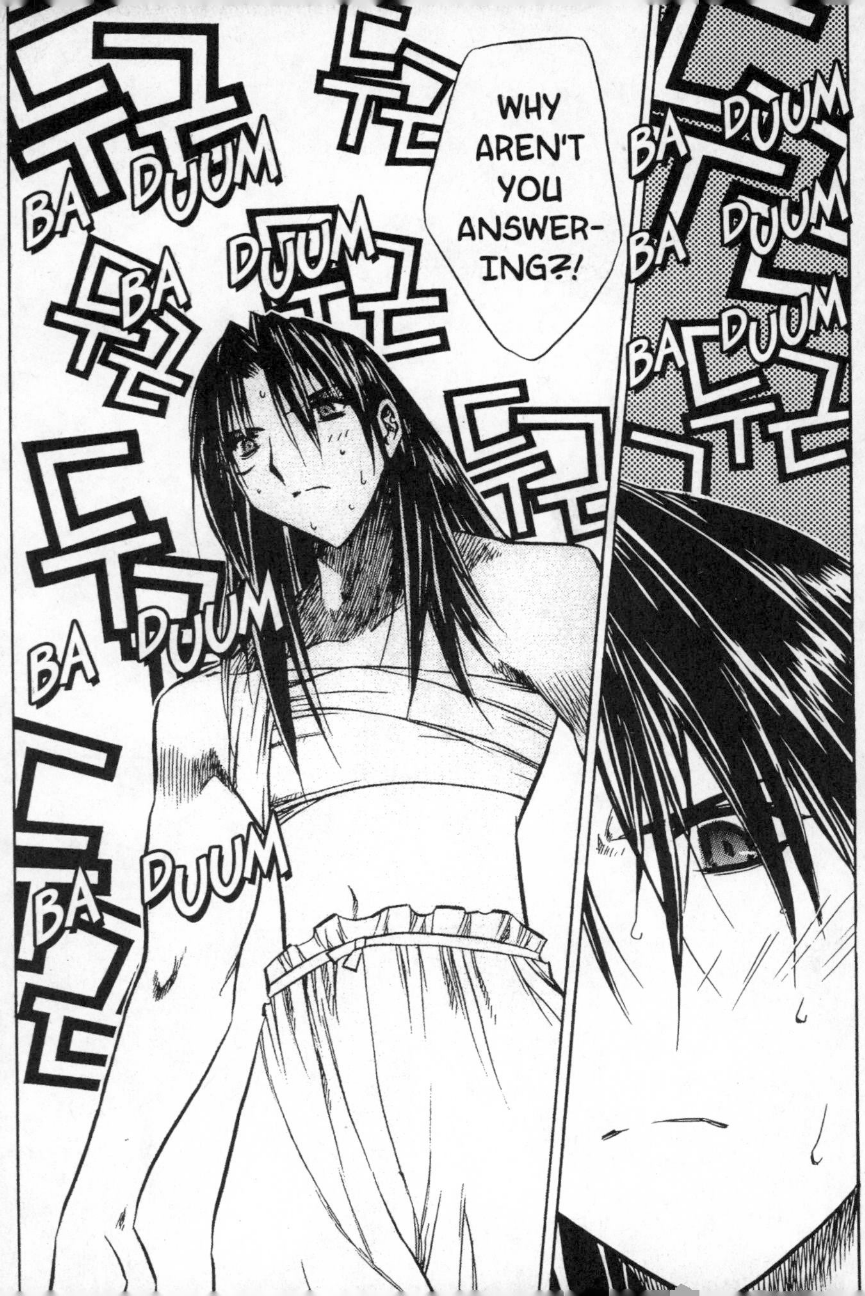
BA DUUM
BA DUUM
BA DUUM
WHY AREN'T YOU ANSWER-ING?!
BA DUUM
BA DUUM
BA DUUM
BA DUUM

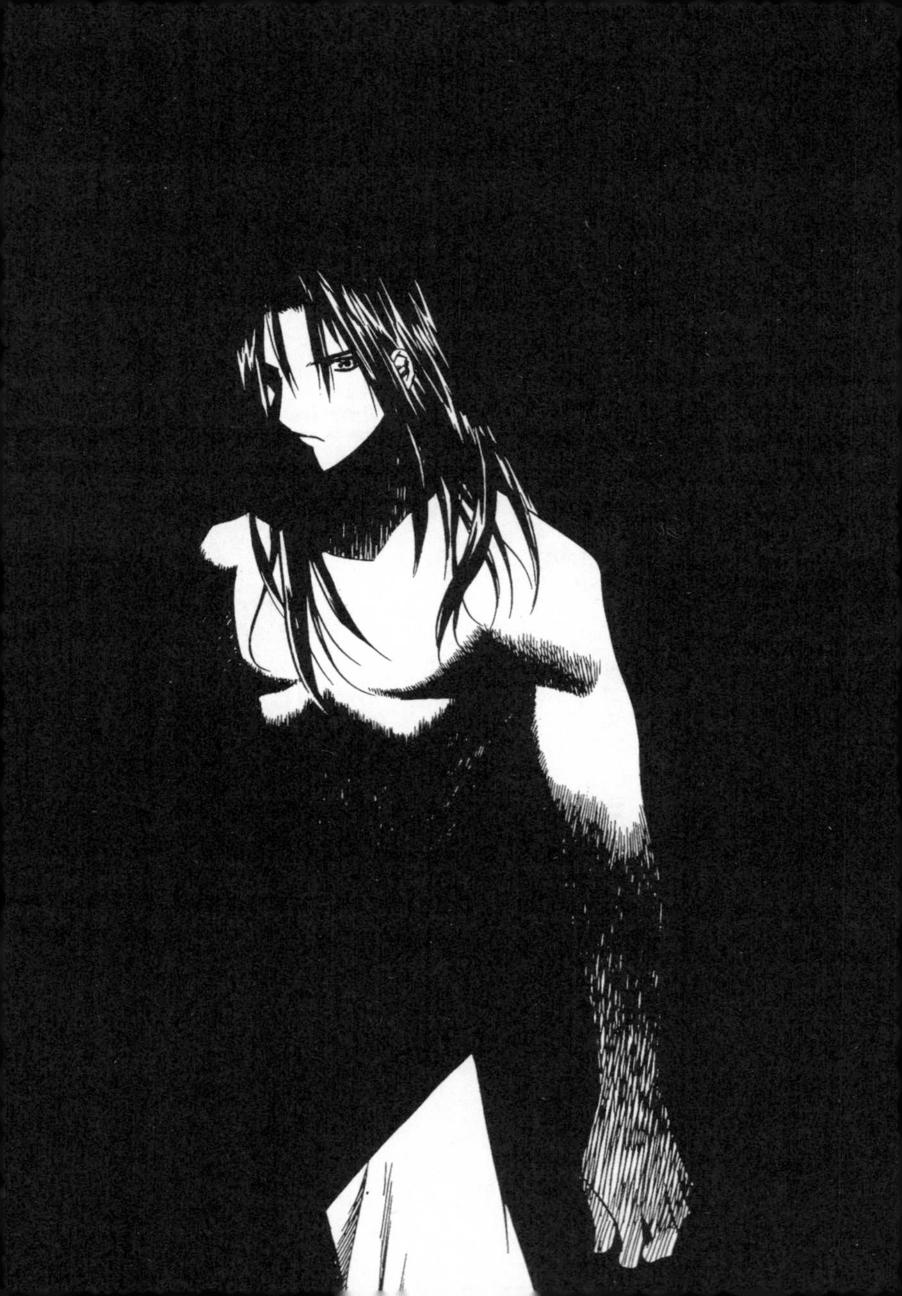

OF COURSE, IF YOU DON'T HAVE THE CONTENTS MEMORIZED, AS I'VE CALCULATED, THEN YOU SHOULD PREPARE YOURSELF FOR WHAT'S COMING!

YOU'LL TASTE A HELL WORSE THAN ANYTHING YOU'VE IMAGINED!

......!!

NOW THEN, ANSWER ME!

MISTRESS, OF COURSE... I HAVE THE CONTENTS MEMORIZED.

LIKE ANYONE ELSE. I WANT TO GET STRONGER!!

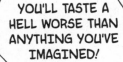

STRENGTH!

......!

...OF...

SMIRK

HOWEVER...

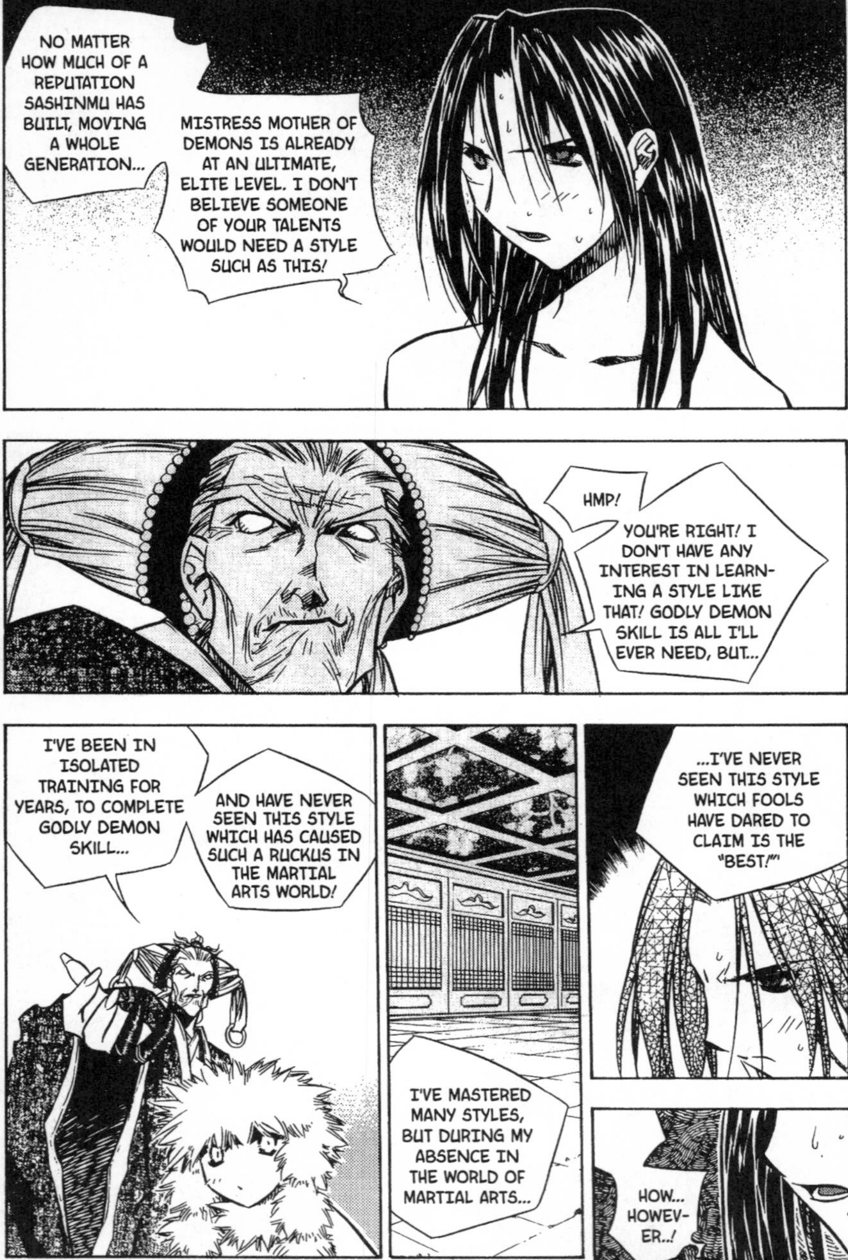
NO MATTER HOW MUCH OF A REPUTATION SASHINMU HAS BUILT, MOVING A WHOLE GENERATION...
MISTRESS MOTHER OF DEMONS IS ALREADY AT AN ULTIMATE, ELITE LEVEL. I DON'T BELIEVE SOMEONE OF YOUR TALENTS WOULD NEED A STYLE SUCH AS THIS!
HMP!
YOU'RE RIGHT! I DON'T HAVE ANY INTEREST IN LEARNING A STYLE LIKE THAT! GODLY DEMON SKILL IS ALL I'LL EVER NEED, BUT...
I'VE BEEN IN ISOLATED TRAINING FOR YEARS, TO COMPLETE GODLY DEMON SKILL...
AND HAVE NEVER SEEN THIS STYLE WHICH HAS CAUSED SUCH A RUCKUS IN THE MARTIAL ARTS WORLD!
I'VE MASTERED MANY STYLES, BUT DURING MY ABSENCE IN THE WORLD OF MARTIAL ARTS...
...I'VE NEVER SEEN THIS STYLE WHICH FOOLS HAVE DARED TO CLAIM IS THE "BEST!"
HOW... HOWEVER..!

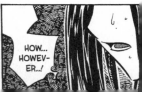

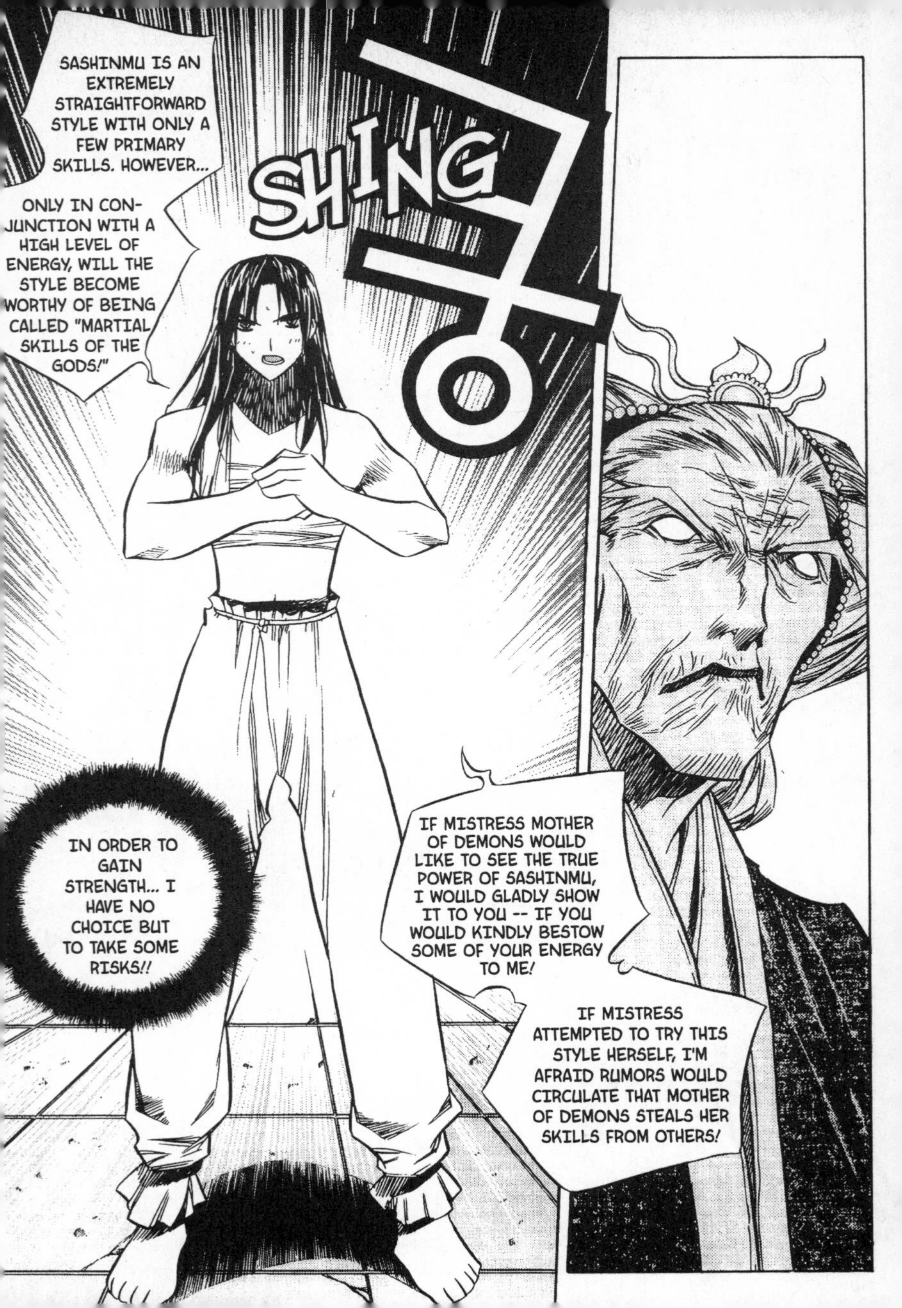
SASHINMU IS AN EXTREMELY STRAIGHTFORWARD STYLE WITH ONLY A FEW PRIMARY SKILLS. HOWEVER...
ONLY IN CON-JUNCTION WITH A HIGH LEVEL OF ENERGY, WILL THE STYLE BECOME WORTHY OF BEING CALLED "MARTIAL SKILLS OF THE GODS!"
SHING
IN ORDER TO GAIN STRENGTH... I HAVE NO CHOICE BUT TO TAKE SOME RISKS!!
IF MISTRESS MOTHER OF DEMONS WOULD LIKE TO SEE THE TRUE POWER OF SASHINMU, I WOULD GLADLY SHOW IT TO YOU -- IF YOU WOULD KINDLY BESTOW SOME OF YOUR ENERGY TO ME!
IF MISTRESS ATTEMPTED TO TRY THIS STYLE HERSELF, I'M AFRAID RUMORS WOULD CIRCULATE THAT MOTHER OF DEMONS STEALS HER SKILLS FROM OTHERS!

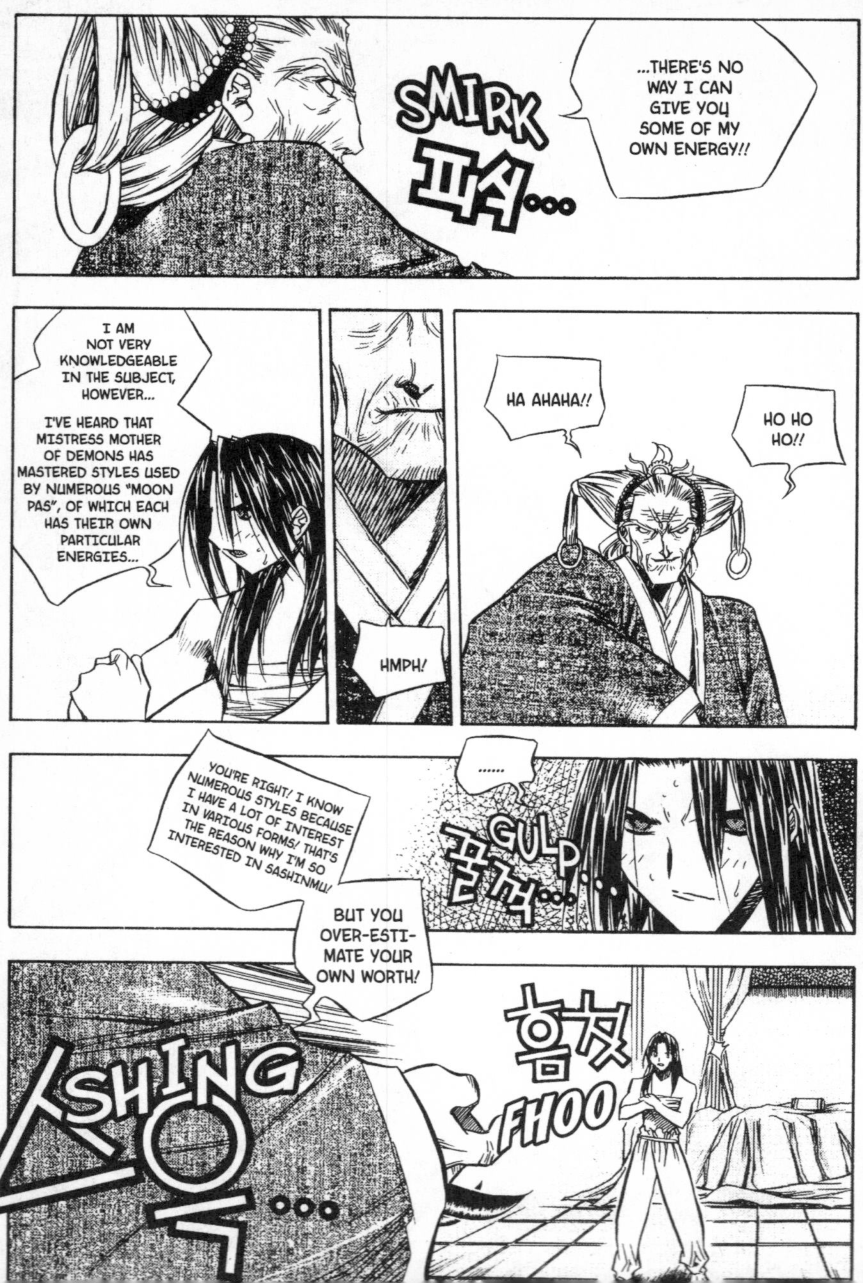

...THERE'S NO WAY I CAN GIVE YOU SOME OF MY OWN ENERGY!!
SMIRK
파삭...
I AM NOT VERY KNOWLEDGEABLE IN THE SUBJECT, HOWEVER...
I'VE HEARD THAT MISTRESS MOTHER OF DEMONS HAS MASTERED STYLES USED BY NUMEROUS "MOON PAS", OF WHICH EACH HAS THEIR OWN PARTICULAR ENERGIES...
HMPH!
HA AHAHA!!
HO HO HO!!
......
YOU'RE RIGHT! I KNOW NUMEROUS STYLES BECAUSE I HAVE A LOT OF INTEREST IN VARIOUS FORMS! THAT'S THE REASON WHY I'M SO INTERESTED IN SASHINMU!
GULP...
꿀꺽...
BUT YOU OVER-ESTI-MATE YOUR OWN WORTH!
흠칫
FHOO
SHING
스윽...

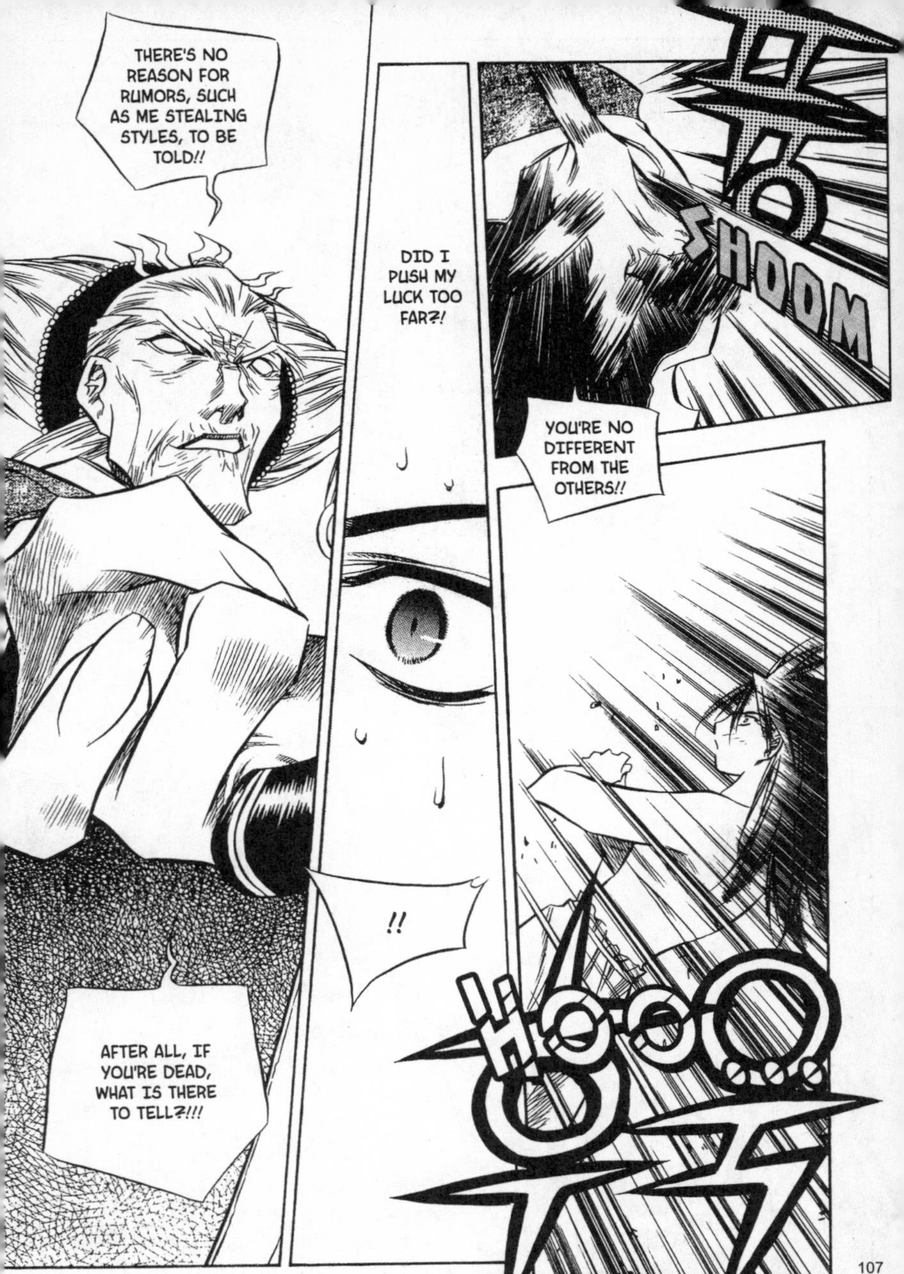
SHOOM
THERE'S NO REASON FOR RUMORS, SUCH AS ME STEALING STYLES, TO BE TOLD!!
DID I PUSH MY LUCK TOO FAR?!
YOU'RE NO DIFFERENT FROM THE OTHERS!!
!!
AFTER ALL, IF YOU'RE DEAD, WHAT IS THERE TO TELL?!!!
HO-O-O...

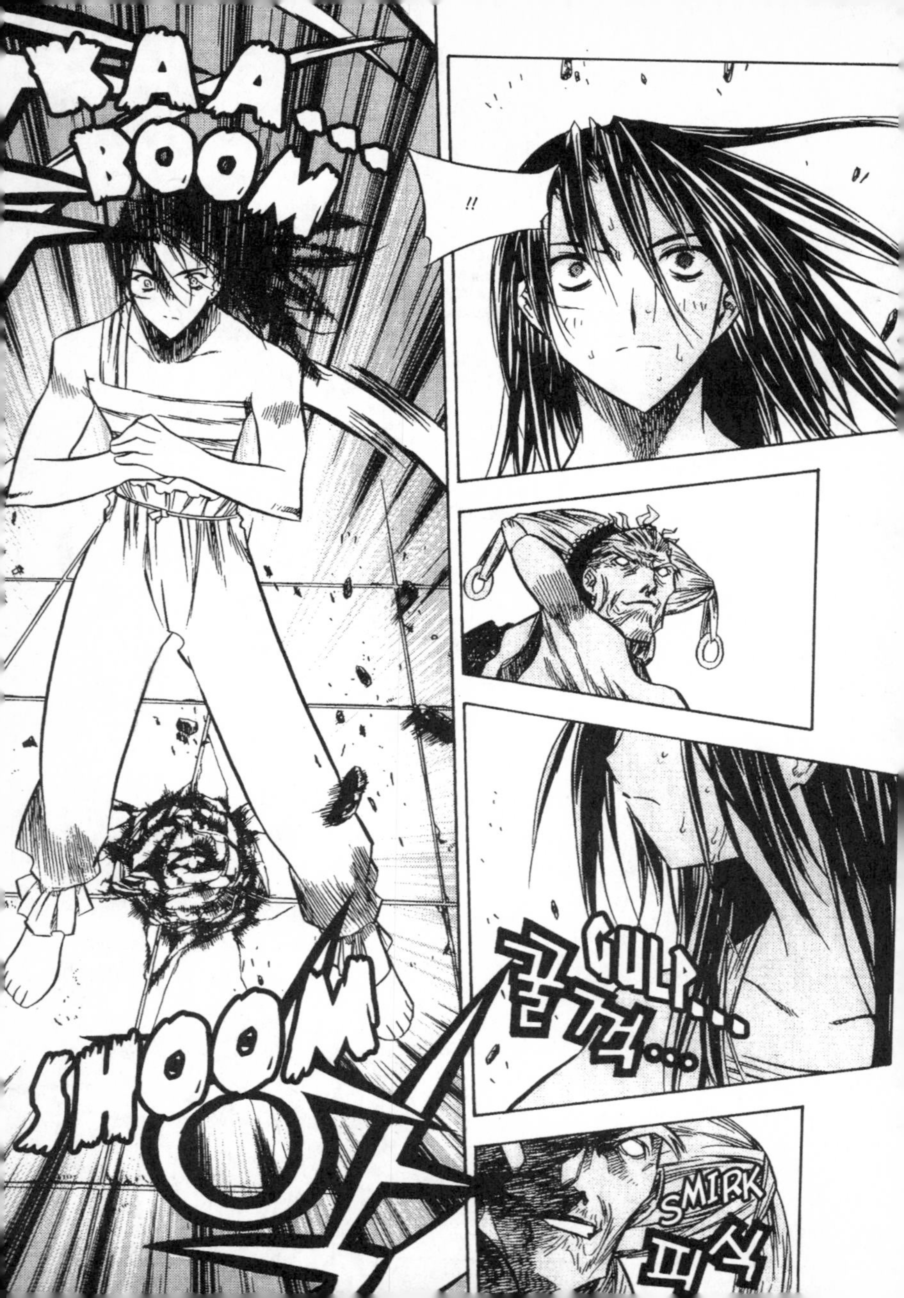
KA-BOOM...
!!
SHOOM
GULP...
꿀꺽...
SMIRK
피식

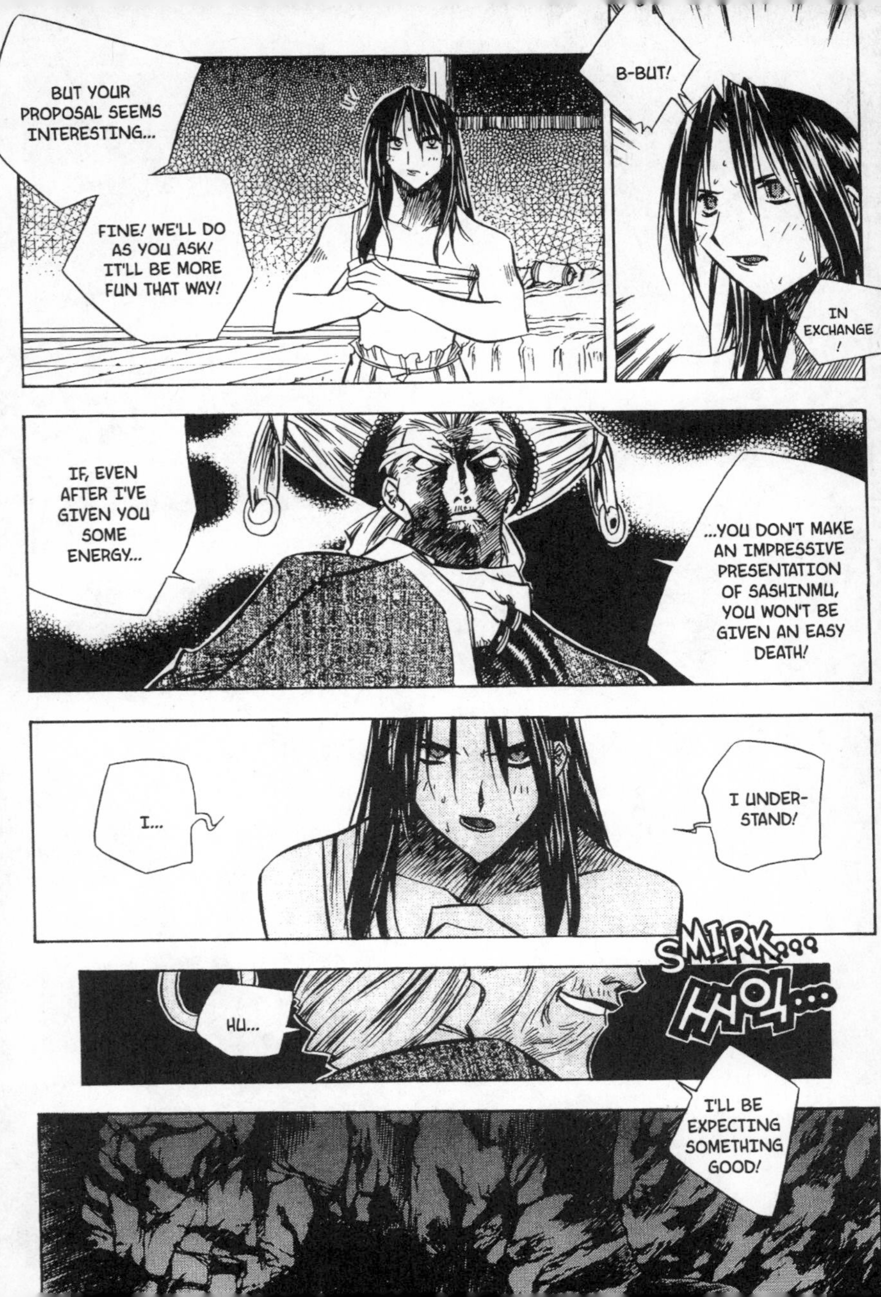
BUT YOUR PROPOSAL SEEMS INTERESTING...
FINE! WE'LL DO AS YOU ASK! IT'LL BE MORE FUN THAT WAY!
B-BUT!
IN EXCHANGE!
IF, EVEN AFTER I'VE GIVEN YOU SOME ENERGY...
...YOU DON'T MAKE AN IMPRESSIVE PRESENTATION OF SASHINMU, YOU WON'T BE GIVEN AN EASY DEATH!
I...
I UNDER-STAND!
SMIRK...
HU...
I'LL BE EXPECTING SOMETHING GOOD!

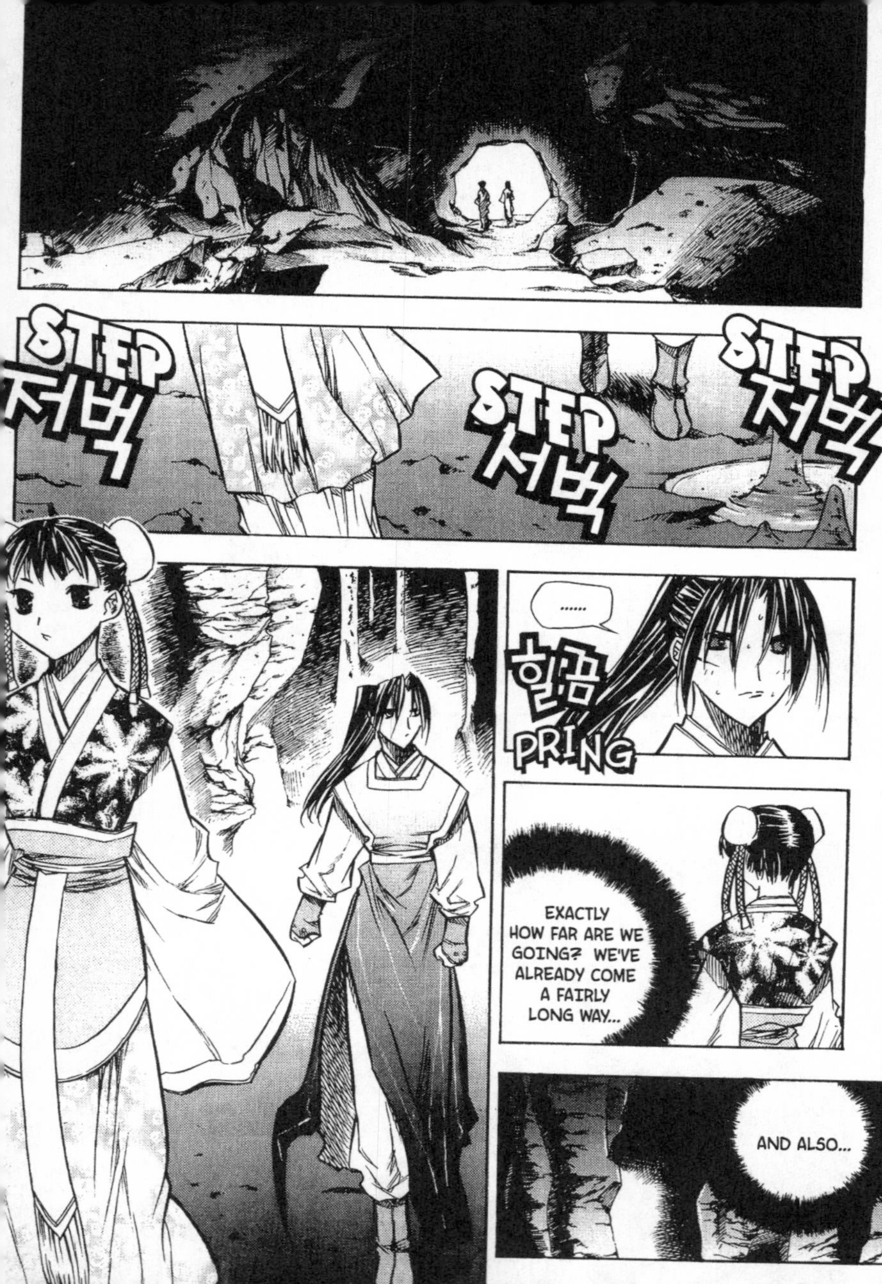
STEP
저벅
STEP
저벅
STEP
저벅
......
힐끔
PRING
EXACTLY HOW FAR ARE WE GOING? WE'VE ALREADY COME A FAIRLY LONG WAY...
AND ALSO...

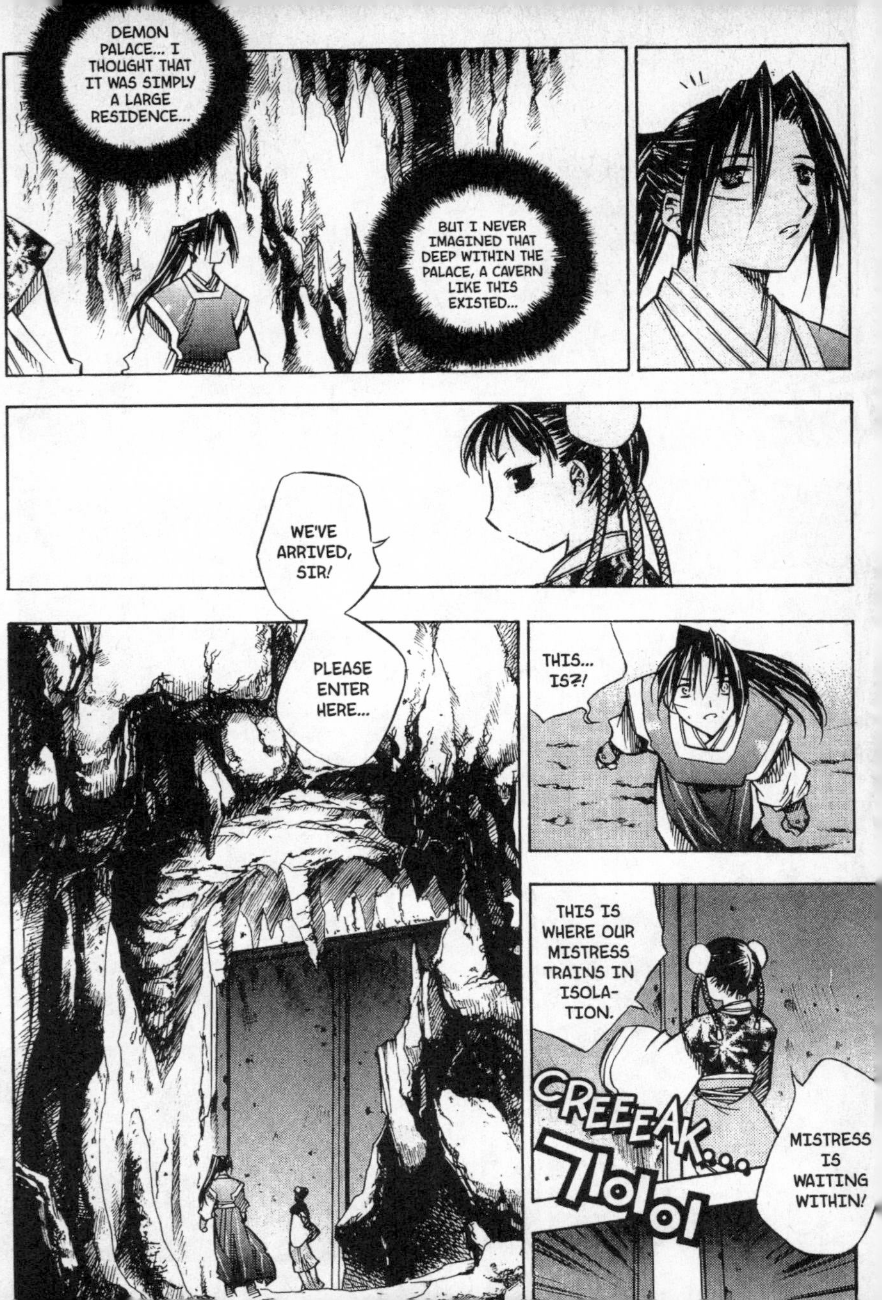
DEMON PALACE... I THOUGHT THAT IT WAS SIMPLY A LARGE RESIDENCE...
BUT I NEVER IMAGINED THAT DEEP WITHIN THE PALACE, A CAVERN LIKE THIS EXISTED...
WE'VE ARRIVED, SIR!
PLEASE ENTER HERE...
THIS... IS?!
THIS IS WHERE OUR MISTRESS TRAINS IN ISOLA-TION.
CREEEAK...
MISTRESS IS WAITING WITHIN!

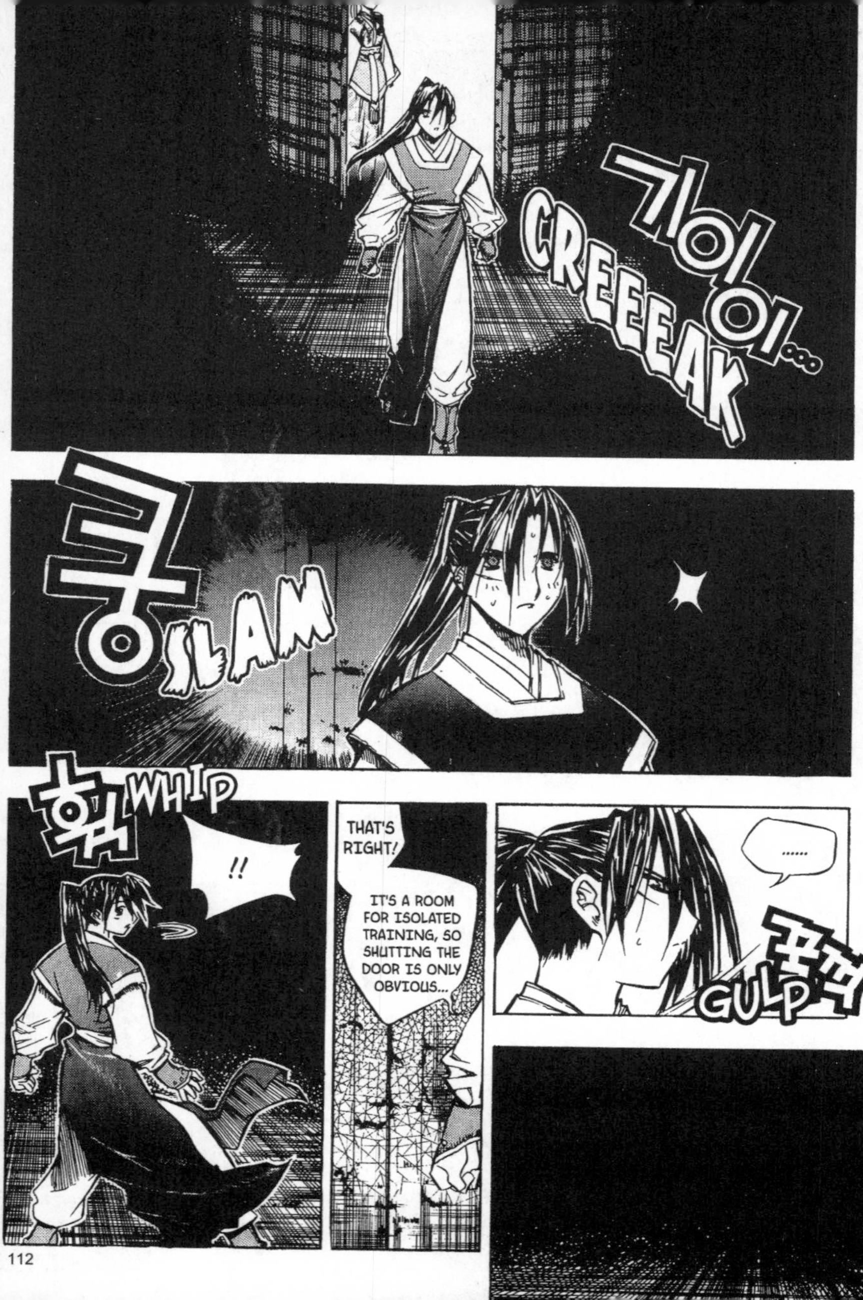

기이이...
CREEEEAK
쿵
SLAM
휙
WHIP
!!
THAT'S RIGHT!
IT'S A ROOM FOR ISOLATED TRAINING, SO SHUTTING THE DOOR IS ONLY OBVIOUS...
......
꼬쩍
GULP

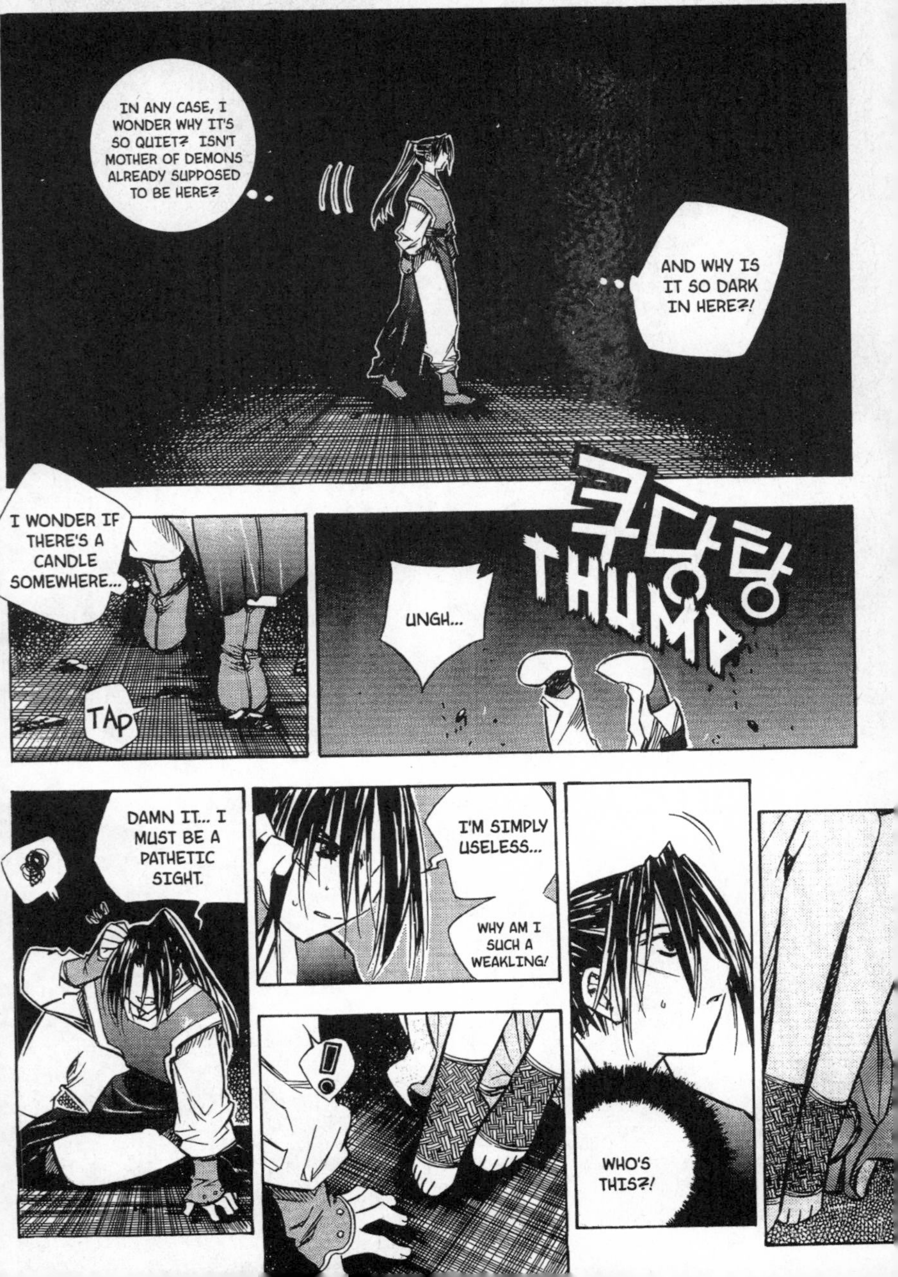
IN ANY CASE, I WONDER WHY IT'S SO QUIET? ISN'T MOTHER OF DEMONS ALREADY SUPPOSED TO BE HERE?
AND WHY IS IT SO DARK IN HERE?!
I WONDER IF THERE'S A CANDLE SOMEWHERE...
TAP
쿠당탕
THUMP
UNGH...
DAMN IT... I MUST BE A PATHETIC SIGHT.
I'M SIMPLY USELESS...
WHY AM I SUCH A WEAKLING!
!
WHO'S THIS?!

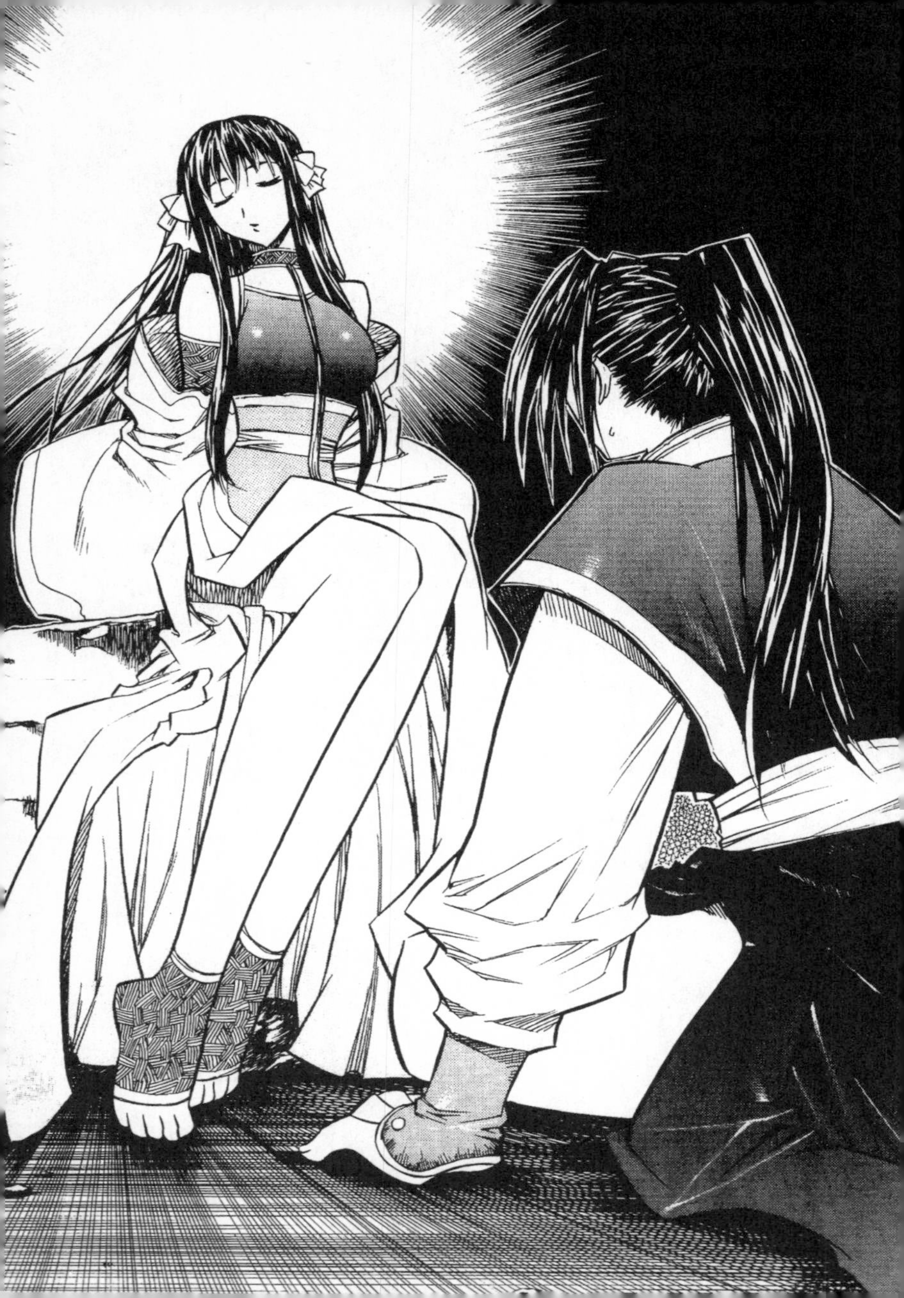

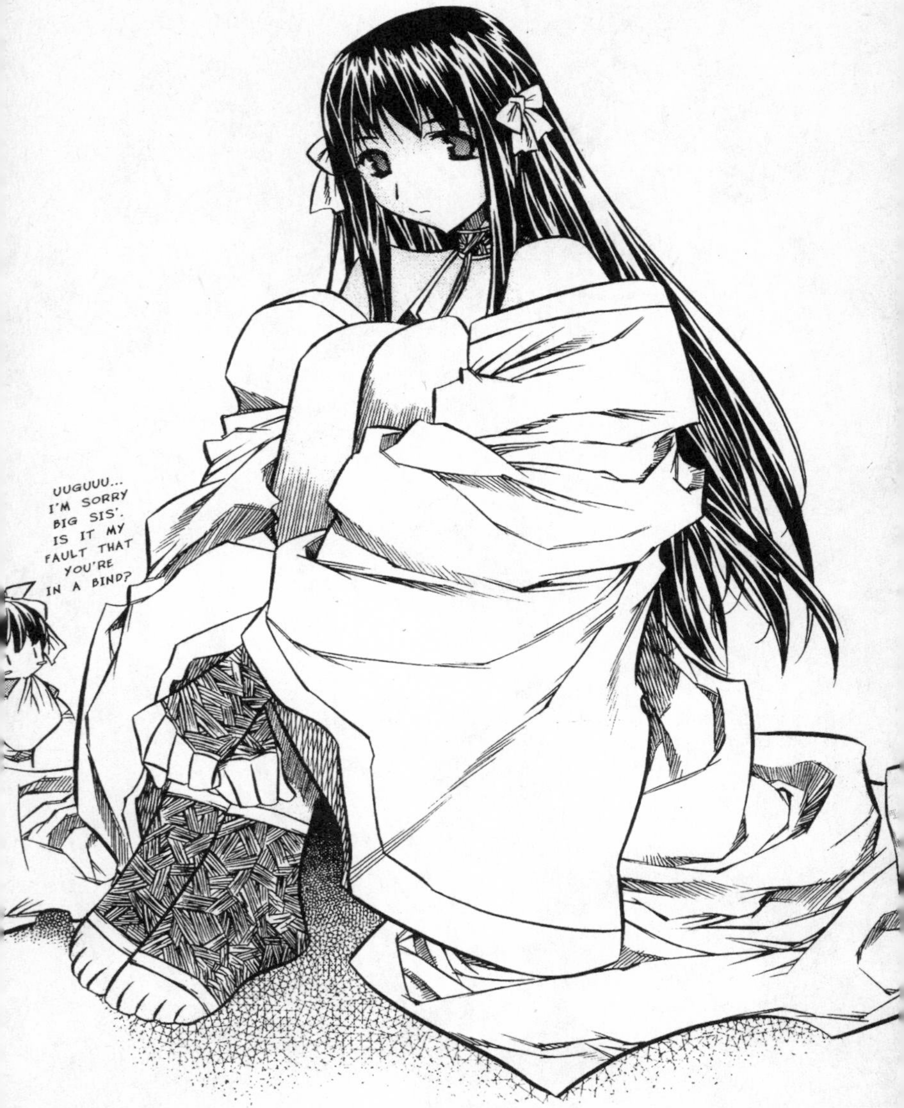
UUGUUU... I'M SORRY BIG SIS'. IS IT MY FAULT THAT YOU'RE IN A BIND?

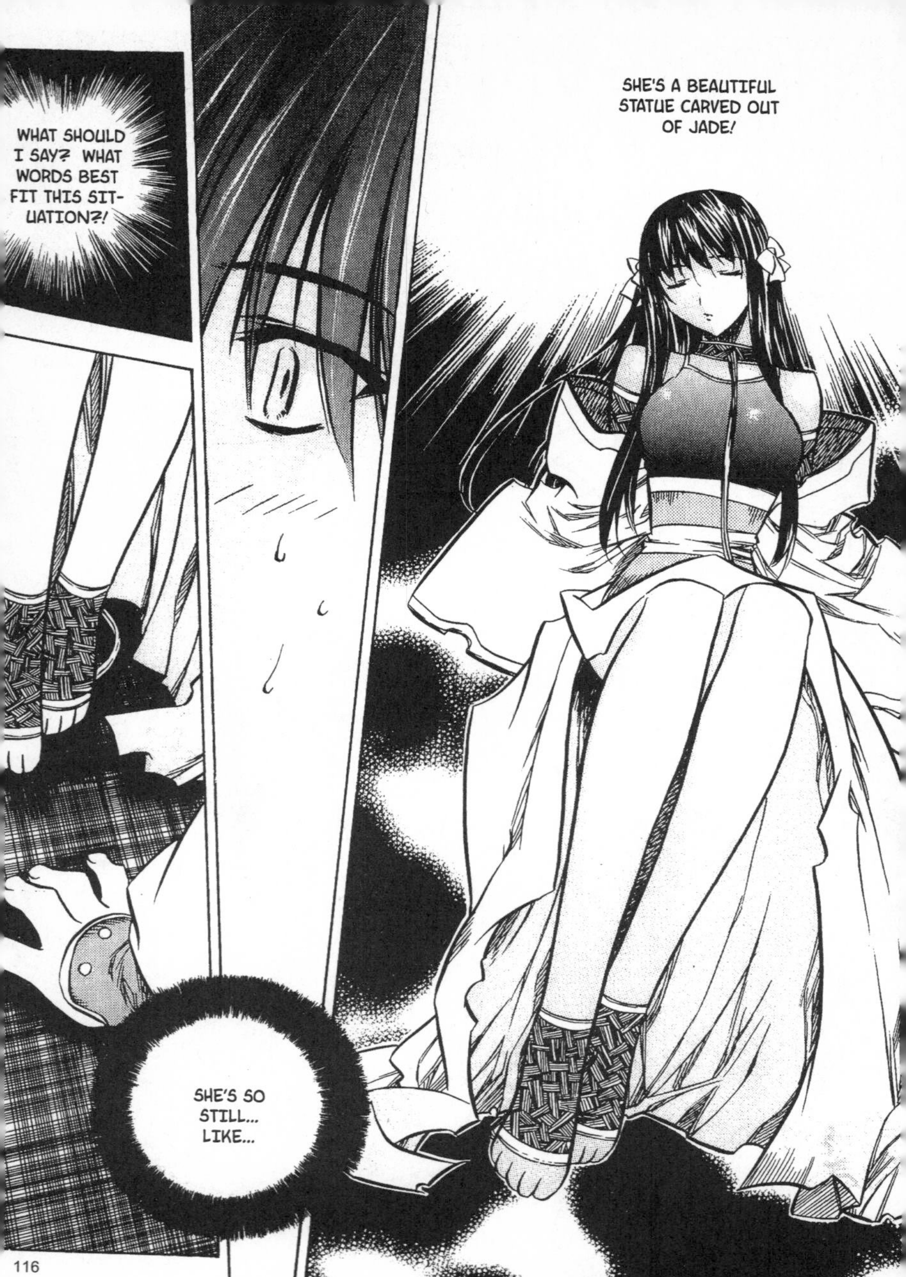

SHE'S A BEAUTIFUL STATUE CARVED OUT OF JADE!
WHAT SHOULD I SAY? WHAT WORDS BEST FIT THIS SIT-UATION?!
SHE'S SO STILL... LIKE...

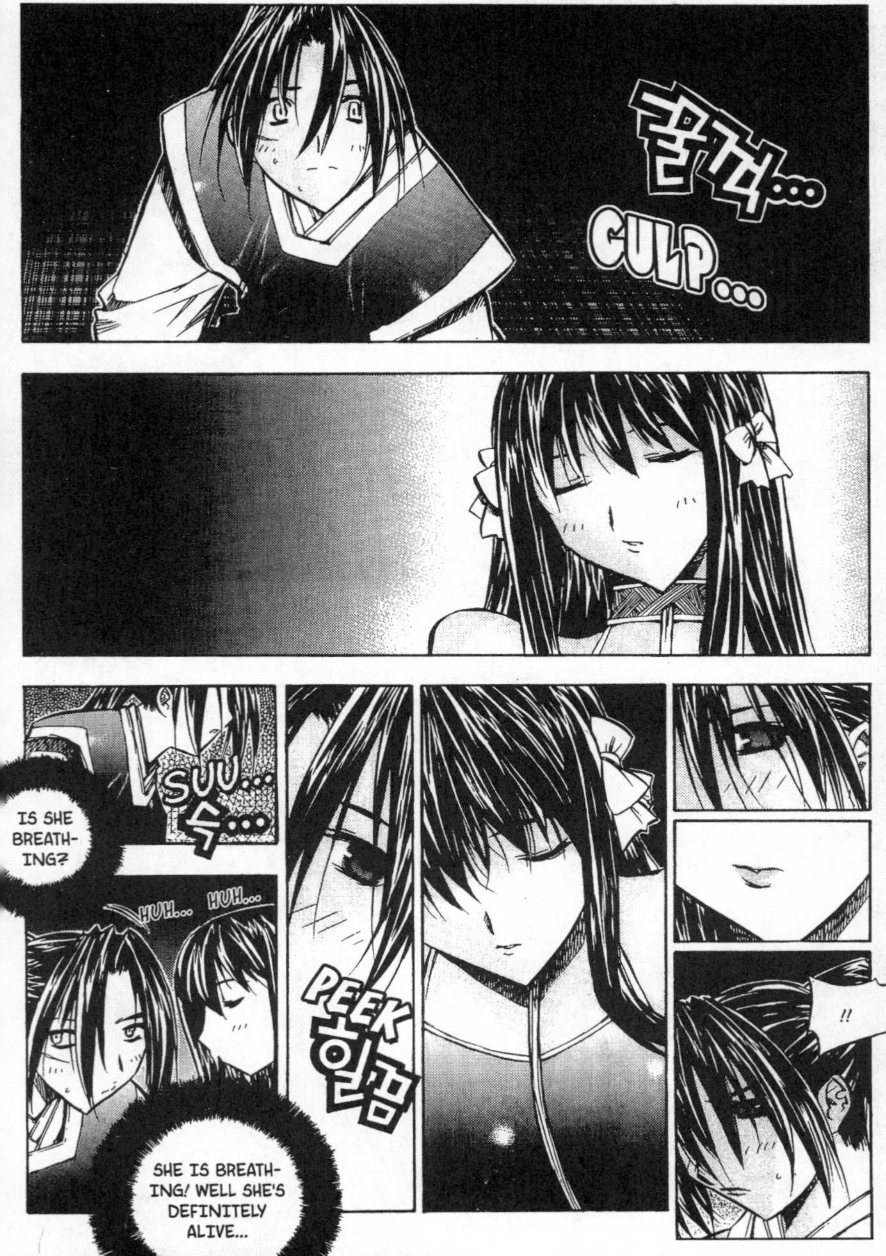
꿀꺽...
CULP...
SUU...
스...
IS SHE BREATHING?
HUH... HUH...
PEEK
힐끔
SHE IS BREATHING! WELL SHE'S DEFINITELY ALIVE...
!!

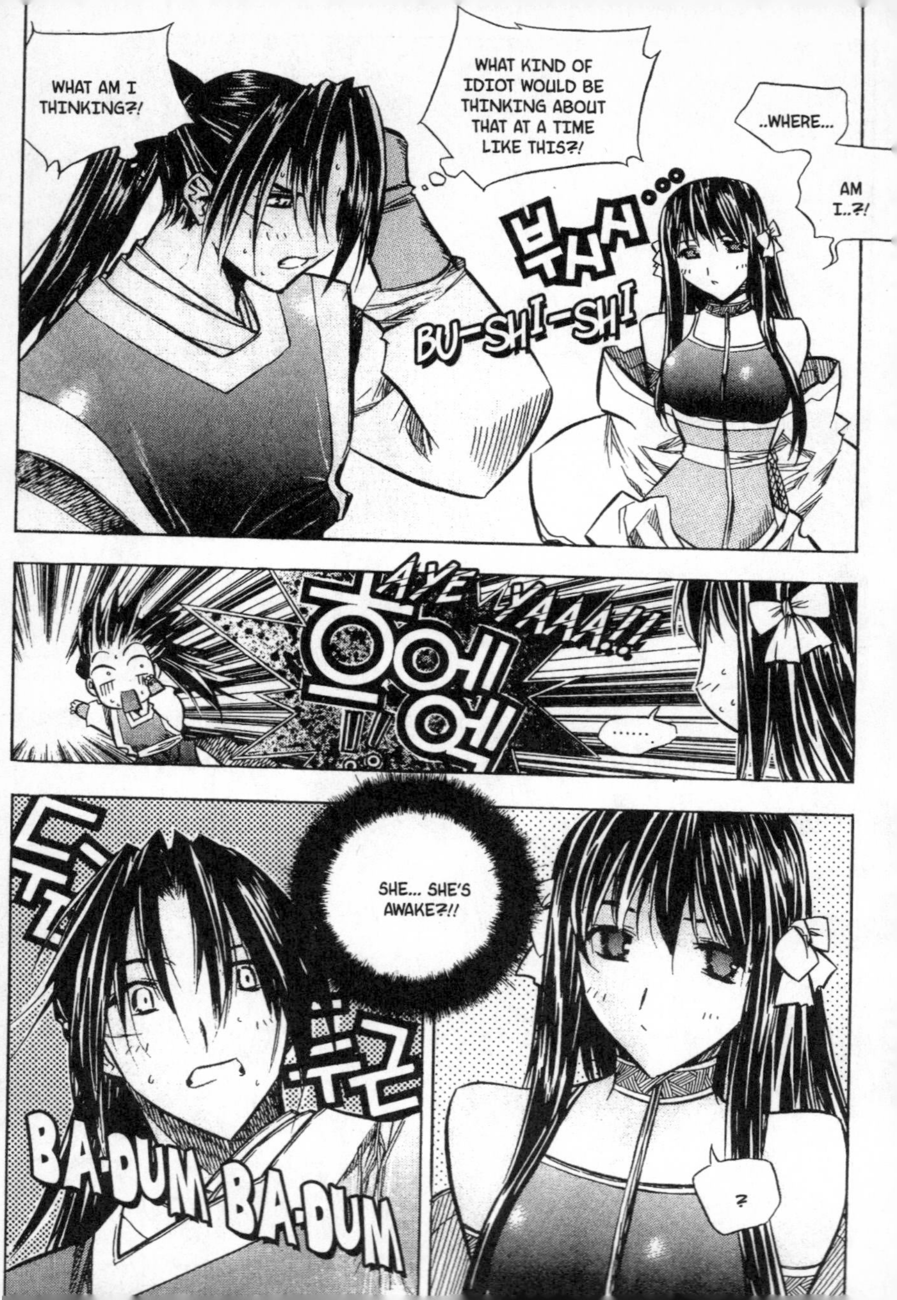

WHAT AM I THINKING?!
WHAT KIND OF IDIOT WOULD BE THINKING ABOUT THAT AT A TIME LIKE THIS?!
..WHERE...
AM I..?!
BU-SHI-SHI
AYE-YAAAA!!
......
SHE... SHE'S AWAKE?!!
BA-DUM BA-DUM
?

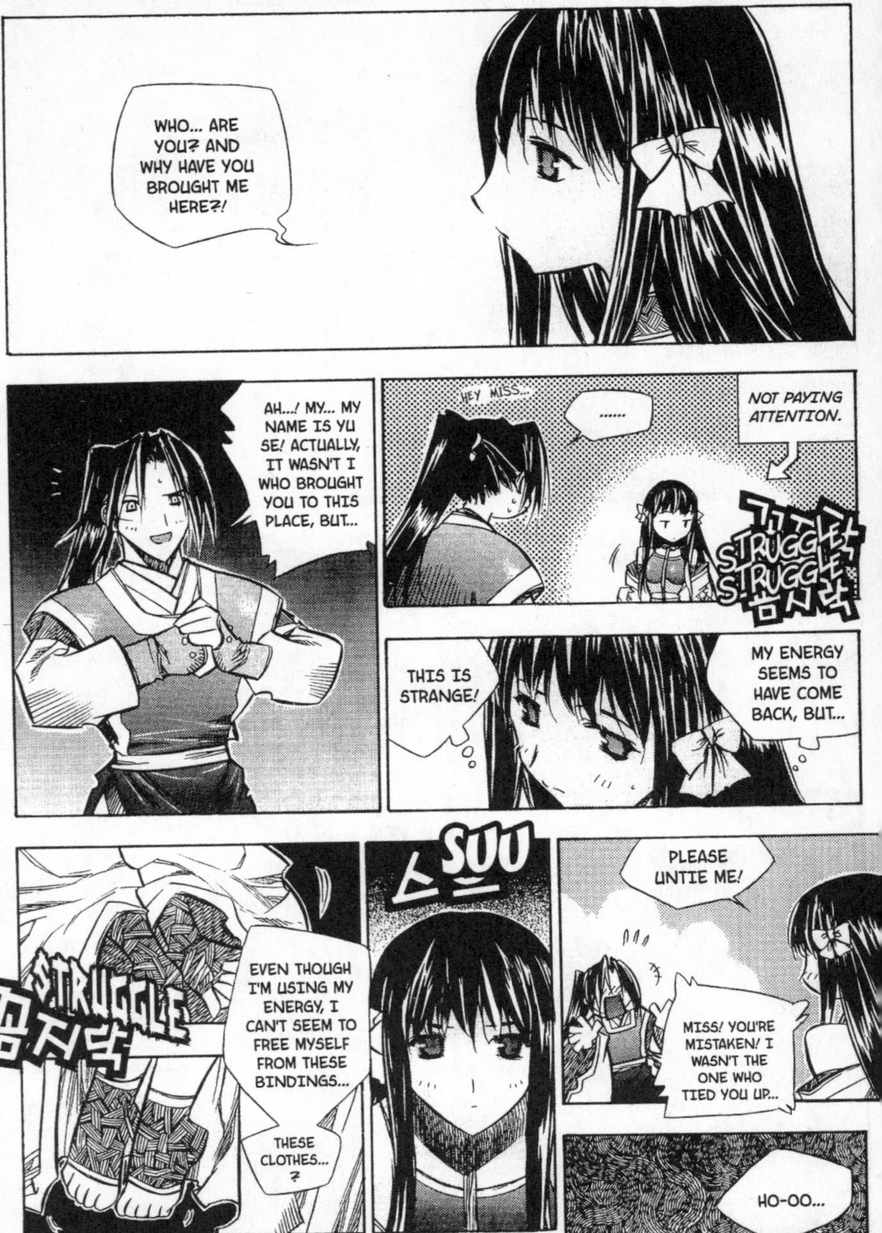
WHO... ARE YOU? AND WHY HAVE YOU BROUGHT ME HERE?!
AH...! MY... MY NAME IS YU SE! ACTUALLY, IT WASN'T I WHO BROUGHT YOU TO THIS PLACE, BUT...
HEY MISS...
......
NOT PAYING ATTENTION.
STRUGGLE STRUGGLE
THIS IS STRANGE!
MY ENERGY SEEMS TO HAVE COME BACK, BUT...
STRUGGLE
EVEN THOUGH I'M USING MY ENERGY, I CAN'T SEEM TO FREE MYSELF FROM THESE BINDINGS...
THESE CLOTHES...?
SUU
PLEASE UNTIE ME!
MISS! YOU'RE MISTAKEN! I WASN'T THE ONE WHO TIED YOU UP...
HO-OO...

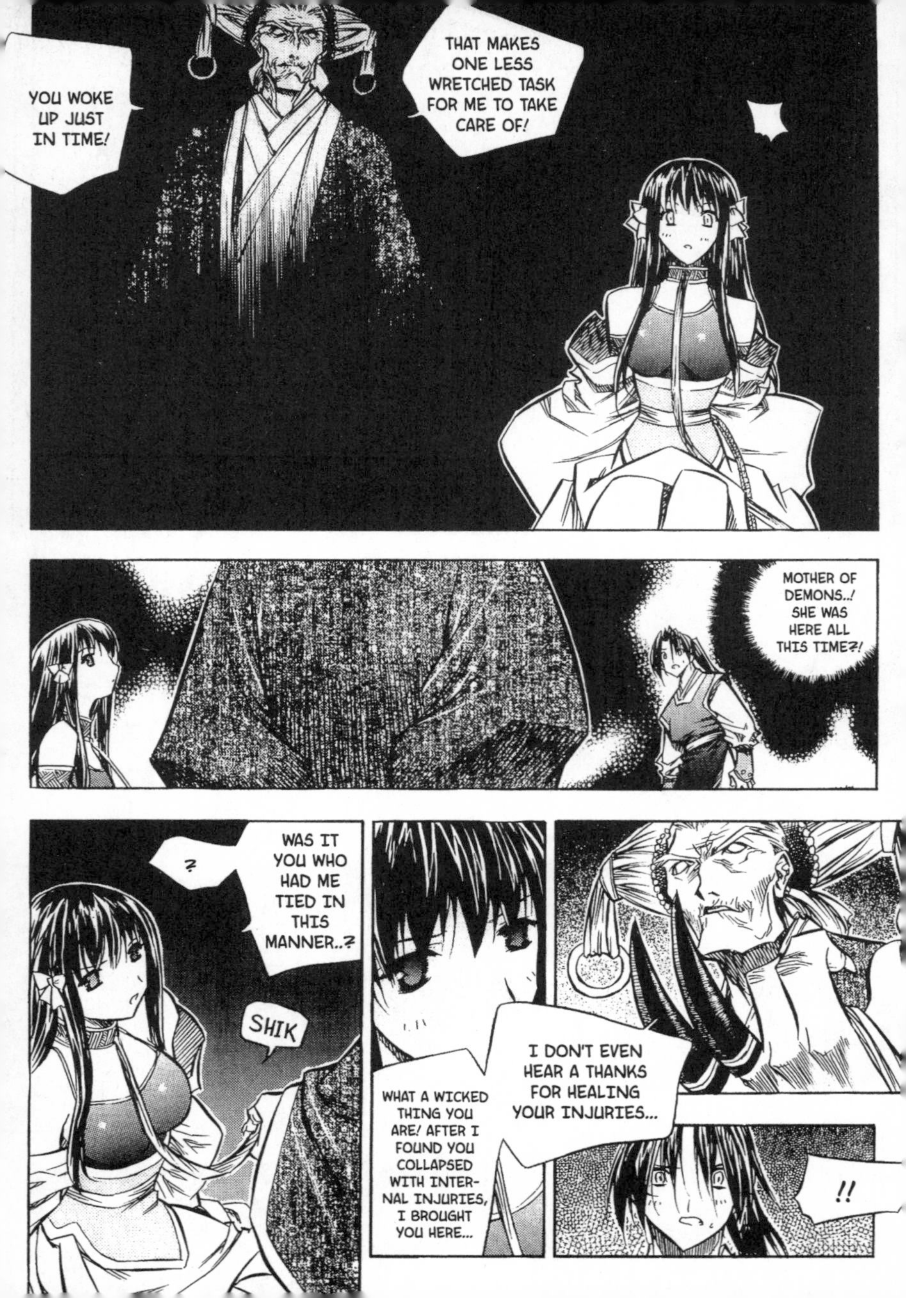
YOU WOKE UP JUST IN TIME!
THAT MAKES ONE LESS WRETCHED TASK FOR ME TO TAKE CARE OF!
MOTHER OF DEMONS..! SHE WAS HERE ALL THIS TIME?!
WAS IT YOU WHO HAD ME TIED IN THIS MANNER..?
?
SHIK
I DON'T EVEN HEAR A THANKS FOR HEALING YOUR INJURIES...
WHAT A WICKED THING YOU ARE! AFTER I FOUND YOU COLLAPSED WITH INTER- NAL INJURIES, I BROUGHT YOU HERE...
!!

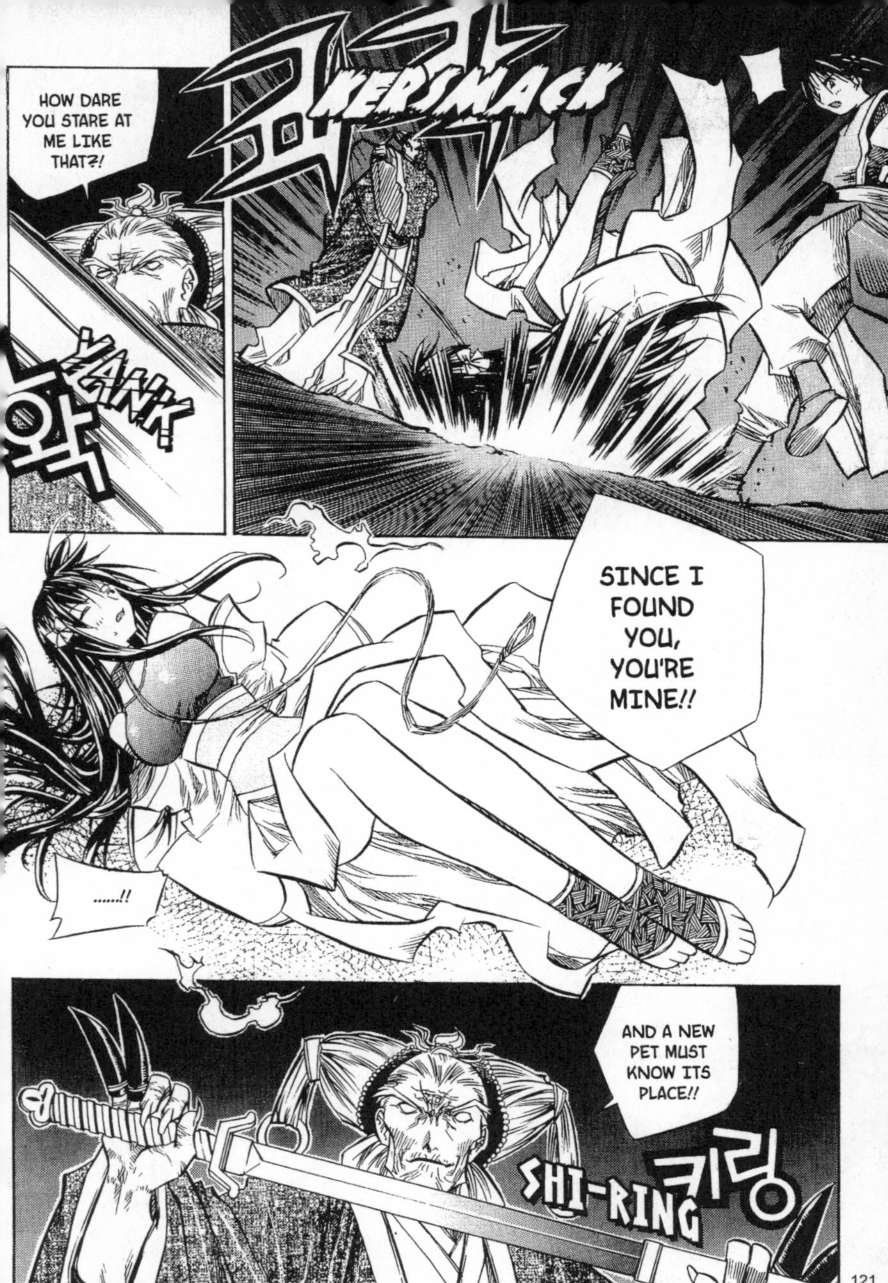

KERSMACK
HOW DARE YOU STARE AT ME LIKE THAT?!
YANK
왁
SINCE I FOUND YOU, YOU'RE MINE!!
......!!
AND A NEW PET MUST KNOW ITS PLACE!!
SHI-RING
키링

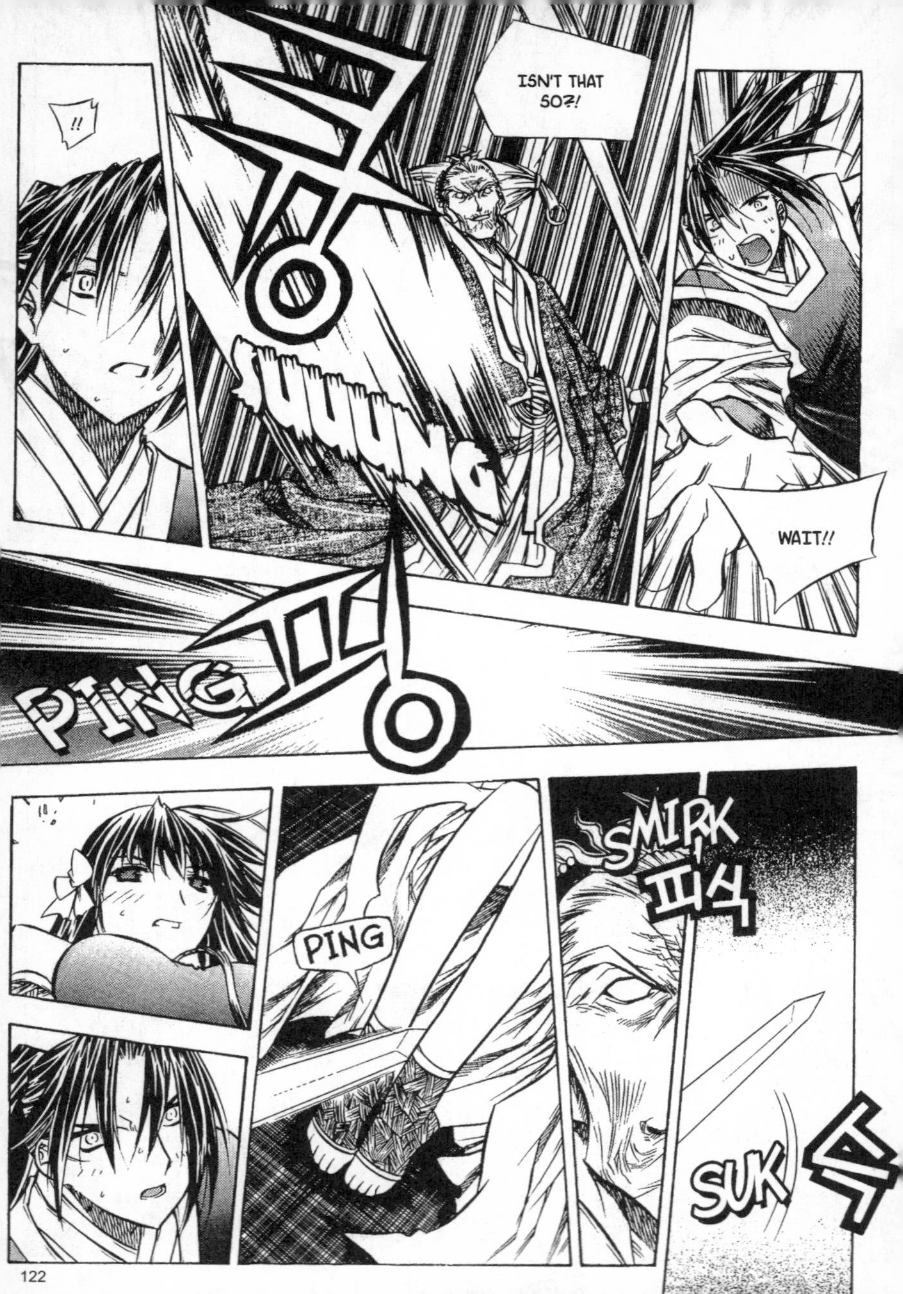
ISN'T THAT SO?!
!!
WAIT!!
VUUUNG
PING
SMIRK
피식
PING
SUK

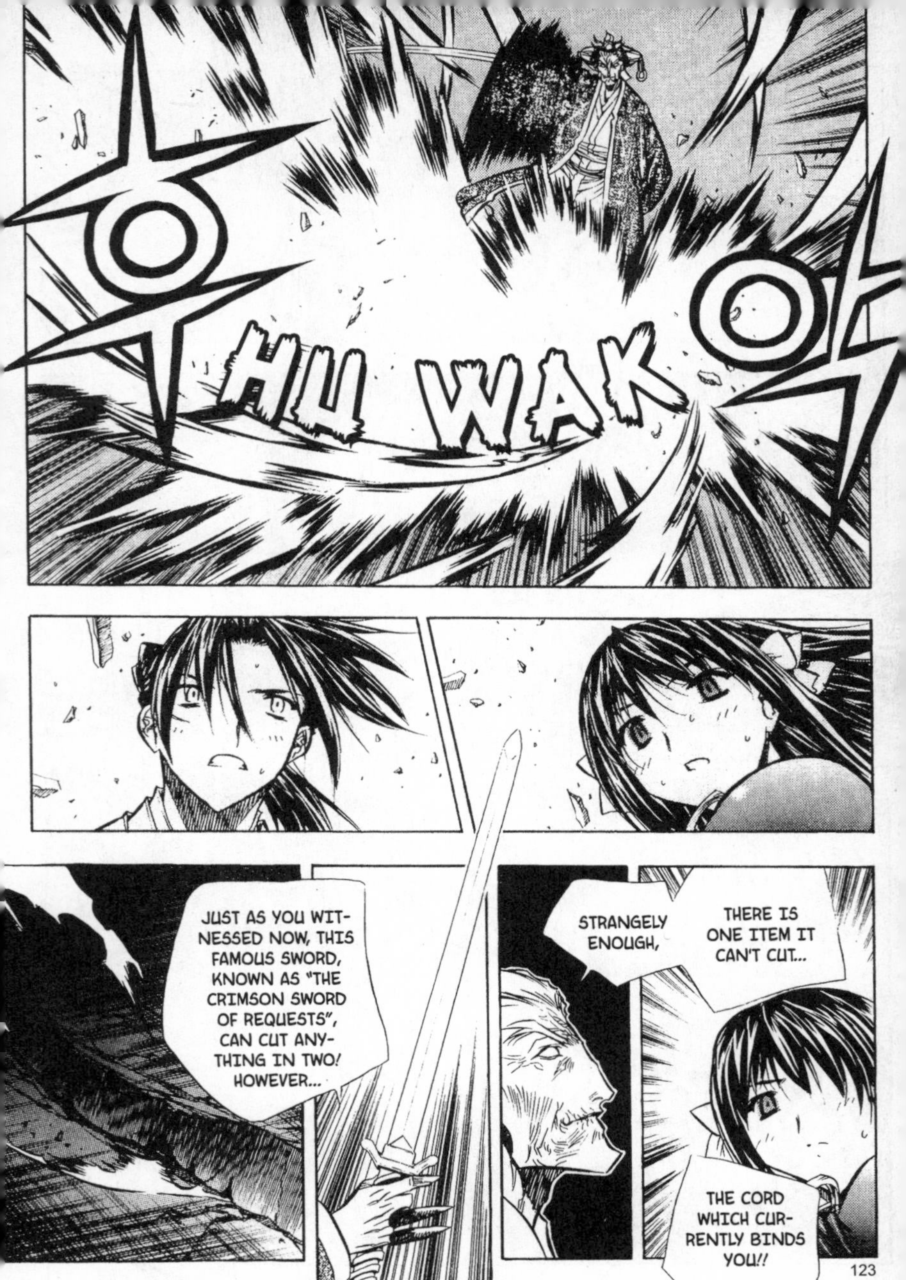
HU WAK
JUST AS YOU WITNESSED NOW, THIS FAMOUS SWORD, KNOWN AS "THE CRIMSON SWORD OF REQUESTS", CAN CUT ANYTHING IN TWO! HOWEVER...
STRANGELY ENOUGH,
THERE IS ONE ITEM IT CAN'T CUT...
THE CORD WHICH CURRENTLY BINDS YOU!!

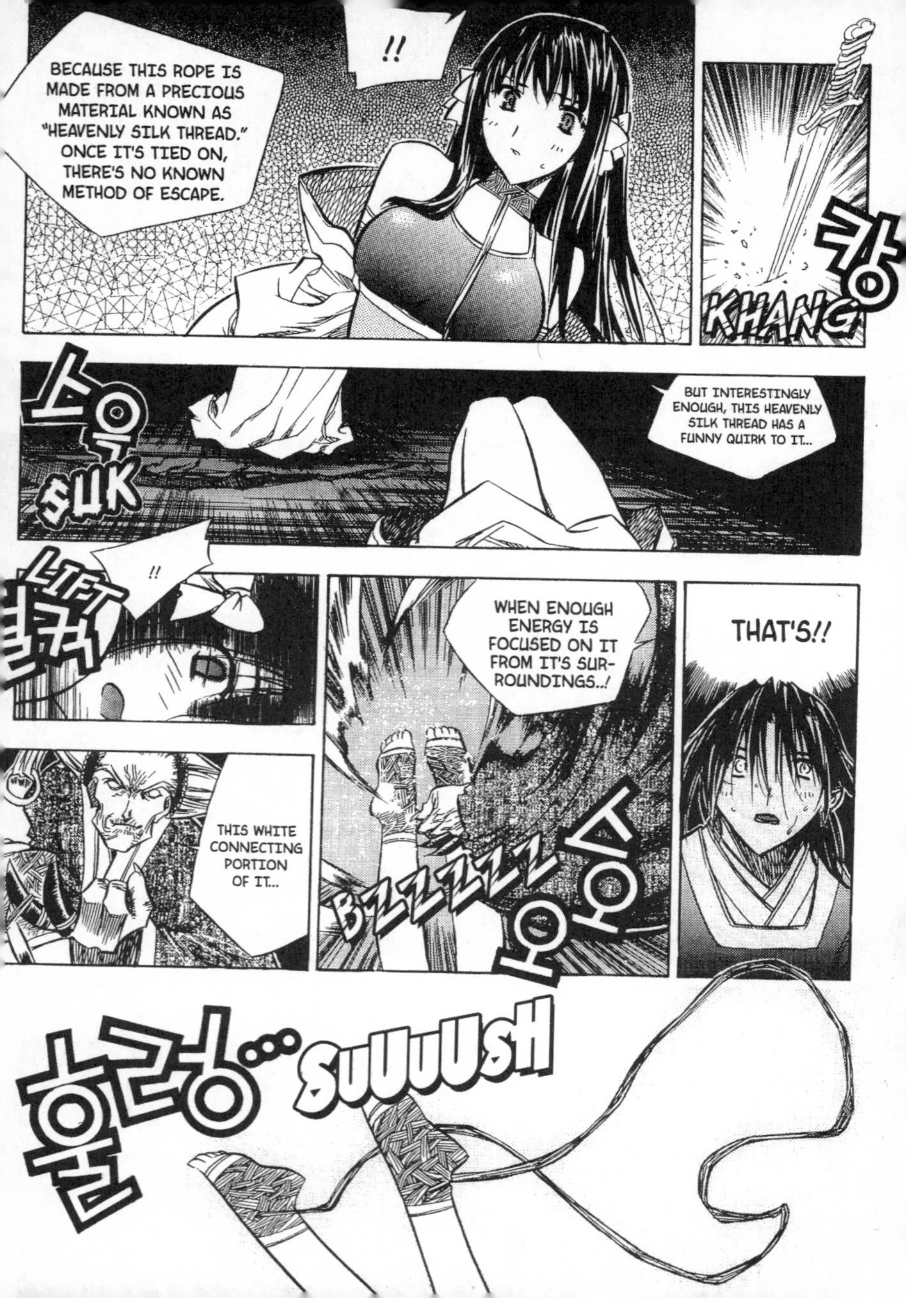
KHANG
!!
BECAUSE THIS ROPE IS MADE FROM A PRECIOUS MATERIAL KNOWN AS "HEAVENLY SILK THREAD." ONCE IT'S TIED ON, THERE'S NO KNOWN METHOD OF ESCAPE.
BUT INTERESTINGLY ENOUGH, THIS HEAVENLY SILK THREAD HAS A FUNNY QUIRK TO IT...
SUK
THAT'S!!
WHEN ENOUGH ENERGY IS FOCUSED ON IT FROM IT'S SURROUNDINGS..!
LIFT
!!
BZZZZZZ
THIS WHITE CONNECTING PORTION OF IT...
SUUUUSH

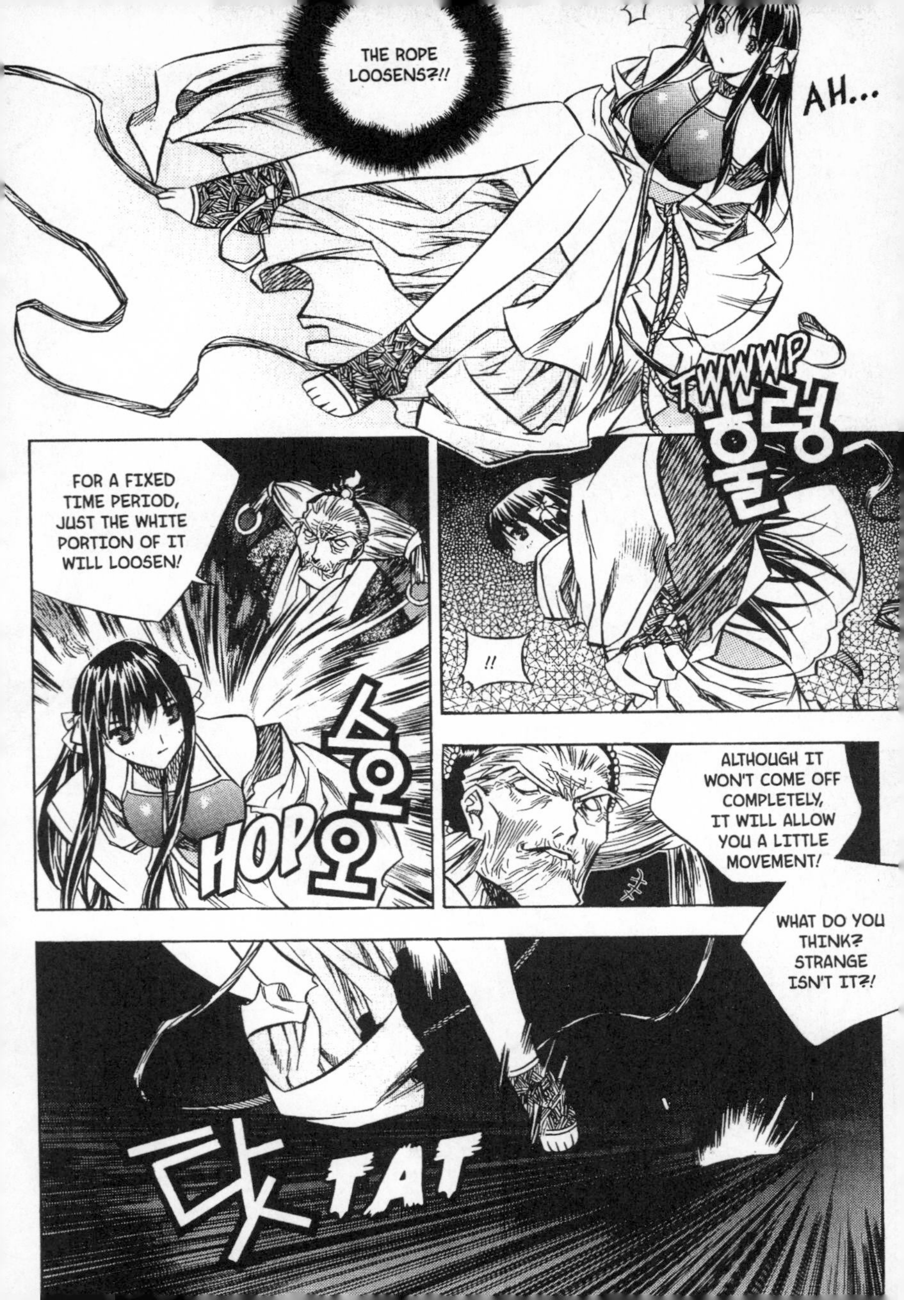
THE ROPE LOOSENS?!!
AH...
TWWWP
훌렁
FOR A FIXED TIME PERIOD, JUST THE WHITE PORTION OF IT WILL LOOSEN!
!!
HOP
ALTHOUGH IT WON'T COME OFF COMPLETELY, IT WILL ALLOW YOU A LITTLE MOVEMENT!
WHAT DO YOU THINK? STRANGE ISN'T IT?!
TAT

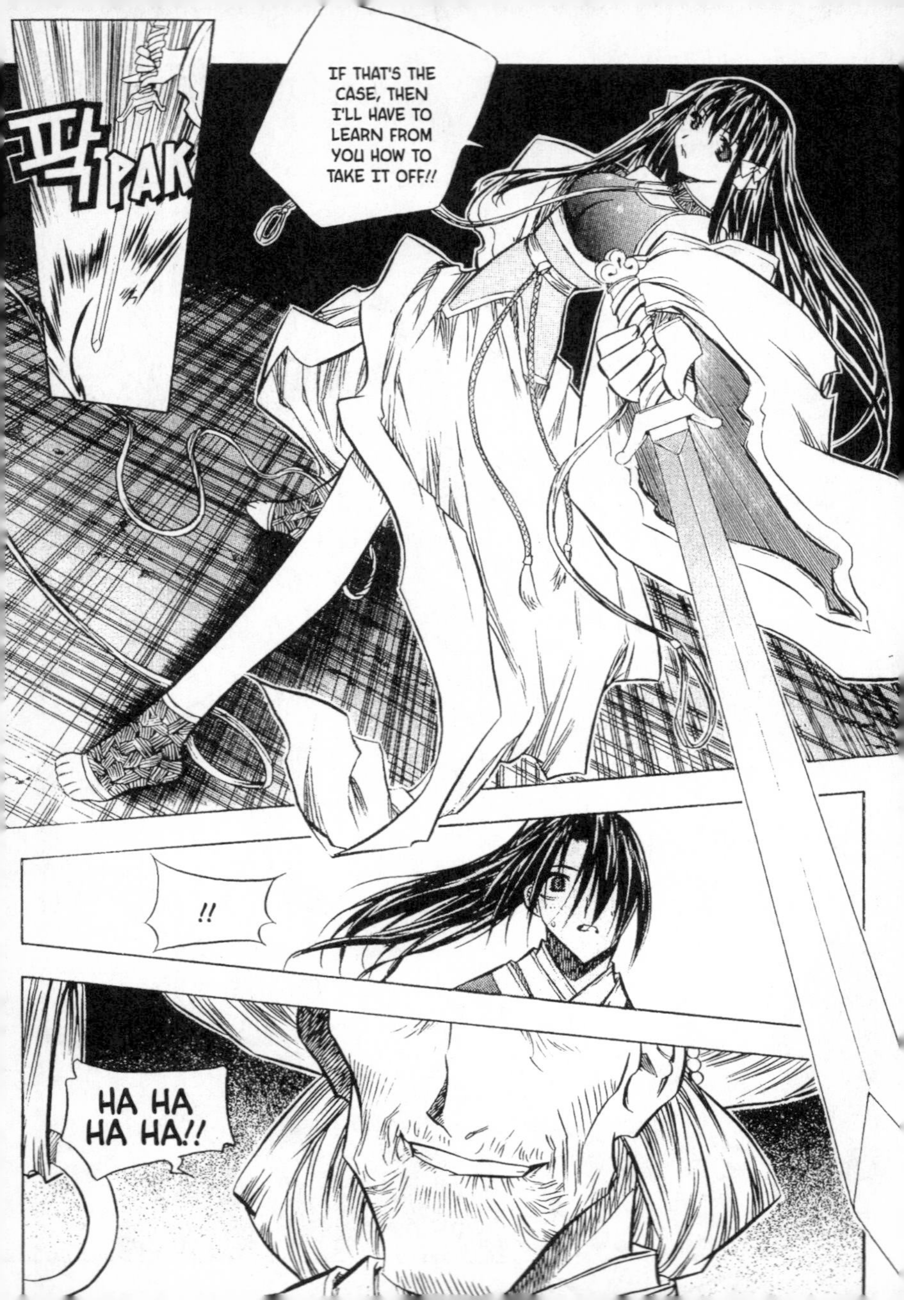
IF THAT'S THE CASE, THEN I'LL HAVE TO LEARN FROM YOU HOW TO TAKE IT OFF!!
팍 PAK
!!
HA HA HA HA!!

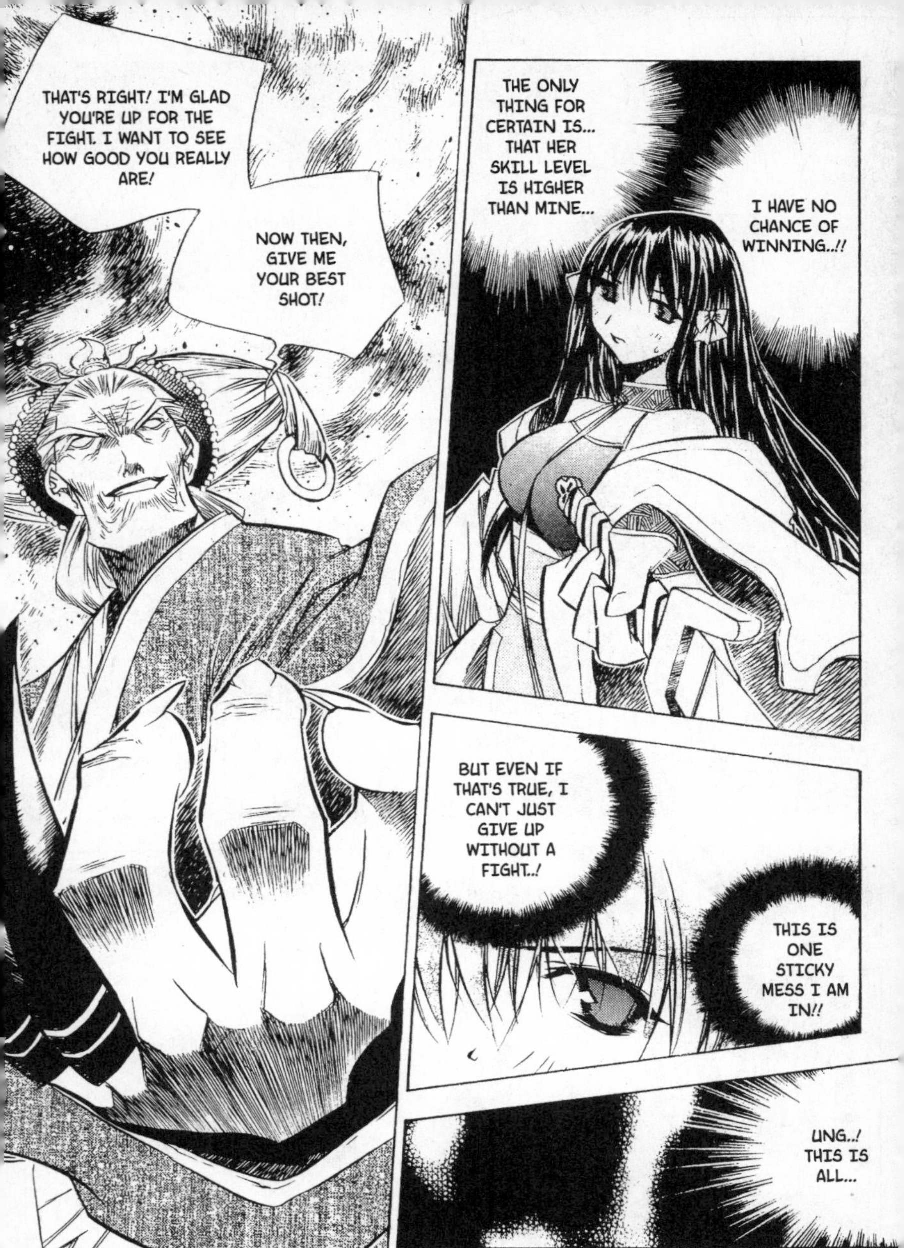
THAT'S RIGHT! I'M GLAD YOU'RE UP FOR THE FIGHT. I WANT TO SEE HOW GOOD YOU REALLY ARE!
NOW THEN, GIVE ME YOUR BEST SHOT!
THE ONLY THING FOR CERTAIN IS... THAT HER SKILL LEVEL IS HIGHER THAN MINE...
I HAVE NO CHANCE OF WINNING..!!
BUT EVEN IF THAT'S TRUE, I CAN'T JUST GIVE UP WITHOUT A FIGHT..!
THIS IS ONE STICKY MESS I AM IN!!
UNG..! THIS IS ALL...

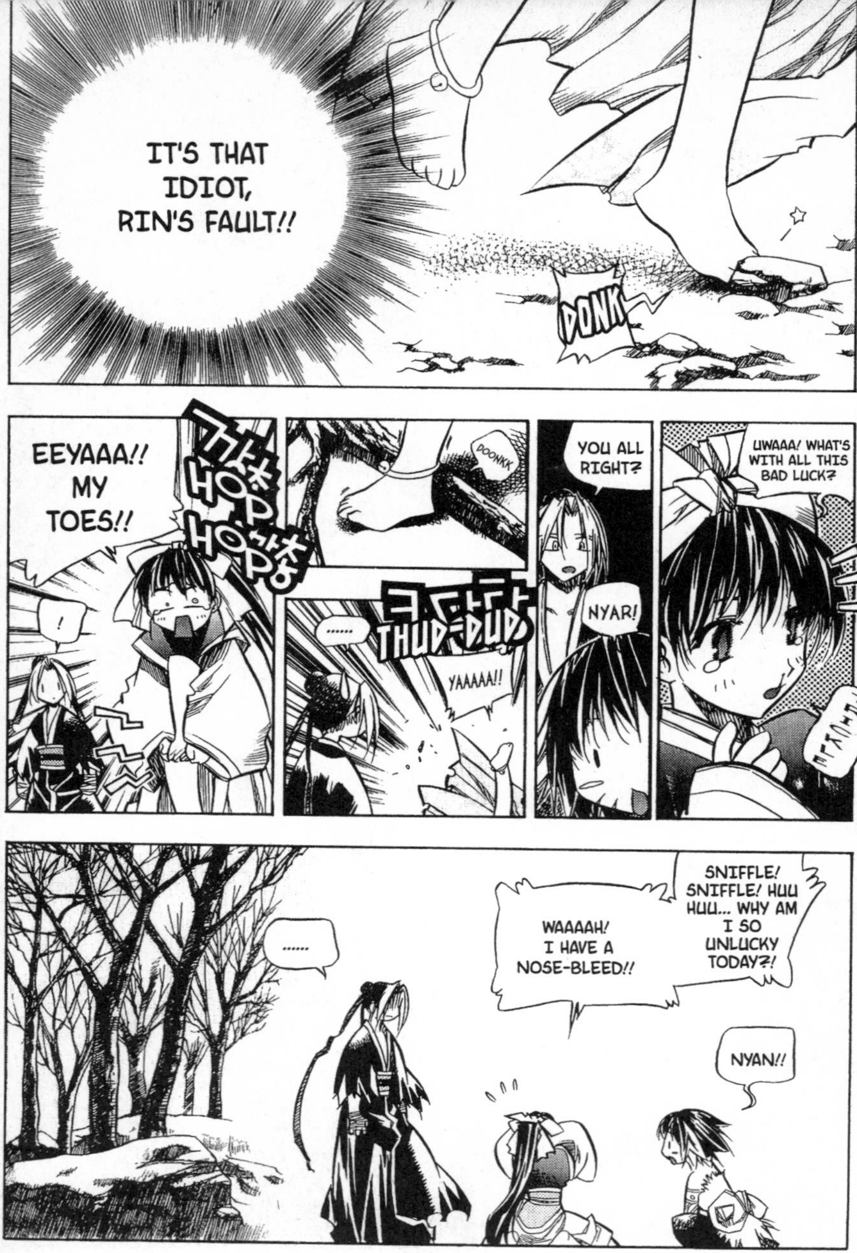
IT'S THAT IDIOT, RIN'S FAULT!!
DONK
EEYAAA!! MY TOES!!
HOP HOP
!
DOONKK
......
THUD-DUD
YAAAAA!!
YOU ALL RIGHT?
NYAR!
UWAAA! WHAT'S WITH ALL THIS BAD LUCK?
......
WAAAAH! I HAVE A NOSE-BLEED!!
SNIFFLE! SNIFFLE! HUU HUU... WHY AM I SO UNLUCKY TODAY?!
NYAN!!

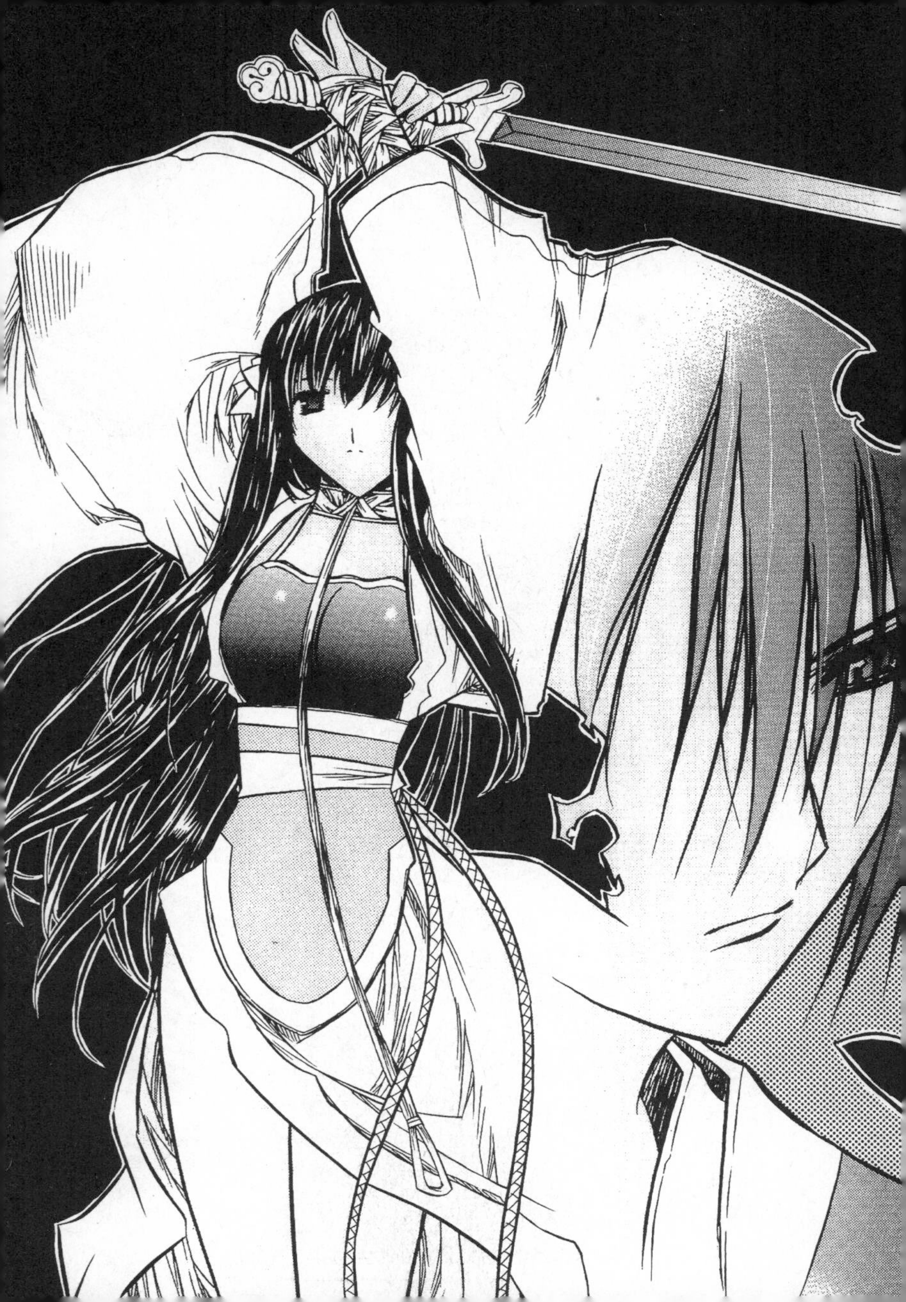

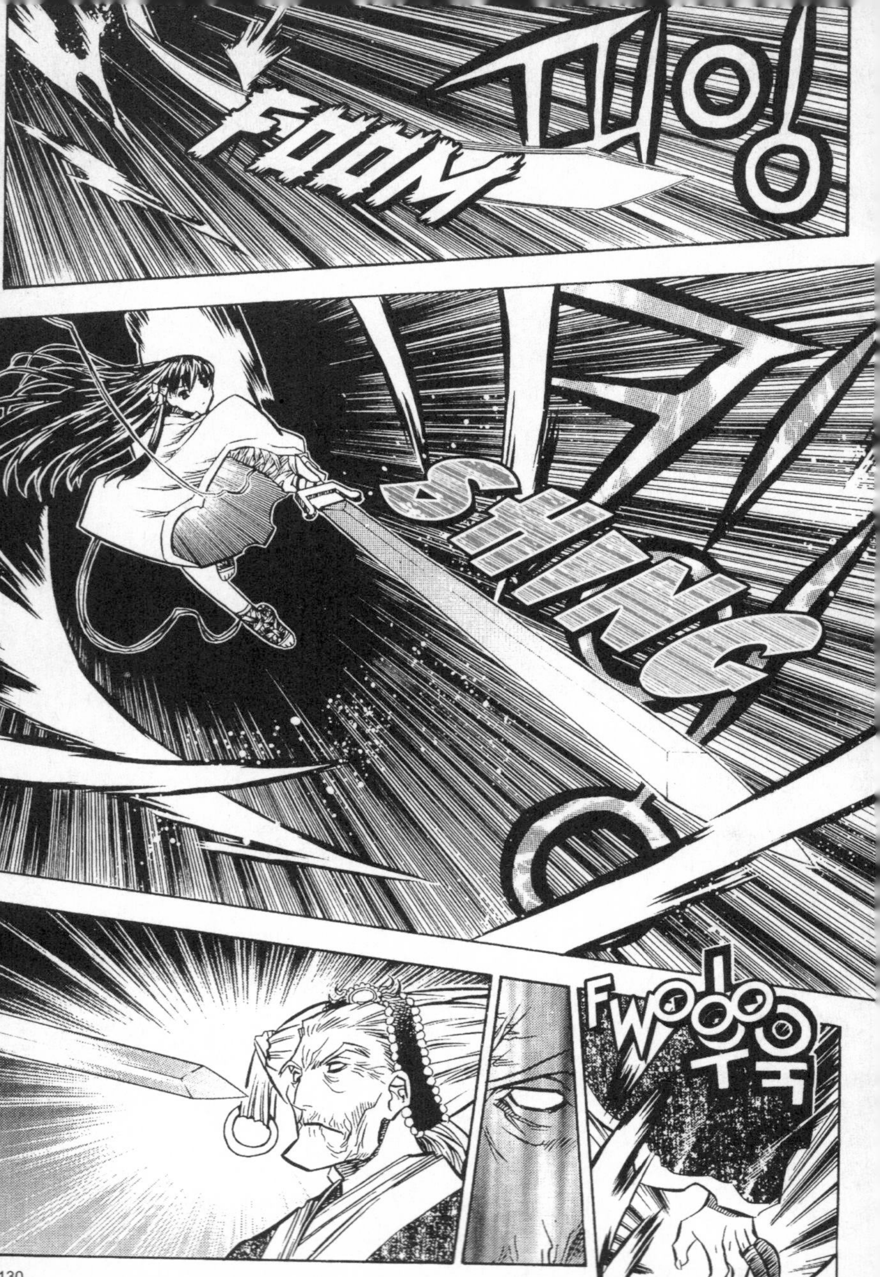
FOOM
SHING

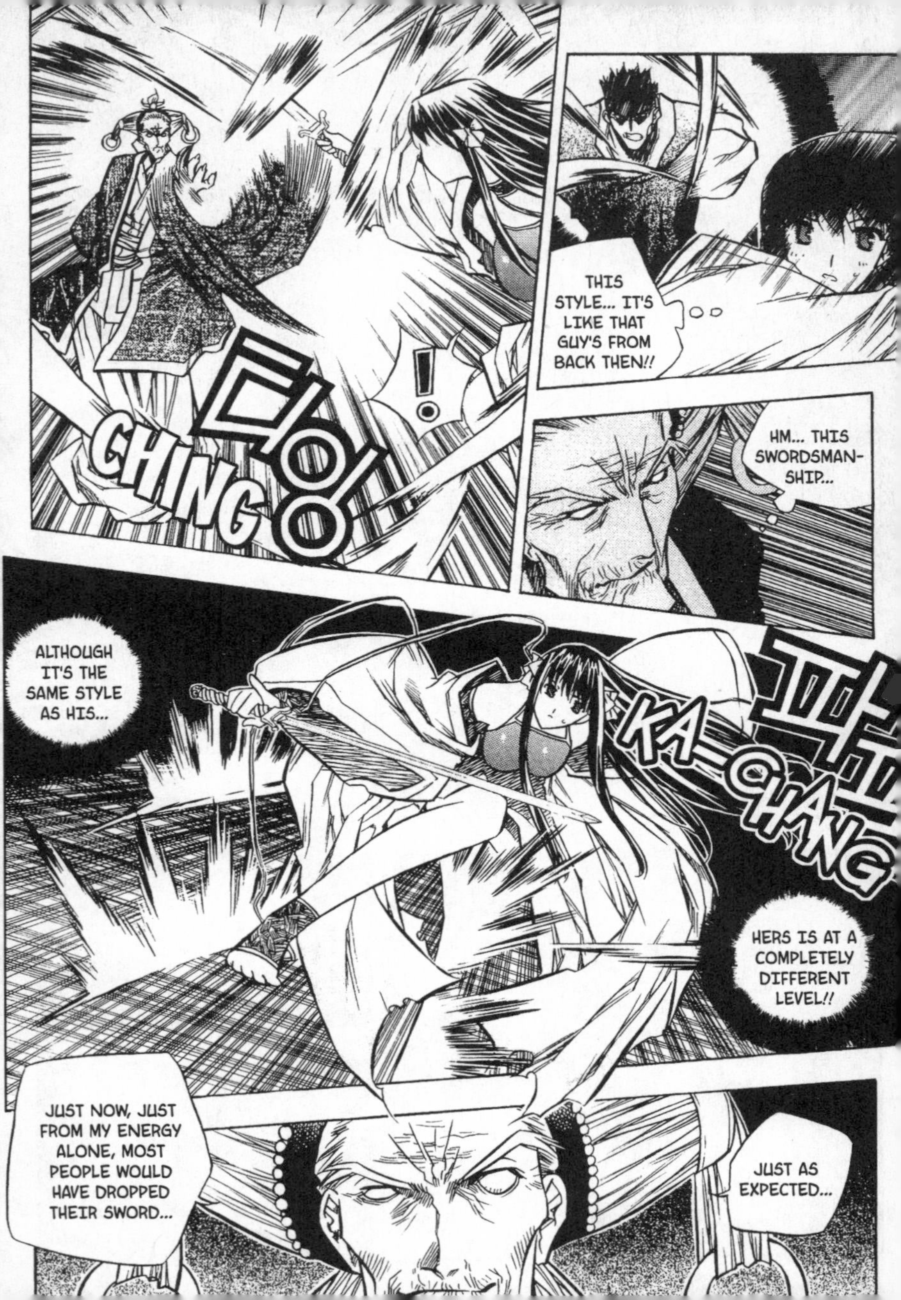
CHING
!
THIS STYLE... IT'S LIKE THAT GUY'S FROM BACK THEN!!
HM... THIS SWORDSMANSHIP...
ALTHOUGH IT'S THE SAME STYLE AS HIS...
KA-CHANG
HERS IS AT A COMPLETELY DIFFERENT LEVEL!!
JUST NOW, JUST FROM MY ENERGY ALONE, MOST PEOPLE WOULD HAVE DROPPED THEIR SWORD...
JUST AS EXPECTED...

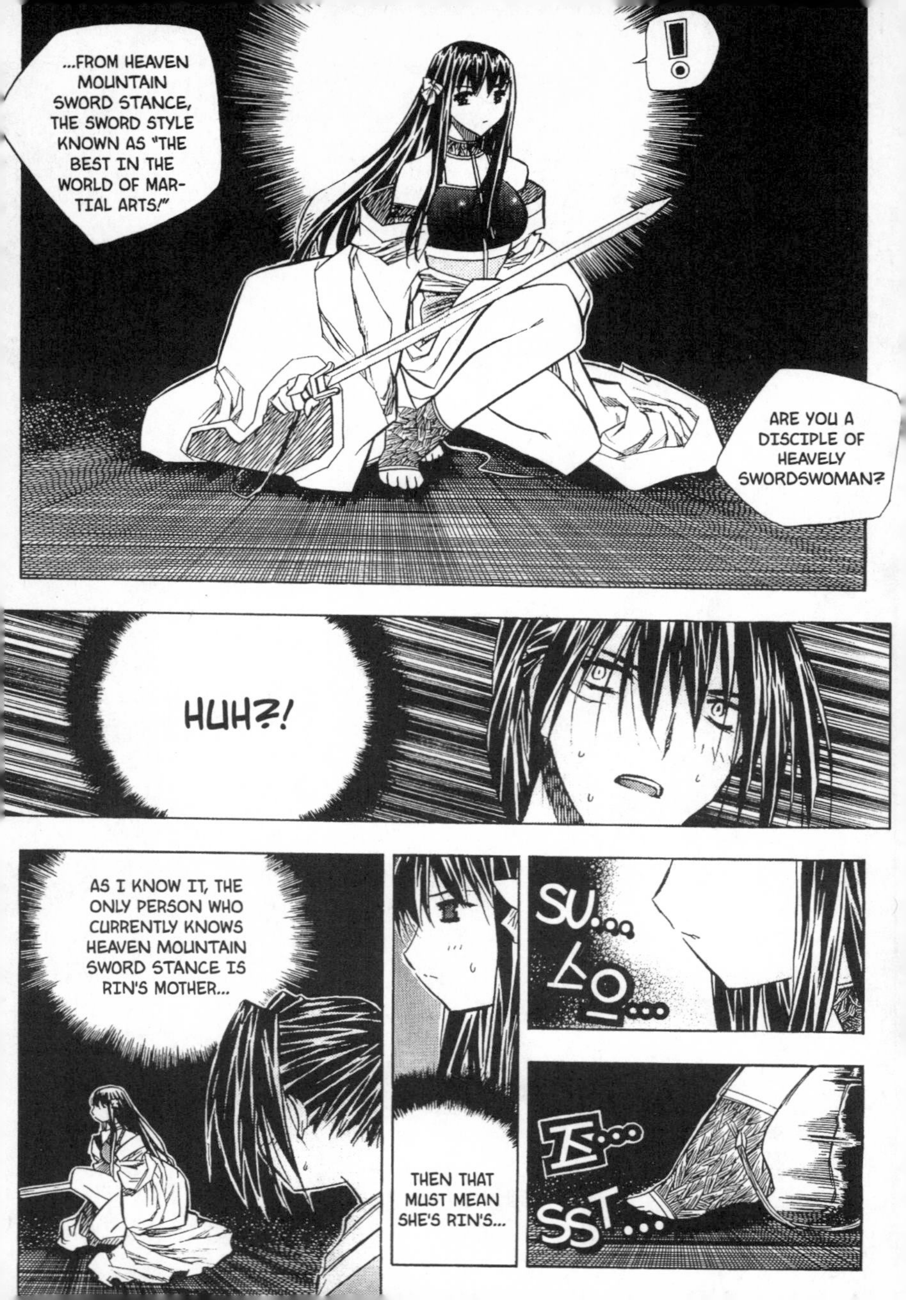
...FROM HEAVEN MOUNTAIN SWORD STANCE, THE SWORD STYLE KNOWN AS "THE BEST IN THE WORLD OF MAR-TIAL ARTS!"
!
ARE YOU A DISCIPLE OF HEAVELY SWORDSWOMAN?
HUH?!
AS I KNOW IT, THE ONLY PERSON WHO CURRENTLY KNOWS HEAVEN MOUNTAIN SWORD STANCE IS RIN'S MOTHER...
THEN THAT MUST MEAN SHE'S RIN'S...
SU...
SST...

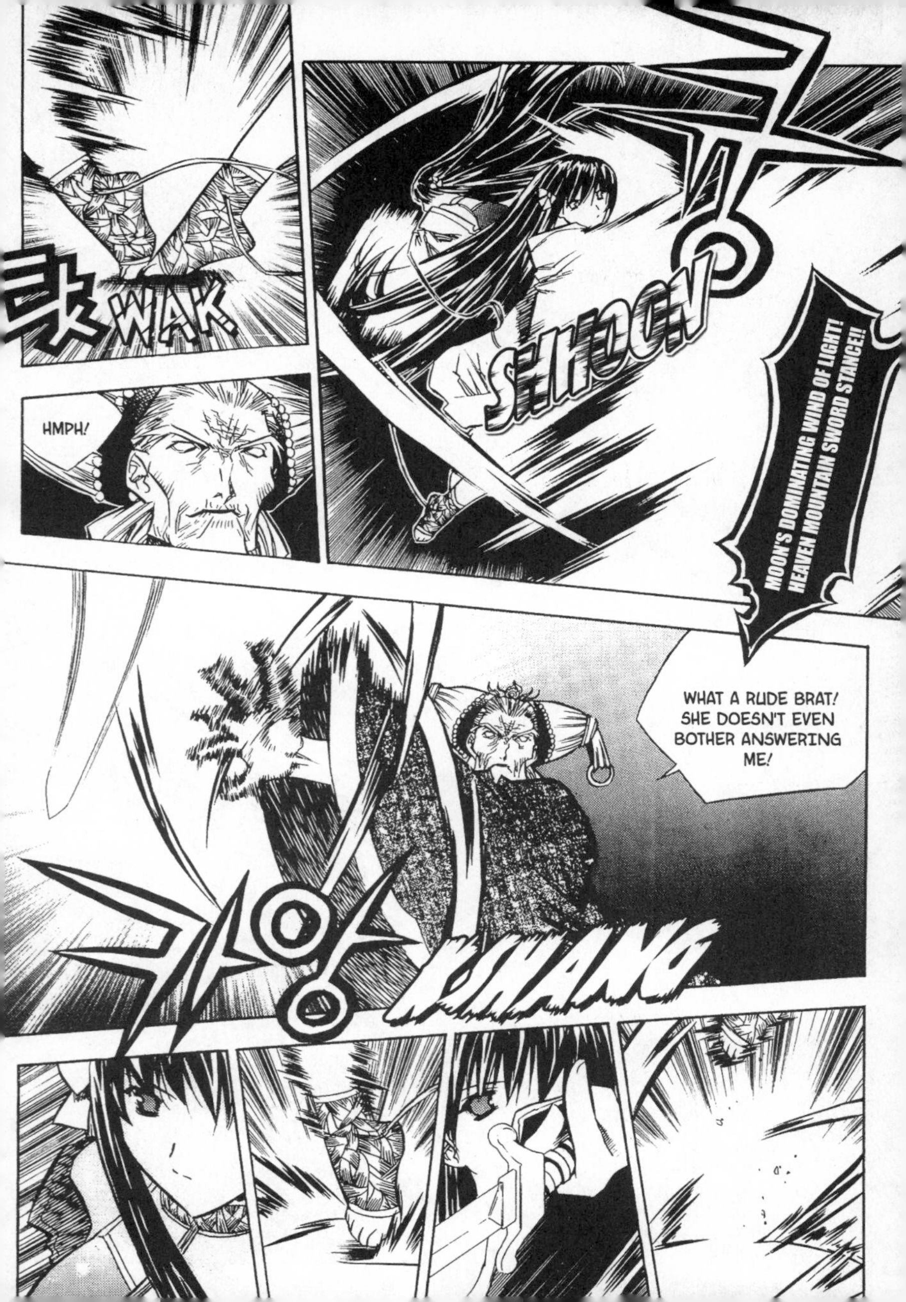

SHHOON
MOON'S DOMINATING WIND OF LIGHT! HEAVEN MOUNTAIN SWORD STANCE!!
WAK
HMPH!
WHAT A RUDE BRAT! SHE DOESN'T EVEN BOTHER ANSWERING ME!
WHANG

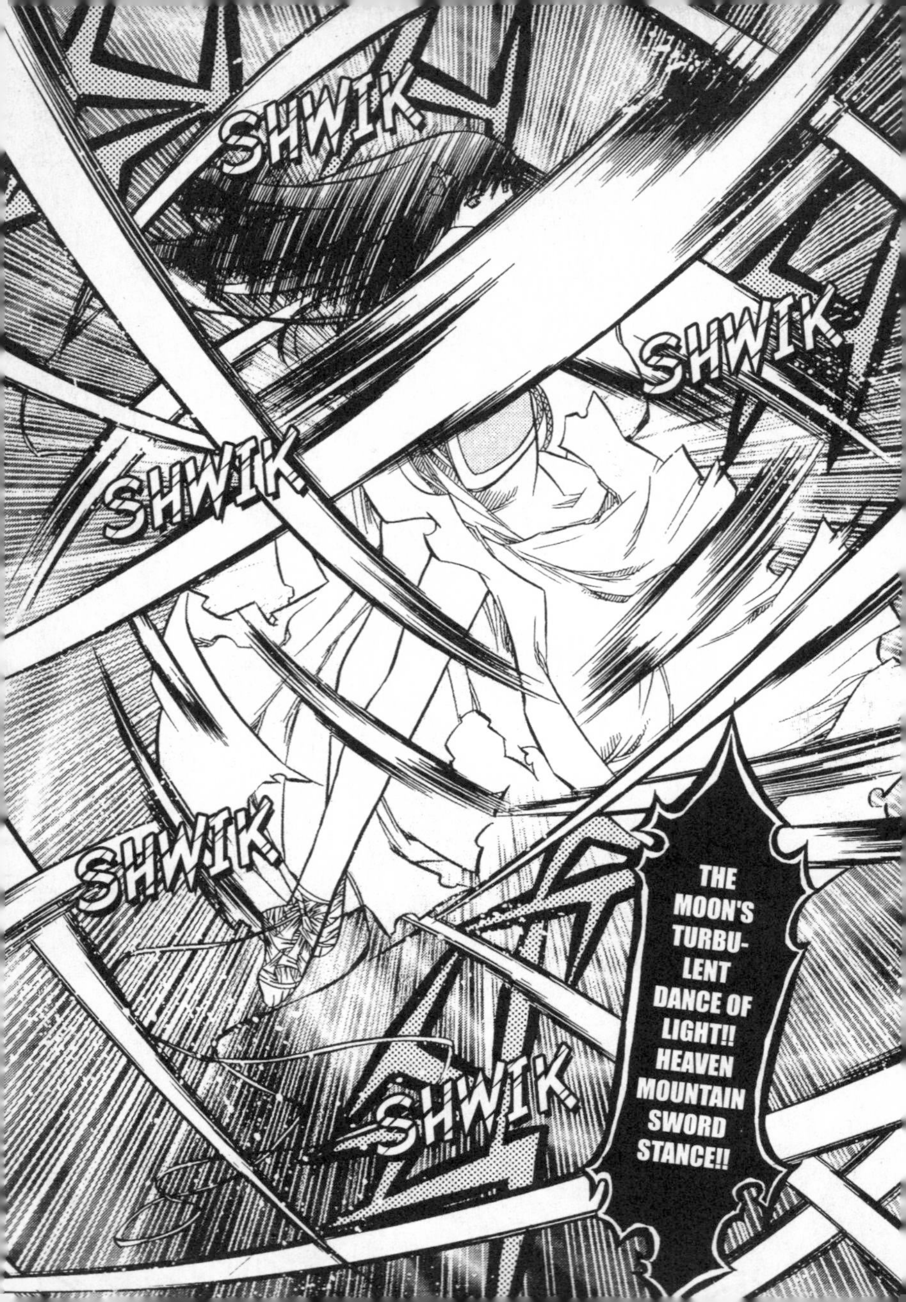
SHWIK
SHWIK
SHWIK
SHWIK
SHWIK
THE MOON'S TURBU-LENT DANCE OF LIGHT!! HEAVEN MOUNTAIN SWORD STANCE!!

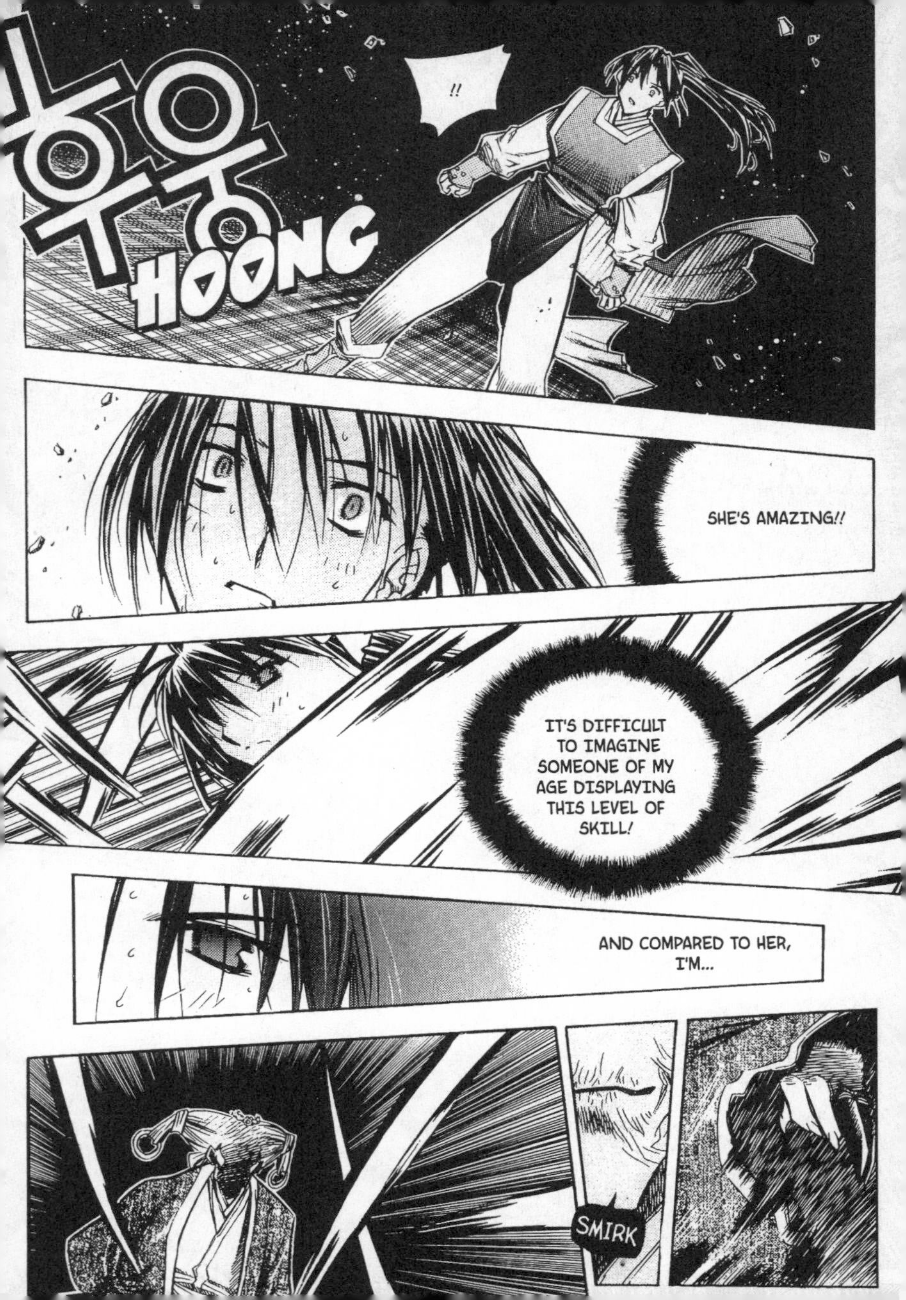

HOONG
!!
SHE'S AMAZING!!
IT'S DIFFICULT TO IMAGINE SOMEONE OF MY AGE DISPLAYING THIS LEVEL OF SKILL!
AND COMPARED TO HER, I'M...
SMIRK

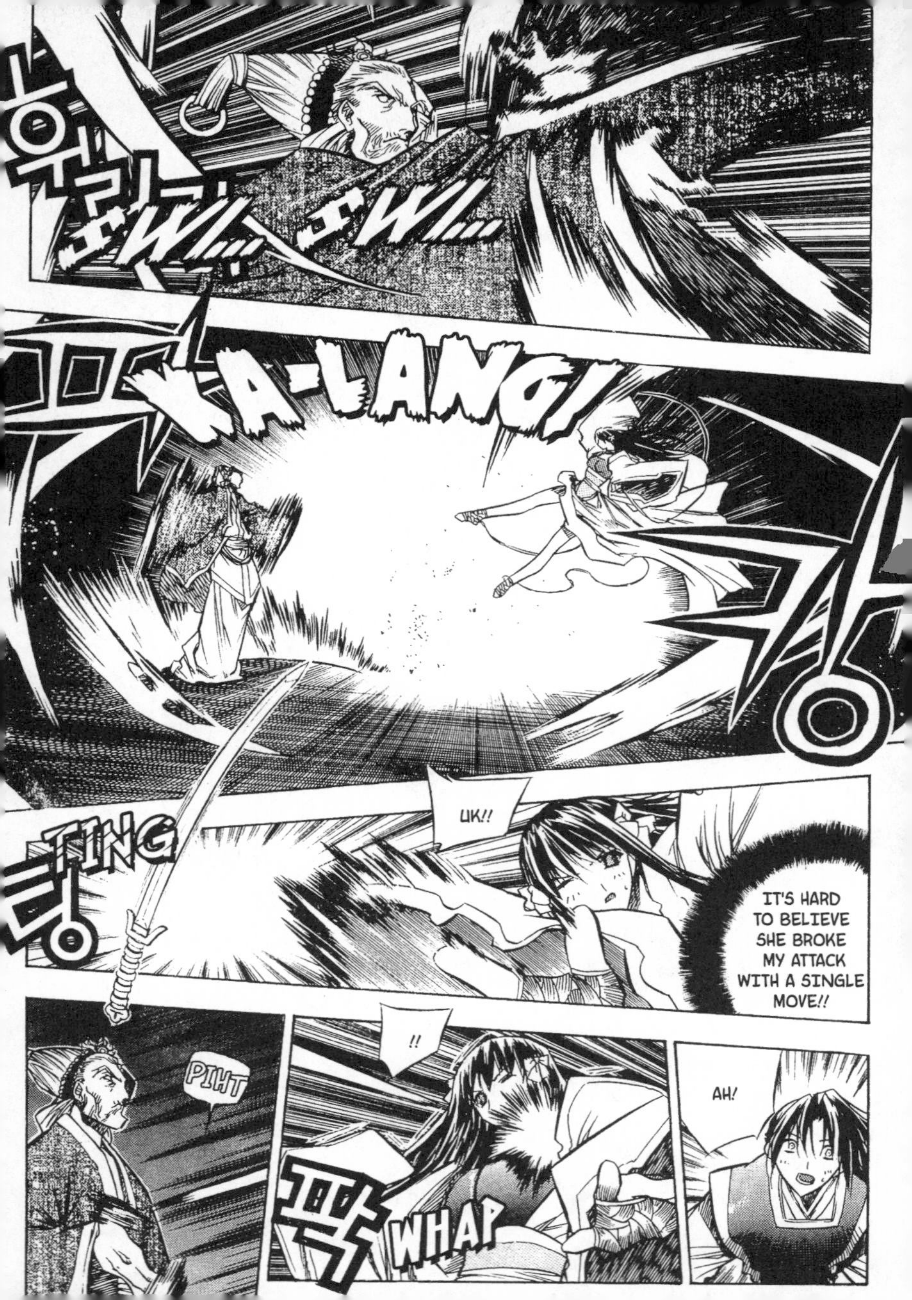
KA-LANG!
UK!!
TING
IT'S HARD TO BELIEVE SHE BROKE MY ATTACK WITH A SINGLE MOVE!!
PIHT
!!
WHAP
AH!

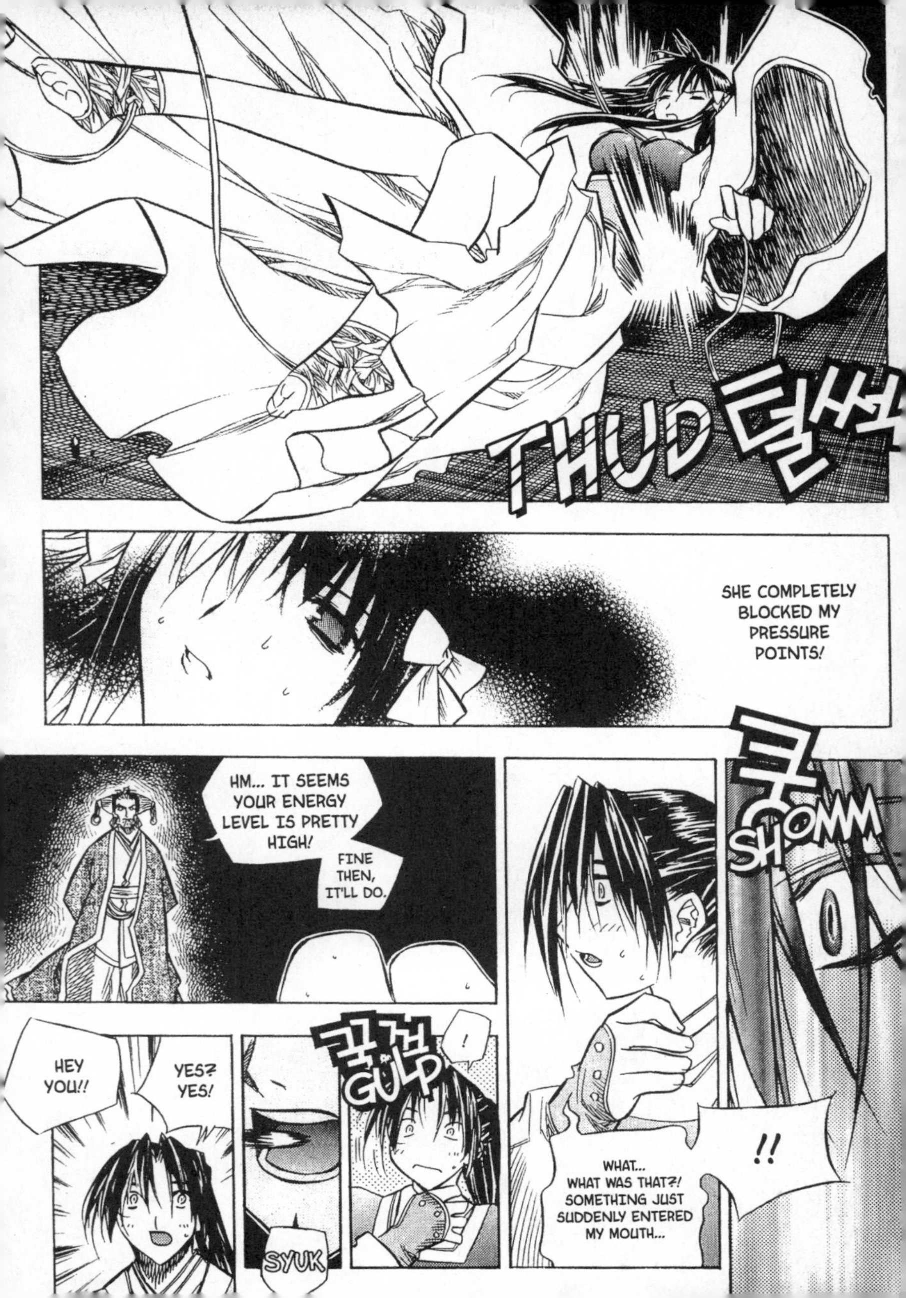
THUD
털썩
SHE COMPLETELY BLOCKED MY PRESSURE POINTS!
HM... IT SEEMS YOUR ENERGY LEVEL IS PRETTY HIGH!
FINE THEN, IT'LL DO.
SHOMM
HEY YOU!!
YES? YES!
SYUK
GULP
!
!!
WHAT... WHAT WAS THAT?! SOMETHING JUST SUDDENLY ENTERED MY MOUTH...

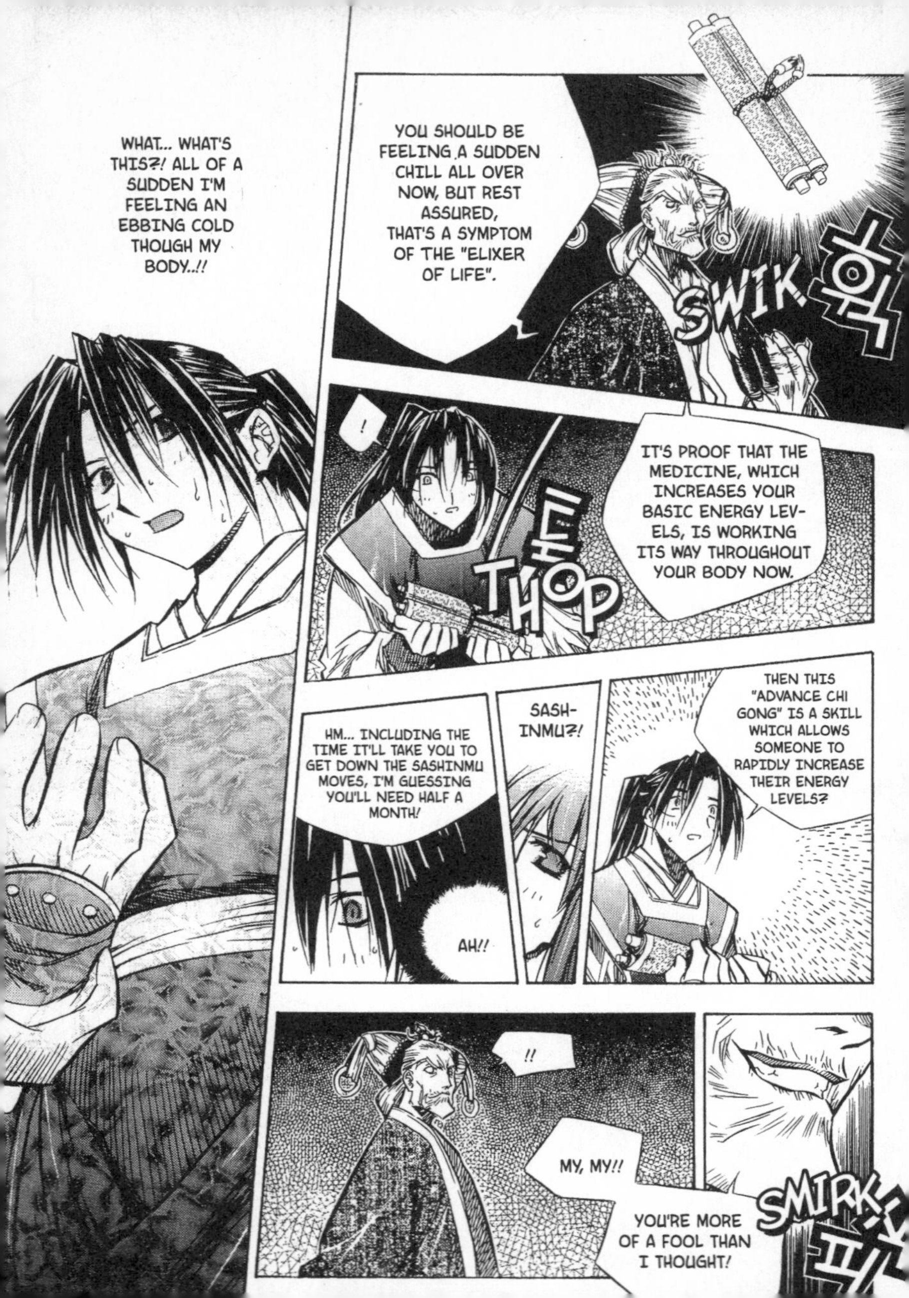
WHAT... WHAT'S THIS?! ALL OF A SUDDEN I'M FEELING AN EBBING COLD THOUGH MY BODY..!!
YOU SHOULD BE FEELING A SUDDEN CHILL ALL OVER NOW, BUT REST ASSURED, THAT'S A SYMPTOM OF THE "ELIXER OF LIFE".
SWIK
!
IT'S PROOF THAT THE MEDICINE, WHICH INCREASES YOUR BASIC ENERGY LEV-ELS, IS WORKING ITS WAY THROUGHOUT YOUR BODY NOW.
THOP
HM... INCLUDING THE TIME IT'LL TAKE YOU TO GET DOWN THE SASHINMU MOVES, I'M GUESSING YOU'LL NEED HALF A MONTH!
AH!!
SASH-INMU?!
THEN THIS "ADVANCE CHI GONG" IS A SKILL WHICH ALLOWS SOMEONE TO RAPIDLY INCREASE THEIR ENERGY LEVELS?
!!
MY, MY!!
SMIRK
YOU'RE MORE OF A FOOL THAN I THOUGHT!

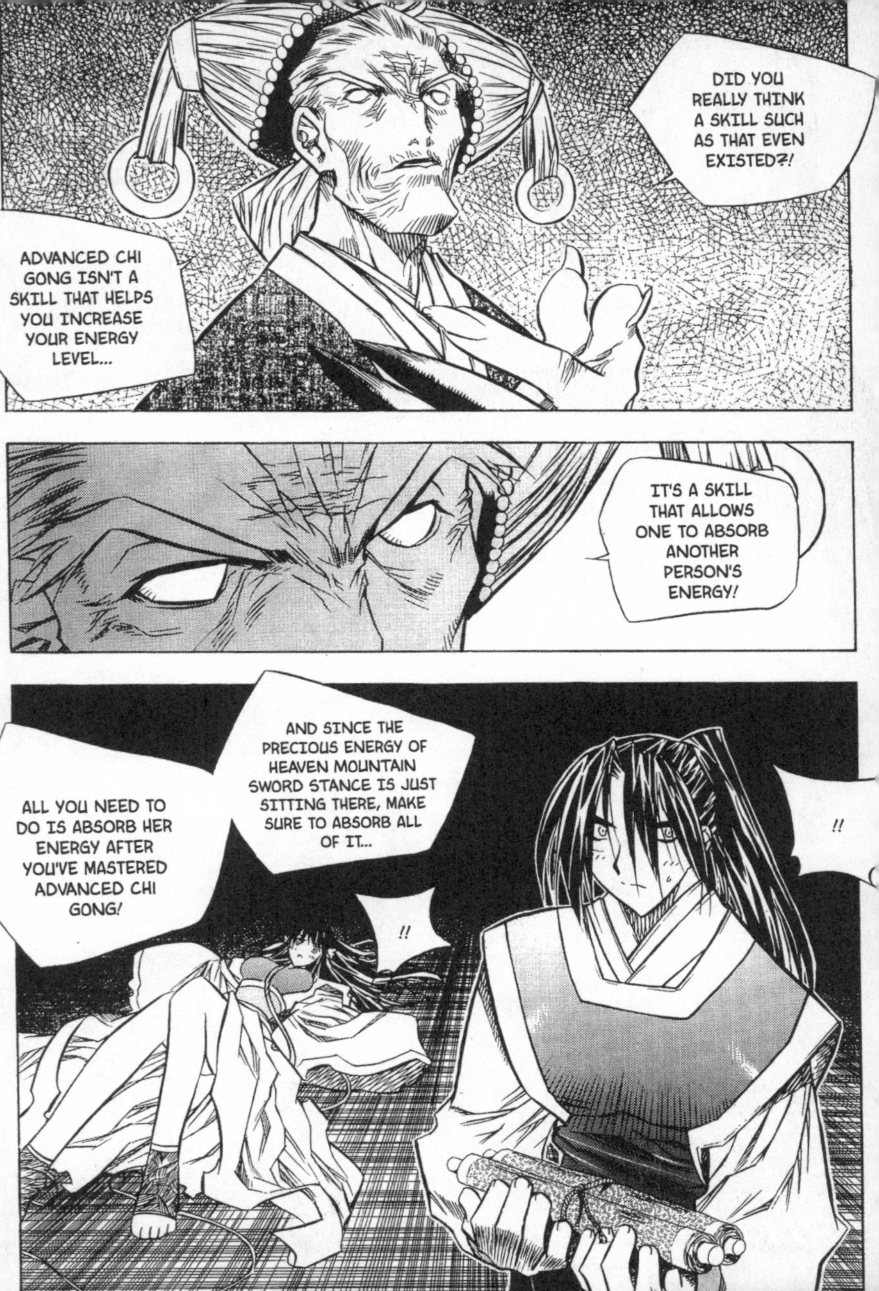
DID YOU REALLY THINK A SKILL SUCH AS THAT EVEN EXISTED?!
ADVANCED CHI GONG ISN'T A SKILL THAT HELPS YOU INCREASE YOUR ENERGY LEVEL...
IT'S A SKILL THAT ALLOWS ONE TO ABSORB ANOTHER PERSON'S ENERGY!
!!
AND SINCE THE PRECIOUS ENERGY OF HEAVEN MOUNTAIN SWORD STANCE IS JUST SITTING THERE, MAKE SURE TO ABSORB ALL OF IT...
ALL YOU NEED TO DO IS ABSORB HER ENERGY AFTER YOU'VE MASTERED ADVANCED CHI GONG!
!!

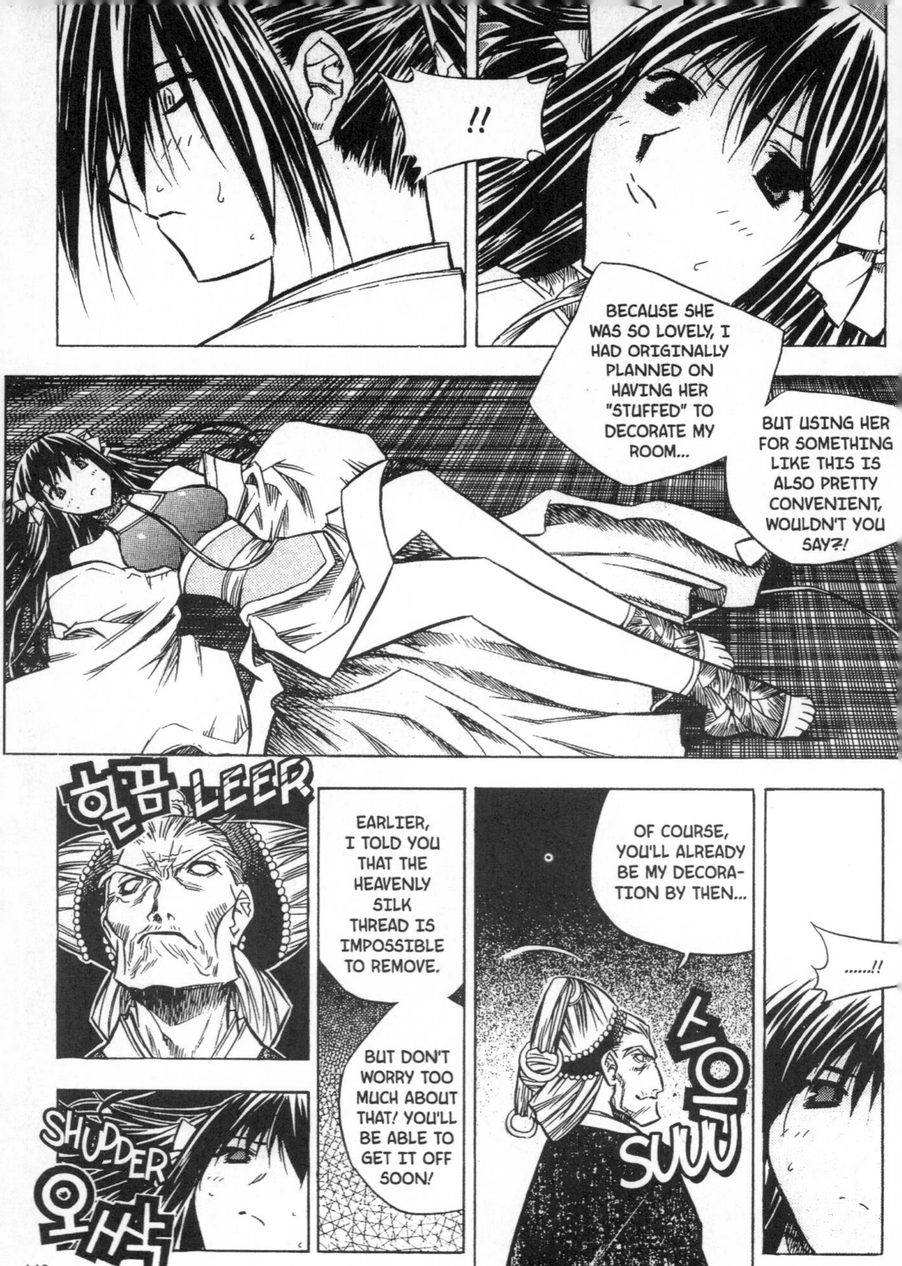
!!
BECAUSE SHE WAS SO LOVELY, I HAD ORIGINALLY PLANNED ON HAVING HER "STUFFED" TO DECORATE MY ROOM...
BUT USING HER FOR SOMETHING LIKE THIS IS ALSO PRETTY CONVENIENT, WOULDN'T YOU SAY?!
힐끔 LEER
EARLIER, I TOLD YOU THAT THE HEAVENLY SILK THREAD IS IMPOSSIBLE TO REMOVE.
BUT DON'T WORRY TOO MUCH ABOUT THAT! YOU'LL BE ABLE TO GET IT OFF SOON!
SHUDDER
오싹
OF COURSE, YOU'LL ALREADY BE MY DECORATION BY THEN...
SUUU
......!!

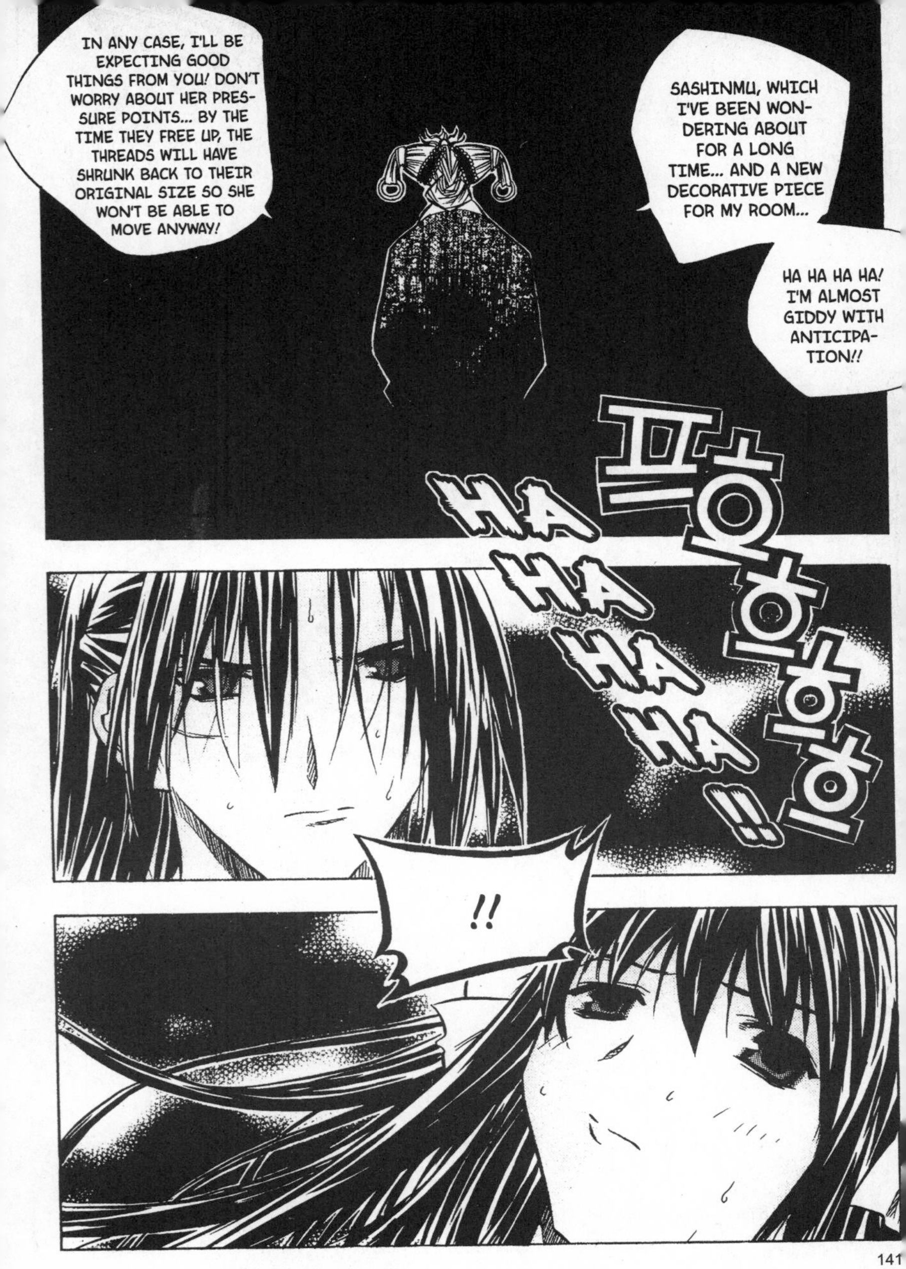
IN ANY CASE, I'LL BE EXPECTING GOOD THINGS FROM YOU! DON'T WORRY ABOUT HER PRES-SURE POINTS... BY THE TIME THEY FREE UP, THE THREADS WILL HAVE SHRUNK BACK TO THEIR ORIGINAL SIZE SO SHE WON'T BE ABLE TO MOVE ANYWAY!
SASHINMU, WHICH I'VE BEEN WON-DERING ABOUT FOR A LONG TIME... AND A NEW DECORATIVE PIECE FOR MY ROOM...
HA HA HA HA! I'M ALMOST GIDDY WITH ANTICIPA-TION!!
프흐흐흐
HA HA HA HA!!
!!

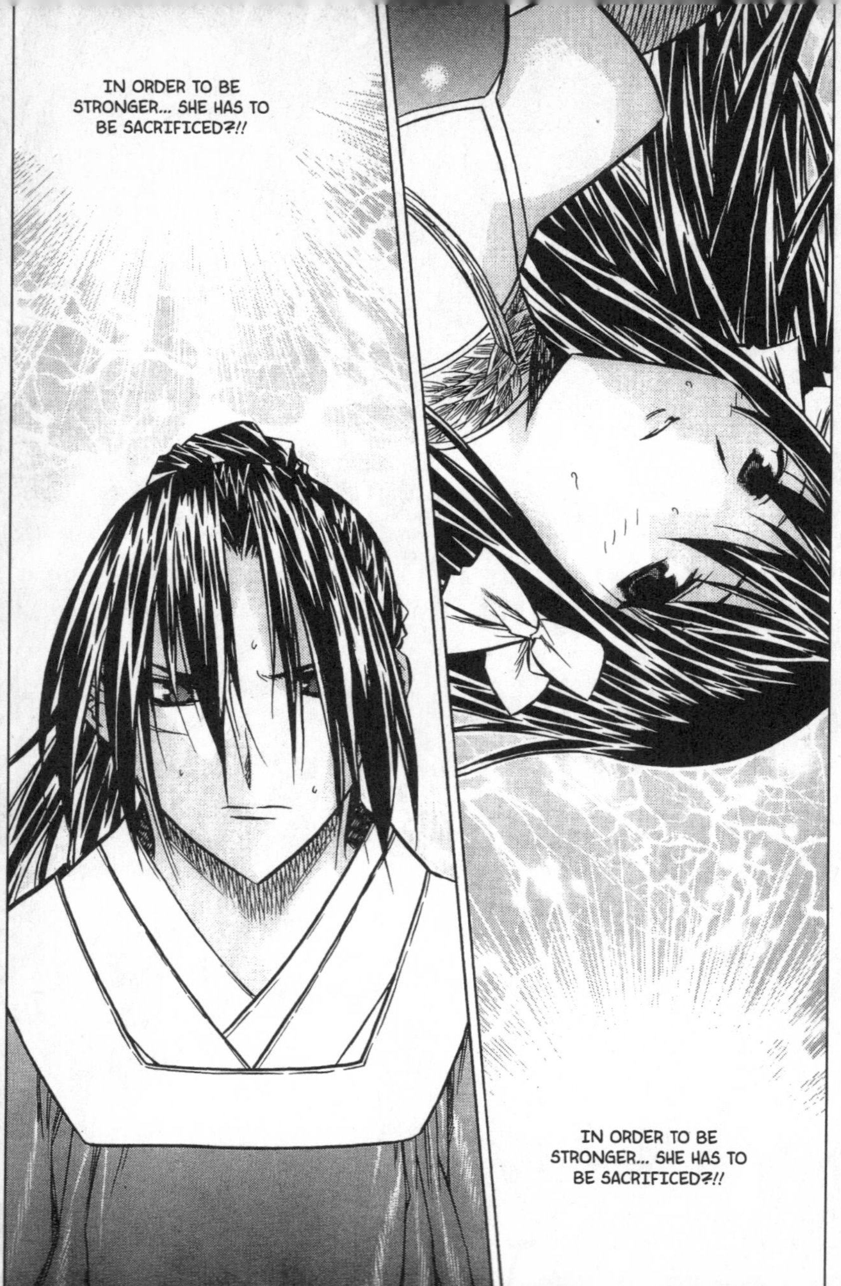
IN ORDER TO BE STRONGER... SHE HAS TO BE SACRIFICED?!!
IN ORDER TO BE STRONGER... SHE HAS TO BE SACRIFICED?!!

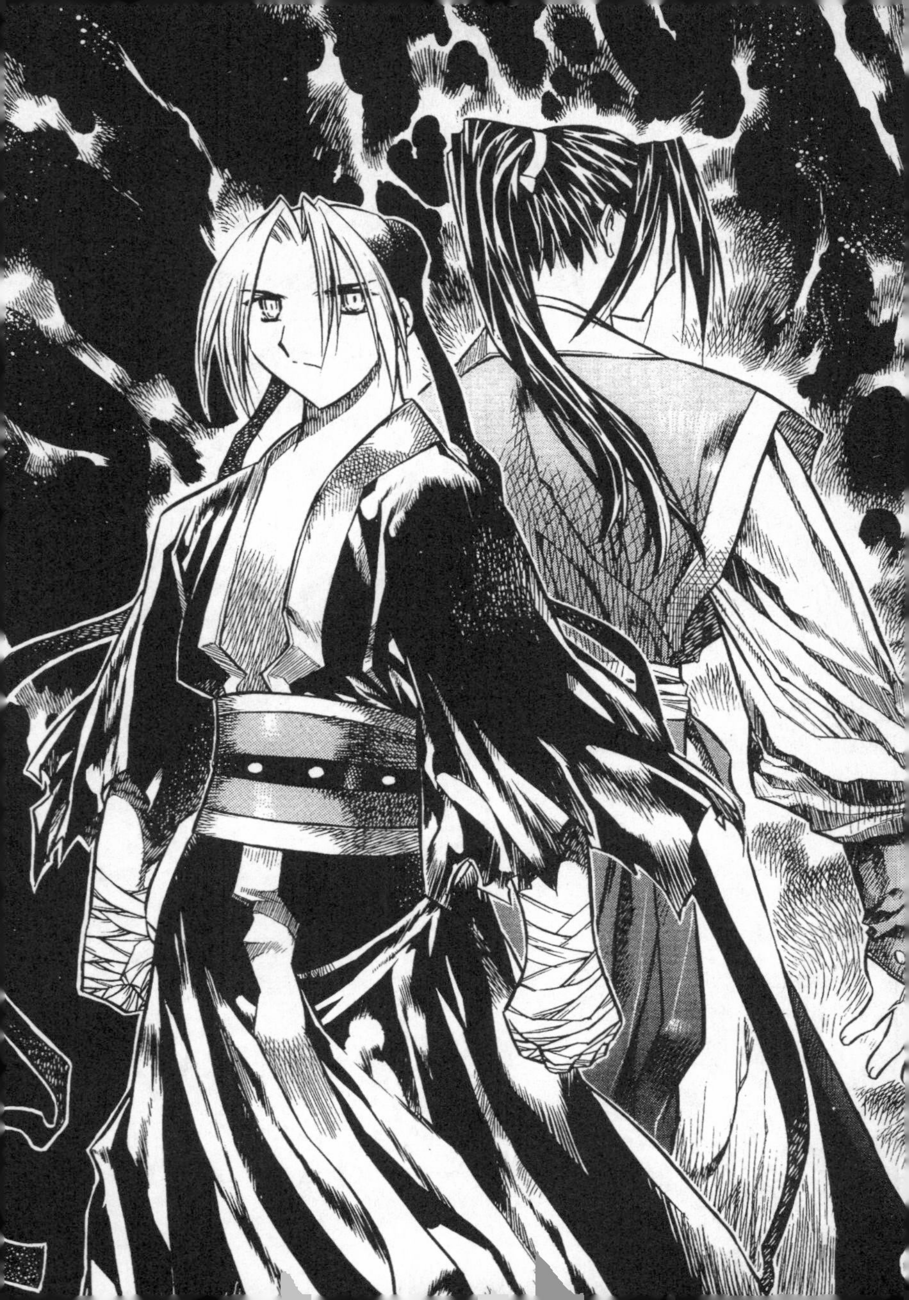

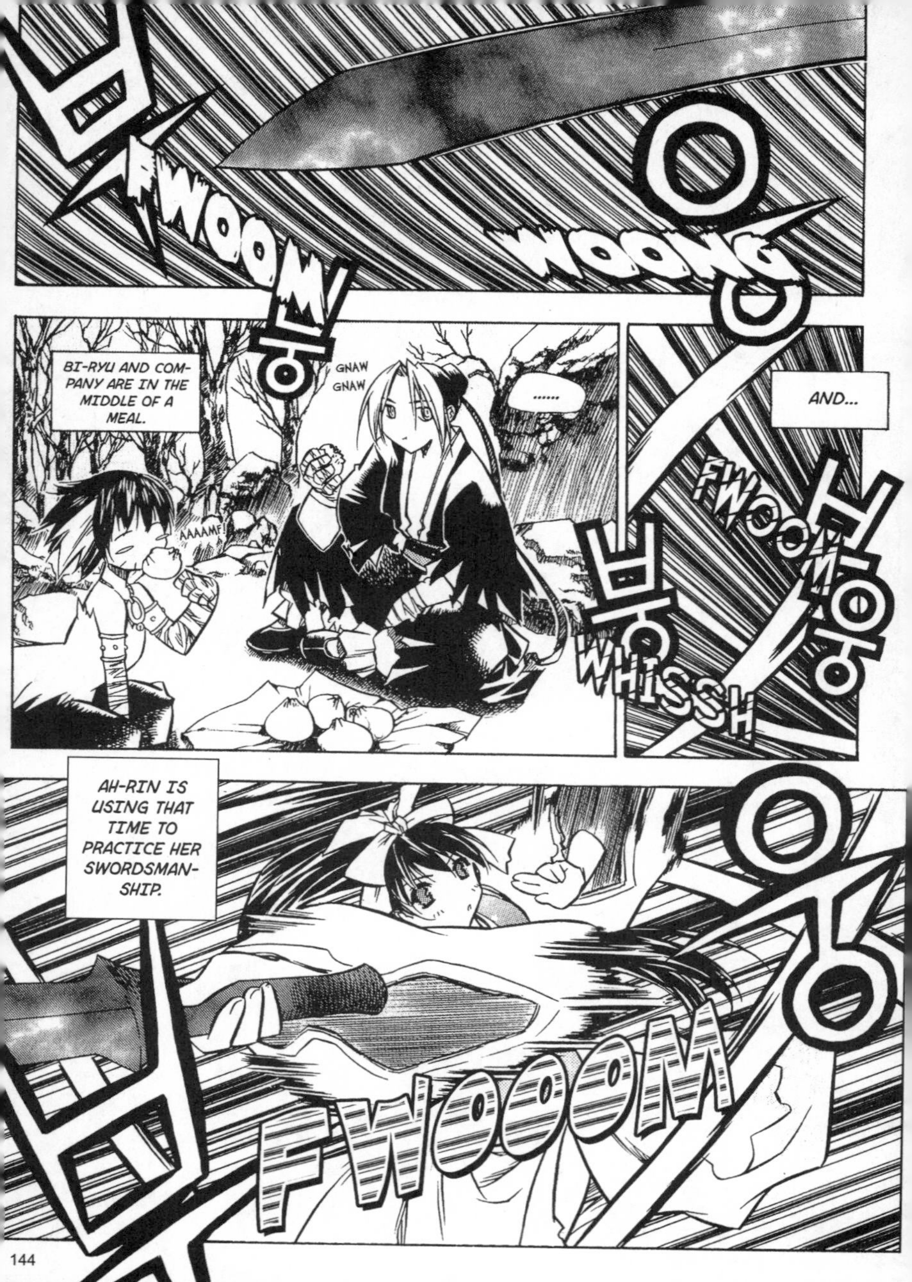
FWOOM
WOOONG
BI-RYU AND COMPANY ARE IN THE MIDDLE OF A MEAL.
GNAW GNAW
......
AAAAMF!
AND...
FWOOM
WHISSH
AH-RIN IS USING THAT TIME TO PRACTICE HER SWORDSMANSHIP.
FWOOOM

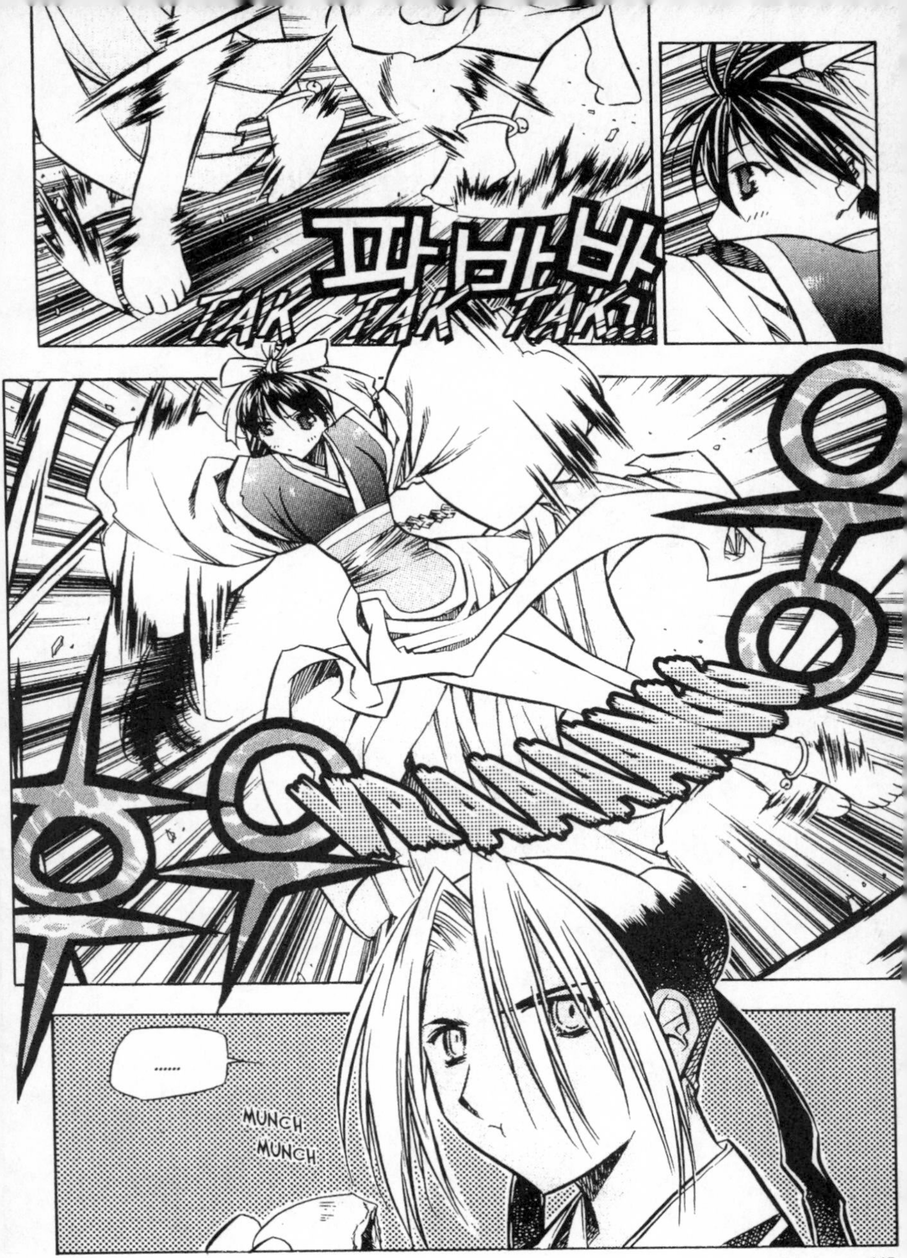
파바밧
TAK TAK TAK!!
......
MUNCH MUNCH

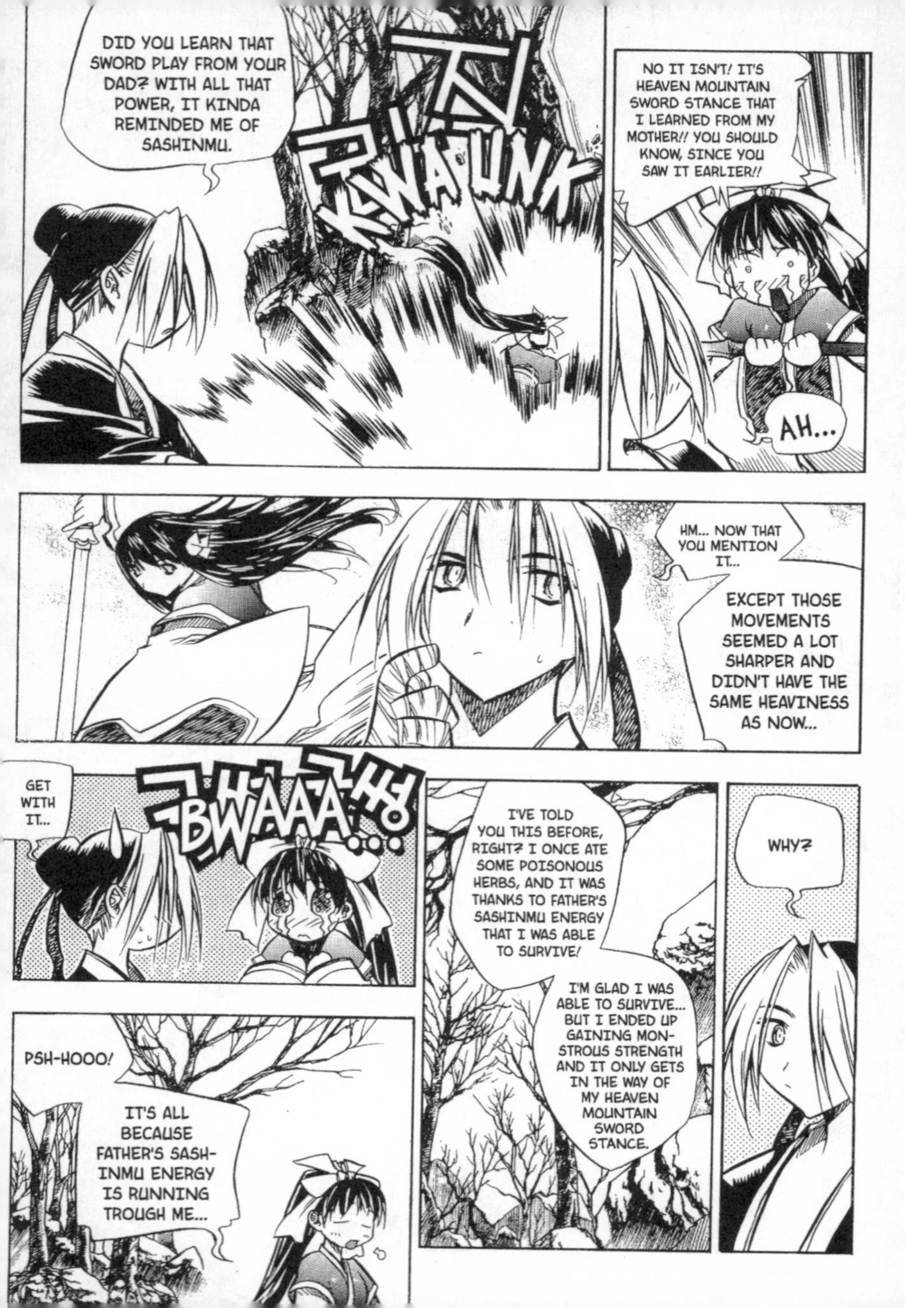
DID YOU LEARN THAT SWORD PLAY FROM YOUR DAD? WITH ALL THAT POWER, IT KINDA REMINDED ME OF SASHINMU.
KWAUNK
NO IT ISN'T! IT'S HEAVEN MOUNTAIN SWORD STANCE THAT I LEARNED FROM MY MOTHER!! YOU SHOULD KNOW, SINCE YOU SAW IT EARLIER!!
AH...
HM... NOW THAT YOU MENTION IT...
EXCEPT THOSE MOVEMENTS SEEMED A LOT SHARPER AND DIDN'T HAVE THE SAME HEAVINESS AS NOW...
GET WITH IT...
BWAAA...
I'VE TOLD YOU THIS BEFORE, RIGHT? I ONCE ATE SOME POISONOUS HERBS, AND IT WAS THANKS TO FATHER'S SASHINMU ENERGY THAT I WAS ABLE TO SURVIVE!
WHY?
I'M GLAD I WAS ABLE TO SURVIVE... BUT I ENDED UP GAINING MONSTROUS STRENGTH AND IT ONLY GETS IN THE WAY OF MY HEAVEN MOUNTAIN SWORD STANCE.
PSH-HOOO!
IT'S ALL BECAUSE FATHER'S SASHINMU ENERGY IS RUNNING TROUGH ME...

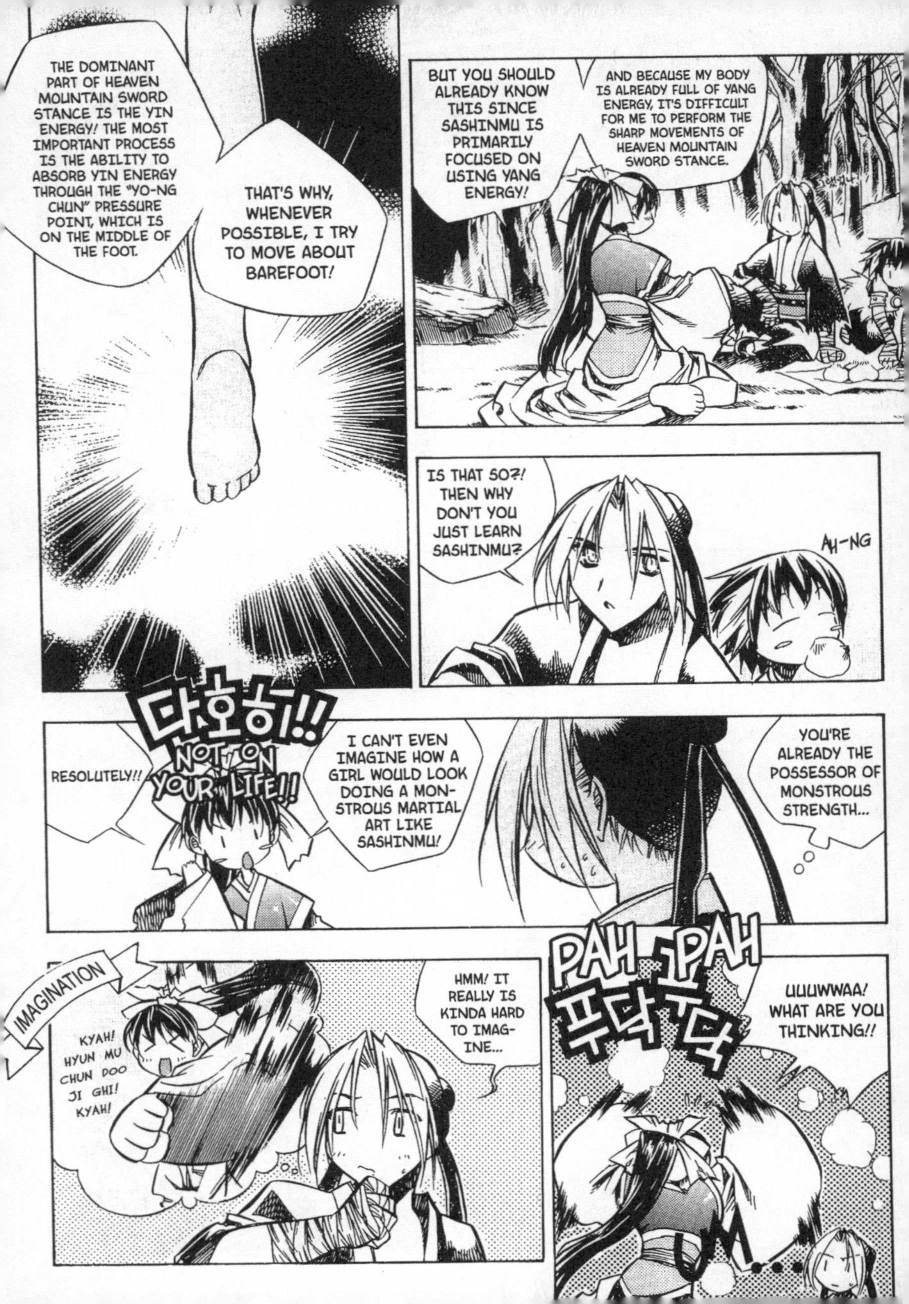
THE DOMINANT PART OF HEAVEN MOUNTAIN SWORD STANCE IS THE YIN ENERGY! THE MOST IMPORTANT PROCESS IS THE ABILITY TO ABSORB YIN ENERGY THROUGH THE "YO-NG CHUN" PRESSURE POINT, WHICH IS ON THE MIDDLE OF THE FOOT.
THAT'S WHY, WHENEVER POSSIBLE, I TRY TO MOVE ABOUT BAREFOOT!
BUT YOU SHOULD ALREADY KNOW THIS SINCE SASHINMU IS PRIMARILY FOCUSED ON USING YANG ENERGY!
AND BECAUSE MY BODY IS ALREADY FULL OF YANG ENERGY, IT'S DIFFICULT FOR ME TO PERFORM THE SHARP MOVEMENTS OF HEAVEN MOUNTAIN SWORD STANCE.
IS THAT SO?! THEN WHY DON'T YOU JUST LEARN SASHINMU?
AH-NG
RESOLUTELY!!
NOT ON YOUR LIFE!!
I CAN'T EVEN IMAGINE HOW A GIRL WOULD LOOK DOING A MONSTROUS MARTIAL ART LIKE SASHINMU!
YOU'RE ALREADY THE POSSESSOR OF MONSTROUS STRENGTH...
IMAGINATION
KYAH! HYUN MU CHUN DOO JI GHI! KYAH!
HMM! IT REALLY IS KINDA HARD TO IMAGINE...
PAH PAH
UUUWWAA! WHAT ARE YOU THINKING!!
UM...

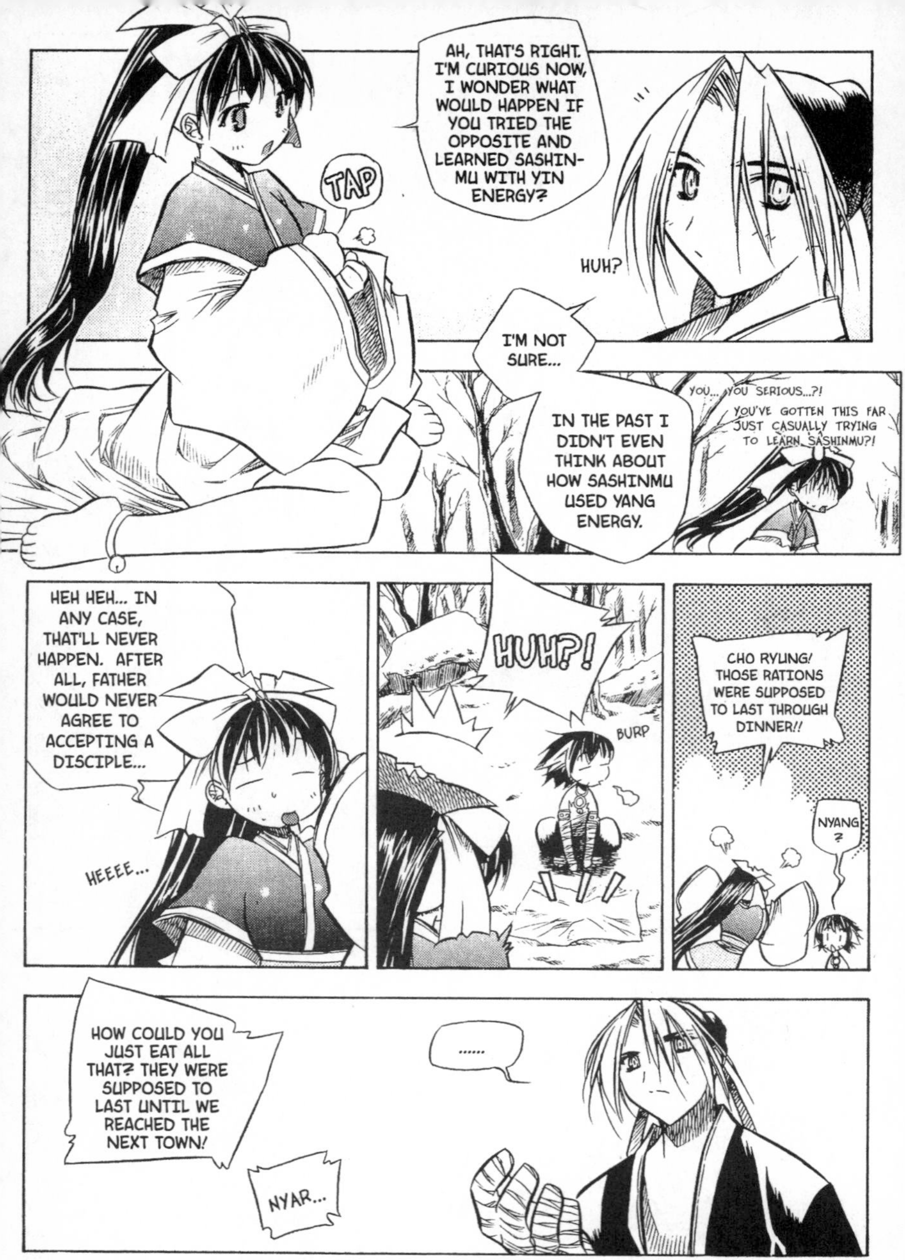
AH, THAT'S RIGHT. I'M CURIOUS NOW, I WONDER WHAT WOULD HAPPEN IF YOU TRIED THE OPPOSITE AND LEARNED SASHIN-MU WITH YIN ENERGY?
TAP
HUH?
I'M NOT SURE...
IN THE PAST I DIDN'T EVEN THINK ABOUT HOW SASHINMU USED YANG ENERGY.
YOU... YOU SERIOUS...?!
YOU'VE GOTTEN THIS FAR JUST CASUALLY TRYING TO LEARN SASHINMU?!
HEH HEH... IN ANY CASE, THAT'LL NEVER HAPPEN. AFTER ALL, FATHER WOULD NEVER AGREE TO ACCEPTING A DISCIPLE...
HEEEE...
HUH?!
BURP
CHO RYUNG! THOSE RATIONS WERE SUPPOSED TO LAST THROUGH DINNER!!
NYANG?
HOW COULD YOU JUST EAT ALL THAT? THEY WERE SUPPOSED TO LAST UNTIL WE REACHED THE NEXT TOWN!
......
NYAR...

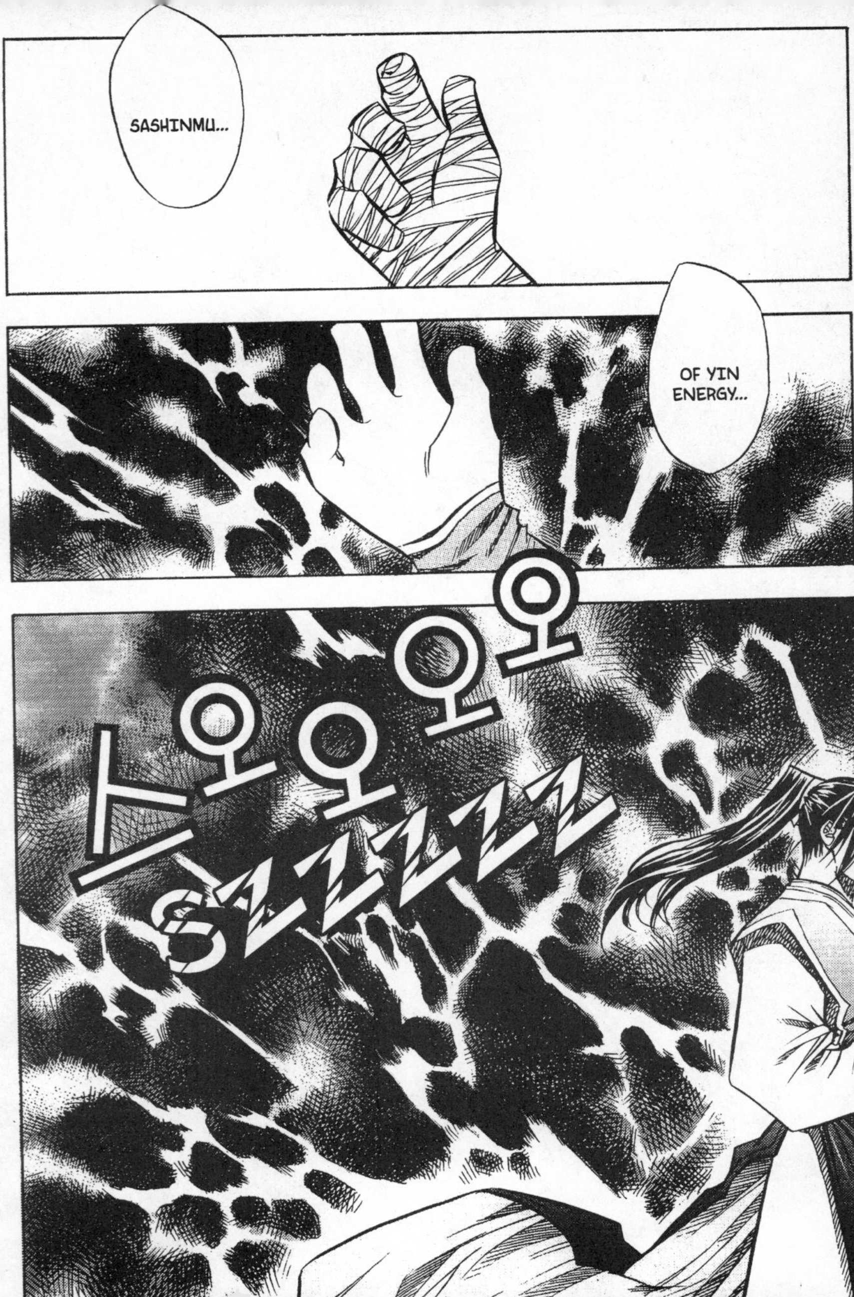
SASHINMU...
OF YIN ENERGY...
VOOOOM
SZZZZZ

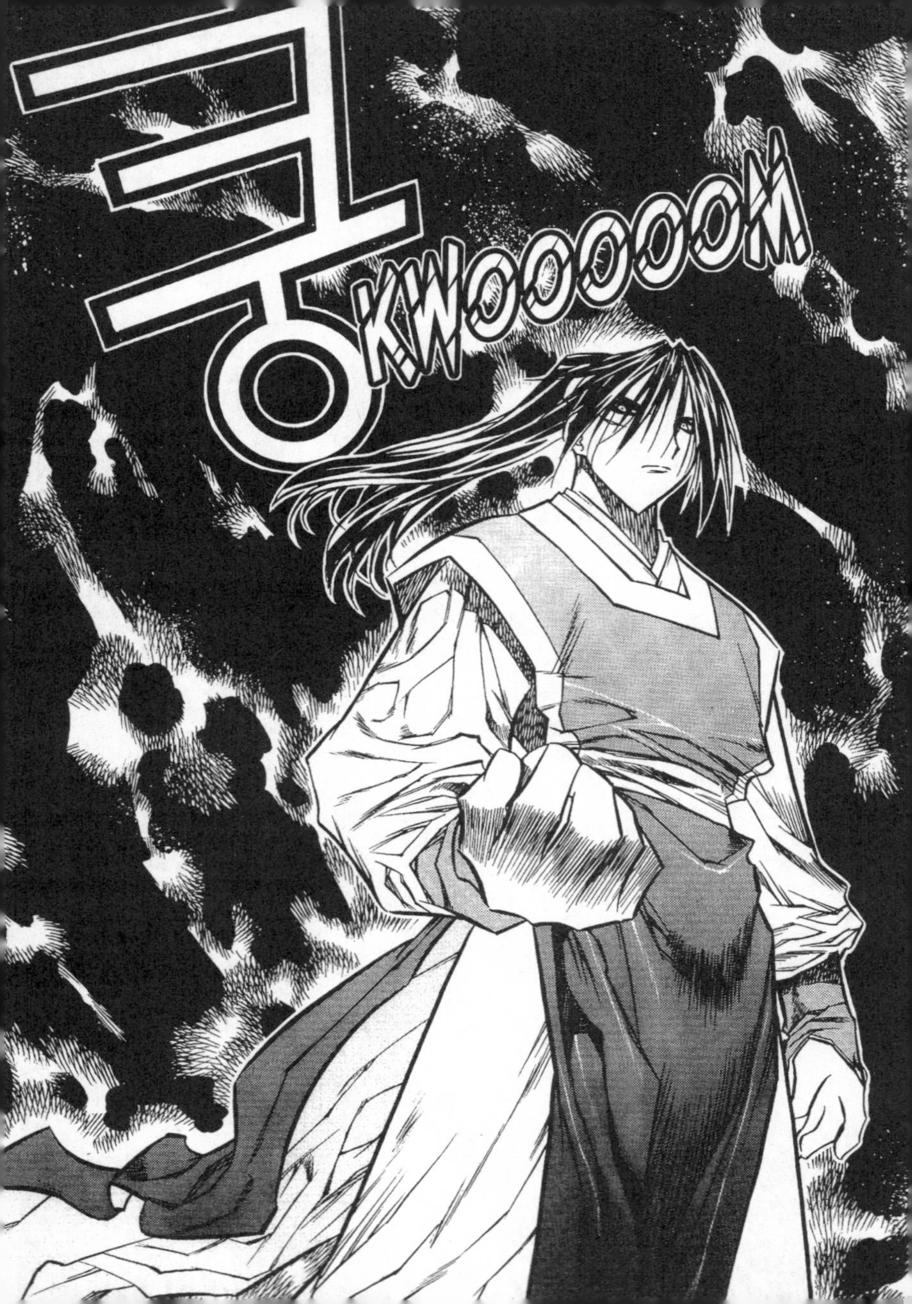
쿠
KWOOOOOOM

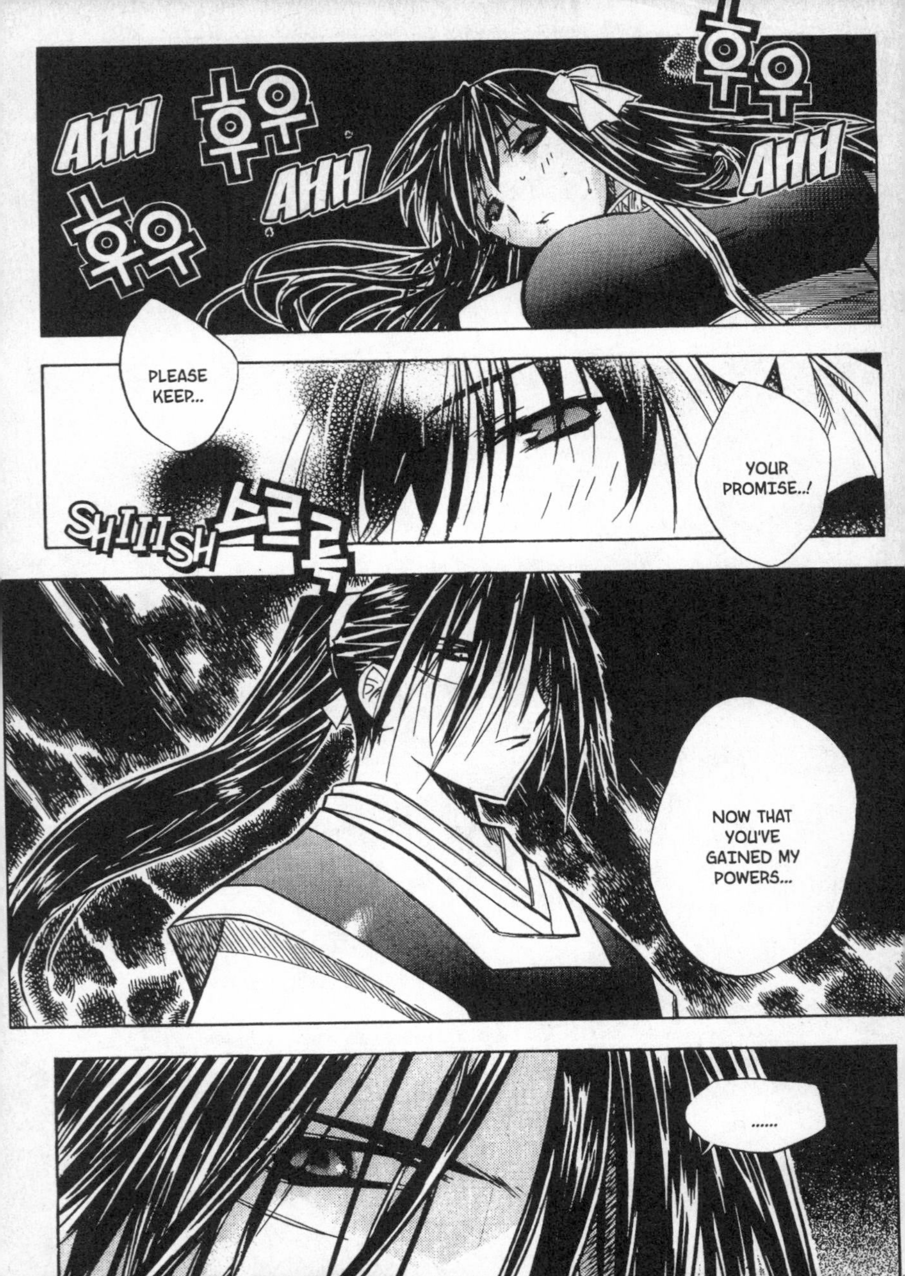
AHH 후우
후우
AHH
후우
AHH
PLEASE KEEP...
YOUR PROMISE..!
SHIIISH 스르륵
NOW THAT YOU'VE GAINED MY POWERS...
......

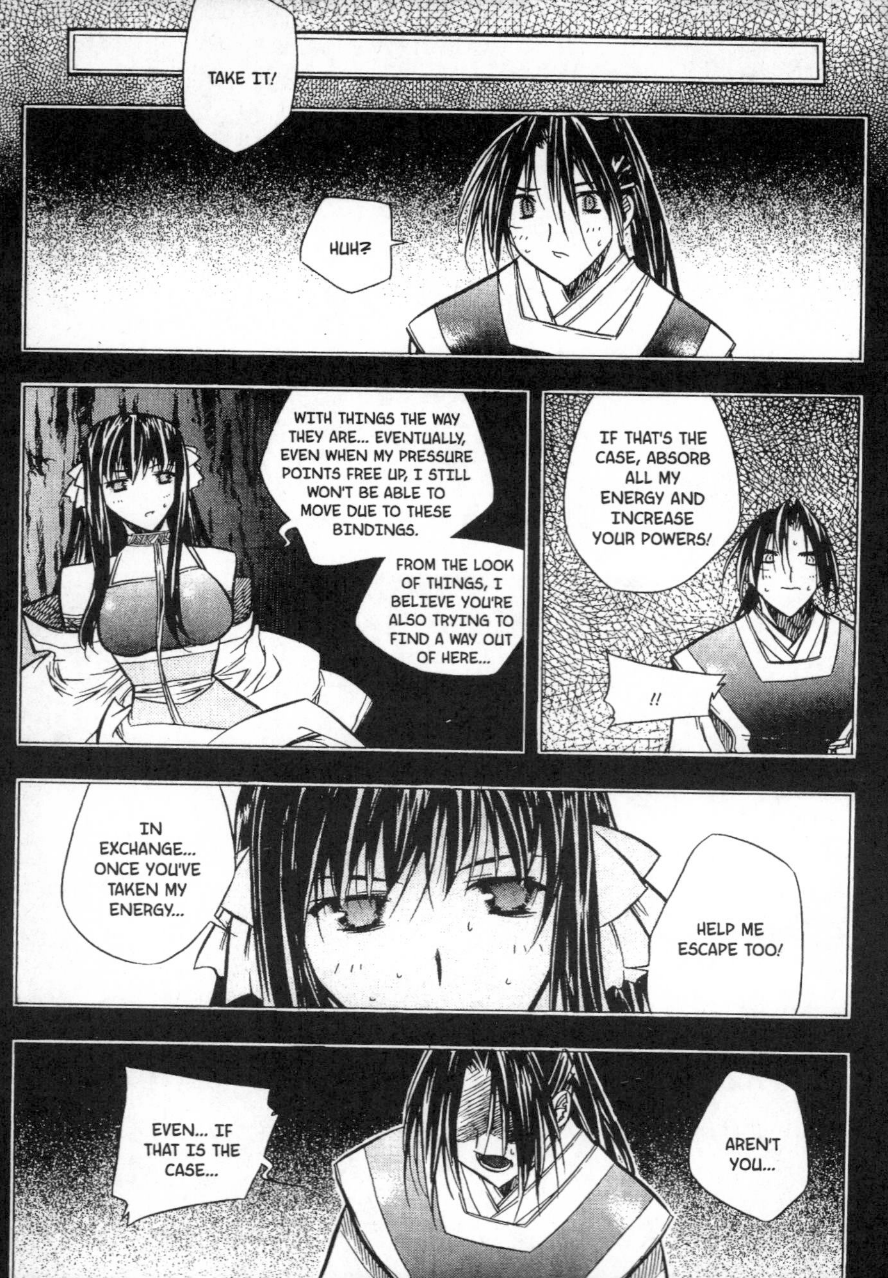
TAKE IT!
HUH?
WITH THINGS THE WAY THEY ARE... EVENTUALLY, EVEN WHEN MY PRESSURE POINTS FREE UP, I STILL WON'T BE ABLE TO MOVE DUE TO THESE BINDINGS.
FROM THE LOOK OF THINGS, I BELIEVE YOU'RE ALSO TRYING TO FIND A WAY OUT OF HERE...
IF THAT'S THE CASE, ABSORB ALL MY ENERGY AND INCREASE YOUR POWERS!
!!
IN EXCHANGE... ONCE YOU'VE TAKEN MY ENERGY...
HELP ME ESCAPE TOO!
EVEN... IF THAT IS THE CASE...
AREN'T YOU...

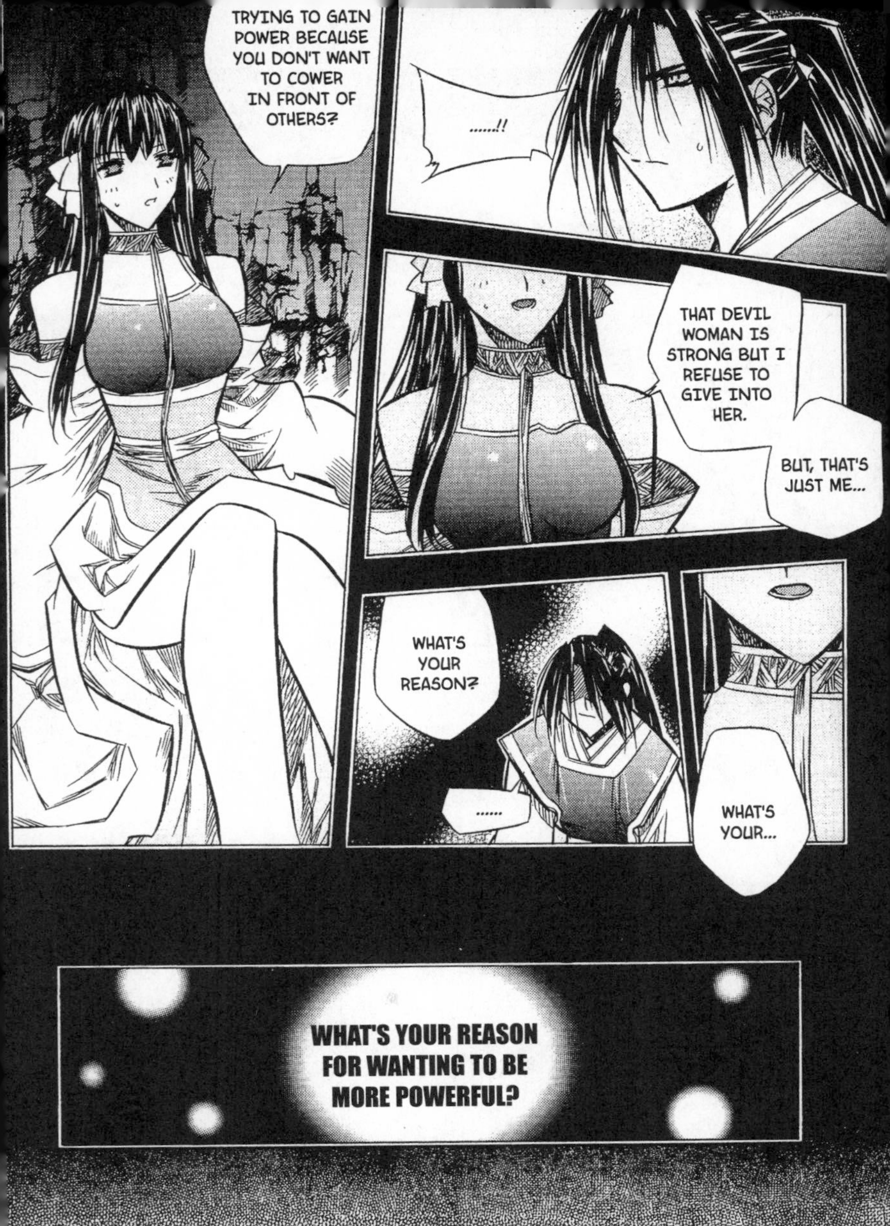
TRYING TO GAIN POWER BECAUSE YOU DON'T WANT TO COWER IN FRONT OF OTHERS?
......!!
THAT DEVIL WOMAN IS STRONG BUT I REFUSE TO GIVE INTO HER.
BUT, THAT'S JUST ME...
WHAT'S YOUR REASON?
......
WHAT'S YOUR...
WHAT'S YOUR REASON FOR WANTING TO BE MORE POWERFUL?

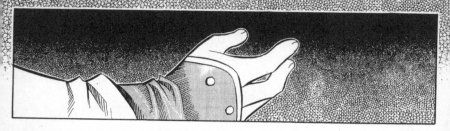

THE ONLY THING THAT CAN CHANGE THIS WORLD...

...IS POWER!

......!!

CLENCH

MY REASON FOR WANTING TO BECOME STRONG...

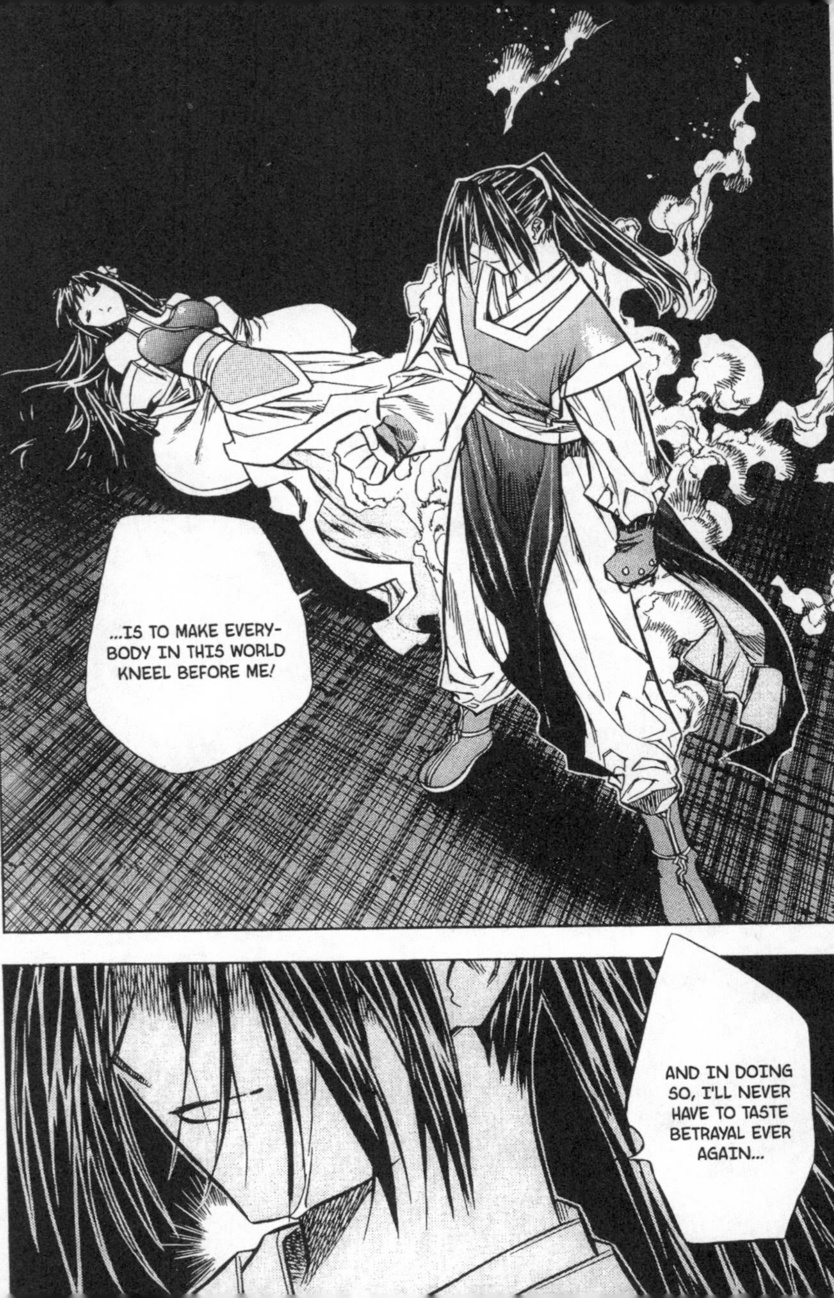
...IS TO MAKE EVERY-BODY IN THIS WORLD KNEEL BEFORE ME!
AND IN DOING SO, I'LL NEVER HAVE TO TASTE BETRAYAL EVER AGAIN...

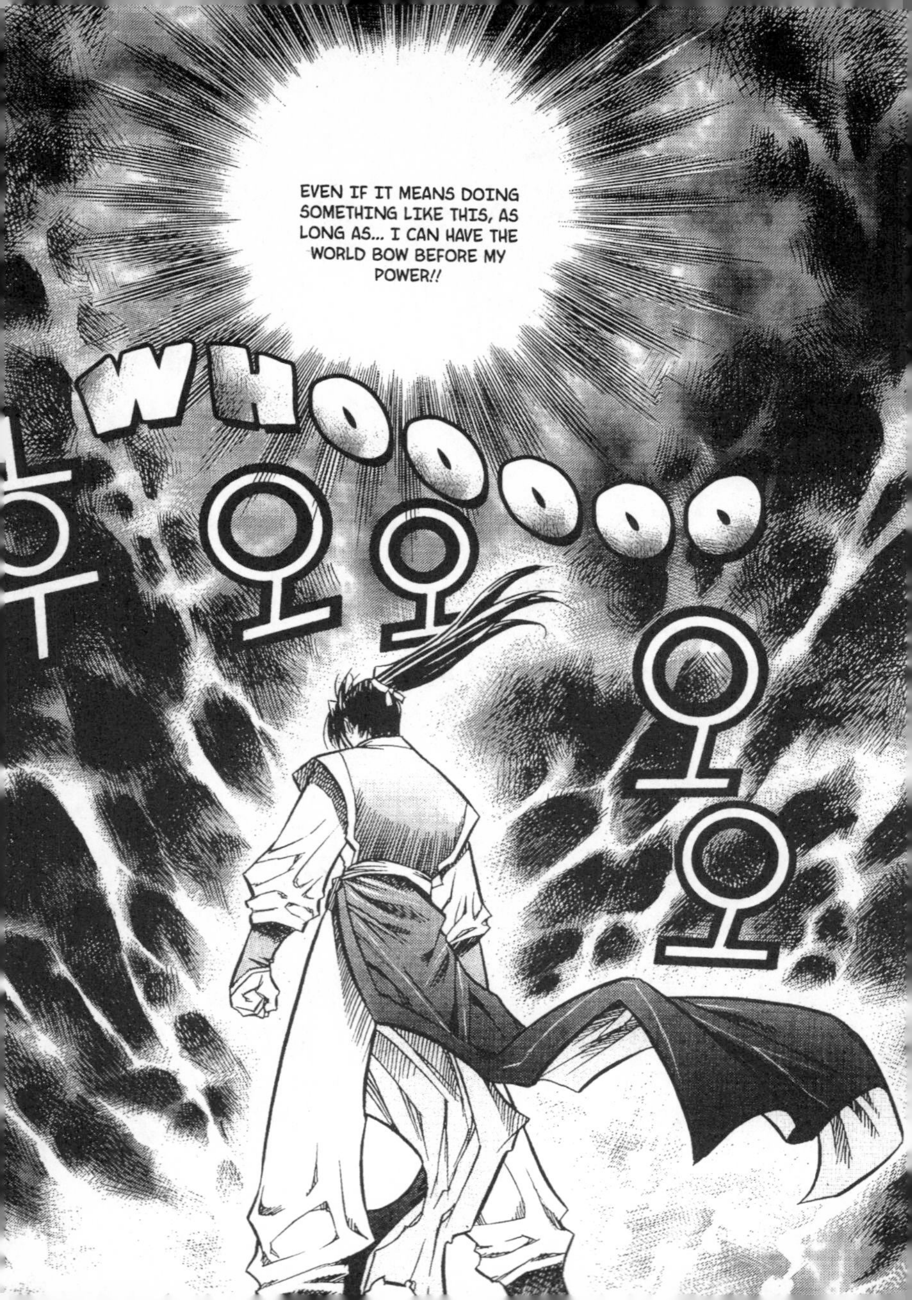
EVEN IF IT MEANS DOING SOMETHING LIKE THIS, AS LONG AS... I CAN HAVE THE WORLD BOW BEFORE MY POWER!!
WHOOOOOOO

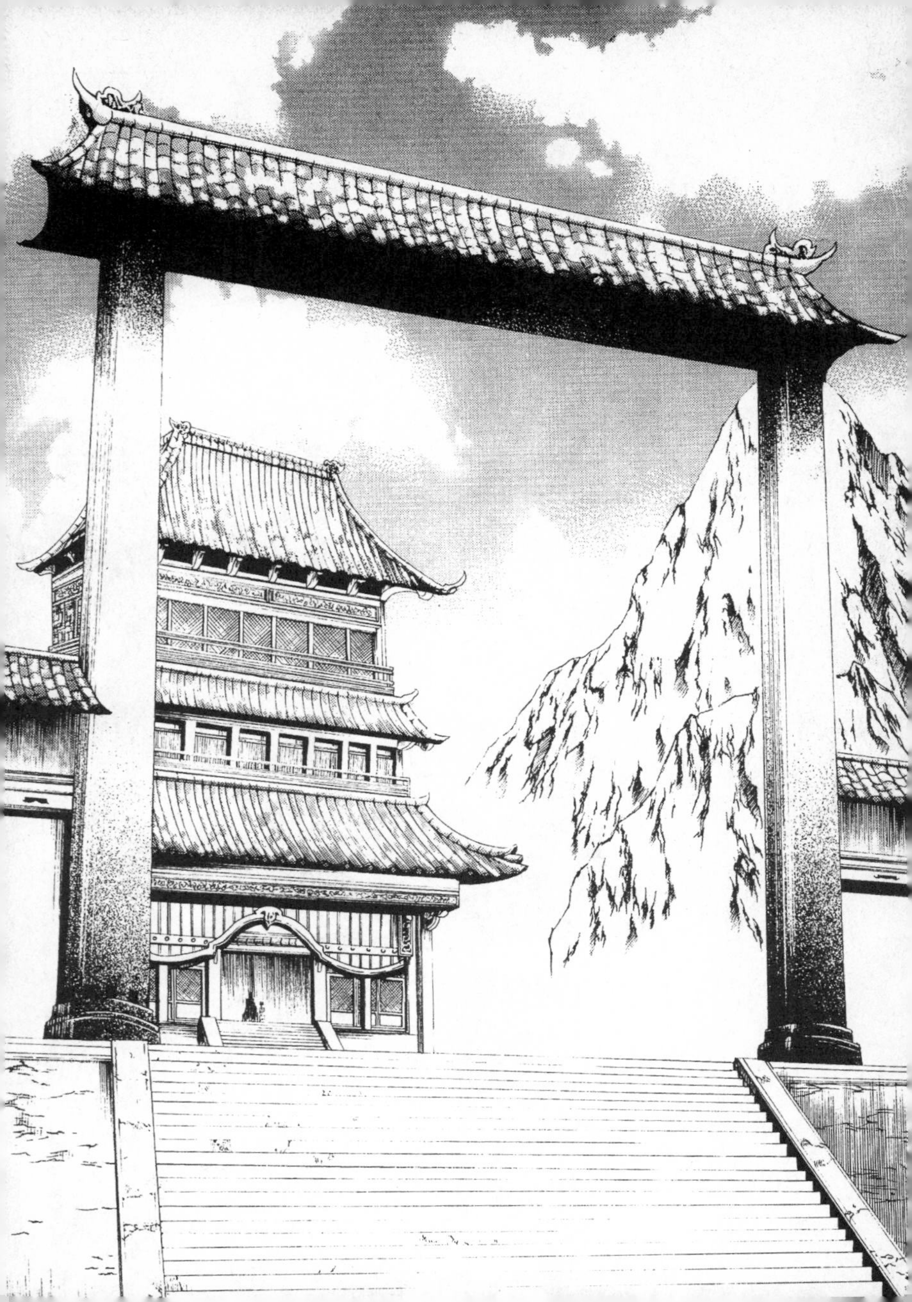

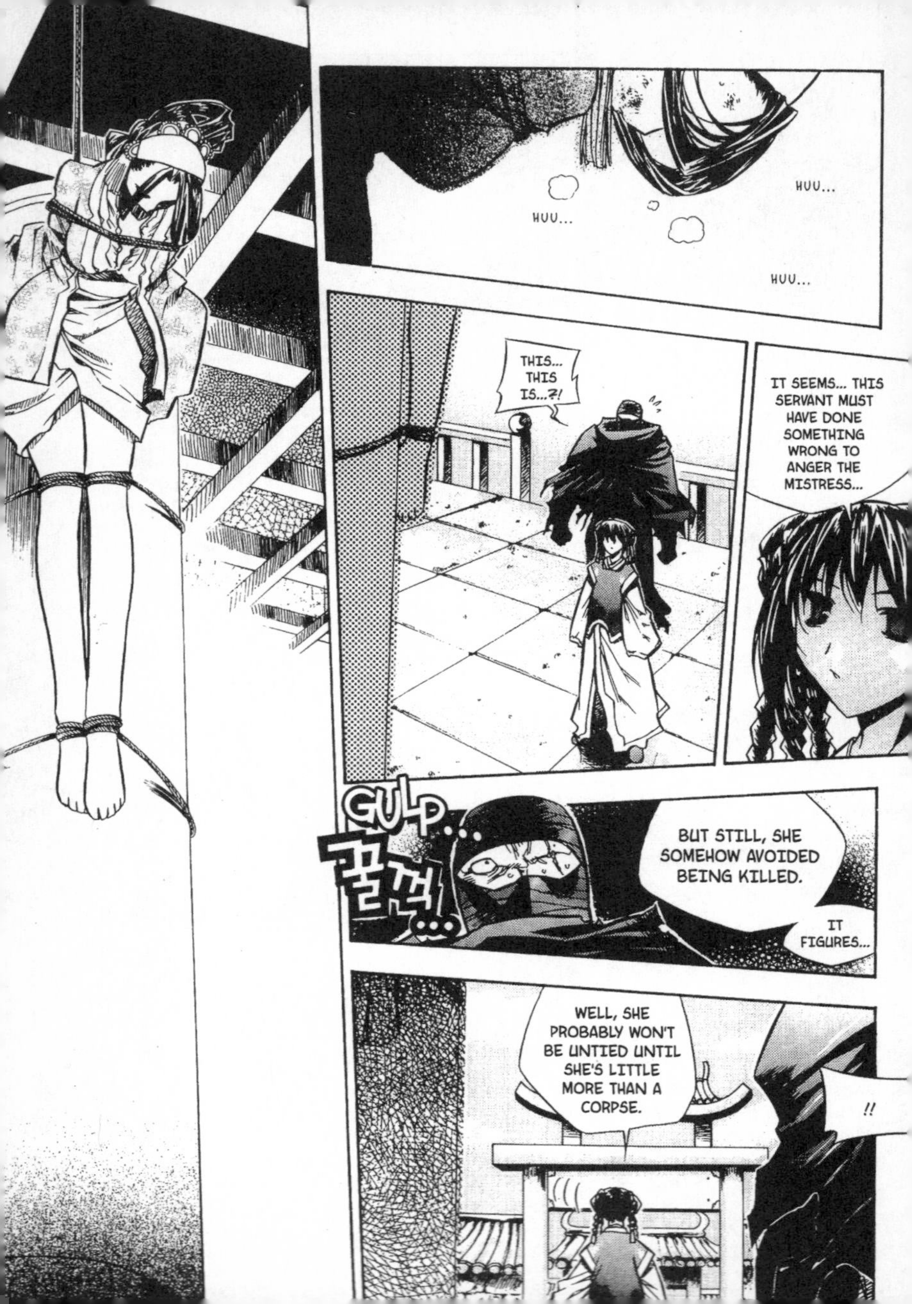
HUU...
HUU...
HUU...
THIS... THIS IS...?!
IT SEEMS... THIS SERVANT MUST HAVE DONE SOMETHING WRONG TO ANGER THE MISTRESS...
GULP...
꿀꺽...
BUT STILL, SHE SOMEHOW AVOIDED BEING KILLED.
IT FIGURES...
WELL, SHE PROBABLY WON'T BE UNTIED UNTIL SHE'S LITTLE MORE THAN A CORPSE.
!!

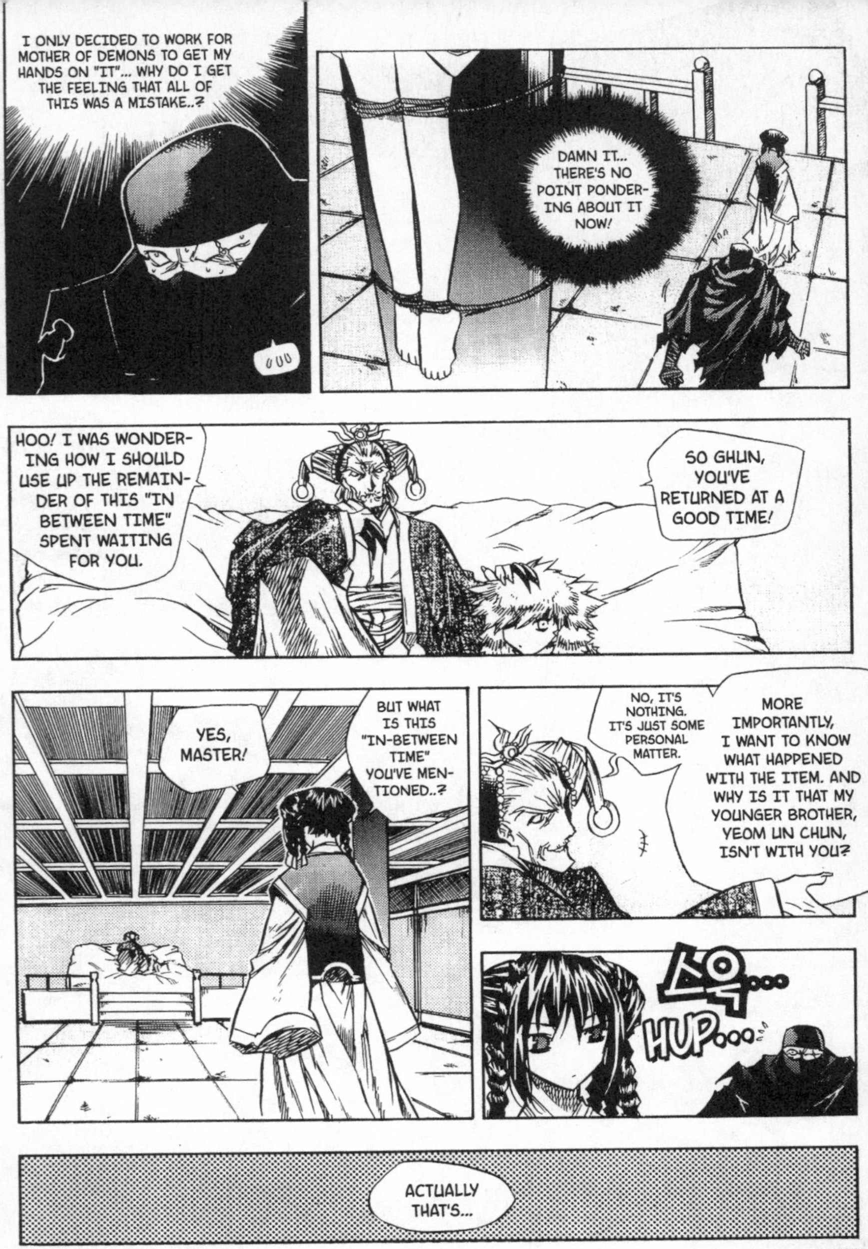

I ONLY DECIDED TO WORK FOR MOTHER OF DEMONS TO GET MY HANDS ON "IT"... WHY DO I GET THE FEELING THAT ALL OF THIS WAS A MISTAKE..?
DAMN IT... THERE'S NO POINT PONDERING ABOUT IT NOW!
HOO! I WAS WONDERING HOW I SHOULD USE UP THE REMAINDER OF THIS "IN BETWEEN TIME" SPENT WAITING FOR YOU.
SO GHUN, YOU'VE RETURNED AT A GOOD TIME!
YES, MASTER!
BUT WHAT IS THIS "IN-BETWEEN TIME" YOU'VE MENTIONED..?
NO, IT'S NOTHING. IT'S JUST SOME PERSONAL MATTER.
MORE IMPORTANTLY, I WANT TO KNOW WHAT HAPPENED WITH THE ITEM. AND WHY IS IT THAT MY YOUNGER BROTHER, YEOM UN CHUN, ISN'T WITH YOU?
HUP...
ACTUALLY THAT'S...

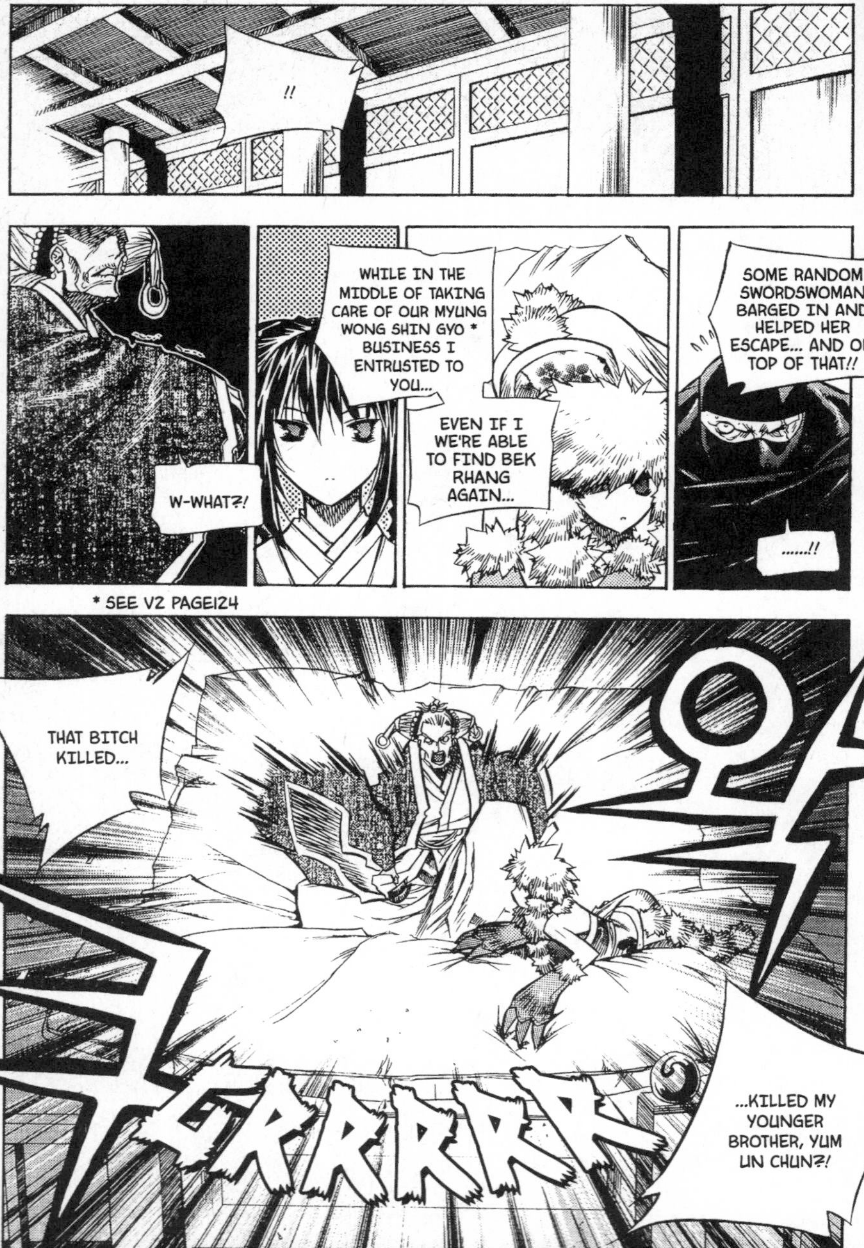
!!
W-WHAT?!
WHILE IN THE MIDDLE OF TAKING CARE OF OUR MYUNG WONG SHIN GYO * BUSINESS I ENTRUSTED TO YOU...
EVEN IF I WE'RE ABLE TO FIND BEK RHANG AGAIN...
SOME RANDOM SWORDSWOMAN BARGED IN AND HELPED HER ESCAPE... AND ON TOP OF THAT!!
......!!
* SEE V2 PAGE124
THAT BITCH KILLED...
CRRRR
...KILLED MY YOUNGER BROTHER, YUM UN CHUN?!

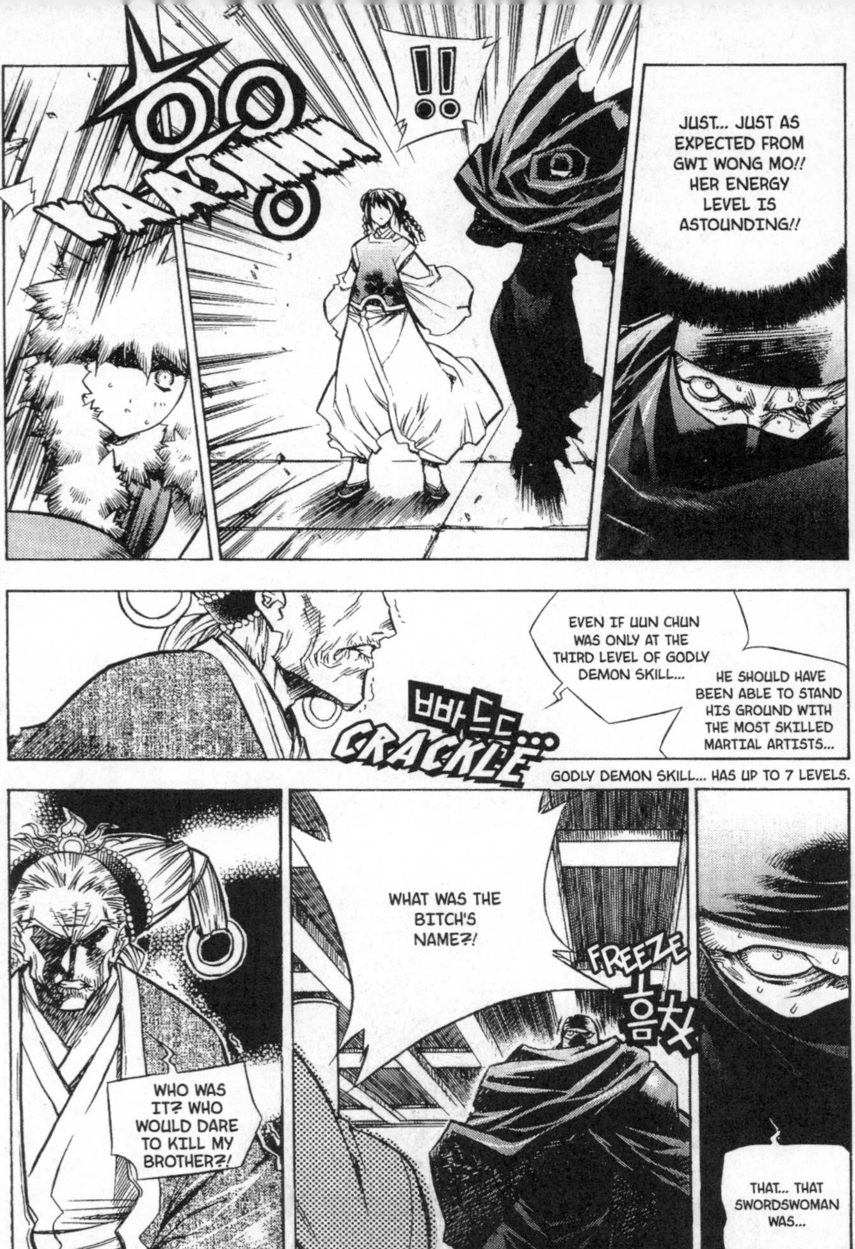
!!
JUST... JUST AS EXPECTED FROM GWI WONG MO!! HER ENERGY LEVEL IS ASTOUNDING!!
EVEN IF UUN CHUN WAS ONLY AT THE THIRD LEVEL OF GODLY DEMON SKILL...
HE SHOULD HAVE BEEN ABLE TO STAND HIS GROUND WITH THE MOST SKILLED MARTIAL ARTISTS...
CRACKLE...
GODLY DEMON SKILL... HAS UP TO 7 LEVELS.
WHO WAS IT? WHO WOULD DARE TO KILL MY BROTHER?!
WHAT WAS THE BITCH'S NAME?!
FREEZE
THAT... THAT SWORDSWOMAN WAS...

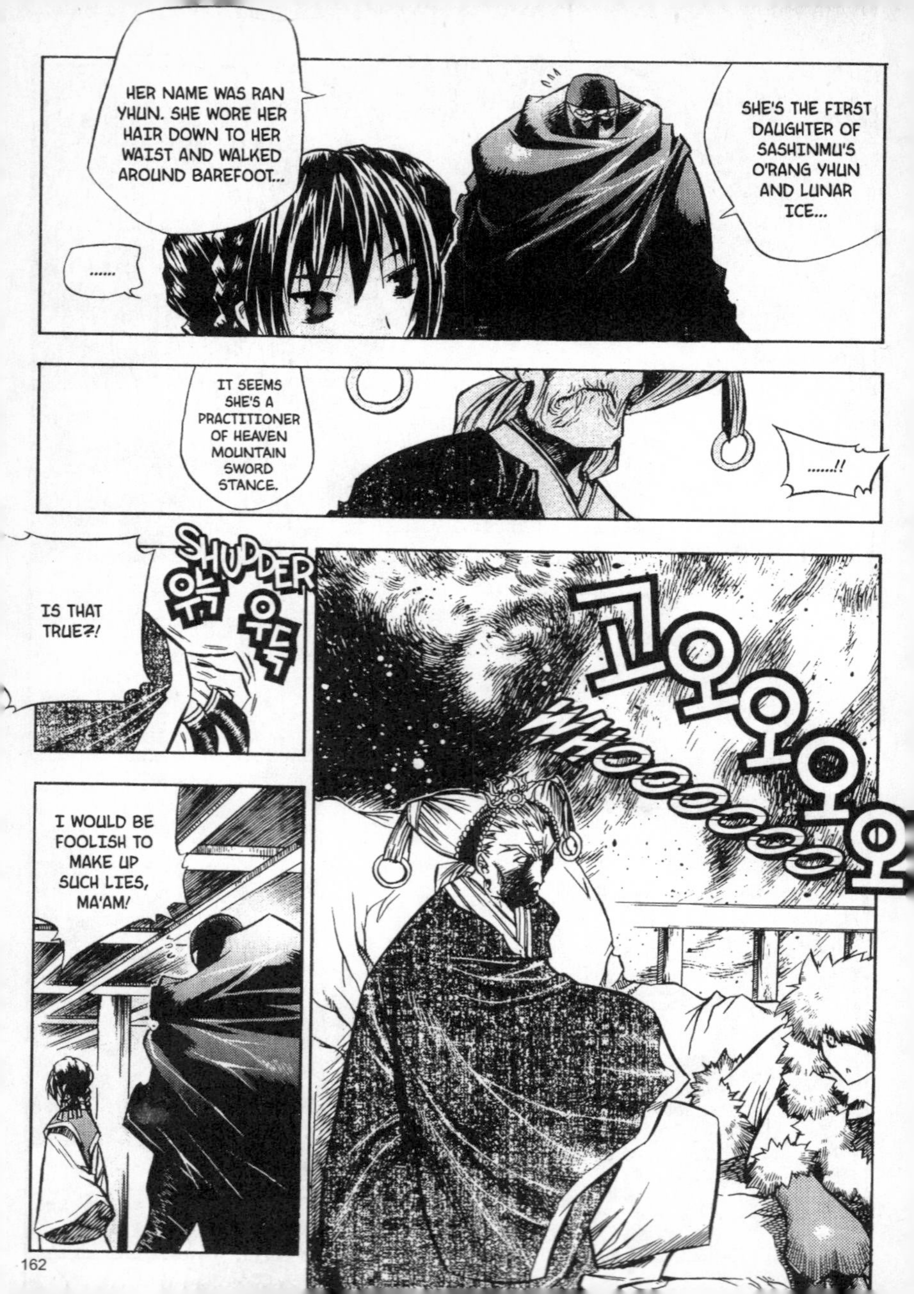
HER NAME WAS RAN YHUN. SHE WORE HER HAIR DOWN TO HER WAIST AND WALKED AROUND BAREFOOT...
SHE'S THE FIRST DAUGHTER OF SASHINMU'S O'RANG YHUN AND LUNAR ICE...
......
IT SEEMS SHE'S A PRACTITIONER OF HEAVEN MOUNTAIN SWORD STANCE.
......!!
SHUDDER
IS THAT TRUE?!
고오오오오
WHOOOOOOOOO
I WOULD BE FOOLISH TO MAKE UP SUCH LIES, MA'AM!

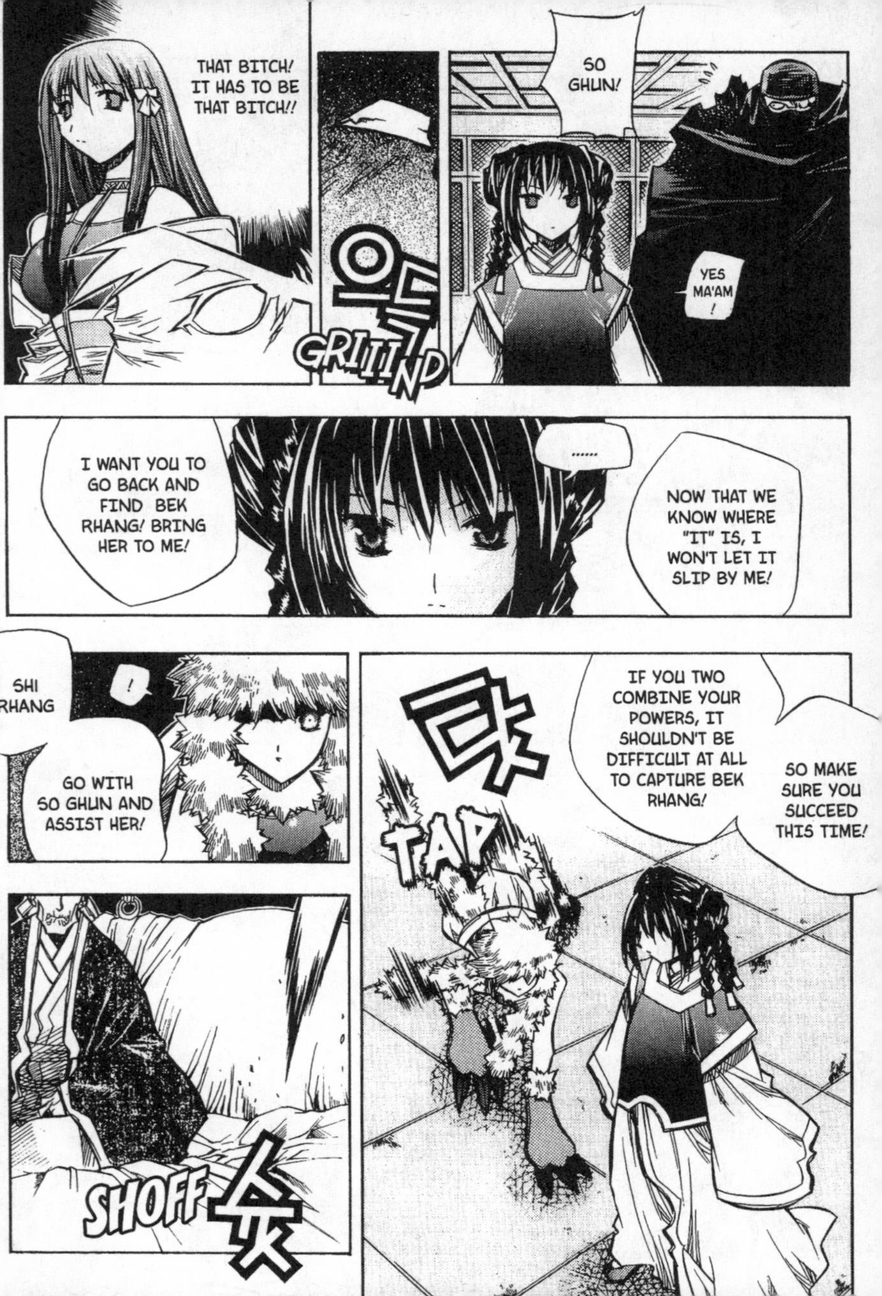
THAT BITCH! IT HAS TO BE THAT BITCH!!
GRIIIND
SO GHUN!
YES MA'AM!
I WANT YOU TO GO BACK AND FIND BEK RHANG! BRING HER TO ME!
......
NOW THAT WE KNOW WHERE "IT" IS, I WON'T LET IT SLIP BY ME!
SHI RHANG
!
GO WITH SO GHUN AND ASSIST HER!
IF YOU TWO COMBINE YOUR POWERS, IT SHOULDN'T BE DIFFICULT AT ALL TO CAPTURE BEK RHANG!
SO MAKE SURE YOU SUCCEED THIS TIME!
TAP
SHOFF

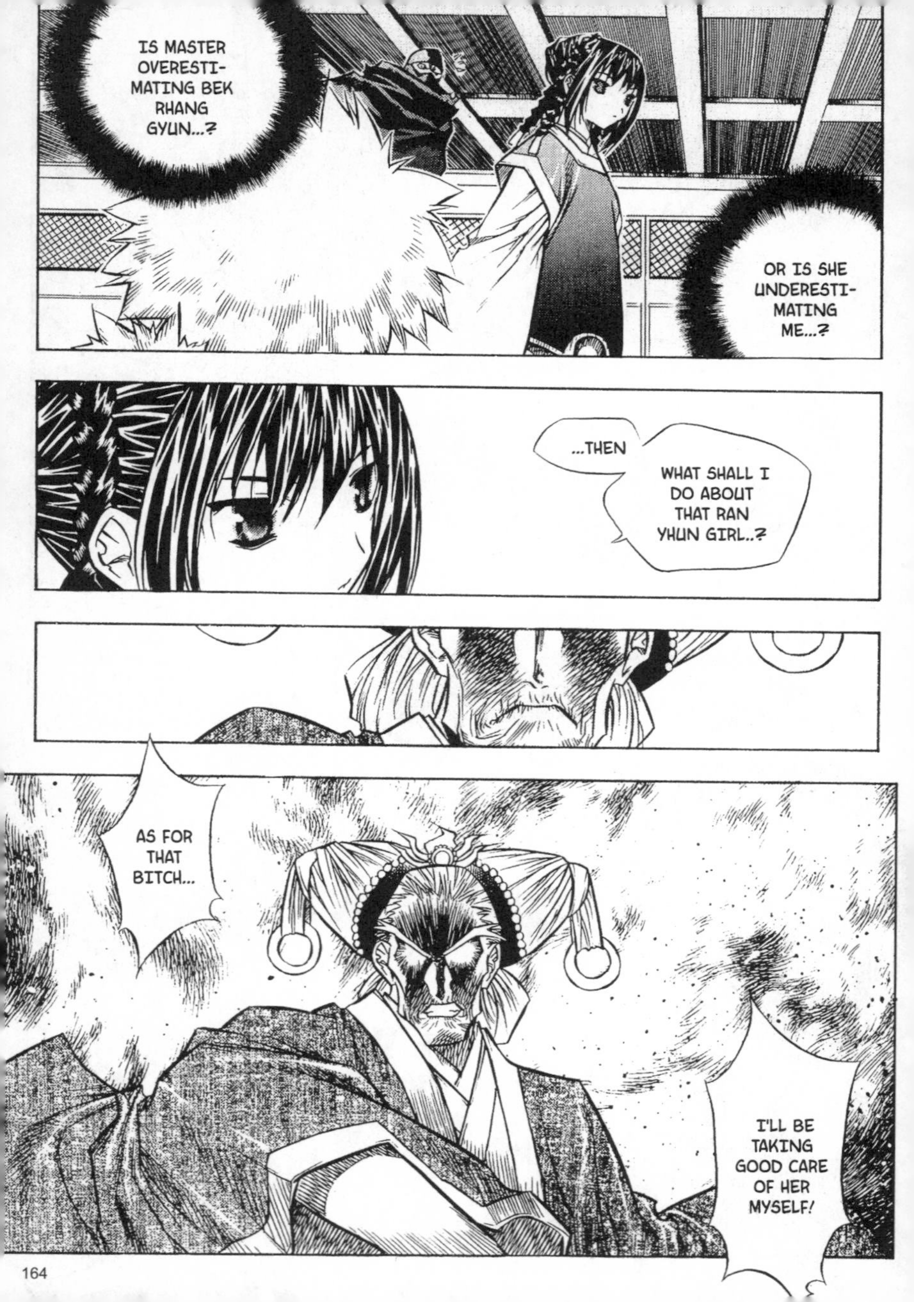
IS MASTER OVERESTI-MATING BEK RHANG GYUN...?
OR IS SHE UNDERESTI-MATING ME...?
...THEN
WHAT SHALL I DO ABOUT THAT RAN YHUN GIRL..?
AS FOR THAT BITCH...
I'LL BE TAKING GOOD CARE OF HER MYSELF!

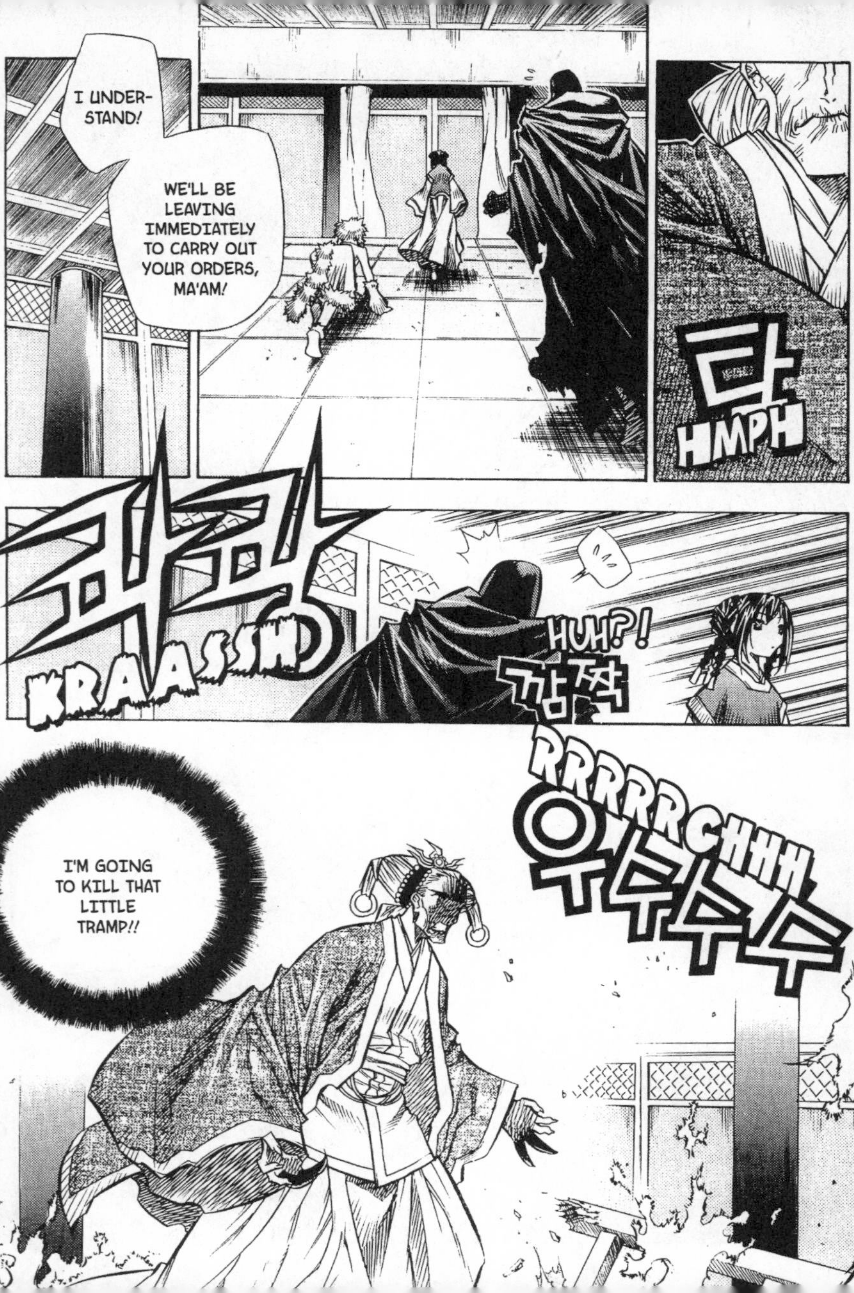
I UNDER-STAND!
WE'LL BE LEAVING IMMEDIATELY TO CARRY OUT YOUR ORDERS, MA'AM!
탁
HMPH
콰직
KRAASSH
HUH?!
깜짝
RRRRRRCHHH
우두두두
I'M GOING TO KILL THAT LITTLE TRAMP!!

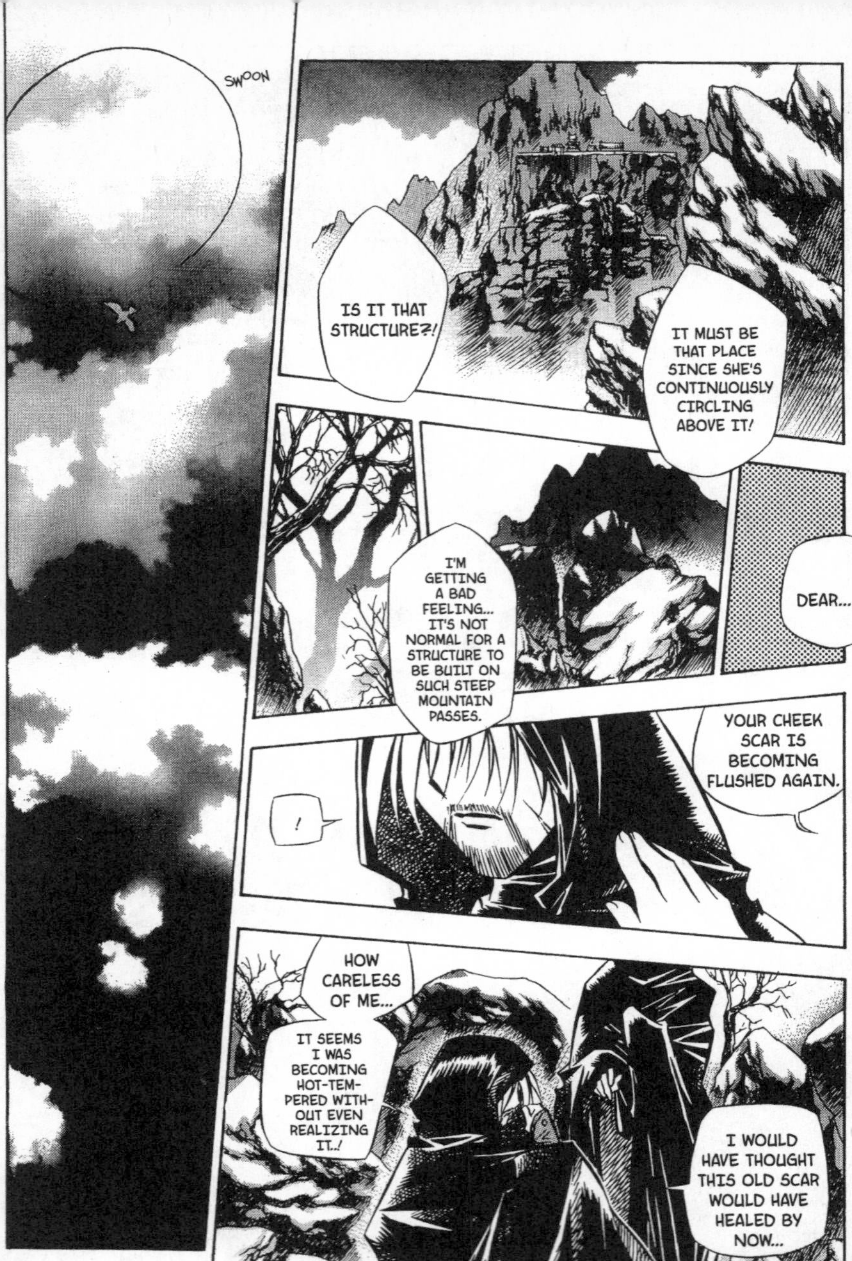
SWOON
IT MUST BE THAT PLACE SINCE SHE'S CONTINUOUSLY CIRCLING ABOVE IT!
IS IT THAT STRUCTURE?!
DEAR...
I'M GETTING A BAD FEELING... IT'S NOT NORMAL FOR A STRUCTURE TO BE BUILT ON SUCH STEEP MOUNTAIN PASSES.
YOUR CHEEK SCAR IS BECOMING FLUSHED AGAIN.
!
I WOULD HAVE THOUGHT THIS OLD SCAR WOULD HAVE HEALED BY NOW...
HOW CARELESS OF ME...
IT SEEMS I WAS BECOMING HOT-TEMPERED WITHOUT EVEN REALIZING IT..!

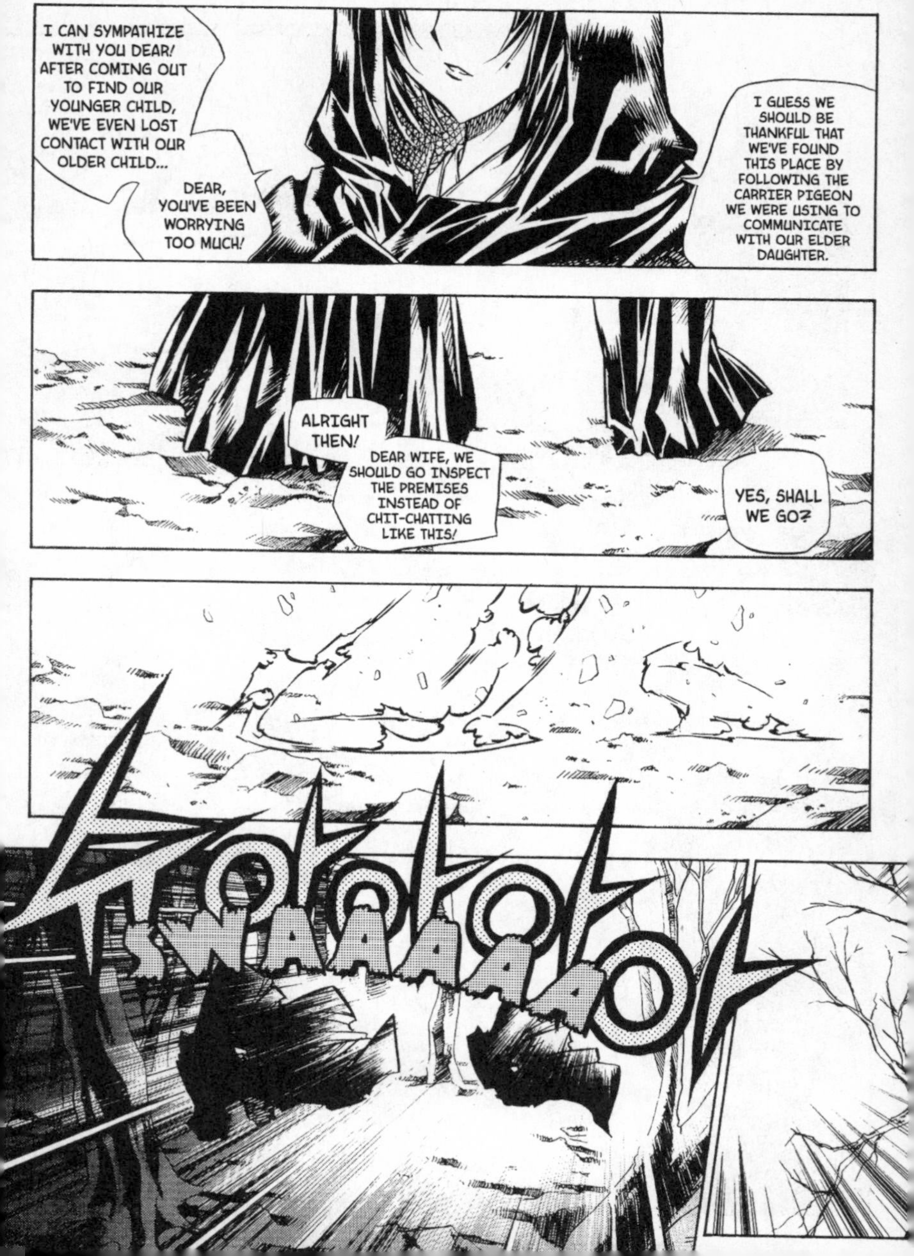
I CAN SYMPATHIZE WITH YOU DEAR! AFTER COMING OUT TO FIND OUR YOUNGER CHILD, WE'VE EVEN LOST CONTACT WITH OUR OLDER CHILD...
DEAR, YOU'VE BEEN WORRYING TOO MUCH!
I GUESS WE SHOULD BE THANKFUL THAT WE'VE FOUND THIS PLACE BY FOLLOWING THE CARRIER PIGEON WE WERE USING TO COMMUNICATE WITH OUR ELDER DAUGHTER.
ALRIGHT THEN!
DEAR WIFE, WE SHOULD GO INSPECT THE PREMISES INSTEAD OF CHIT-CHATTING LIKE THIS!
YES, SHALL WE GO?
SWAAAAAO

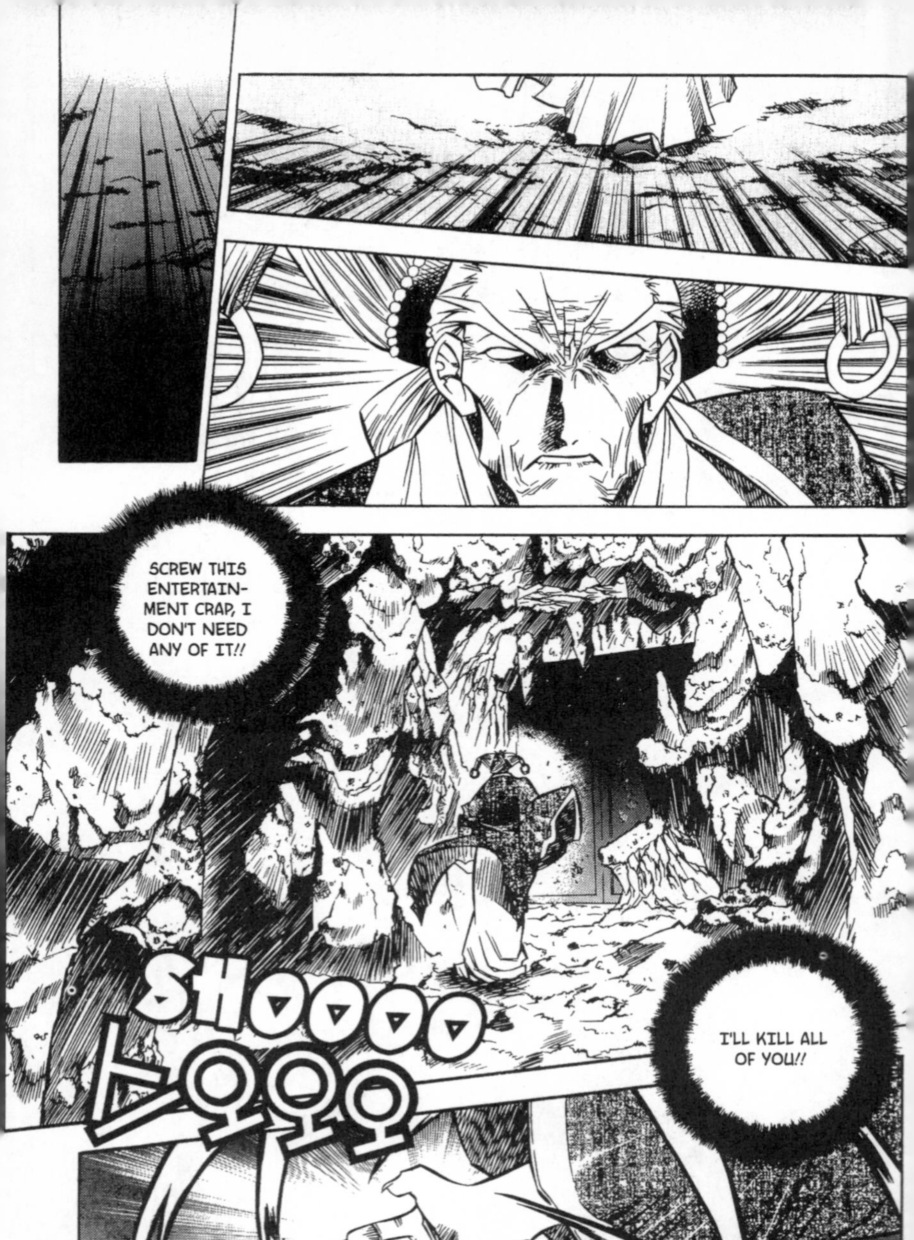
SCREW THIS ENTERTAINMENT CRAP, I DON'T NEED ANY OF IT!!
SHOOOOOOOOO
I'LL KILL ALL OF YOU!!

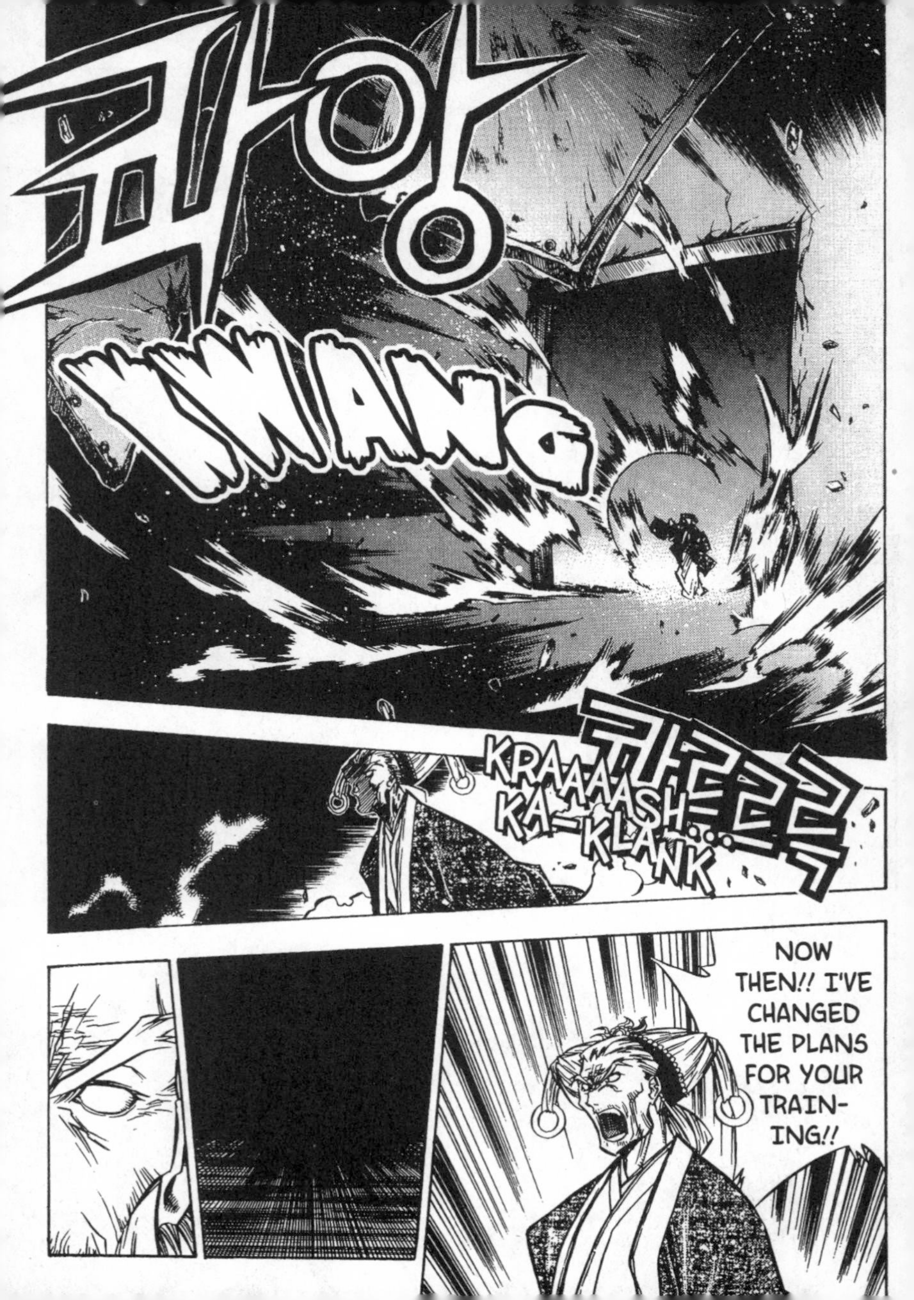
WWANG
KRAAAAASH...
KA-KLANK
NOW THEN!! I'VE CHANGED THE PLANS FOR YOUR TRAIN-ING!!

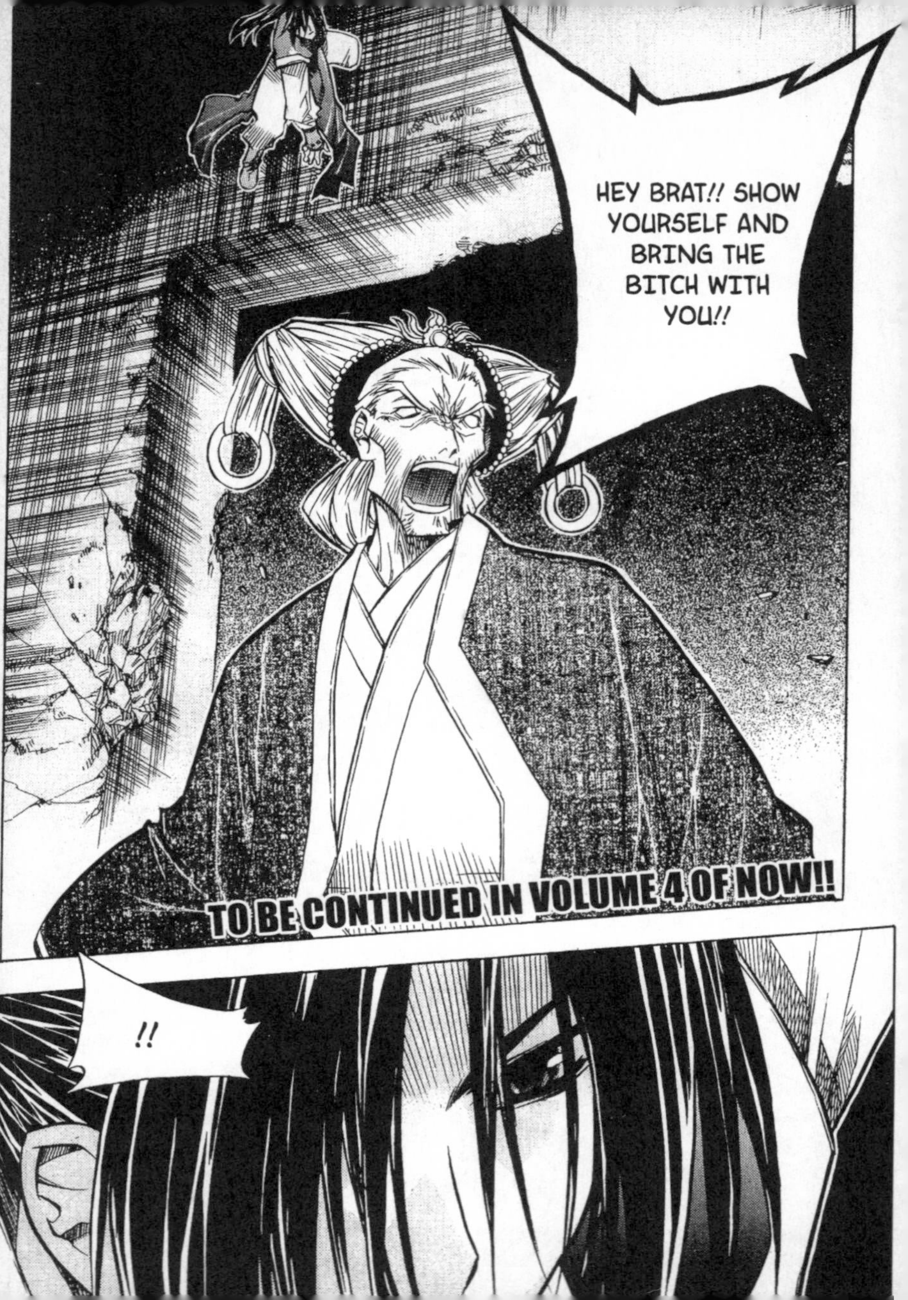
HEY BRAT!! SHOW YOURSELF AND BRING THE BITCH WITH YOU!!
TO BE CONTINUED IN VOLUME 4 OF NOW!!
!!

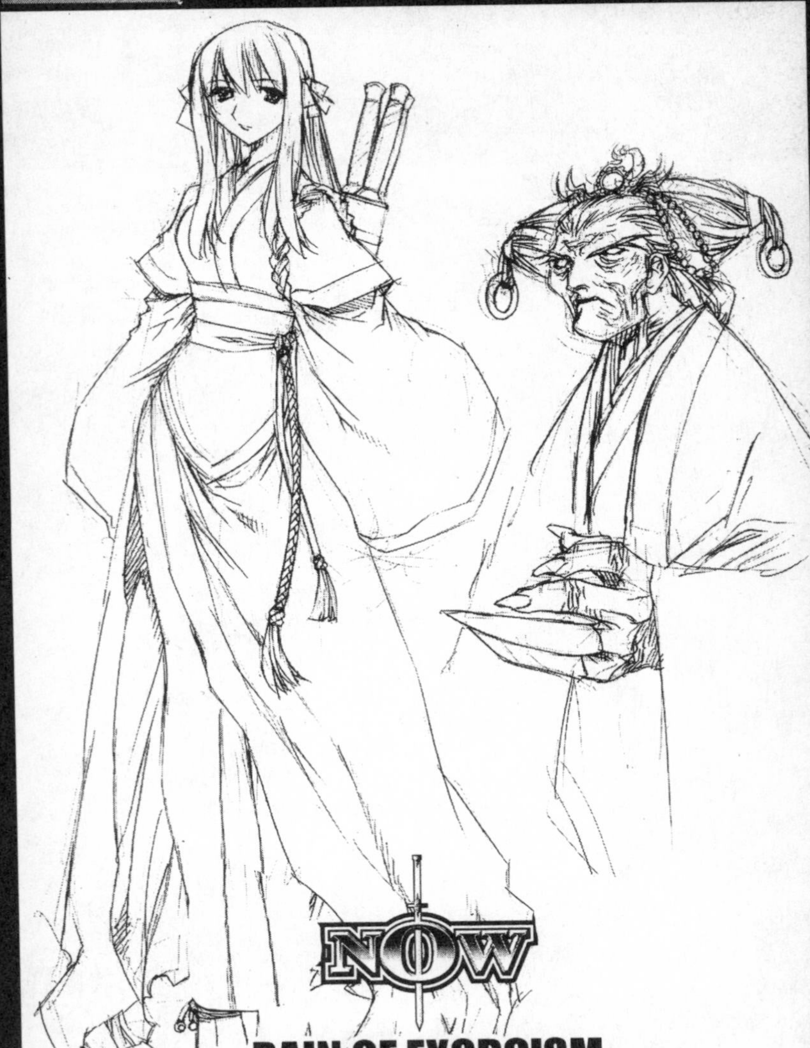
NOW

RAIN OF EXORCISM CHARACTER INTRODUCTION

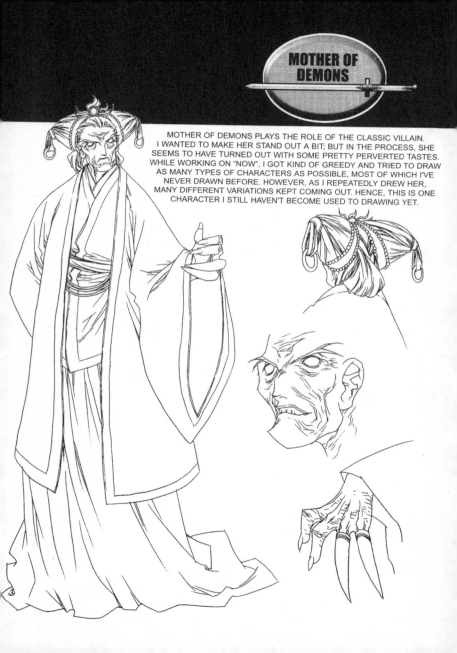

MOTHER OF DEMONS

MOTHER OF DEMONS PLAYS THE ROLE OF THE CLASSIC VILLAIN. I WANTED TO MAKE HER STAND OUT A BIT; BUT IN THE PROCESS, SHE SEEMS TO HAVE TURNED OUT WITH SOME PRETTY PERVERTED TASTES. WHILE WORKING ON "NOW", I GOT KIND OF GREEDY AND TRIED TO DRAW AS MANY TYPES OF CHARACTERS AS POSSIBLE, MOST OF WHICH I'VE NEVER DRAWN BEFORE. HOWEVER, AS I REPEATEDLY DREW HER, MANY DIFFERENT VARIATIONS KEPT COMING OUT. HENCE, THIS IS ONE CHARACTER I STILL HAVEN'T BECOME USED TO DRAWING YET.

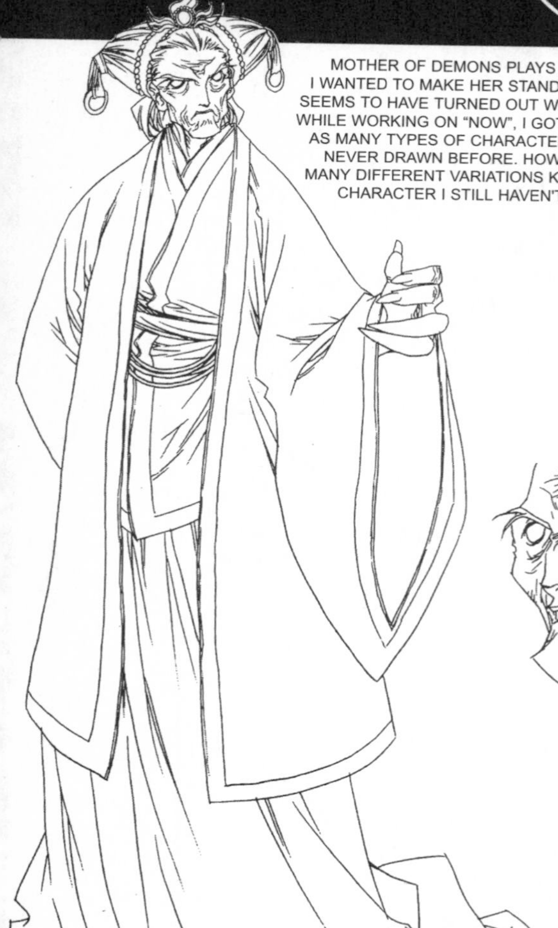

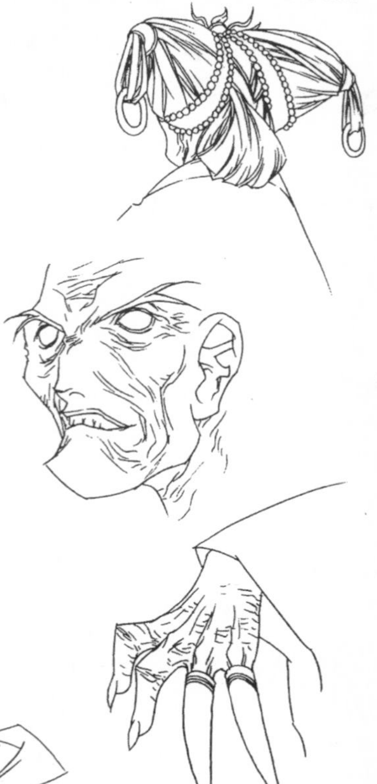

SHI RHANG

AFTER MOTHER OF DEMONS LOST HER PRIZED BEK RHANG, SHI RHANG WAS TRAINED AND RAISED AS HER REPLACEMENT. WHILE SHE NORMALLY FOLLOWS MOTHER OF DEMONS EVERYWHERE SHE GOES,SHE LEAVES WITH SO GHUN TO BRING BACK BEK RHANG (CHO RYUNG) UNDER MOTHER OF DEMONS' ORDERS.

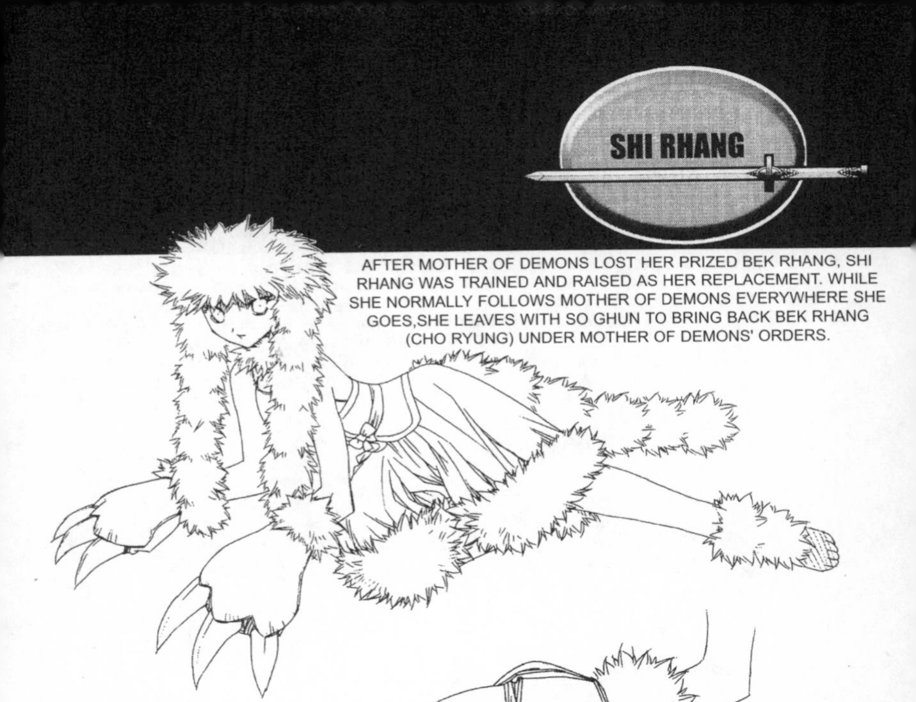

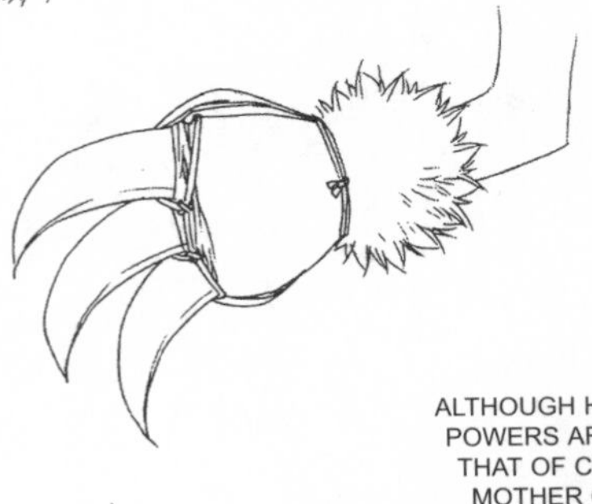

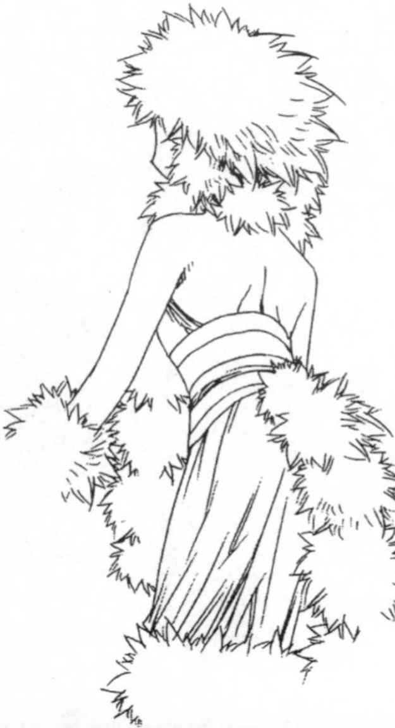

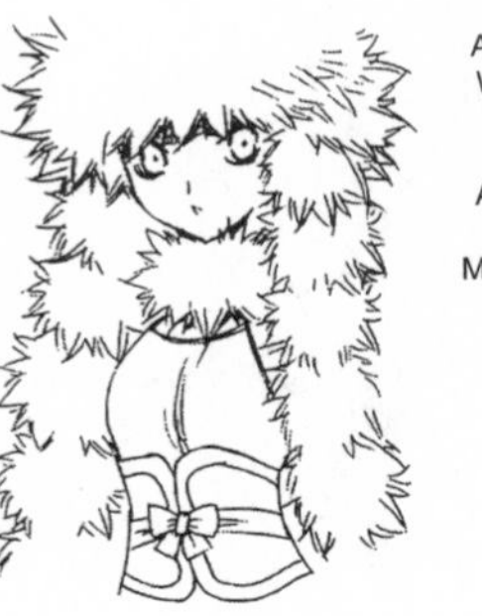

ALTHOUGH HER PRINCIPLE POWERS ARE LESS THAN THAT OF CHO RYUNG'S, MOTHER OF DEMONS ARMS HER WITH A RAKE WEAPON TO LEVEL THE PLAYING FIELD. THESE CLAWS GIVE HER AN ADVANTAGE IN COMBAT.

MY INSPIRATION FOR HER DESIGN WAS... A POODLE...HEHE!!

HEAVENLY SILK

AS IT WAS ALREADY EXPLAINED IN THE STORY, THE HEAVENLY SILK (CHUN JHAM SA) IS AN ACCESSORY THAT PREVENTS THE APPLICATION OF ENERGY AGAINST IT PHYSICALLY. AS YOU MIGHT ALREADY KNOW FROM THE WORD "JHAM (SILK)," "CHUN JHAM (HEAVENLY SILK)" IN THE STORY IS A PRODUCT OF SILK-WORMS. OF COURSE NO SUCH ITEM REALLY EXISTS. ON OUR HOME PAGE, WHICH WE RECENTLY CREATED, WE REVEALED THAT NOW WOULD BE A FANTASY TYPE STORY THAT INCLUDED ITEMS SUCH AS THIS.

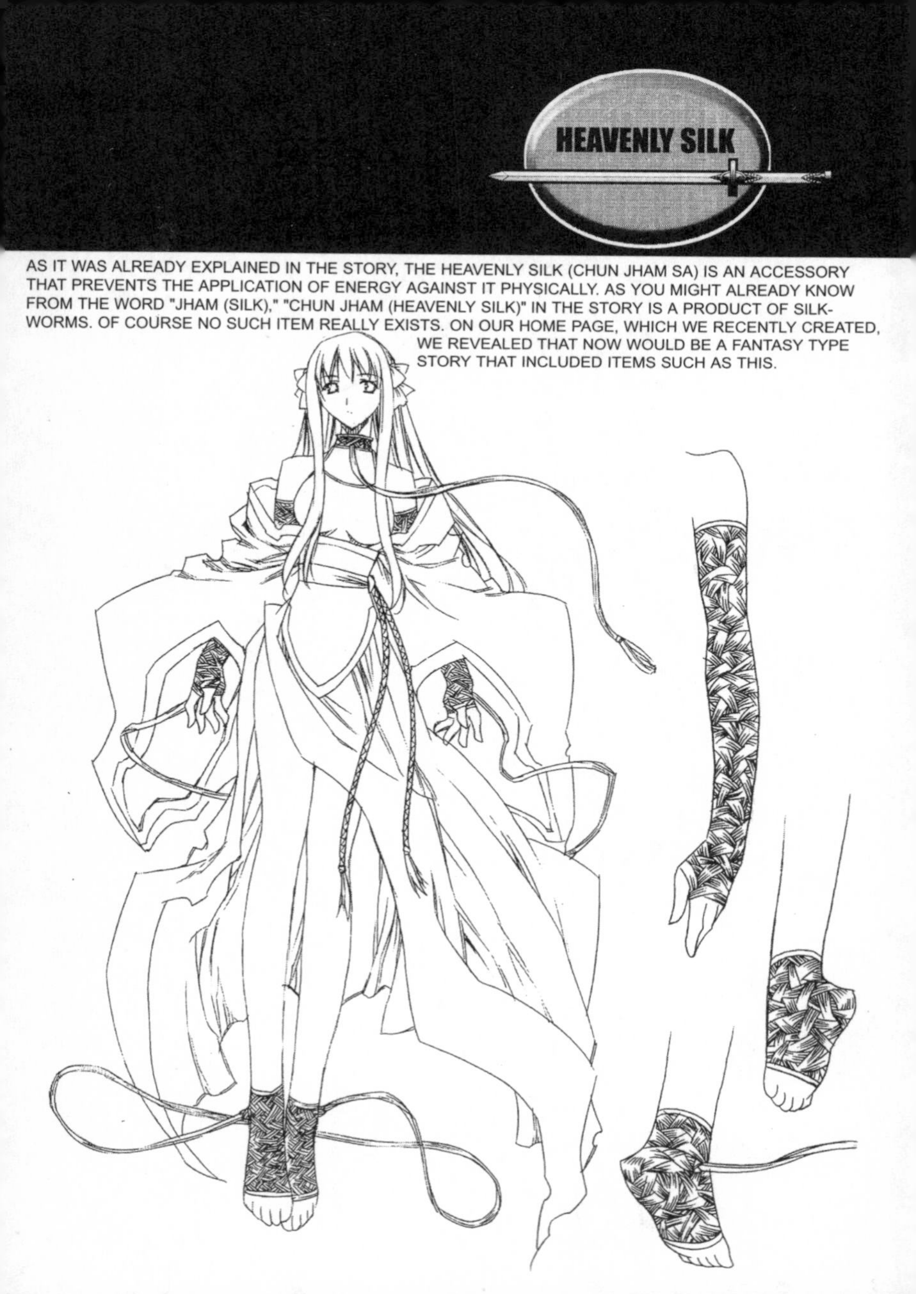

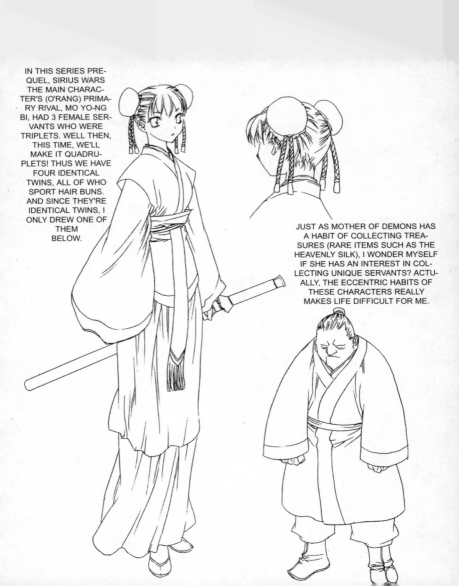

IN THIS SERIES PRE-QUEL, SIRIUS WARS THE MAIN CHARAC-TER'S (O'RANG) PRIMA-RY RIVAL, MO YO-NG BI, HAD 3 FEMALE SER-VANTS WHO WERE TRIPLETS. WELL THEN, THIS TIME, WE'LL MAKE IT QUADRU-PLETS! THUS WE HAVE FOUR IDENTICAL TWINS, ALL OF WHO SPORT HAIR BUNS. AND SINCE THEY'RE IDENTICAL TWINS, I ONLY DREW ONE OF THEM BELOW.

JUST AS MOTHER OF DEMONS HAS A HABIT OF COLLECTING TREA-SURES (RARE ITEMS SUCH AS THE HEAVENLY SILK), I WONDER MYSELF IF SHE HAS AN INTEREST IN COL-LECTING UNIQUE SERVANTS? ACTU-ALLY, THE ECCENTRIC HABITS OF THESE CHARACTERS REALLY MAKES LIFE DIFFICULT FOR ME.

YU SE HA

HE IS NOW'S OTHER PROTAGONIST. FROM MY VIEWPOINT, AS I DRAW THIS SERIES, HE'S A CHARACTER WHOM I HAVE A LOT OF AFFECTION FOR. WHILE BI RYU EXISTS IN THIS STORY AS THE TYPICAL HERO YOUNG BOYS LOOK UP TO, SE HA IS A CONSTANTLY MATURING CHARACTER WHO'S MORE IN TUNE WITH REALITY. OF COURSE, WHEN I MENTION THIS ASPECT OF "REALITY," A READER MUST UNDERSTAND THAT SOME SO CALLED "HEROES" SHED THE STEREOTYPICAL IMAGE OF A MAN-OF-JUSTICE.
AS FOR HIS DESIGN, IT WAS SIMPLY MIRRORED FROM MO YO-NG BI, THE PRIMARY RIVAL OF O' RANG YHUN, THE PROTAGONIST OF THIS BOOK'S PRE-QUEL. I GUESS I SHOULD SAY THAT THIS IS A TYPE OF "CODE" I'VE STARTED TO USE...

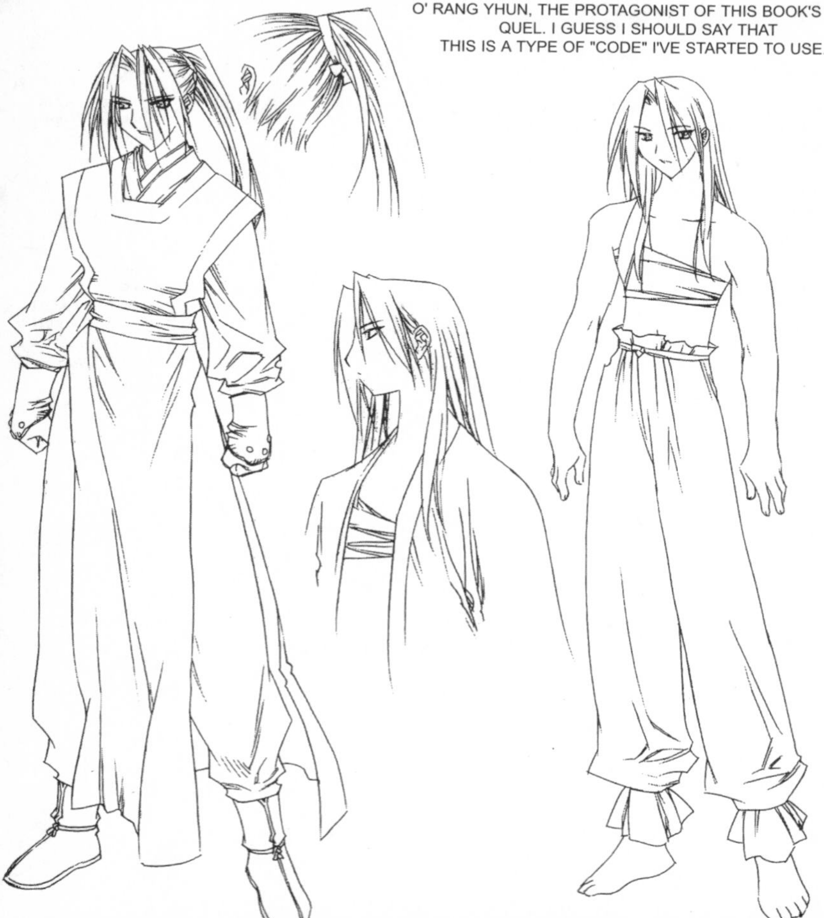

MOTHER OF DEMONS' HAND MAID AND OTHERS

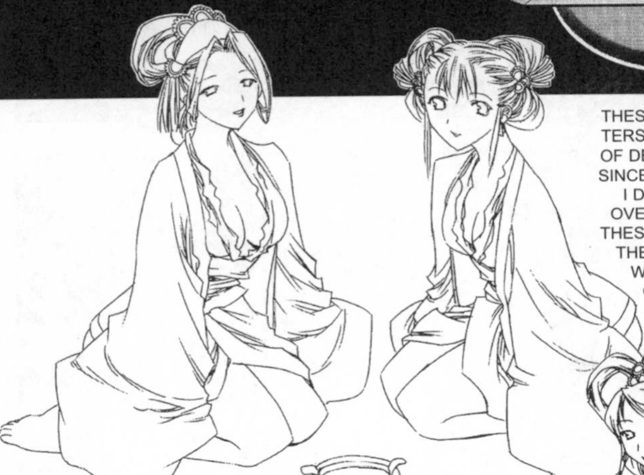

THESE WERE OPTIONAL CHARACTERS I DESIGNED TO FIT MOTHER OF DEMONS' PERVERTED TASTES. SINCE THEY ARE MERELY EXTRAS, I DECIDED TO USE A SIMILAR OVERALL DESIGN FOR BOTH OF THESE CHARACTERS. ORIGINALLY, THE HANDMAIDEN ON THE LEFT WAS SUPPOSED TO BE KILLED OFF WHILE THE HANDMAIDEN ON THE RIGHT WAS TO SURVIVE. HOWEVER, DUE TO MY CO-WORKERS' POPULAR SUPPORT, I HAD TO KILL OFF THE HANDMAIDEN ON THE RIGHT. I GUESS MY CO-WORKERS REALLY LIKE THE HANDMAIDEN ON THE LEFT.

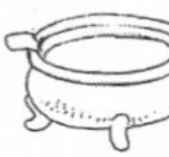

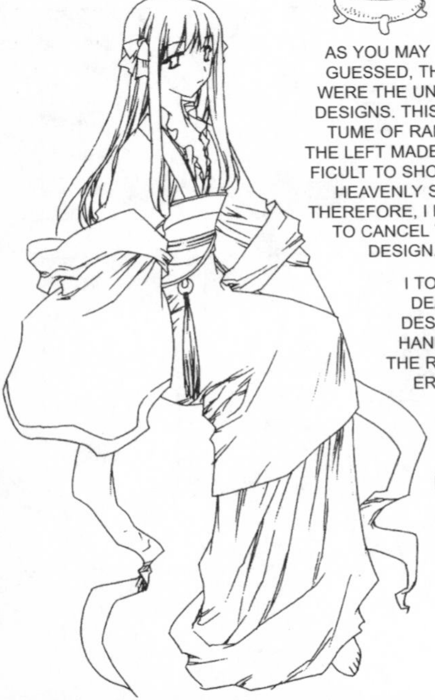

AS YOU MAY HAVE GUESSED, THESE WERE THE UNUSED DESIGNS. THIS COSTUME OF RAN ON THE LEFT MADE IT DIFFICULT TO SHOW THE HEAVENLY SILK. THEREFORE, I DECIDE TO CANCEL THIS DESIGN.

I TOOK A GREAT DEAL OF TIME DESIGNING THIS HANDMAIDEN ON THE RIGHT. HOWEVER, DUE TO HER EXTRAVAGANCE, HER USAGE WAS CANCELLED. BUT I WANTED TO AT LEAST SHOW HER DESIGN.

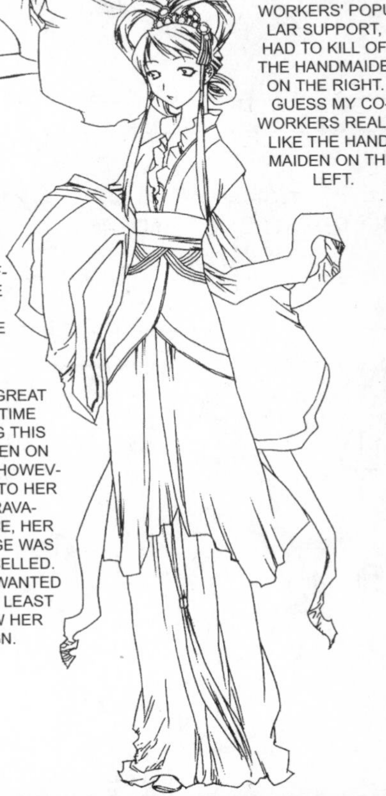

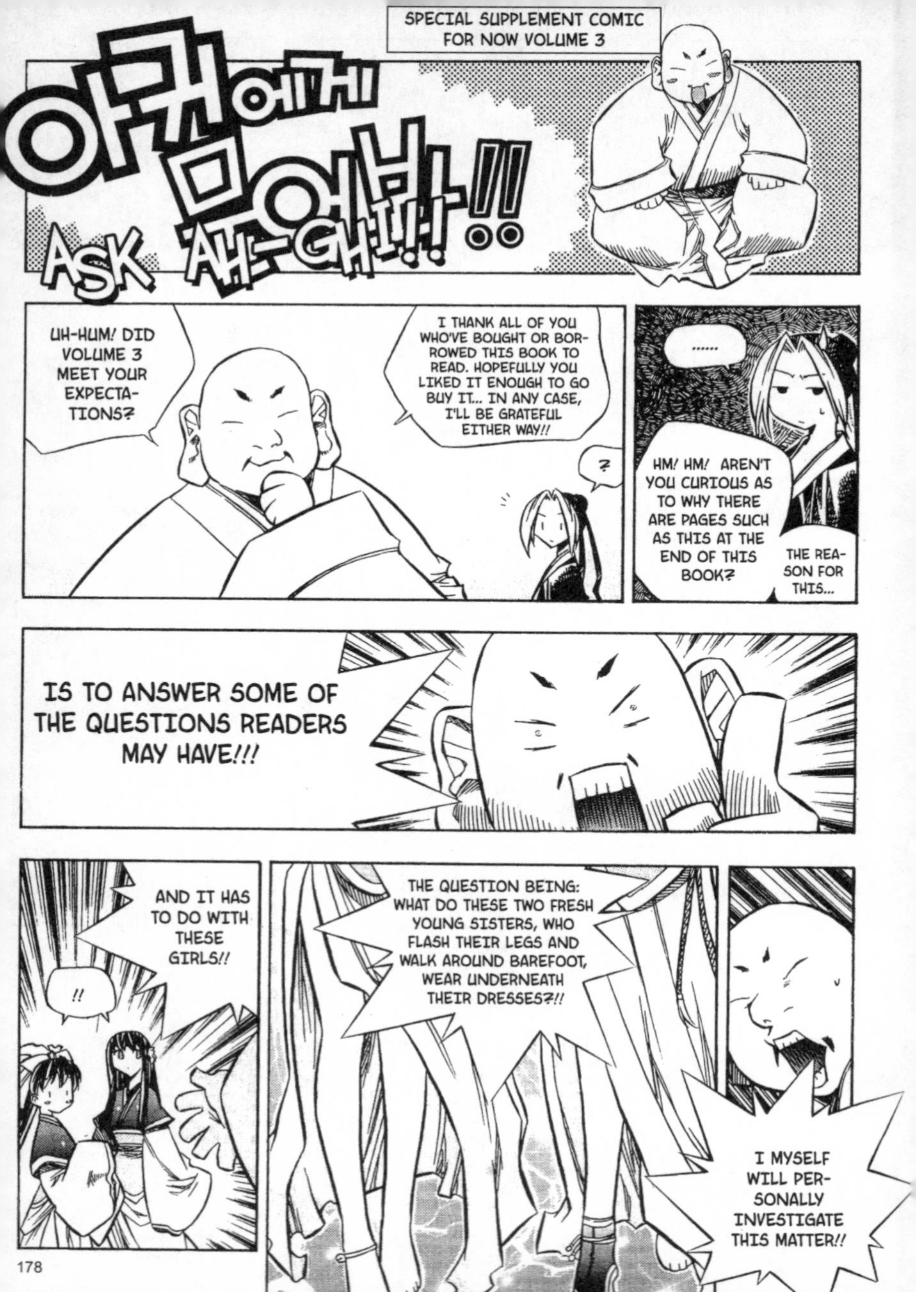

SPECIAL SUPPLEMENT COMIC
FOR NOW VOLUME 3
ASK AH-GHI!!
UH-HUM! DID VOLUME 3 MEET YOUR EXPECTATIONS?
I THANK ALL OF YOU WHO'VE BOUGHT OR BORROWED THIS BOOK TO READ. HOPEFULLY YOU LIKED IT ENOUGH TO GO BUY IT... IN ANY CASE, I'LL BE GRATEFUL EITHER WAY!!
?
......
HM! HM! AREN'T YOU CURIOUS AS TO WHY THERE ARE PAGES SUCH AS THIS AT THE END OF THIS BOOK?
THE REASON FOR THIS...
IS TO ANSWER SOME OF THE QUESTIONS READERS MAY HAVE!!!
AND IT HAS TO DO WITH THESE GIRLS!!
!!
THE QUESTION BEING: WHAT DO THESE TWO FRESH YOUNG SISTERS, WHO FLASH THEIR LEGS AND WALK AROUND BAREFOOT, WEAR UNDERNEATH THEIR DRESSES?!!
I MYSELF WILL PERSONALLY INVESTIGATE THIS MATTER!!

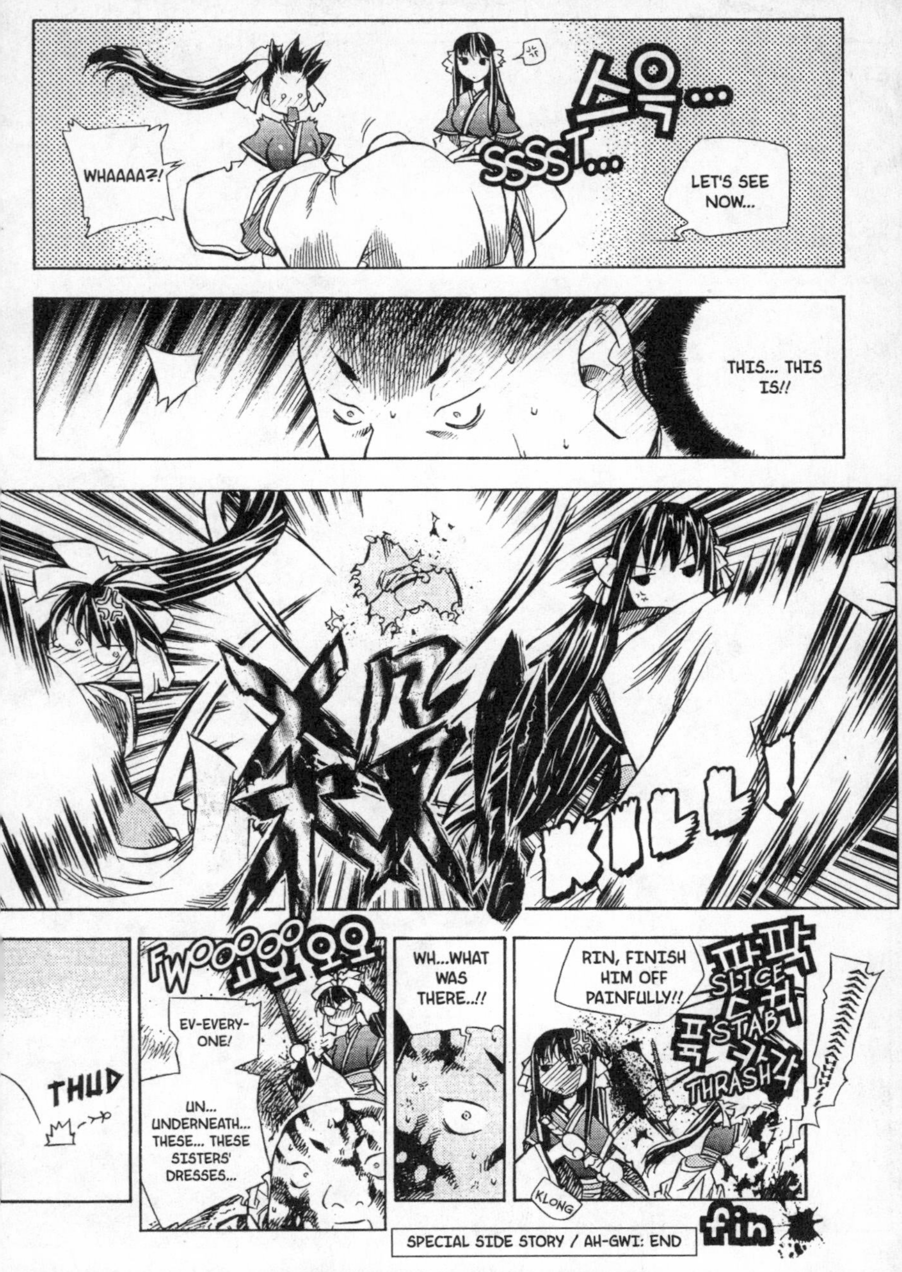
WHAAAA?!
스윽...
SSSST...
LET'S SEE NOW...
THIS... THIS IS!!
KILL
FWOOOOO
EV-EVERY-ONE!
UN... UNDERNEATH... THESE... THESE SISTERS' DRESSES...
THUD
WH...WHAT WAS THERE..!!
RIN, FINISH HIM OFF PAINFULLY!!
SLICE
STAB
THRASH
KLONG
fin
SPECIAL SIDE STORY / AH-GWI: END

got manga? ™

SISTER RED

シスターレッド

Mahito lives at home with her father and her cousin Erika, who came to live with Mahito's family several years ago after the death of her parents. One fateful stormy night Mahito is fatally run down by a reckless motorist. Upon her death she is reborn with the help of a strange woman. This woman shared a part of her "Sacred Heart" with Mahito, giving her life as a Median, or Undead.

It is a strange world Mahito is introduced to. As a Median, Mahito possesses unique powers and sees the world around her for what it really is - a place quite different than what we humans perceive. It is a darker more foreboding plane where danger can lurk behind any given corner.

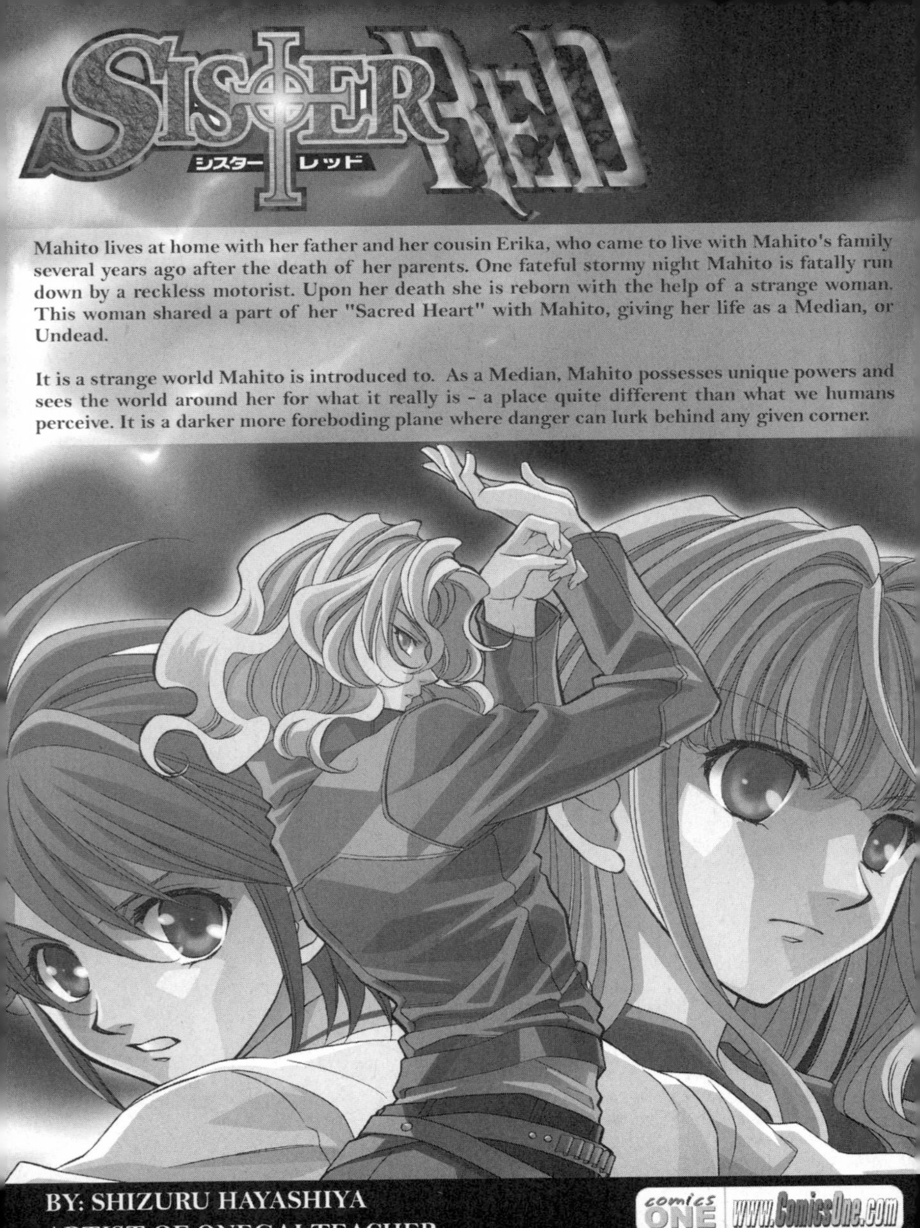

BY: SHIZURU HAYASHIYA
ARTIST OF ONEGAI TEACHER

TOP SPEED

PACIFIC ROAD IS THE MEETING PLACE FOR THOSE WHO HUNGER FOR SPEED. FOUR GROUPS CONSTANTLY CHALLENGE EACH OTHER FOR DOMINANCE, WHILE THE SPECTATORS PLACE THEIR BETS. ONE NIGHT, A UNKNOWN TAXICAB LEAVES EVERYONE IN THE DUST. BEHIND THE WHEEL IS TIAN, A YOUNG MAN WHO LOST HIS FAMOUS RACING FATHER TO AN ACCIDENT DURING A RACE. LITTLE DOES HE KNOW THAT HIS JOB AS A TAXI DRIVER, WILL SOON EXPOSE HIS UNBELIEVABLE DRIVING SKILLS. NATURALLY, EVERYONE WANTS A PIECE OF THIS SUPERIOR DRIVER – THIS DRIVER WITH NOTHING BUT HATRED FOR RACING.

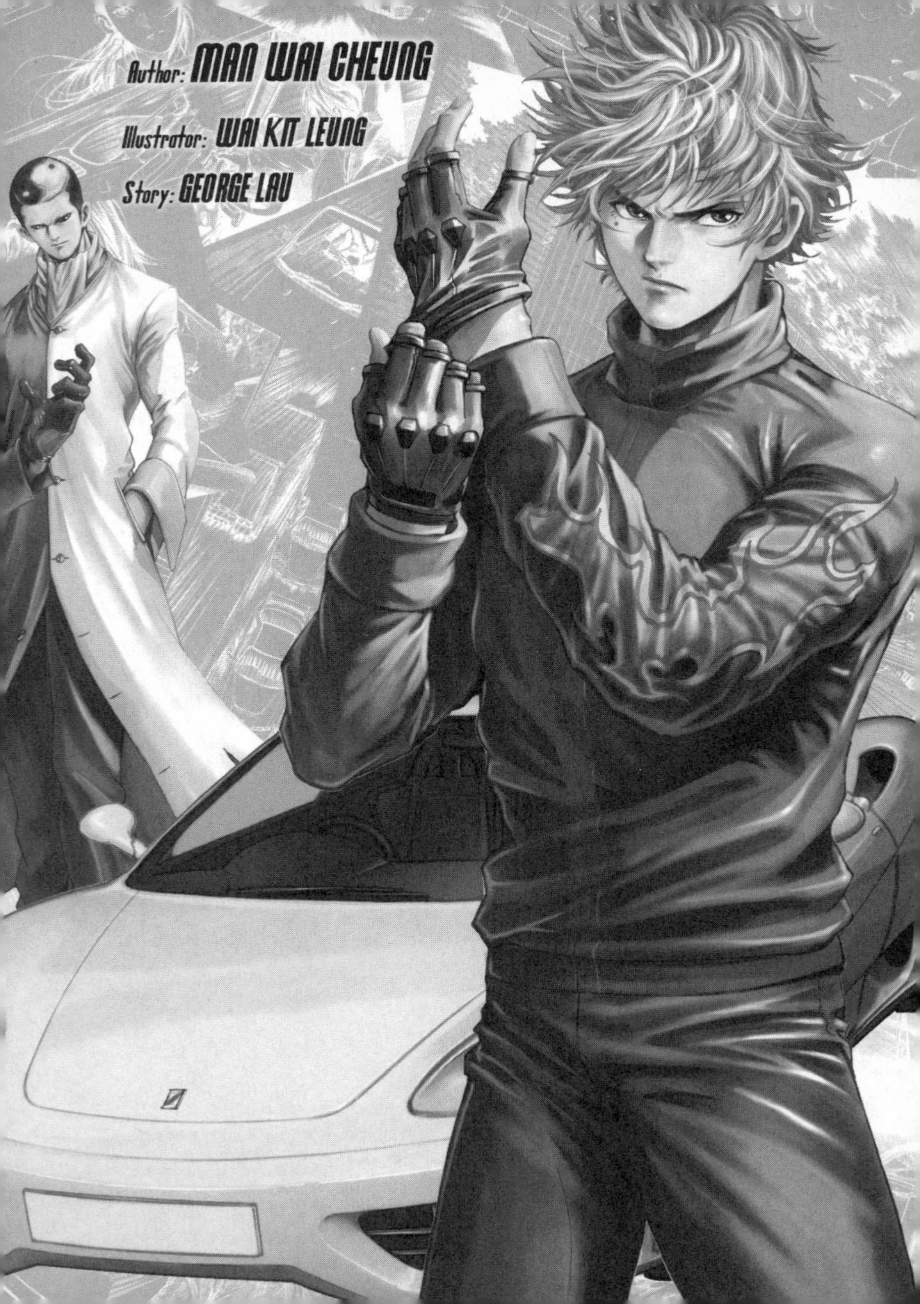
Author: MAN WAI CHEUNG
Illustrator: WAI KIT LEUNG
Story: GEORGE LAU

SVC Chaos draws on characters from the world's three most popular fighting game series - Street Fighter, King of Fighters and SNK vs. Capcom. There exists a limbo realm where the cost of admission is death! Here a new battlefield is populated by the most powerful and fearsome martial artists the world has ever known.

the Four Constables

ANDY SETO & TONY WONG

When it comes to creative team-ups, you can't get more impressive than comic giant Tony Wong locking pencils with rising star - Andy Seto. They have come together to produce the comic adaptation of The 4 Constables - the critically acclaimed novel by Wen Rui-An. Four of China's supremely skilled assassin/detectives serve only their Master Zhuge Zhen-Wo - The Little Flower, who in turn is head bodyguard and advisor for China's all-powerful Emperor. These Imperial Constables act as protectors. With their venerable skill they root out potential usurpers and discern the cause of many strange occurrences happening during the Sung Dynasty!

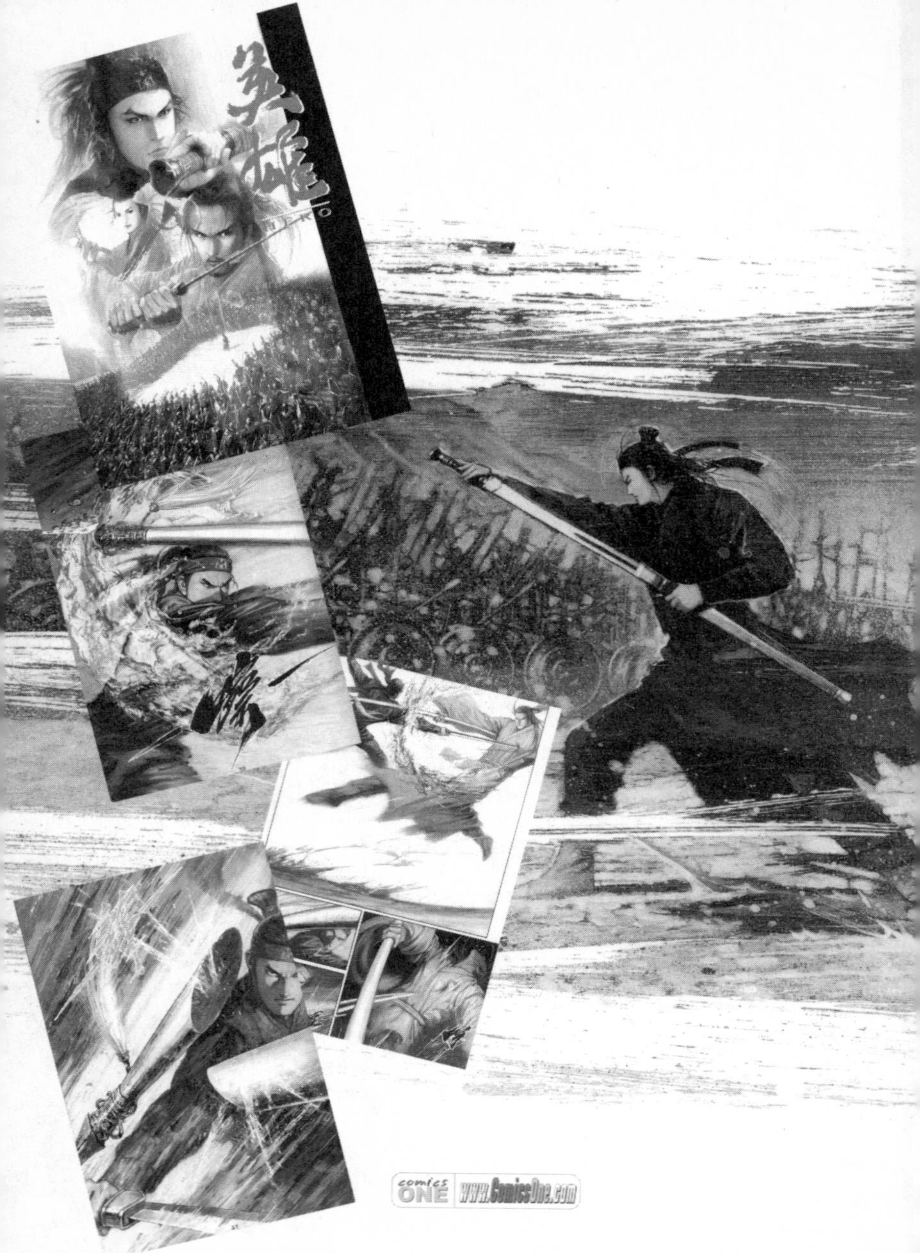
英雄

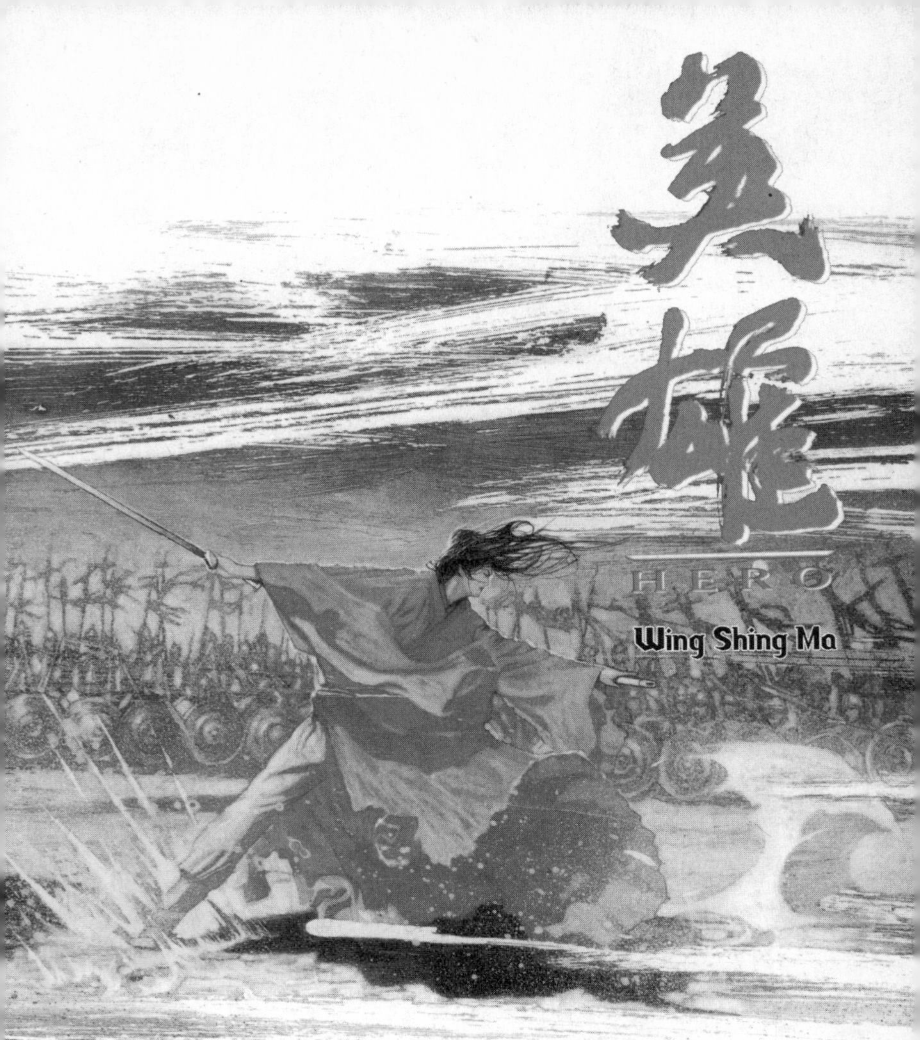
英雄
HERO
Wing Shing Ma

Hero illustrated by Wing Shing Ma, is the graphic novel adaptation of Zhang Yimou's breath-taking Oscar nominated feature length martial arts movie. At the height of China's Warring States period, the country was splintered into seven kingdoms: Qin, Zhao, Han,Wei, Yan, Chu and Qi. For years, the separate kingdoms fought ruthlessly for supremacy. This brought decades of death and suffering. The soon-to-be first Emperor of China is on the cusp of conquering the war-torn land, yet three martial arts masters are determined to assassinate him. However one loyal subject stands in their way, ironically in the name of peace for all the land.

How To Draw
KUNG FU COMICS

Ever wonder how the great kung fu comic creators like Tony Wong, Andy Seto and Wing Shing Ma work their magic? Well now you can learn how it's done. *How to Draw Kung Fu Comics* will identify all steps necessary to create a complete kung fu comic. Chapters cover drawing tools and materials, character development (bodies,heads,hair,clothing), background images (backdrops/scenery) and special effects (action sequences/battles).

Novel

ONEGAI TWINS 1

GO ZAPPA

The highly anticipated follow-up to the Onegai Teacher series is here! Maiku Kamishiro is an orphan, whose only memory of his childhood is a picture of his house, himself, and his twin sister. In an attempt to find out about his past Maiku moves into his childhood home. Soon after two girls suddenly enter into Maiku's single life. One of them is his twin sister, and the other is a perfect stranger. But which is which? From there begins a tangled give-and-take relationship between Maiku and the blue-eyed girls. Find out who is Maiku's real blood relative.

What is THE PRESS Saying?

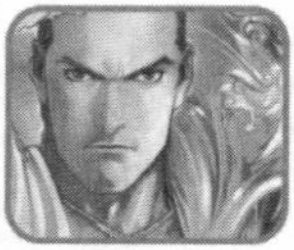

Crouching Tiger, Hidden Dragon

"The artwork in this comic is simply phenomenal. The color is rich without being overpowering, and Andy Seto's drawings are done with very,very fine lines and close attention to detail." **Javier Lopez, NewType USA, Jan 2003**

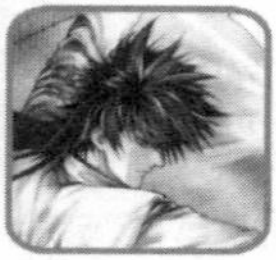

Saint Legend

"...beautiful and very dramatic... Seto has always been a fan of Yoshikazu Yazuhiko, but he now shows some interest in Masamune Shirow's style. [Saint Legend] should be read for the fantastic artwork, which would put about any American superhero comic to shame...." **3-Star Review Protoculture Addicts, March/April 2003**

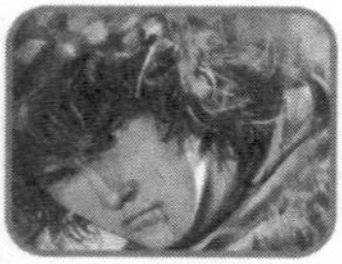

Storm Riders

"Much like the best martial arts movies, the art uses familiar objects merely as the starting point in its design. The combat scenes are phantasmagoric, swirling ballets. Ma shatters and reshapes landscapes and human faces for dramatic effect and uses nature as raw material for visual experimentation." **Publishers Weekly, March 2003**

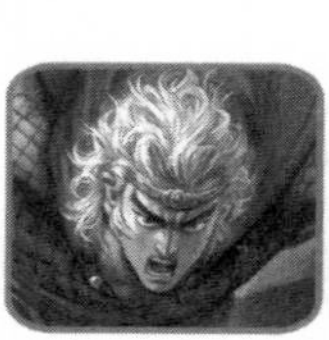

Weapons of the Gods

"The first volume in this Hong Kong kung fu comic has all the elements of a major epic: detailed, dynamic artwork; a ferociously complicated plot; and a large cast of characters who need serious counseling." **Publishers Weekly, March 2003**

We know ComicsOne Series are good, but don't take our word for it. Here is what others think:

Heaven Sword & Dragon Sabre
"If a pit fight or tournament should be held to determine the Best of the Best of Hong Kong comics, I'm certain that Heaven Sword & Dragon Sabre would emerge from the fracas looking good and utterly victorious. " **PATRICK MACIAS, Animerica, Dec 2002**

Story of the Tao
"This fusion of several distinctly different styles of comic book art melded together with fascinating and relevant story about religion and its pitfalls is well suited to the times we live in. The result of all this is one of the best comics I have read in my life. " **Dr. Brown, Animerica, Jan 2003**

Mega Dragon & Tiger
"A better ride for truly jaded thrill seekers would be hard to find." **Patrick Macias, Animerica**

Legendary Couple
"...you'd have to be nuts not to get a blast out of the highlight of Volume One: a knock-down drag-out battle between Dragon style and Toad style that seems to go on even when you put the book down." **Patrick Macias, Animerica**

Iron Wok Jan!
"If you're entertained by the Japanese T.V. import Iron Chef, you'll no doubt fall in love with Iron Wok Jan. When you put it down, I guarantee you'll have a craving for Chinese." **Ain't it Cool News**

Bride of Deimos
"Bride of Deimos is comparable in formula to Narumi Kakinouchi's Vampire Princess Miyu, but surpasses that manga in inventiveness and charm, achieving the right balance between moody atmospherics and stuff actually happening." **Jason Thompson, Animerica , Dec 2002**

Red Prowling Devil
"Despite my lack of affinity for jet movies in the past, I actually found myself getting into the story of Red Prowling Devil. ...the characters are interesting and the plot is adequately complex." **Pat King, Animefringe June 2003**

Crayon Shinchan
"Mix equal parts Calvin (from Calvin & Hobbes), Dee Dee (from Dexter's Laboratory) and Dennis the Menace, and the end result is pretty close to Shinchan." **Wizard, April 2003**

Onegai Teacher
"Overall, the series has a good storyline that works around the typical love-drama story, but adds its own twist. The character and story format is a familiar one but it is better accomplished than most series of this nature." **Francis Li, The Ticker, March 2003**

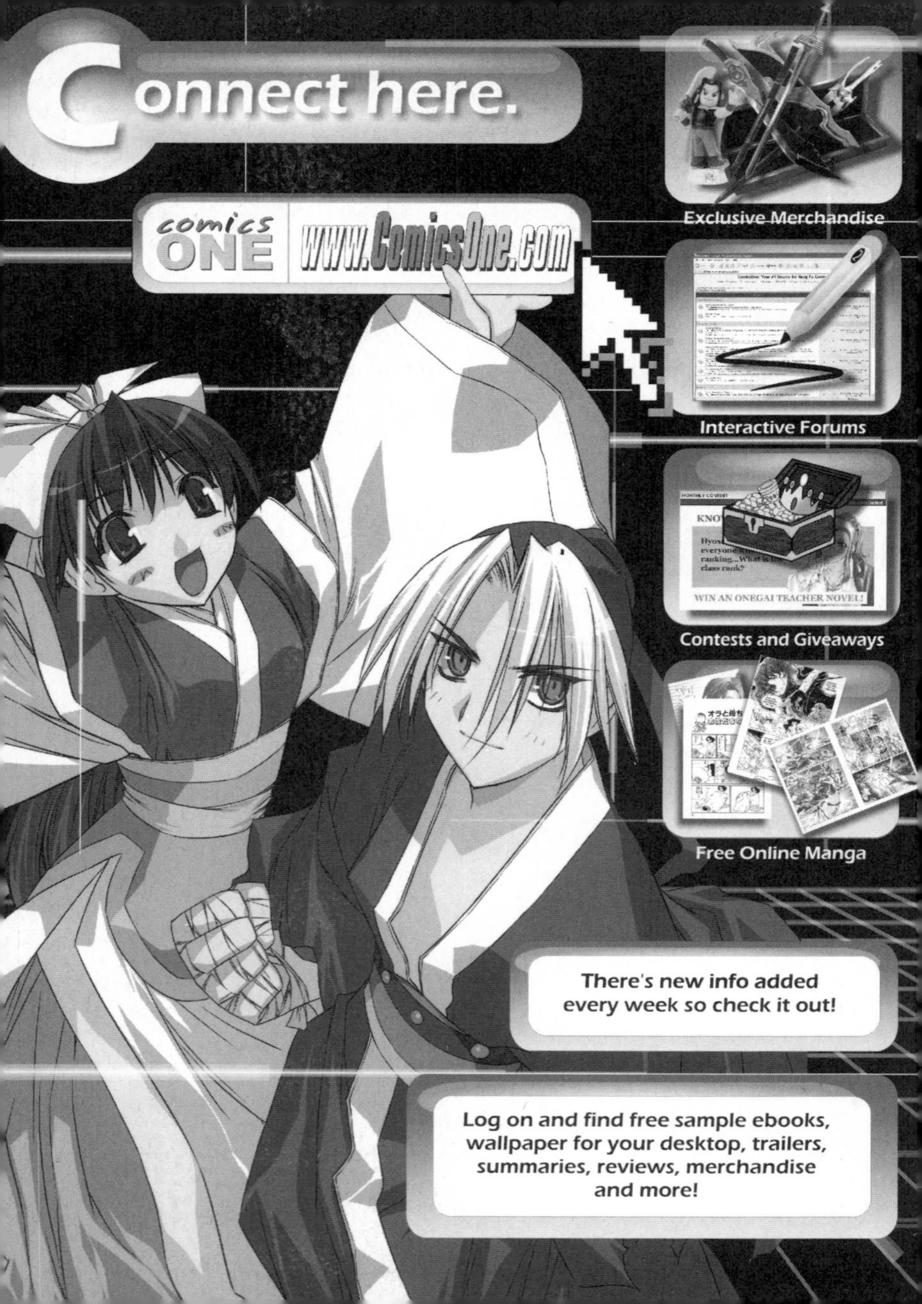